Development without Destruction

United Nations Intellectual History Project

Ahead of the Curve? UN Ideas and Global Challenges
Louis Emmerij, Richard Jolly, and Thomas G. Weiss

Unity and Diversity in Development Ideas: Perspectives from the UN Regional Commissions
Edited by Yves Berthelot

Quantifying the World: UN Ideas and Statistics
Michael Ward

The UN and Global Political Economy: Trade, Finance, and Development
John Toye and Richard Toye

UN Contributions to Development Thinking and Practice
Richard Jolly, Louis Emmerij, Dharam Ghai, and Frédéric Lapeyre

UN Voices: The Struggle for Development and Social Justice
Thomas G. Weiss, Tatiana Carayannis, Louis Emmerij, and Richard Jolly

Women, Development, and the UN: A Sixty-Year Quest for Equality and Justice
Devaki Jain

Human Security and the UN: A Critical History
S. Neil MacFarlane and Yuen Foong Khong

Human Rights at the UN: The Political History of Universal Justice
Roger Normand and Sarah Zaidi

Preventive Diplomacy at the UN
Bertrand G. Ramcharan

The UN and Transnational Corporations: From Code of Conduct to Global Compact
Tagi Sagafi-nejad in collaboration with John H. Dunning

The UN and Development: From Aid to Cooperation
Olav Stokke

UN Ideas That Changed the World
Richard Jolly, Louis Emmerij, and Thomas G. Weiss, Foreword by Kofi A. Annan

Global Governance and the UN: An Unfinished Journey
Thomas G. Weiss and Ramesh Thakur

Development without Destruction

The UN and Global Resource Management

Nico Schrijver

Forewords by
James Crawford and Supachai Panitchpakdi

Indiana University Press
Bloomington and Indianapolis

This book is a publication of

Indiana University Press
601 North Morton Street
Bloomington, Indiana 47404-3797 USA

www.iupress.indiana.edu

Telephone orders	800-842-6796
Fax orders	812-855-7931
Orders by e-mail	iuporder@indiana.edu

♾ *The paper used in this publication meets the minimum requirements of the American National Standard for Information Sciences—Permanence of Paper for Printed Library Materials, ANSI Z39.48-1992.*

MANUFACTURED IN THE UNITED STATES OF AMERICA

Library of Congress Cataloging-in-Publication Data

Schrijver, Nico, [date]
Development without destruction : the UN and global resource management / Nico Schrijver ; forewords by James Crawford and Supachai Panitchpakdi.
p. cm. — (United Nations intellectual history project)
Includes bibliographical references and index.
ISBN 978-0-253-35488-4 (cloth : alk. paper) — ISBN 978-0-253-22197-1 (pbk. : alk. paper) 1. Conservation of natural resources—International cooperation. 2. Natural resources—International cooperation. 3. Sustainable development—International cooperation. 4. United Nations. I. Title.
JZ4972.5.S37 2010
333.7—dc22

2010007344

1 2 3 4 5 15 14 13 12 11 10

To Yuwen

Sustainable development is development that meets the needs of the present without compromising the ability of future generations to meet their own needs.

—World Commission on Environment and Development

Contents

Figures and Tables

Series Editors' Foreword

We began the United Nations Intellectual History Project (UNIHP) ten years ago to fill a surprising and serious omission—there was no comprehensive study of the history of the UN's contributions to economic and social thinking and action. With some satisfaction we can look back as the entire series of seventeen books has now been published.

The project has unearthed important findings: that ideas have been among the UN's most important contributions; that the quality of the world organization's work has at times been outstanding; that the United Nations has often been ahead of the curve in its intellectual work; and finally that in terms of impact, the world body's leading contributions have literally changed history. The final conclusion is reflected in the title of the project's capstone volume that presents the major conclusions of the entire project, *UN Ideas That Changed the World.*[1]

We are also pleased that over the last decade, the landscape of UN history has been changing due to the work of others. Books documenting the history of the United Nations Development Programme, the World Food Programme, the International Labour Organization, and other UN funds and specialized agencies have been produced or are in the process of being written.[2] The record of UN contributions is now more accessible. But though all this is welcome, we should underline that it is no more than what should be expected of all public organizations, especially internationally accountable ones. Enhanced efforts to organize, improve, and open the archives so that independent researchers can analyze dispassionately their efforts and achievements are also most welcome. All this is an essential part of what is needed to improve nascent global governance, the title of yet another volume in this series.[3]

The United Nations Intellectual History Project, launched in 1999, is an independent research effort based in the Ralph Bunche Institute for International Studies at The Graduate Center of The City University of New York. We are grateful for the enthusiastic backing from Kofi Annan, the UN Secretary-General when the project was launched, and of many staff within the UN system. Generous financial support from five foundations and eight governments has ensured total intellectual and financial independence. Details of this and other aspects of the project can be found on our Web site: www.UNhistory.org.

The UN's work can be divided into two broad categories: economic and social development, on the one hand, and international peace and security, on the other. Although UNIHP started by focusing on the former, the project grew to encompass three volumes on the latter topic, given the increasingly recognized interrelationships among these spheres of activity. All the volumes have been published in a series by Indiana University Press. In addition, the project has completed an oral history collection of seventy-nine lengthy interviews of persons who have played major roles in launching and nurturing UN ideas—and sometimes in hindering them! Extracts from these interviews were published in 2005 as *UN Voices: The Struggle for Development and Social Justice.*[4] Authors of various UNIHP volumes, including this one, have drawn on these interviews to highlight substantive points made in their texts. Full transcripts of the oral histories are also available in electronic form as a CD-ROM to facilitate work by other researchers and interested persons worldwide.[5]

There is no single way to organize research, especially for such an ambitious undertaking as this one. This UN history of ideas has been structured for the most part by topics—ranging from trade and finance to human rights, from transnational corporations to development assistance, from regional perspectives to sustainability. We have selected world-class experts for each topic, and the presentation and arguments in all of the volumes are the responsibility of the authors whose names appear on the cover. All have been given freedom and responsibility to organize their own digging, analysis, and presentation. Our guidance as project directors as well as from peer review groups has ensured accuracy and fairness in depicting where the ideas came from, how they were developed and disseminated within the UN system, and what happened afterward. We trust that future analyses will build upon our series and go beyond. Our intellectual history project is the first, not the last, installment in depicting the history of the UN's contributions to ideas.

The present volume, *Development without Destruction: The United Nations and Global Resource Management,* by Nico Schrijver, fills an important gap in the UNIHP series. Its legal approach to resource management and the environment makes for an illuminating take on these problems. This international legal approach supplements the social science nature of most of the earlier books in the UNIHP series. Professor Schrijver is uniquely qualified to write about the subject. He occupies the oldest and most prestigious chair of public international law at Leiden University and is the academic director of the Grotius Centre for International Legal Studies at The Hague. He has pleaded before the International Court of Justice, the International Tribunal for the Law of the Sea, and many other legal bodies.

The book uses a broad historical perspective to present the context for the problems of the last sixty-five years. It treats the UN's involvement in natural resource management from national and international points of view before dealing with the issue of global commons. He discusses the international architecture for environmental governance as a prelude to the crucial problem of natural resources and armed conflict. A special chapter is devoted to the role of the International Court of Justice in natural resource disputes.

Readers may be surprised—we hope agreeably—by many topics addressed in the following pages. These include:

- the codification of sovereign rights to natural resources with decolonization and the later evolution toward a balance of rights and duties in the exercise of sovereignty over natural resources to legal obligations;
- the concern for the protection of marine resources in law of the sea treaties that preceded many of the environmental concerns of the late 1960s and the 1972 Stockholm Conference on the Human Environment;
- the importance and range of issues involved in the protection of marine resources;
- the permanent sovereignty and rights over natural resources linked to the right of countries to retain the means of subsistence for their populations and what this implies for action to tackle poverty;
- the evolution of concern from "the province of all mankind" to "the common heritage of all mankind";
- the significance of the Outer Space Treaty to keep the claims of national sovereignty at bay; and
- the measureable impact and success in many areas of the UN's work, notably in negotiating the Montreal Protocol, which has reduced ozone pollution by an important extent since 1984 and led to the considerable restoration of the planet's ozone layer.

The legal story of all this in action, with judges and courts exploring and ruling on what it means in practice, is a stimulating contrast to the perspectives and recommendations for action that we have seen in the social science–based books in the series and in many UN resolutions. International law may sometimes be flouted, but it has spelled out state obligations very specifically.

This book in our series is, therefore, different from previous ones, but at the same time it complements them. It makes the UNIHP series an even better-rounded whole by looking at the history of UN ideas not only from the economic, social, and political aspects, but also from a legal perspective. Nico Schrijver has written an extremely well-documented book that provides an enormous amount of detailed and indispensable information. This first-rate contribution covers many areas not addressed elsewhere in the series.

We are persuaded that the UN system needs to be greatly strengthened to meet the challenges of the years ahead. *Development without Destruction* provides us with yet another policy approach and instrument to face these challenges. Kofi Annan wrote in the "Foreword" to *Ahead of the Curve? UN Ideas and Global Challenges:* "With the publication of this first volume in the United Nations Intellectual History Project, a significant lacuna in twentieth-century scholarship and international relations begins to be filled."[6] With this last volume in the series, a further gap in that record is now closed.

We hope that readers will enjoy this account, at once a journey through time and an analysis of the strengths and weaknesses of today's attempts to tackle many of the priority issues on the global agenda. As always, we welcome comments from our readers.

Louis Emmerij, Richard Jolly, and Thomas G. Weiss
New York, March 2009

Foreword

The term "United Nations," substituted for "Associated Powers" in an early draft of the Atlantic Charter, was coined by Winston Churchill while he was sitting in the bath, a place where the British prime minister was known to do some of his best thinking. No longer in the bath, Churchill showed Roosevelt the text of Byron's *Childe Harold,* which read in part:

> Here, where the sword United Nations drew,
> Our countrymen were warring on that day!
> And this much—and all—which will not pass away;

The two agreed the term was fitting; after all, security was the preoccupation of the time. But of course the United Nations as it has evolved seeks to fulfill functions quite distinct from the maintenance of military peace and security. The extent to which it has influenced, directed, and contributed to the management of natural resources is the subject of examination in this book.

The sustainable management of natural resources is one of the greatest challenges facing governments and peoples. For governments, the management of resources is a long-standing concern, but with increasing awareness of the need to protect and preserve the natural environment and the knowledge of the inevitable dramatic consequences of a failure to do so, management of natural resources is increasingly becoming a concern of all.

Professor Schrijver's study addresses the ways the United Nations has contributed to the development of the law, practice, and policy relating to management of natural resources and the extent to which the concepts so developed have tended to become universalized: development, sustainability, peace and security itself. Attempts to regulate management of natural resources confront tensions between environmental protection and economic development, between sovereignty and communitarian objectives, and between conservation and exploitation. His study provides a valuable survey of the work of the United Nations in this field, but it also exposes the limitations of that work, which can produce solutions only with the cooperation of member states. Professor Schrijver's thorough account of the achievements of the organization across the field of natural resource management enables him both to assess that contribution and to make realistic, practical suggestions for improvement. His thoughtful and well-researched contribution to the problem of the management of natural resources is a contribution both in itself and in adding to an appreciation of the work of the United Nations more generally.

James Crawford
Lauterpacht Centre for International Law
Cambridge
August 2009

Foreword

This study examines the role of the United Nations in global resource management, whose influence and activities in this area include data collection, policy analysis, advisory services, and operational activities. Most of all, however, the United Nations—through the activities of its programs and agencies—is able to exercise the power of an idea: that balanced economic development can be achieved with the prudent and sustainable use of natural resources.

The United Nations Conference on Trade and Development (UNCTAD) has been one of the principal advocates within the UN system of balanced and sustainable economic development since its establishment in 1964. Indeed, the original intellectual hypothesis underpinning its creation, elaborated by the economists Raúl Prebisch and Hans Singer, focused on a structural imbalance in global economic relations. The organization's earliest activities focused on how to remedy the long-term decline in the terms of trade between mainly primary commodity-exporting developing countries and manufactures-exporting developed countries. In the past, falling and highly volatile prices for key commodities made countries' dependence on commodities particularly problematic, and even today, 86 out of 144 developing countries depend on commodities for more than half their export earnings.

For many developing countries that have managed to diversify their economies, this situation has improved—partly helped by policy prescriptions UNCTAD has developed, such as an emphasis on preferential market access and nonreciprocity in trade relations and attempts to stabilize world commodity markets. Additionally, the recent boom in commodity prices created by new demand in emerging economies has opened up new opportunities for commodity-rich countries. Since the 1960s, the bipolar characterization of economic relations has become more complex and new challenges have emerged. One such challenge is to ensure that policies and institutions are in place that allow new opportunities to be seized for the benefit of all countries while at the same time managing the consumption of global resources.

To address this challenge, UNCTAD has consistently drawn attention to the role of sound investment policies and laws in the area of primary commodity production to secure long-term national and global benefits and the better management of natural resource endowments. In the area of foreign direct investment by multinational companies, host countries (receiving the investment) could do more to ensure that the benefits are better spread over the long term. More transparency and accountability of international revenue payments within the sector are also needed to distribute revenues more equitably among the population so that everyone shares the benefits of their country's resources.

This timely study makes a seminal contribution to understanding the management of natural resources in the context of changing economic, environmental, and social realities. The author, Professor Nico Schrijver, is a distinguished independent expert on the right to development who has contributed to the United Nations' efforts on development through his participation as a member of the High-level Task Force on the Right to Development and the UN Committee on Economic, Social and Cultural Rights. In his work, he has drawn on UNCTAD's research on policies and strategies for economic development. Professor Schrijver's work shows how research undertaken in the past by the United Nations is contributing to the search for solutions to today's main challenge: safeguarding the global commons for tomorrow while providing a decent quality of life for all.

Supachai Panitchpakdi
Secretary-General of the United Nations
Conference on Trade and Development

Acknowledgments

This book did not come to fruition overnight but underwent a long incubation period. It builds on my long-standing research in this field and was written in the midst of many other and diverse duties that often distracted me. I am very grateful for the trust, admirable patience, and constructive comments at several phases of this book project from the three senior editors and intellectual fathers of UNIHP: Louis Emmerij, Richard Jolly, and Thomas G. Weiss. I owe them a great deal.

I would like to record my deep appreciation for three reviewers of the entire manuscript: Arthur H. Westing, who has inspired me for several decades with his pioneering work on environmental conservation and the nexus between natural resources and armed conflict at the Stockholm International Peace Research Institute (SIPRI), the Peace Research Institute, Oslo (PRIO), and elsewhere and who greatly honored me by welcoming and introducing me to his natural habitat in the hills of Vermont (United States); Elisabeth DeSombre of Wellesley College (United States), the author of the fine book *Global Environmental Institutions* (2005), who graciously shared with me her advanced knowledge of and insights into international environmental governance and the relationship between natural resources and armed conflict; and Sabine von Schorlemer of the Technical University of Dresden (Germany), a very knowledgeable colleague in the field of international law with whom I share a passion for promoting the relevance of our field of study in alleviating poverty and achieving the recognition of a human right to development. I am also very grateful to my friends Rob van Schaik (formerly the Dutch Permanent Representative to the United Nations in Nairobi, Geneva, and New York) and Rob van den Berg (Director of the Evaluation Unit of the Global Environment Facility) for their comments on a draft of chapter 4. My colleagues at the Vrije Universiteit Amsterdam and later at Leiden University, particularly Larissa van den Herik, Carel Stolker, and Carsten Stahn, have often encouraged me and provided me with an academic environment conducive to research. I am aware that my appetite for hard copies of books, journal articles, and documents is somewhat dated, and I gratefully acknowledge the very kind assistance I have always been privileged to receive for this and other research projects from the Peace Palace Library in The Hague (Jeroen Vervliet and his staff);

the Library of the United Nations Office in Geneva in the Palais des Nations, especially in the Salle juridique from Irina Gerassimova (Chief); and from Albert Dekker and his colleagues at the Law Library of Leiden University.

This book would probably never have been successfully completed if I hadn't had the great benefit of being assisted by research fellow, colleague, and friend Vid Prislan of the Grotius Centre for International Legal Studies at Leiden University. His dedication to this project, his detailed knowledge, and his remarkable skills in composing tables and figures have been invaluable. In earlier phases, I also received support from Gary Debus, Daniëlla Dam, and various student assistants for which I am grateful. I am also indebted to Danielle Zach Kalbacher of The Graduate Center of The City University of New York and Kate Babbitt of Indiana University Press for their skillful editorial assistance.

Any remaining errors and mistakes are entirely my own responsibility.

This book is dedicated to my sustainable partner in life, Yuwen Li, who has accompanied me all the way on this project, as she has on past and I hope will on future projects. Her dedication to academic study and to advancing human dignity and the rule of law in China and beyond has always been a source of great inspiration in my own endeavors.

Nico Schrijver
Leiden/Beijing
August 2009

Abbreviations

ACCOBAMS	Agreement on the Conservation of the Cetaceans of the Black Sea, Mediterranean Sea and Contiguous Atlantic Area
ASCOBANS	Agreement on the Conservation of Small Cetaceans of the Baltic and North Seas
CCAMLR	Convention on the Conservation of Antarctic Marine Living Resources
CFCs	chlorofluorocarbons
CITES	Convention on International Trade in Endangered Species of Wild Fauna and Flora
CLRTAP	Convention on Long-Range Transboundary Air Pollution
COFI	Committee on Fisheries (of the FAO)
COP	Conference of the Parties
CRAMRA	Convention on the Regulation of Antarctic Mineral Resource Activities
CSD	Commission on Sustainable Development
ECA	Economic Commission for Africa
ECE	Economic Commission for Europe
ECLAC	Economic Commission for Latin America and the Caribbean
ECOSOC	Economic and Social Council
EEZs	exclusive economic zones
EMEP	Co-operative Programme for Monitoring and Evaluation of the Long-Range Transmission of Air Pollutants in Europe
ESCAP	Economic and Social Commission for Asia and the Pacific
ESCWA	Economic and Social Commission for Western Asia
EU	European Union
FAO	Food and Agriculture Organization
FSA	United Nations Agreement for the Implementation of the Provisions of the United Nations Convention on the Law of the Sea of 10 December 1982 relating to the Conservation and Management of Straddling Fish Stocks and Highly Migratory Fish Stocks (Fish Stocks Agreement)
GEF	Global Environment Facility
IBRD	International Bank for Reconstruction and Development
ICA	International Co-operative Alliance
ICES	International Council for the Exploration of the Sea
ICJ	International Court of Justice

IDA	International Development Association
ICRW	International Convention for the Regulation of Whaling
IFAD	International Fund for Agricultural Development
IJC	Canada-United States International Joint Commission
ILC	International Law Commission
IOC	International Oceanographic Commission
IPCC	Intergovernmental Panel on Climate Change
ISA	International Seabed Authority
ITLOS	International Tribunal for the Law of the Sea
IUCN	International Union for Conservation of Nature
IWC	International Whaling Commission
MDGs	Millennium Development Goals
NAMMCO	North Atlantic Marine Mammal Commission
NGO	nongovernmental organization
NIEO	New International Economic Order
ODS	ozone-depleting substances
OECD	Organisation for Economic Co-operation and Development
OPEC	Organization of the Petroleum Exporting Countries
PCIJ	Permanent Court of International Justice
RFMO/As	regional fisheries management organizations and institutionalized arrangements
RMP	Revised Management Procedure
UNCC	United Nations Compensation Commission
UNCED	United Nations Conference on Environment and Development
UNCHE	United Nations Conference on the Human Environment
UNCLOS	United Nations Convention on the Law of the Sea
UNCTAD	United Nations Conference on Trade and Development
UNDP	United Nations Development Programme
UNEP	United Nations Environment Programme
UNESCO	United Nations Educational, Scientific and Cultural Organization
UNFF	United Nations Forum on Forests
UNIDO	United Nations Industrial Development Organization
UNIHP	United Nations Intellectual History Project
UNITA	União Nacional para a Independência Total de Angola
WMO	World Meteorological Organization

Development without Destruction

Introduction: Concepts and Principles

- **Concepts and Principles**
- **Chapter Outline**
- **Methodology**

This book is about the United Nations and global resource management, in particular the maintenance of the natural adaptability of ecosystems and the sustainable use of natural resources for the benefit of present and future generations of humankind. It seeks to analyze the role of the United Nations system in developing and consolidating universal values, principles of international law, and concepts of international governance to promote sustainable development. It hence focuses on natural resource management in areas both within and beyond the national jurisdiction of states as well as on the global commons, such as the high seas, outer space, and the climate system.

The management of natural resources and the environment is not an issue that features in the UN Charter, yet since 1945 the United Nations has had a profound impact on how natural resources are viewed and how they are used. Various principal actors within the UN proper as well as several specialized agencies are involved in resource management, bringing in different perceptions and emphases from the particular set of responsibilities of each of these institutions. The conceptual contribution of the UN to international approaches to natural resource management has been extensive and includes the generation of new concepts for resource management, such as resource sovereignty (on land and in the sea), the common heritage of humankind, the sharing of natural resources, sustainable development, and the use of collective sanctions to address resource conflicts. This study identifies the extent to which these concepts reflect and to a certain extent also shaped universal values such as development, respect for nature, sustainability, and peace and security.

At the same time, these global resource concepts constantly face important challenges, such as the tensions between development and the environment, conservation and exploitation, sovereignty and internationalism, territoriality and functionality, and armed conflict and access to natural resources and between a value-driven and an interest-driven international society. Such tensions have had a profound impact on the actual content of UN-generated concepts related to natural resources.

The objective of this book is to demonstrate the role of international organizations, particularly the United Nations, in developing universal values about global natural resource management for sustainable development. Key values are a duties-based as well as a rights-based concept of national resource sovereignty, sustainability, peace, international management of the global commons, and recognition of the notion of global public goods. I demonstrate that these values derive from the same tradition within the United Nations that attempts to foster economic and social progress. Yet proponents of these values now pay increasing attention to equitable and sustainable development and the interests of future generations of humankind.

Concepts and Principles

At the outset of this study, it seems appropriate to briefly present a number of basic concepts and principles that will be regularly referred to and further elaborated in the following chapters.

Basic Concepts

The basic concepts of this study include natural resources, natural wealth, ecosystem, environment, sustainable use, and global commons.

Natural Resources

Whereas the term "natural resources" does not appear in the UN Charter, the constitutive acts of various bodies within the UN system established in the aftermath of World War II do refer to "natural resources." Thus, for example, one of the purposes of the International Bank for Reconstruction and Development was to develop "the productive resources of its members,"[1] while the Food and Agriculture Organization of the United Nations was mandated to promote "the conservation of natural resources."[2] The work of these institutions will be presented in chapter 4.

Dictionaries define "natural resources" as "materials or substances of a place which can be used to sustain life or for economic exploitation"[3] or as "material from nature having potential economic value or providing for the sustenance of life."[4] Natural resources are generally classified into nonrenewable (stock) and renewable (flow) resources or into nonliving and living resources. Nonrenewable resources, such as minerals, are resources that are consumed as they are used; the quantity of these resources (at least from a human perspective) is fixed. In contrast, renewable resources are resources that are naturally generated and provide new supply units within at least one human generation. Nonetheless, renewable resources are not necessarily inconsumable; in certain circumstances they can indeed be susceptible to depletion, exhaustion, and extinction, frequently because of human activities. As a consequence, they can be just as "finite" as minerals and other nonrenewable resources. Usually the categories of nonrenewable/renewable resources coincide with the categories of nonliving/living natural resources, but this is not always the case. Certain nonliving resources can be as renewable as animals or plants. Polymetallic nodules on the deep seabed, for example, can grow in approximately forty years.

Natural Wealth

In UN resolutions, the term "natural wealth" is often used in connection with "natural resources." An example is the 1962 Declaration on Permanent Sovereignty over Natural Resources, which extends the right of permanent sovereignty to "natural wealth and resources."[5] No authoritative definition of the notion of "natural wealth" exists, which makes it difficult to determine the precise scope and content of the concept. Nevertheless, it is clear that "natural wealth," such as forests or the sea, often consists of several "natural resources," such as timber, oil, or fish.

Ecosystem

The notion of "natural wealth" is often related to the concepts of "ecosystem" and "environment." The 1992 Convention on Biological Diversity defines "ecosystem" as "a dynamic complex of plant, animal and micro-organism communities and their non-living environment interacting as a functional unit."[6] A similar definition is regularly used in the publications of the United Nations Environment Programme (UNEP).[7] Alternatively, the International Law Commission (ILC) has described "ecosystem" as "an ecological unit consisting of living and nonliving components that are interdependent and function as a community."[8]

Environment

In its advisory opinion on the legality of the threat or use of nuclear weapons, the International Court of Justice (ICJ) recognized that "the environment is not an abstraction but represents the living space, the quality of life and the very health of human beings, including generations unborn."[9] The relation between human beings and their "environment" is the point of departure of many UN activities in this field. As early as 1949, for example, the Economic and Social Council (ECOSOC) convened a scientific conference that dealt with the relationship between conservation of natural resources and the use of such resources by humans.[10] It was not until the late 1960s, however, that the "environment" as such emerged on the UN agenda. In response to a growing awareness that the "human environment" was at risk, the General Assembly decided to convene a conference on the human environment (which was subsequently held in Stockholm in 1972) to address the issue in a comprehensive way. The Declaration of the United Nations Conference on the Human Environment, which resulted from the conference, proclaimed the human being to be "both creature and moulder of *his* environment" and defined the "human environment" as comprised of both the natural and the manmade environment.[11] Twenty years later, the Conference on Environment and Development—which convened in Rio de Janeiro as a follow-up to the Stockholm conference—adopted the Rio Declaration on Environment and Development, which articulated "the integral . . . nature of the Earth," and further emphasizing that the earth is "our home."[12] The World Summit on Sustainable Development—which convened in Johannesburg in 2002 to take stock of the action taken since the Rio conference—adopted a political declaration that proclaimed the "collective responsibility" of humanity for protecting the environment as part of a broader effort toward sustainable development.[13] Few people would dispute that nowadays promoting environmental protection and pursuing sustainable development belong to the special tasks and fields of activity of the United Nations.

Biological Diversity

A leading textbook defines biological diversity or biodiversity as "the variety of life, in all of its manifestations. It encompasses all forms, levels and combinations of natural variation and thus serves as a broad unifying concept."[14] Another, more extensive formulation is provided by the 1992 Convention on Biological Diversity, which describes it as "the variability among living organisms from all sources including, inter alia, terrestrial, marine and other aquatic ecosystems and the ecological complexes of which they are part; this includes diversity within species, between species and of ecosystems."[15]

Climate

"Climate" refers to the atmospheric conditions of the regions of the earth. According to the 1992 United Nations Framework Convention on Climate Change, the climate system is comprised of "the totality of the atmosphere, hydrosphere, biosphere and geosphere and their interactions."[16]

Sustainability

"Sustainability" is the general norm underlying the effort to protect natural resources and conserve the environment through sustainable development. As such, it is based on other general norms such as respect for human life, for nature and its flora and fauna, for justice, and for development, all of which have roots in various cultures and civilizations.[17] The basic idea of sustainability is quite straightforward: "a sustainable system is one which survives or persists."[18]

Economists and moral philosophers are currently engaged in a debate between advocates of "strong" and "weak" sustainability.[19] Proponents of weak sustainability want to conserve the total capital base, including natural capital, as a guarantee of a welfare level that at least will remain the same, although this implies the possibility that the loss of natural capital could be replaced by economic capital. Many economists argue that new knowledge and technology will enable humankind to replace nonrenewable natural resources and thus continue to live with different forms of damage to nature and the environment. On the other hand, strong sustainability requires that each type of capital be maintained separately. To achieve this, it is essential to conserve biodiversity, to prevent significant and irreversible damage to the environment, and to use exhaustible natural resources economically. At present, the various international legal instruments and the body of international law relating to sustainable development appear to be based more on "weak" than on "strong" sustainability.

Types of Jurisdiction over Natural Resources

Natural resources are spread over the planet, albeit not evenly. Some are fully under the jurisdiction of one particular state; others are either shared by two or more states or are beyond the limits of national jurisdiction in international areas.

National Jurisdiction

Resources in areas under national jurisdiction are located within the territorial boundaries of a single state and under the permanent sovereignty and exclusive authority of that state. In addition to the resources on land, this also includes resources located in internal waters, such as rivers, canals and lakes, and those in the seas adjacent to the coast (i.e., in territorial seas and archipelagic waters), on the seabed and subsoil of the continental shelf, and, in cases where a state proclaims an exclusive economic zone, those located in the waters up to a distance of 200 nautical miles from a coast. These various maritime zones—and the extent of coastal states' powers therein—will be discussed in chapter 2.

Shared or Transboundary Resources

Shared or transboundary resources transcend the boundaries of a single state and are therefore shared by two or more states. In the more narrow understanding, shared resources refer to resources that form a unitary whole by virtue of their physical relationship. This is mostly the case with nonliving resources, such as international rivers and other watercourses; shared bodies of underground waters ("aquifers"); single geological structures of oil, gas, or other mineral resources in liquid state; adjacent bodies of seas, particularly enclosed or semi-enclosed seas; or the airshed or air mass above the territories of a limited number of states.[20] Under a more broad understanding, transboundary resources also include living resources, such as highly migratory fish stocks; migratory birds and other fauna that straddle the boundaries of two or more states; or special ecosystems that span the frontiers between two or more states. In the broadest meaning, shared resources also include global commons, such as the atmosphere or the resources of the high seas. As shared or transboundary resources are not under the national jurisdiction of one single state, it is necessary for states to cooperate with regard to their conservation and harmonious and equitable utilization.[21]

Resources in International Areas

Resources in international areas can be found in areas beyond national jurisdiction and hence no state can claim or exercise sovereignty or sovereign rights over them. Some of these resources—such as the living resources of the high seas—can be subject to appropriation by any state or company (unless otherwise regulated by international agreement); others belong to the "common heritage of humankind" and are subject to a special international regime of exploitation. The latter include the resources of the deep seabed area and the resources of the moon and other celestial bodies. The natural resources of Antarctica are in a special position, inasmuch as sovereign claims to parts of Antarctica have been "frozen" for the time being, while the exploitation of some of its resources—namely seals, fisheries, and other marine living resources—is subject to special rules. Chapter 3 presents in greater detail the management of these resources.

Global Commons

In old English and Dutch law, the term "commons" denoted an arrangement under which property or resources were held in common and jointly exploited, such as the village square or shared grazing grounds. From the perspective of property law, "commons" represent resource domains in which "common pool resources" are found, in the sense that access to them or the exploitation of them cannot be efficiently limited to a "pool" of users. Following this logic, "global commons" denote natural resources that are not subject to the national jurisdiction of a particular state but belong to the international community as a whole; all nations have legal access to them.[22] The climate, outer space, the atmosphere, and the high seas may be designated as part of the "global commons." As such, they resemble the "common goods" (*res communes*) identified by Hugo Grotius in his seminal 1609 work *Mare Liberum*, in that they belong to everyone and yet are from no one. In contemporary context, global commons are defined by the Organisation for Economic Co-operation and Development (OECD) as "natural assets outside national jurisdiction."[23] In certain respects, the global commons can be viewed as the natural wealth beyond national borders (i.e., beyond the areas that nation-states control) and will be regarded in this book as encompassing the resources in international areas.

Principles in Natural Resource Management

Several principles of international law are relevant for global resource management: sovereignty, permanent sovereignty over natural resources, self-determination, the common heritage of humankind, and sustainable development.

Sovereignty

Since the Peace of Westphalia in 1648, sovereignty has been the most fundamental characteristic of statehood. In the classic *Island of Palmas* case, sole arbitrator Max Huber described the concept in the following way: "Sovereignty in the relations between States signifies independence. Independence in regard to a portion of the globe is the right to exercise therein, to the exclusion of any other State, the functions of a State."[24] In this sense, sovereignty may be described as "supreme authority within a territory."[25]

Sovereignty has also been regarded as the core principle on which contemporary international law is based. As observed by the International Court of Justice in the *Corfu Channel* case of 1949, "Between independent States, respect for territorial sovereignty is an essential foundation of international relations."[26] Nonetheless, the establishment of the United Nations with its broad mandate—including international cooperation in the economic, social, cultural, and humanitarian fields—has had a great bearing on the scope of state sovereignty. This was perhaps sensed by Judge Alejandro Alvarez, who in a separate opinion to the same judgment in the *Corfu Channel* case considered that "we can no longer regard sovereignty as an absolute and individual right of every State, as used to be the case under the old law founded on the individualist regime, according to which States were only bound by the rules which they had accepted. Today, owing to social interdependence and to the predominance of general interest, the States are bound by many rules which have not been ordered by their will."[27] This statement is truer than ever today, with over 530 major multilateral treaties deposited with the UN Secretary-General.

Permanent Sovereignty over Natural Resources

Taking root in the concept of state sovereignty, the concept of "permanent sovereignty over natural resources" evolved in the postwar era as a new principle of international economic law. It was generated within General Assembly debates as a right of states and peoples, and its objective was to safeguard the rights of newly independent and developing countries over their natural wealth and resources against foreign infringement.[28] The resolutions resulting from these debates—which will be analyzed in greater detail in chapter 2—have largely defined the content of the principle. The most authoritative resolution in this respect is the 1962 Declaration on Permanent Sovereignty over Natural Resources.[29] As a right of peoples, "permanent sovereignty over natural resources" is also part of the right to self-determination as laid down in common Article 1 of the Covenant on Economic, Social and Cultural Rights and the Covenant on Civil and Political Rights (both 1966). Paragraph 2 of this provision determines that "all peoples may, for their own ends, freely dispose of their natural wealth and resources." It adds: "In no case may a people be deprived of its own means of subsistence.[30]

The principle—which today is widely accepted as part of general international law[31]—entails several rights related to resources, including the right to explore and exploit natural resources freely and the right to regulate foreign investment. Over time, the objects to which the principle applies have ranged from "natural resources" and "natural wealth and resources"[32] to "all its wealth, natural resources and economic activities."[33] In recent General Assembly resolutions, the scope of the concept has again been confined to "natural wealth and resources."[34] Apart from rights, the principle has also come to entail obligations, in particular as a result of developments in the fields of international economic cooperation, environmental conservation, and human rights. These include a duty to exercise sovereignty over resources for the development of a nation and the well-being of the population, an obligation to respect the rights and interests of indigenous peoples, and a duty to use natural wealth and resources in a sustainable way.[35]

Self-Determination

The principle of self-determination—as included in Article 1(1) of the Covenant on Economic, Social and Cultural Rights and the Covenant on Civil and Political Rights—entails the right of peoples to "freely determine their political status and freely pursue their economic, social and cultural development." While the concept of "self-determination" was anticipated in 1918 in a speech by U.S. president Woodrow Wilson, it is within the United Nations that it has evolved into a principle of international law.[36] Referred to in Articles 1(2) and 55 of the UN Charter as a foundation for "friendly relations among nations," it has received practical meaning in the context of the process of decolonization. The principle of self-determination has especially found expression in the landmark Declaration on the Granting of Independence to Colonial Countries and Peoples of 1960 as a legal right of colonial peoples "to freely determine their political status and freely pursue their economic, social and cultural development."[37] Within the anticolonial context, the right to self-determination has widely been interpreted as entailing a right of secession for peoples under colonial administration.

Outside the colonial context, a right to self-determination exists for all peoples, although it is not equated with a right to secession and a right to political independence. The UN Declaration on the Rights of Indigenous Peoples, adopted after nearly twenty-five years of deliberation in 2007, now also acknowledges a right of self-determination to indigenous peoples, by virtue of which "they freely determine their political status and freely pursue their economic, social and cultural development."[38] However, the declaration limits the right to self-determination of indigenous peoples to autonomy within the state territory.[39]

Common Heritage of Humankind

In 1967, UN Ambassador Arvid Pardo of Malta proposed that the General Assembly declare that the seabed and the ocean floor beyond the limits of national jurisdiction was "the common heritage of mankind." Earlier in the same year, the General Assembly had declared outer space, including the moon and other celestial bodies, to be "the province of all mankind."[40] Pardo's remarkable proposal eventually led to the adoption in 1970 of the Declaration of Principles Governing the Sea-bed and the Ocean Floor, and the Subsoil Thereof, Beyond the Limits of National Jurisdiction, in which the General Assembly proclaimed the seabed area and its resources as the "common heritage of humankind,"[41] and to the incorporation of the same principle in the UN Convention on the Law of the Sea in 1982. With the adoption of the Agreement Governing the Activities of States on the Moon and Other Celestial Bodies in 1979, the principle of the "common heritage of humankind" was also applied to the natural resources of the moon and other celestial bodies.

Today, there is no precise definition of what the principle of "common heritage of humankind" entails. In general, it implies that certain areas and resources beyond national jurisdiction should not be exploited for the national or private gain of states or corporations. The principle thus certainly entails the ideas of nonappropriation (in contrast to the principle of "first come, first served"), common management, sharing benefits, using resources for peaceful purposes, preserving resources for future generations, and freedom of scientific research.

It is interesting to note that the principle does not figure in the new multilateral environmental agreements of the 1990s. The UN Framework Convention on Climate Change (1992), the UN Convention on Biological Diversity (1992), and the UN Convention to Combat Desertification in Countries Experiencing Serious Drought and/or Desertification, Particularly in Africa (1994) instead refer to the notion of the "common concern of humankind." This idea is not associated with a special international regime, but it still carries the connotation of the global nature of the problems at stake.[42]

Sustainable Development

The concept of sustainable development was introduced to the international agenda in 1987 through the report of the World Commission on Environment and Development, *Our Common Future*. The commission (also known as the Brundtland Commission) defined sustainable development as "development that meets the needs of the present without compromising the ability of future generations to meet their own needs."[43] Over time, the concept of sustainable development has been broadened and deepened.[44]

The origins of the concept lie in provisions relating to the sustainable use of natural resources, such as those found in international fishery regulation and in forestry. In this context, the core issue was preserving the regenerative capacity of a school of fish or a forest in order to achieve optimal economic production. Under the influence of the publication in 1972 of the Club of Rome's report *Limits to Growth*[45] and the Stockholm conference of the same year, the concept of optimal and rational use of natural resources began to be considered in a more general sense and applied to all natural resources—living and nonliving, renewable and nonrenewable. (With regard to nonrenewable resources, the main concern was rational consumption and the avoidance of waste). The concept was thus essentially a principle of conserving nonrenewable resources through rational and prudent use and maintaining the productivity of renewable resources indefinitely.

Since the Declaration on the Human Environment of the Stockholm conference of 1972, however, the concept has been expanded to the general need to protect nature and the environment and the ecological system of the earth, taking into consideration the interests of future generations. Gradually, these concerns began to be related not only to maintaining productive ecosystems, both terrestrial and marine, but also to protecting the ozone layer, the climate system, and other ecological functions of the planet that are vital for humankind.

The Stockholm conference also struck a compromise: environmental protection and economic development must go hand in hand regardless of the different environmental problems of developing and industrialized countries. Since then, it has become generally recognized that economic growth is indispensable and is an important engine of sustainable development, but only after taking into consideration environmental demands and the sustainable use of natural resources. At the 1992 Rio conference, the scope of sustainable development was broadened to include poverty reduction and economic development for developing countries and economic growth for all countries, thus striking a balance between the concerns of the industrialized and the developing countries.

Sustainable development has come a long way from the original meaning of sustainable use of natural resources. Although the definition now includes more anthropocentric and socioeconomic substance, it is fair to say that sustainable use of natural resources continues to be the core of the concept of sustainable development. Alertness is called for to prevent sustainable development from becoming an all-encompassing concept, if not a mantra, and there should be an accurate and continuous reconsideration of what can and cannot be part of the concept. The remarkably concise definition of the Brundtland Commission still provides the best guidance in this discussion.[46]

Chapter Outline

Chapter 1 provides a historical background and demonstrates that early forms of international organization in the pre-UN period often included schemes for natural resource management. Attention is paid to the early river commissions for the Danube and Rhine, to the early steps in fisheries conservation, and to early efforts to protect international wildlife. It also examines efforts within the League of Nations to address the issue of access to natural resources and world economic development and to settle international resource conflicts, partly through the Permanent Court of International Justice. Such experiences influenced the ideas for setting up the post–World War II international organization and are reflected, inter alia, in the establishment of ECOSOC and various specialized agencies, most notably the Food and Agriculture Organization (FAO), the World Bank, and the United Nations Educational, Scientific and Cultural Organization (UNESCO).

The next two chapters address in some detail the evolution of UN concerns regarding global resource management. Chapter 2 starts with a more general discussion of the responsibilities the UN Charter established in the economic and social field. Subsequently, the chapter focuses on national resource management and maps out the evolution of the main themes and trends in UN concerns about natural resource management. These include unsuccessful early postwar ideas on international management of national natural resources, the rise of economic nationalism reflected in the genesis of the concept of permanent sovereignty over natural resources, the broadening of sovereignty over resources by extending national jurisdiction to marine resources and the deepening of natural resource sovereignty, for example through nationalization of the natural resource sector as a key element of the effort to establish a New International Economic Order (NIEO). This is followed by a discussion of the evolution of the law of the sea and an analysis of the inception of the concept of sustainable development in the United Nations and of the contribution of the concept of proper global resource management to the achievement of the Millennium Development Goals (MDGs), particularly Goal 7 on ensuring environmental sustainability.

Chapter 3 addresses UN concerns about natural resource management from a global perspective. It examines the management of the areas and resources beyond the limits of national jurisdiction, often referred to as the global commons. These include the high seas, the ocean floor, the Antarctic environment and the Arctic region, the atmosphere, and outer space, particularly the moon and other celestial bodies. These areas have been used by the United Nations as a kind of laboratory for testing new ideas on the sharing of resources, such as the common heritage of humankind, the common concern of humankind, and international administration.

Chapter 4 reviews the international architecture of environmental governance and global resource management. It pays considerable attention to the United Nations Environment Programme and deals with other environment-related institutions, including the Commission on Sustainable Development (CSD) and the Global Environment Facility (GEF). The chapter also reviews the role of various specialized agencies in natural resource management, particularly the FAO, the International Fund for Agricultural Development (IFAD), the World Meteorological Organization (WMO), the World Bank, and UNESCO, and that of the secretariats of multilateral environmental and commodity agreements. It concludes that consultation and decision making about natural resource management is rather poorly organized within the UN system. Therefore, it proposes some alternative ideas for proper global resource management, including the idea of establishing a new UN world environmental organization.

Chapter 5 discusses recent concerns about the relationship between natural resources and armed conflict. While it seems logical that plentiful natural resources should engender prosperity, the record of instability and violence in countries such as Angola, Sierra Leone, Liberia, and the Democratic Republic of the Congo suggests a correlation between resource abundance and conflict—the so-called resource curse. In the early years of the twenty-first century, this has given rise to a shift in thinking about the role of natural resources in stability and development. This relates first of all to internal armed conflict to gain control over natural resources, an issue addressed by the Security Council through its sanctions on conflict trade and blood diamonds. Second, it relates to changing geopolitical relations, such as instability in the resource-rich Russian Federation and the rise of China as an economic power and its quest for access to natural resources in Africa and Asia.

The last two chapters are more reflective and prospective. Chapter 6 sketches the role of the International Court of Justice in settling natural resource disputes. It examines the jurisprudence of the court from the perspective of natural resources and analyzes cases concerning maritime delimitation and fishery disputes, land boundary disputes, disputes over water management, and international armed conflicts. Chapter 7 summarizes the four main roots of the UN's involvement with natural resource management. These are, in nearly consecutive order: the post–World War II concern about the security of the supply of and access to natural resources; the quest for permanent sovereignty over natural resources as part of the push for decolonization; the growing concern over the nonsustainable use of natural resources; and the role of natural resources in armed conflict as well as the protection of the environment and natural resources during times of armed conflict. Chapter 7 also reviews the principal actors within the UN system involved in resource management. Attention is also paid to the role of international commissions and of particular individuals.

Lastly, the chapter highlights the conceptual contribution of the UN to international approaches to managing natural resources and conserving the environment. The UN has been instrumental in generating widespread interest in rational resource management, taking into account developmental, environmental, and social dimensions. UN organs as well as its specialized agencies have made intellectual investments and undertaken numerous operational activities to foster economic development and a sustainable use of natural resources. Moreover, the political debates in various UN forums and conferences have resulted in new concepts for managing resources, such as resource sovereignty (on land and in the sea), duties as well as rights, the sharing of transboundary natural resources, the management of the global commons, and sustainable development. In examining the UN's conceptual contributions, the chapter seeks to identify the factors, circumstances, continents, institutions, and even particular persons that were instrumental in generating ideas on national and global resource management and the bringing of change.

Methodology

A major part of the study is based on the records of relevant debates within the United Nations and within other international organizations; an analysis of the related documents, including treaties, UN resolutions, and other legally or politically relevant instruments and reports; and literature and other relevant secondary sources in the fields of economics, political science, and international law. Furthermore, and in the spirit of the UN oral history project, this book builds on the materials available through the oral interviews conducted within the context of United Nations Intellectual History Project.

1

Historical Background: Formative Phases of International Organization during the Pre–UN Period

- **Early History of International Organization**
- **Early Examples of International Natural Resource Management**
- **The League of Nations**
- **Assessment**

In order to understand contemporary patterns of global resource management, it is useful to examine the historical evolution of the concept of international organization as it exists today. For this purpose, this chapter first reviews the roots and early history of international organization. It also introduces early organizational forms set up to manage natural resources. Next, this chapter examines the period of the League of Nations, with particular attention to natural resource regulation and access to raw materials.

Early History of International Organization

Before the nineteenth century, forms of international organization were relatively rare. In ancient Egypt and Mesopotamia, there are a few known cases of independent communities that collaborated in the management of rivers for agricultural purposes, but their cooperation lacked organizational structure. Moreover, conflicts between these communities soon ended any form of cooperation.[1] In ancient Greece, some forms of international organization existed, the political confederations being the most advanced. These leagues of cities had councils that were authorized to make majority decisions and sometimes even had an assembly that could levy contributions for military expenditure. Also in ancient Italy primitive forms of international organization existed. Yet the rise of the Roman empire ended this development. In the Middle Ages, examples of international organization include the Hanseatic League, a trade coalition of cities in the North of Europe, and the league of Swiss cantons (the Everlasting League), which was set up for defensive purposes. Any form of international cooperation between states, however, proved impossible due to continuous power struggles between the European empires. From the seventeenth century on, international relations were based on the principle of the balance of power, which in practice could only be challenged by waging war.[2]

Averse to the continuing threat of war, various seventeenth- and eighteenth-century philosophers elaborated on the idea of a general peace organization. As early as 1623, a French monk named Émeric Crucé proposed that a federation of states be established consisting of a council of ambassadors that could settle disputes between members.[3] Around the same time, the Dutch jurist Hugo Grotius suggested that "it would be advantageous, indeed in a degree necessary, to hold certain conferences of Christian powers, where those who have no interest at stake may settle the disputes of others, and where, in fact, steps may be taken to compel parties to accept peace on fair terms."[4] More than half a century later, William Penn went a step further and proposed a federal union or "European diet." This diet was to have a parliament with broad powers. The number of representatives of each state in the parliament was to be determined by the state's income. The idea of an international court of arbitration was further elaborated by Abbé de Saint-Pierre. In his 1713 book entitled *Projet pour rendre la paix perpétuelle en Europe,* he introduced the idea of a "union of sovereigns" for the settlement of legal disputes and assigned decision-making functions to the union's principal organ, the congress of envoys. Rousseau's "federation of states" as well as Kant's "alliance of peace" or "league of nations" built on this idea.[5]

When the modern concept of international organization finally emerged in the nineteenth century, it did so as a response to political needs rather than as a matter of ideology. For present purposes, it suffices to identify three main streams in the evolution of international organization: the Concert of Europe, the Hague system, and public international unions.

The Concert of Europe

The Concert of Europe refers to the system of multilateral high-level political conferences that replaced the system of predominantly bilateral consultations between states. This system goes back to the Congress of Vienna, which was convened in the period November 1814 to June 1815. The Congress of Vienna aimed to reshape the European order after the defeat of the French emperor Napoleon. In order to prevent a relapse into war, the congress sought to create a balance of power between the European states. The efforts of the European powers resulted in the 1815 Treaty of Paris, which set new borders for the European continent and established the Quadruple Alliance among Great Britain, Prussia, Austria, and Russia.

The Congress of Vienna proved significant in more than one way. It marked the beginning of a system that may be referred to as diplomacy by conference. This concert system aimed to promote peaceful coexistence between states, including through the negotiation of international regulations. In this regard, the regulation of navigation on international rivers is significant. In addition, the Congress of Vienna gave meaning to the term "great power" as a distinct category based on the idea that powerful states should assume greater responsibility than other states. Finally, the conference laid the foundations for the modern concept of "Europe." It defined Europe not only as a geographical area but also (and foremost) as a social and political community of independent states that adhered to certain social principles. In this way, the concert system established a "European family."[6]

The Hague System

Whereas the Concert of Europe was an entirely European affair, the Hague system opened international diplomacy to the larger community of states. The two peace conferences held in The Hague in 1899 and 1907 constituted the first "global" political summits in history in the sense that countries from all five continents that at the time contained sovereign states were represented. They further replaced the hegemonic power of the Concert of Europe with a system in which small states were also given the opportunity to voice their interests on an equal footing with the great powers. Thus, the Hague peace conferences marked the beginning of the modern system based on the sovereign equality of states. In 1899 twenty-six states participated and in 1907 forty-six states did so, thus marking the expansion of the number of states participating in international consultations and in international lawmaking.

Yet the principal significance of the Hague conferences lies in their contribution to the establishment of a comprehensive system to promote peace and regulate war *in abstracto* (and to a lesser extent the prevention of war). Rather than focusing on a particular crisis, the Hague conferences intended to formulate instruments for preventing war, conducting hostilities, and peacefully settling disputes in general. The 1899 conference created the Permanent Court of Arbitration with general authority to deal with arbitration cases brought before it by the parties to the Convention (1) on the Pacific Settlement of International Disputes (1899). Plans to set up a really permanent court were disappointed, though. At the 1907 peace conference, proposals to establish a general court of arbitral justice or an international prize court did not materialize.[7] In reality, the Permanent Court of Arbitration has been neither a proper nor a permanent court. Its function is to serve as a secretariat and registry providing legal and administrative support to arbitral tribunals or commissions of inquiry that are established ad hoc for each specific case. To date, the **Permanent Court of Arbitration** still functions in this role as the oldest international body for settling disputes.

Public International Unions

Public international unions constitute the third main stream in the nineteenth-century evolution of the modern concept of international organization. These were permanent associations of governments or administrations (such as national railway or postal bureaus) that were established on the basis of a multilateral treaty in fields where cooperation between governments had become imperative, such as transportation or telecommunication.[8] Early examples include the International Telegraphic Union (founded in 1865) and the Universal Postal Union (founded in 1874). Although they were still far away from advanced intergovernmental institutions of modern times, the public international unions were the first functional organizations in history and have been characterized as "rudimentary pieces of a system of intergovernmental collaboration."[9]

Whereas the Concert of Europe and the Hague system were primarily occupied with high-level political and diplomatic issues, the public international unions were set up primarily to deal with the practical aspects of international cooperation. They served inter alia as clearinghouses for information, as centers for discussion between governments on particular issues, and as instruments for coordinating national policies and practices. However, the diverse working fields of the public international unions—which ranged from agriculture to railroads and even narcotic drugs—paved the way for the modern system of specialized international organizations. Moreover, their structure—which included a conference of states for general decision making, a secretariat with a permanent staff, and a governing body to manage the organization—served as an example for modern international organizations.

Early Examples of International Natural Resource Management

Institutional management of natural resources has its origins in early organizations set up to manage rivers, fisheries, nature, and wildlife. These early attempts to manage shared natural resources provide important early examples of interstate cooperation,[10] particularly elaborating fundamental management principles. Furthermore, they created models of institutional structure.

The River Commissions

The river commissions are among the earliest examples of interstate cooperation to manage a natural resource. Their origin can be traced back to the Administration générale de l'Octroi de navigation du Rhin, which was established by a treaty between France and the Holy Empire dated 15 August 1804.[11] Whereas that organization was only concerned with the management of one particular river, the foundations for a comprehensive system to manage European rivers were created by the Vienna Congress of 1815. In Articles 108 to 117 of its Final Act—also characterized as the "constitutional charter" for European river navigation law[12]—the congress adopted the principle of free and nondiscriminatory navigation on international rivers and established basic rules for navigation on such rivers.[13]

Some rivers, including the Rhine, the Elbe and the Po, were specifically mentioned in the Final Act. The navigation of these and other rivers was to be regulated by common instruments that were based on the rules established in the Final Act.[14] In the years following the congress, several of these instruments were adopted. Examples include the Convention . . . Relative to the Free Navigation of the Elbe (1821) and the Mainz Convention (1831) relating to the Rhine. The latter convention established a supervisory Central Commission for Navigating on the Rhine, which still exists today. Other examples of early river commissions include the European Commission of the Danube, established through the 1856 Treaty of Paris. Although a commission for the Elbe was not established until after the conclusion of the 1919 Treaty of Versailles, it was preceded by a Commission of Revision that was charged with supervising the 1821 convention.[15] The regime of free navigation was also extended to watercourses in colonial Africa and Asia, but without transposing the system of river commissions to these watercourses. The International Commission of the Congo, established by the Treaty of Berlin in 1885, is a rare example of a nineteenth-century river commission outside Europe.[16]

The principal task of the early river commissions was to implement the principle of free navigation as developed within the specific conventions. They represented in a way the "community of riparians" of transboundary rivers—a notion denoting the idea of common ownership of an international watercourse by the riparians.[17] The competences of the commissions ranged widely, from issuing permits to establishing and enforcing navigation rules to setting the rules for levying tolls, although their mandates remained generally limited to navigation and related matters. With the exception of the first organization that dealt with the management of rivers, the Administration générale de l'Octroi de navigation du Rhin, the exploitation of freshwater resources and the control of pollution were not among the responsibilities of the nineteenth-century river commissions.

As a result of the industrial revolution in Europe and the United States, the use of rivers for other purposes than navigation grew considerably. Examples include using water for irrigation, for generating hydroelectric power, and for drinking water and sanitation.[18] These developments made apparent the need to initiate new forms of international cooperation, aimed specifically at managing freshwater resources. In 1911, the Institut de Droit international recommended the appointment of permanent joint commissions that would render decisions and opinions about situations where building new installations or altering existing installations in a shared watercourse would have a harmful impact on the portion of the watercourse located in the territory of another state or states.[19] In subsequent years, various special commissions were established to supervise the equitable utilization of the freshwater resources by all riparians. An early example of such a commission is the International Joint Commission (IJC) of Canada and the United States, which was established by the Boundary Waters Treaty concluded in 1909 between the United States and Great Britain and still exists today. The treaty endowed the IJC with a broad mandate that includes settling disputes involving the use of waters and was the first instrument to commit its parties to preventing pollution.[20] In 1920, a draft treaty on pollution prevention was drawn up under the auspices of the IJC, although it was never adopted.[21] Nevertheless, the attempt indicated growing awareness that the process of industrialization affected the quality of the water itself. Over the course of the twentieth century, specialized commissions were set up to deal with the issue of water pollution.[22]

International Regulation of Fishery and Sealing

The regulation of fishery and sealing is another example of early interstate cooperation to conserve and manage shared natural resources. A number of conventions regarding freshwater fishery were concluded beginning in the middle of the nineteenth century. These were of a bilateral character, such as the 1892 Convention between the Grand Duchy of Luxembourg and Prussia Concerning the Regulation of Fisheries in Boundary Waters (1892) [23] or the Convention Concerning Fishing in the Bidassoa between Spain and France (1886),[24] but also multilateral, as for example the Treaty Concerning the Regulation of Salmon Fishery in the Rhine River Basin (1885),[25] the Berne Convention Establishing Uniform Regulations Concerning Fishing in the Rhine Between Constance and Basel (1860),[26] or the Convention Concernant l'Exploitation et la Conservation des Pêcheries dans la Partie-Frontière du Danube (1902).[27] While none of these conventions set up special commissions to regulate freshwater fisheries, the conventions are relevant as early examples of institutionalized cooperation between states with regard to living natural resources.

Around the same time, the first steps were taken with to conserve marine fisheries and other resources of the seas. Fisheries treaties had in fact been concluded since the Middle Ages but were mostly concerned with ensuring freedom from molestation while fishing or were limited to coastal waters. In the nineteenth century, the need to more systematically regulate fishing and the harvesting of marine resources on the high seas became apparent after the first signs of overharvesting began to be seen with some valuable species. This development was attributable particularly to advancements in fishery techniques and the improvement of fishing capacity with the introduction of steam engines.

Yet the first steps in the multilateral management of living marine resources were not made in the context of fisheries but in relation to the preservation of seals. Like fish, seals were hunted on the high seas and efforts to conserve them suffered from the same problems as did efforts to manage fisheries. In 1876, Britain, Germany, Norway, the Netherlands, and Sweden attempted concurrent international regulation when they designated closed seasons for seals around eastern Greenland

and Jan Mayen Island.[28] It was also in the context of sealing that one of the first "environmental disputes" was settled by interstate arbitration. In the seminal Bering Sea controversy over fur sealing, an arbitral tribunal was established to solve a dispute that arose after the United States unilaterally sought to impose conservation measures on sealing on the high seas to prevent the alleged overexploitation of fur seals by Great Britain. The arbitral tribunal eventually decided that the United States had no property rights with regard to the seals and no right to unilaterally prohibit sealing beyond the three nautical mile limit of the territorial sea (a limit that originates from the cannon-shot rule advocated by the Dutch jurist Cornelis van Bynkershoek in his seminal work *De Dominio Maris* of 1703), upholding the doctrine of freedom of the high seas.[29] Nevertheless, the controversy is relevant at least in two aspects. First, it showed the potential for disputes over valuable natural resources lying beyond the national jurisdiction of any state. Second, it marked the beginning of unilateral attempts to regulate resource exploitation—a tenet that would be common in subsequent attempts to regulate exploitation of marine resources. Moreover, this late-nineteenth-century dispute showed that the motive behind conservation then was merely to protect fur seals as an economic asset.[30]

Signs of overexploitation soon became evident with regard to fisheries as well, and this resulted in various attempts to regulate them multilaterally. In 1881, a major conference was convened on fisheries of the North Sea that was attended by all the major powers of the time. The conference led to the adoption of the North Sea Fisheries Convention of 1882 and its 1887 supplement, perhaps the earliest multilateral conventions on fisheries. These conventions mostly emphasized policing and enforcement measures within a carefully defined area, although it is important to note that the conference itself was triggered by the perception that the North Sea was being overfished.[31] The emerging perception that marine species could become overharvested and depleted also triggered the establishment in 1902 of the first organization entrusted with the coordination of scientific research on fisheries, the International Council for the Exploration of the Sea (ICES),[32] which later began to provide scientific advice under a number of fisheries conventions. The establishment of the ICES indicated that the prevailing idea of inexhaustibility of living resources had begun to change and that people were beginning to see scientific information as the necessary basis for conservation measures.

A further step in the evolution of fishery management was the adoption of a number of multilateral conventions that were aimed at conserving commercially valuable species, the abundance of which had begun to be threatened. One such example was the Convention for Preservation and Protection of Fur Seals in the North Pacific (1911),[33] which prohibited pelagic sealing and introduced a number of measures that resembled modern environmental treaties (i.e., setting quotas and regulating trade in objects from seal hunting). Another important development in the management of shared fishery resources was the adoption of the Convention for the Preservation of Halibut Fishery of the Northern Pacific Ocean (1923),[34] which established one of the earliest marine fishery commissions, the International Fisheries Commission. While initially entrusted merely with conducting research into the halibut fishery, the powers of the commission were gradually increased to include the authority to limit catches in certain areas, regulate fishing gear, close areas to protect immature halibut, and establish closed seasons.[35] The Convention for the Protection, Preservation and Extension of Sockeye Salmon Fishery of the Fraser River System (1930)[36] similarly established the International Pacific Salmon Fisheries Commission in 1937 and gave it important regulatory powers.

International Protection of Nature and Wildlife

A third area where early concerns with natural resource management and conservation emerged was with regard to the protection of migratory birds and other migratory animals on land. The early steps focused on species of flora and fauna that were useful to human beings. Protection of nature and wildlife was hence motivated by economic rather than ecological reasons. A typical example of these concerns was the Convention for the Protection of Birds Useful to Agriculture (1902),[37] its title tellingly revealing its purpose. Although limited in its approach, the convention adopted conservation techniques that would later be used in modern environmental treaties, such as the total protection of certain birds and the prohibition of certain methods of killing. The convention could also be considered the first multilateral convention that protected certain *species* of wildlife. However, the first treaty that was aimed at the protection of wildlife in a *particular region* was the 1900 Convention Destinée à Assurer la Conservation des Diverses Espèces Animales Vivant à l'Etat Sauvage en Afrique qui sont Utiles à l'Homme ou Inoffensives,[38] the purpose

Table 1.1. Early Institutions for International Management of Natural Resources

River Commissions
- L'Administration générale de l'Octroi de navigation du Rhin (1804)
- Central Commission for Navigation on the Rhine (1831)
- European Commission of the Danube (1856)
- Commission of Revision (1821) for the Elbe (replaced by the International Commission for the Elbe in 1919)
- International Navigation Commission of the Congo (1885)
- International Joint Commission (1909; Canada and the United States)

Fishery Commissions
- International Council for the Exploration of the Sea (1902)
- International Fisheries Commission (1923)
- International Pacific Salmon Fisheries Commission (1930)

of which was protecting natural resources in Africa, particularly by imposing limitations on trade in furs and skins.

Common to all these early efforts in natural resource management is that they were sporadic, concerned only with specific aspects of resource use, and, in the case of living natural resources, directed at species that had already become endangered. In addition to this, the accompanying institutional arrangements were rudimentary and fragmented in nature. Nevertheless, they can be regarded as important milestones in the development of institutionalized cooperation because they were early instruments for regulating the exploitation and conservation of shared natural resources—although they were resources that were commercially valuable or otherwise useful. These initial steps laid the foundations of institutionalized management of natural resources that would evolve in the United Nations era. The first contours of this institutionalized management, however, began to take shape during the League of Nations.

The League of Nations

Established in 1919, the League of Nations was the first worldwide international organization vested with the general duty of containing conflict and promoting international peace and security. Although the Covenant of the League of Nations was limited to political issues—especially to peace and security matters—its organs nonetheless undertook considerable activity in the economic field. This included policies about natural resources. As a result, a number of important developments took place with regard to natural resource management during the League era. Early attempts took place under the auspices of the League to lay down general rules about the exploitation of living marine resources. In addition, the League concluded a number of multilateral conventions on natural resources. During the League years, the regulation of commodities and related discussions on access to raw materials began to develop. Of particular interest are the first examples to solve disputes involving natural resources through judicial means.

Early Attempts at Codification: The Exploitation of Products of the Sea

The early attempts at codification were an important episode in the League's involvement in natural resource management. In 1924, the assembly requested that the council convene a committee of experts "to prepare a provisional list of the subjects of international law[,] the regulation of which by international agreement would seem to be most desirable and realizable at the present moment."[39] The seriousness of the endeavor was underlined by the fact that these experts should "not merely [possess] individually the required qualifications but also as a body [represent] the main forms of civilization and the principal legal systems of the world," a requirement later followed in the United Nations era with the International Law Commission. The Committee of Experts for the Progressive Codification of International Law, as it was called, prepared an initial list of topics that included the question of "exploitation of the products of the sea." It appointed Argentinean professor José León Suárez as special rapporteur on the topic.[40]

In 1926, Suárez submitted his first report,[41] which deserves special attention because a number of his observations still hold true today. Suárez noted that the existing international regulation of the exploitation of the products of the sea, though it had proved valuable on occasion, was no longer adequate because it "has hitherto been of a limited and local character and has, except in two or three cases, been directed not solely to the protection of species from extinction but mainly to establish police measures and to ensure reciprocity and *commerce,* regardless of biological interests, which in this case are inseparable from *economic* and *general* interests." In Suárez's view, the result of such regulation had been "the useful but by no means sufficient one of delaying, but not preventing, the extinction of some of the principal species." As a result, "marine species of use to man will become extinct unless their exploitation is subject to international regulation." This would have detrimental consequences: "as, if we consider the life of all the species in the animal kingdom, biological solidarity is even closer among the denizens of the ocean than among land animals, the disappearance of certain species would destroy the balance in the struggle for existence and would bring about the extinction of other species also."

Suárez noted a truism that would trouble efforts to regulate fisheries throughout the twentieth century, particularly stocks of highly migratory fish: "The majority of aquatic animals are essentially migratory, and it is this characteristic which creates the biologico-geographical solidarity of species, which should find its counterpart in a legal solidarity in the sphere of international law in which we are working." International regulation should take account of that fact, "for animals, happier in this than men, are ignorant of jurisdictions and national frontiers and observe not international law but internationalism; the sea for them is a single realm, like Ovid's dream of a world forming a single fatherland for humanity."

In Suárez's opinion, the exploitation of the products of the sea required regulation most urgently in the waters nearest to the coasts, as those waters contain species most useful to humankind. Among "the most economically important species which should be preserved for the use of humanity," Suárez included herring, salmon, cod, mackerel, and hake. He also drew attention to seals, which were in danger of extinction, and to the modern whaling industry, which was rapidly exterminating the whale. With regard to the latter, Suárez observed a number of issues that would become characteristic for other fisheries as well with the increase of industrial fishing: the use of "the perfected form of weapon and special craft" and the great increase of "floating factories," which accelerates the production process and renders national control impossible, "since no action can be taken in the open sea."[42]

Suárez thereby pointed out to what for a long time would be considered the greatest obstacle to effective conservation of marine resources—the principle of the freedom of the seas. The principle, which for centuries had governed the use of the high seas, implied that everyone could navigate, conduct commerce, and fish as long as the rights of others were not hindered. Decisive in establishing this principle was a booklet called *Mare Liberum* (1609) in which the Dutch jurist Hugo Grotius had opposed the claims to sovereignty over oceans that Portugal, Spain, and some other countries of his time had advanced.[43] The booklet—which won a great reputation and decisively influenced the development of the law of the sea—was based on the premise that the sea must be free because it is impossible to occupy infinite and boundless natural elements such as air and marine waters. While this made perfect sense with regard to navigation, applying the same logic to the use of marine resources had different implications, for it meant that states could not regulate the exploitation of the resources of the high seas unless they did so by common agreement. Of course, this did not raise serious problems when the exploitation of the seas was limited to a few users, but as improvements in fishing techniques resulted in overexploitation of marine resources, the limitations of the principle became rather apparent. Throughout the twentieth century these same limitations were used as arguments in favor of extending the sovereignty of coastal states over extensive maritime areas.

Calling upon the Committee of Experts, Suárez observed that "the riches of the sea, and especially the immense wealth of the Antarctic region, are the patrimony of the whole human race, and our Committee is the body best qualified to suggest to the Governments what steps should be taken before it is too late." In his view, "To save this wealth, which, being to-day the uncontrolled property of all, belongs to nobody, the only thing to be done is to discard the obsolete rules of the existing treaties, which were drawn up with other objects, to take a wider view, and to base a new jurisprudence, not on the defective legislation which has failed to see justice done but on the scientific and economic considerations which, after all the necessary data has been collected, may be put forward, compared and discussed at a technical conference by the countries concerned." Suárez's posture in this respect was remarkable. As he himself proclaimed, he was "not considering . . . the interests of the moment or of any particular country but the general interest of mankind, which before long will have to draw upon the reserves of the sea to make good the inadequacy of the food production of the land. It is our business to see that this step is not taken too late."[44]

Suárez concluded that it was possible through adequate regulation to exploit the products of the sea economically; that such regulation could not fail to be in the general interest; that existing treaties "have not always taken into account the point of greatest importance to humanity, which is to find means to prevent the disappearance of species, and not infrequently they concern measures of police or purely commercial measures, without considering the biologico-economic aspect, which is the essential aspect"; and that the attention of all maritime powers should be called to the urgent need to establish regulations by holding a conference.[45]

After discussing the report, however, the Committee of Experts felt that a special procedure should be followed because of "the extremely technical nature of the subject" and because a number of governments had indicated that the question needed to be studied at greater length and in greater detail. The committee felt that a conference of experts was the proper body for formulating an opinion on these problems and on the best method of creating rules without undesirable delay. Such a conference should include experts in maritime zoology, representatives of the marine products industry, and jurists and should draw on the cooperation of institutions such as the ICES.[46] These recommendations remarkably resemble modern international rule making in regulating natural resources, where the input of science has come to play a crucial role. These suggestions were taken up by the Council and the General Assembly of the League,[47] and the latter instructed the Economic Committee of the League to study, in collaboration with the ICES and any other organization especially interested in the matter, "the question whether and in what terms, for what species and in what areas, international protection of marine fauna could be established."[48]

The conference on the Progressive Codification of International Law, which in the meantime had convened at The Hague in 1930, examined only three topics that were ultimately considered suitable for codification—the questions of nationality, territorial waters, and responsibility of states for damage to foreigners. However, even with regard to these three topics the conference mostly failed to achieve its aim; it succeeded in adopting international instruments only on the topic of nationality. In contrast, a draft convention on territorial waters did not garner sufficient support, as states were unable to agree on the breadth of the territorial sea. For centuries, sovereignty was accepted only for internal waters (lakes, rivers, canals, ports) and a narrow belt of sea next to the shore—the territorial sea. However, no uniform agreement existed on the extent of the latter. While the major maritime powers insisted on a limit of three nautical miles, some other coastal states claimed a wider area. The Scandinavian countries, for instance, claimed a maritime *dominium* of four miles along the whole coastline, while Russia for some purposes even claimed twelve nautical miles.[49]

The failure of the codification conference of 1930 was to a great extent attributable to the diversity of interests, the protection of which was the object of the claims states made to territorial waters. An important place among these interests was given to fisheries and more generally to the use of the products of the sea. This was evident not only from the draft articles prepared on the topic by German rapporteur Walther

Schücking[50] but also by the recommendations adopted by the drafting committee of the conference, which, recognizing "that the protection of the various products of the sea must be considered not only in relation to the territorial sea, but also the waters beyond it," affirmed the desirability of "measures of protection and collaboration which may be recognized as necessary for the safeguarding of riches constituting the common patrimony."[51]

Multilateral Natural Resource Conventions

Further treatment of the topic of exploitation of the products of the sea was undertaken by the League's Economic Committee, which decided, in cooperation with the ICES, that only whaling appeared to lend itself to international action.[52] This eventually led to the conclusion of the Convention for the Regulation of Whaling in 1931,[53] which was negotiated on the basis of a draft prepared by the ICES and the League's organs. Although applicable only to baleen (or whalebone) whales, the convention was a remarkable achievement because it prohibited the taking of certain species of whale as well as the taking of immature or suckling whales and required an optimal use of whale carcasses. The convention also required vessels hunting whales to be authorized by permit and required parties to keep records and make regular reports to the Bureau of International Whaling Statistics. Remarkably, it applied these regulations, for the first time, to "all the waters of the world, including both the high seas and territorial and national waters."[54] The convention attracted quite a bit of support,[55] including from Great Britain and Norway, the two major whaling nations of the time, but it did not include among its parties states that had begun to develop their whaling industries—namely, Japan, Germany, Chile, Argentina, and Russia. In spite of its innovative provisions, the convention was thus not considered a success and a new convention had to be adopted in 1937 and a further protocol had to be adopted in 1938. However, this happened outside the context of the League of Nations.[56]

The 1931 whaling convention was not the only multilateral treaty to deal with natural resources that was adopted under the auspices of the League of Nations. An earlier example of an international convention that specifically dealt with the management of natural resources was the International Convention Concerning the Regime of Navigable Waterways of International Concern (1921).[57] This convention was concerned primarily with navigation on international waterways above other possible uses and could thus be said to have resumed the task of codifying the body of rules relating to freedom of navigation and equality of treatment on international rivers that was begun by the Congress of Vienna. The convention required parties to refrain from impairing the navigability of a waterway, to eliminate obstacles to navigation, and even to carry out works for improving navigability if asked to do so by another riparian state. It also stipulated that navigable waterways could be closed only with the consent of all the riparian states.

Another notable achievement of this period was the Convention Relative to the Preservation of Fauna and Flora in the Nature State (1933),[58] which was concluded by League members with the objective of preserving the natural fauna and flora of certain parts of the world, particularly Africa. While it excluded from its provisions the metropolitan areas of colonial powers, the convention is an important milestone in the development of wildlife and nature protection and is considered to be a "precursor to our present environmental concepts."[59] The convention could be said to have started the modern approach to ecological issues; it envisaged the establishment of national parks and reserves, the introduction of strict protection of certain species (listed in an annex), and the regulation of hunting and collection of species. Moreover, it stipulated some limitations on trade.

The League of Nations period thus marks the beginning of an era of treaty making during which international organizations played a role in facilitating the drafting and conclusion of multilateral conventions and, as in the case of the League's secretariat, acted as registrars of treaties, a role that would be later taken up by the United Nations and its specialized agencies.

Access to Raw Materials and the Emerging Regulation of Commodities

A third important development with regard to the management of natural resources relates to the regulation of access to raw materials that began to take place in the League period. Owing to sharp fluctuations in the prices of primary products, the first commodity regulation schemes were created in the years after World War I. These included the Bandoeng Pool to regulate the quantities of tin that could be released on the market, and the Stevenson Plan, which limited the tonnage of exported rubber, later to be followed by control schemes for sugar, copper, petroleum, lead, zinc, wheat, and tea that were initiated in the late 1920s and early 1930s.[60] As a result of overproduction of whale oil in the early 1930s, a series of multicompany agreements was developed to stabilize the market for that commodity. The major whaling companies, which were mainly of Norwegian and British origin, decided to impose regulations upon themselves to limit whale catches. However, these agreements, which were developed simultaneously with interstate agreements under the League of Nations, were not aimed at conservation as such but were designed to prevent overexploitation and bring economic stability to the whaling industry.[61]

The emergence of industrial agreements regulating the supply of commodities generated certain concerns. These were voiced, for example, in the report of the World Economic Conference of 1927 that took place under the auspices of the League of Nations, which noted that international industrial agreements "should not, either in intention or effect, restrict the supply to any particular country of raw materials or basic products, or without just cause create unequal conditions between the finishing industries of the consuming and producing countries or other countries situated in the same conditions."[62]

In 1936, the League's General Assembly decided that the time was ripe for studying the question of equal commercial access to certain raw materials. The following year, the council appointed the Committee for the Study of the Problem of Raw Materials, which in the same year produced a report on the topic. It is interesting to note the initial observation of the committee that it was not its function "to discuss the question of restricting raw-material supplies in order to discourage aggression"; rather, it felt that its job was to study "the possibility of international co-operation in facilitating commercial access to raw materials for all countries in the world engaged in peaceful trade."[63] For its purposes, the committee noticed that the problems with raw materials fell into two categories: on the one hand, there were difficulties in obtaining a sufficient and secure supply of raw materials; on the other hand, certain countries had difficulty paying for the raw materials they needed. The committee observed that the regulation schemes relating to raw materials in operation had been an important factor in the improvement in economic conditions producing countries had experienced during the depression and in the development of international trade. But it felt that it was very important that consuming countries be given every assurance that the schemes would be operated in a reasonable manner. While certain prohibitions and restrictions could be justified, the committee felt that serious objections could be made to prohibitions or restrictions that were designed to apply pressure to other countries, to preserve industries that were not economical, or to maintain artificial price levels by creating an excessive supply in the internal market, by starving the market, or by maintaining monopolies or quasi-monopolies.[64]

Economic advancement to a large degree depends on a progressive development of natural resources, the committee argued, and it noted that although immense progress had been made in this direction, it was not uniform: "While some countries command natural resources in excess of their need; others are less favoured."[65] As industrialization could only be built upon a basis of imported raw materials, it was in the committee's view of vital concern to those countries that they be assured that they would have unrestricted supplies of raw materials and a market for their increased output. "It should be recognized," remarked the committee, "that the Governments of countries which are important suppliers, actual or potential, of raw materials have a responsibility not unreasonably to hamper the development of their raw materials," taking into account the "interdependence of all countries."[66]

The committee concluded that the difficulties that existed with supply of raw materials were not insuperable and that the problems with regard to payments were much more difficult to solve. On a more general note, it added:

> There is no doubt that there is an inequality in the distribution of raw materials and that certain countries have particularly serious difficulties in supplying their requirements. . . . But the only general and permanent solution of the problem of commercial access to raw materials is to be found in a restoration of international exchanges on the widest basis.[67]

The Economic Committee of the League's General Assembly, however, did not consider it necessary to frame an international convention on the subject. Instead, it formulated principles regarding commercial access to raw materials, including foodstuffs. Those principles stipulated that raw materials should not be subjected to any export prohibition or restriction except in pursuance of an international regulation scheme. They also stipulated that raw materials should not be subject to any export duties. The principles also stated that foreigners should have equal rights in the development of natural resources of sovereign countries and colonial territories and called for the establishment of international regulation schemes to take account of the interests of consumers, provide consumers with adequate supplies of the regulated material, and prevent (so far as possible) excessive increases in the price of the regulated material and keep the price reasonably stable.[68]

Access to natural resources remained a preoccupation throughout the League period and became of acute importance during World War II. The Allied Powers realized that both the supply of raw materials and access to overseas natural resources were very vulnerable and that free access to natural resources would be an essential part of postwar reconstruction. This concern was first expressed in the Atlantic Charter of 1941, in which the Allies (in fact, the United Kingdom and the United States) agreed "to further the enjoyment by all States, great or small, victor or vanquished, of access, on equal terms, to the trade and to the raw materials of the world which are needed for their prosperity."[69] At the United Nations Conference on Food and Agriculture in 1943, it was thus repeatedly stressed "that the world, after the war, should follow a bold policy of economic expansion instead of the timid regime of scarcity which characterized the 1930s."[70] These concerns led to various postwar initiatives in the newly established United Nations organization.

Settlement of Disputes Related to Resources

Last but not least, the League of Nations period was also characterized by the increased resort to judicial mechanisms to settle disputes relating to the exploitation and use of natural resources—a development that was reflected in the docket of the Permanent Court of International Justice (PCIJ), located in The Hague. From an institutional perspective, the PCIJ was not a League organ to the same extent that the International Court of Justice is one of the principal organs of the United Nations. Its statute was drawn up separately and did not form an integral part of the Covenant of the League of Nations in a similar fashion as the statute of the ICJ forms part of the UN Charter.[71]

Nevertheless, the PCIJ played an important role in the functioning of the League: the court's main purpose was to settle disputes between member states (and, subject to special provisions, other states as well),[72] and the League of Nations' Council or its General Assembly could ask the court for advisory opinions.

One of the earliest disputes brought before the court—the Mavrommatis concessions case—involved questions regarding the exploitation of natural resources. The case concerned a dispute that began with the alleged refusal of the government of Palestine, and consequently also of the British government as the mandatory of the territory, to recognize the right of the Greek national Euripides Mavrommatis to concessions for constructing electric and water works in the cities of Jerusalem and Jaffa. Mavrommatis had acquired the concessions under contracts and agreements with the Ottoman authorities before World War I but was prevented from implementing them after Palestine became a mandated territory of Great Britain. In 1924, the Greek government took Mavrommatis's claim to the PCIJ, which subsequently decided that the concession granted to Mavrommatis with regard to utilities works in Jerusalem were valid and that certain rights that were granted to another concessionaire, Pinhas Rutenberg, did not conform with international obligations that the British Mandate of Palestine had accepted. However, the court found that no loss had accrued to Mavrommatis as a result of that circumstance and that, therefore, the Greek government's claim for an indemnity had to be dismissed.[73] On the basis of the judgment, Mavrommatis was entitled to require that the concession be readapted to the new economic conditions, but the British government delayed in approving the readaptation plans for the concessions. As a result, the dispute was again brought to the court, but this time, because of the changed nature of the dispute, the court found that it had no jurisdiction.[74]

Concessions were involved in another dispute that was decided by the court in the 1938, the phosphates in Morocco case. The dispute arose after a legislative decree (*dahir*) reserved for the Moroccan government the exclusive right to prospect for and work phosphates, thereby infringing upon the rights of the Italian company Miniere e Fosfati, which had previously acquired licenses to prospect for phosphates in certain areas of Morocco, which was then a French protectorate. The Italian government subsequently instituted proceedings against the French government, claiming that the monopolization of Moroccan phosphates was inconsistent with certain international obligations of Morocco and France. Moreover, Italy claimed that Morocco and France had to respect the rights acquired by the Italian company, which should have been recognized as discoverer, and had to invite tenders to work the deposits covered by the company's licenses. In the event that they did not do so, Italy demanded fair compensation for the expropriation. The dispute, however, could not be decided by the court, which had found that the conventions and treaties upon which Italy had relied to establish the court's jurisdiction were not applicable. Consequently, the court ruled that it had no jurisdiction to entertain the Italian claims.[75]

On two occasions the PCIJ also played a role in solving disputes relating to the use of shared or international watercourses. One was the 1929 case concerning the International Commission of the River Oder, in which the court had to determine whether the jurisdiction of the international commission extended to the sections of the Oder's tributaries Warthe (Warta) and Netze Noteć, which were situated in Polish territory, and if so, which principle had to be adopted for determining the upstream limits of the commission's jurisdiction. In providing an answer to these questions, the court referred to "the principles governing international fluvial law in general," and noted, first, that "the desire to provide the upstream States with the possibility of free access to the sea played a considerable part in the formation of the principle of freedom of navigation on so-called international rivers." At the same time, however, the court observed that:

> when consideration is given to the manner in which States have regarded the concrete situations arising out of the fact that a single waterway traverses or separates the territory of more than one State, and the possibility of fulfilling the requirements of justice and the considerations of utility which this fact places in relief, it is at once seen that a solution of the problem has been sought not in the idea of a right of passage in favour of upstream States, but in that of a community of interest of riparian States. This community of interest in a navigable river becomes the basis of a common legal right, the essential features of which are the perfect equality of all riparian States in the use of the whole course of the river and the exclusion of any preferential privilege of any one riparian State in relation to the others.[76]

The principle of "perfect equality of all riparian States," which became one of the fundamental principles of the international law of watercourses, enabled the court to conclude that the jurisdiction of the international commission extended to tributaries of the Oder river, inasmuch as the common right extends to the whole navigable course of the river and does not stop short at the boundaries of Poland.

In another case involving a dispute relating to an international watercourse, the 1937 case concerning the diversion of waters from the Meuse river, the PCIJ was required to determine whether Belgium's construction of certain canals and the manner in which Belgium supplied and intended to supply existing or projected canals in its territory with water violated the rights of the Netherlands under an 1863 treaty that established a regime for taking water from the river. The dispute therefore involved a variety of questions connected with the use of the waters of the Meuse, a watercourse that Belgium and the Netherlands as well as France shared. In deciding the dispute, the court confined itself exclusively to the interpretation and application of the 1863 water treaty concluded between the two parties and after finding no violation of the 1863 treaty dismissed the contentions of both parties. In contrast with the Oder river decision, the court did not find it necessary to rely upon any general principles of "fluvial law" or to further develop them.[77]

Resort to judicial mechanisms to settle disputes relating to the exploitation and use of natural resources was observable not only in the case law of the Permanent Court of International Justice but also in arbitral practice. An important example is the landmark Trail smelter arbitration of 1938–1941, which can be regarded as the first international decision on transboundary air pollution. The case arose out of a dispute between the United States and Canada with regard to a zinc and lead smelter located in Trail, British Columbia, in the vicinity of the international boundary with the U.S. state of Washington. The United States objected that sulfur dioxide emissions from the operation of the smelter were causing damage to the land and the trees of the Columbia River Valley, which were used for logging, farming, and cattle grazing. The dispute was initially referred for settlement to the International Joint Commission of the United States and Canada, which in 1931 had prescribed limitations on sulfur dioxide emissions from the smelter and demanded that Canada pay compensation for damages.

As conditions did not improve, however, the two states submitted the dispute to an ad hoc arbitral tribunal in 1933. In an initial decision of 1938, the arbitral tribunal made provisional restrictions on the smelting operation while it studied the effects of its sulfur dioxide emissions. The tribunal reached its final decision in 1941, in which it observed that

> under the principles of international law, . . . no State has the right to use or permit the use of its territory in such a manner as to cause injury by fumes in or to the territory of another or the properties or persons therein, when the case is of serious consequence and the injury is established by clear and convincing evidence.[78]

The tribunal decided that Canada should pay compensation for damages that the smelter had caused during the period from 1932 to 1937, primarily to land along the Columbia River Valley, and that the smelter should refrain from causing future damage from its sulfur dioxide emissions. To that purpose, the tribunal prescribed a monitoring regime for measuring the emissions and provided that further compensation could be awarded to the United States if the smelter was unable to adhere to the prescribed sulfur dioxide levels. While the importance of the decision for the development of international environmental law has perhaps been exaggerated, the arbitral award continues to be relied upon as an important precedent that spelled out the obligation not to cause significant transboundary harm, which crystallized into one of the fundamental principles of international environmental law.[79] Moreover, it is a leading example of two states voluntarily submitting their differences to international arbitration.

Assessment

The establishment of the League of Nations was an important milestone in both the evolution of international organization and in natural resource management. The League's organs served as permanent forums where various topics involving natural resource management could be discussed. There was a move toward a more systematic approach to certain aspects of natural resource management, as is evident from the discussions that took place with regard to topics such as the exploitation of the resources of the sea or access to raw materials. The work of the League's organs generated an important impetus for states to adopt various multilateral conventions governing natural resource exploitation and conservation, many of which were drafted by the organs of the League. During the League of Nations period, the first disputes related to natural resources were submitted to institutionalized forms of international dispute settlement. The early decisions of the PCIJ and arbitral tribunals demonstrated the utility of international procedures for settling resource disputes and identified a number of substantive principles and rules, such as the "perfect equality of the riparian states" in the management of international watercourses or the importance of respecting acquired rights in the context of mineral and other concessions related to natural resources. As is demonstrated in the forthcoming chapters, after 1945 many of these activities were taken up by the United Nations and its specialized agencies.

2

UN Involvement with Natural Resource Management at the National and Transboundary Levels

- **UN Charter Responsibilities in the Economic and Social Field**
- **Early Postwar Concerns**
- **The Rise of Economic Nationalism**
- **Deepening Resource Sovereignty: Protection for Newly Independent States**
- **Broadening Resource Sovereignty: The Rush to Exploit Marine Resources**
- **A Major Milestone: The Stockholm Conference on the Human Environment**
- **Toward a New International Economic Order?**
- **A New Constitution for the Seas and the Oceans**
- **UNEP Guidelines and the Management of Shared Natural Resources**
- **The 1992 Earth Summit**
- **Post-Rio Developments**
- **Indigenous Sovereignty over Natural Resources**
- **Assessment**

This chapter maps the history of the involvement of the United Nations with natural resource management at the national and transboundary levels, from the organization's early days up to recent times.[1] The term "natural resources" does not figure in the UN Charter, nor does "environment" or "sustainable development." Yet the UN soon became involved with issues relating to the management of natural resources as part of postwar efforts to reconstruct war-torn Europe. Since then, natural resource management has gradually become one of the main concerns of the United Nations. This chapter briefly presents the Charter responsibilities of the UN in the economic and social field. It then sketches the various stages that marked the movement toward strengthening, deepening, and broadening national sovereignty over natural resources as well as the opposite movement that led to the gradual qualification of a state's sovereignty over its resources with provisions to protect the environment. While these developments never followed a single path and cannot be neatly separated into historic periods, the chapter nevertheless tries to present a coherent narrative that brings the reader from early postwar concerns with natural resource management to the rise of economic nationalism, the protection of newly independent states, and the extension of sovereignty over marine resources. It discusses the beginnings of an environmental regime with the Stockholm conference, the debates on a New International Economic Order, the negotiation of a new constitution for the oceans, the Rio Conference on Environment and Development, the various post-Rio summits, and finally the Declaration of the Rights of Indigenous Peoples of 2007.

UN Charter Responsibilities in the Economic and Social Field

The Charter of the United Nations does not refer at all to the concept of natural resources or to the goal of conservation of the environment. Obviously, the new world organization was first of all meant to restore and maintain peace and security. Only in this specific field was the organization vested with far-reaching enforcement powers. However, one of the Charter's main differences from the Covenant of the League of Nations was that it included the promotion of international economic and social cooperation.[2] Thus, the preamble refers to the organization's determination to employ "international machinery for the promotion of economic and social advancement of all peoples." Moreover, Article 1 states that one of the purposes of the United Nations is to achieve international cooperation in solving international economic and social problems. This is elaborated in Chapter IX, "International Economic and Social Co-operation," most notably in Articles 55 and 56. Article 55 states that the economic and social purposes of the United Nations include "higher standards of living, full employment, and conditions of economic and social progress and development." It is noteworthy that these economic and social objectives are subordinated to the all-embracing goal of "the creation of conditions of stability and well-being which are necessary for peaceful and friendly relations among nations based on respect for the principle of equal rights and self-determination of peoples."[3] ECOSOC was established to implement these functions of the United Nations.[4]

Reference may also be made to similar objectives that are applicable to non-self-governing territories and trust territories. Charter article 73 stipulates that member states with responsibilities for such non-self-governing territories have "a sacred obligation to promote to the utmost . . . the well-being of the inhabitants of these territories."[5] This includes the duty "to promote constructive measures of development." In a similar vein, Chapter XII of the Charter states that one of the basic objectives of the international trusteeship system is the promotion of the "political, economic, social and educational advancement of the inhabitants of the trust territories."

While there can be little doubt that maintaining peace and security was at the forefront of the minds of the founders of the United Nations, in practice the organization began to focus on economic and social issues as well from the very beginning.

Early Postwar Concerns

Especially during World War II, the Allied Powers, particularly the United States, became aware of their dependence on overseas raw materials and of the vulnerability of their supply lines. Such concerns were outlined in the Atlantic Charter of 1941, in which the Allies advocated the principle of equal access of all states to the raw materials of the world. The Allied Powers stated that they would endeavor "with due respect for existing obligations, to further the enjoyment by all States, great or small, victor and vanquished, of access, on equal terms, to the trade and to the raw materials of the world which are needed for their economic prosperity."[6] This concern was one of the reasons for establishing the Bretton Woods institutions as well as the General Agreement on Tariffs and Trade. The ultimate goal of all these institutions was to contribute to a balanced and expanding world economy, and a secure supply of resources was an important precondition toward that end. Thus, the articles of agreement of both the International Bank for Reconstruction and Development and the International Monetary Fund refer to the need to develop "the productive resources of all members," while the preamble to the General Agreement on Tariffs and Trade includes among its objectives "the full use of the resources of the world."[7]

Illustrative of the spirit prevailing during the postwar period was the initiative of the International Co-operative Alliance (ICA), a U.S.-based consumers' organization that in 1947 submitted a proposal to ECOSOC concerning control over world oil resources.[8] In 1946, the ICA had adopted a resolution that emphasized the need to place control and administration of the world's oil resources under the authority of an organ of the United Nations. As a first step in that direction, the resolution proposed that the oil resources of the Middle East be the first to be administered by the world body. The ICA proposed that a UN petroleum commission be established under the authority of ECOSOC. In its report to ECOSOC, it referred to the Atlantic Charter principle of equal access for all states to the raw materials of the world and stated:

> From the consumers' viewpoint it is absolutely necessary that raw materials should be made available to the whole of humanity on equal terms. No valid reason can be constructed for regarding every raw material as the monopoly of the State within whose boundaries it happens to exist or can be produced. On the contrary, raw materials should be first thing after armaments to be placed under the control of the United Nations.[9]

The ICA further proposed that the United Nations draw up a convention on international control over oil resources, especially those in the Middle East, where the greater part of the unexploited oil resources of the world appeared to be located. The ICA felt that the convention should stipulate that oil resources were to be exploited in the public interest, that all should have equal access to these resources, and that sufficient reserves should be left for the needs of future generations.[10] The convention should also be agreed to by the countries of the Middle East. The alliance pointed out that its proposals did not purport to infringe on the sovereign rights of these states, since these proposals left the property titles intact. The ICA asked the United Nations to consider this question an urgent matter inasmuch as rivalry for the acquisition of new oil fields might endanger world peace, equitable access to world resources was a vital condition for the world's economic reconstruction, and there was a tendency on the part of large oil enterprises to fix prices without considering the interests of the consumer. However, the proposals for extending UN control over oil resources were not viewed favorably in ECOSOC.[11]

Increasingly, the attention of the United Nations and its specialized agencies was devoted to questions of conservation and effective utilization of natural resources, particularly with regard to the growing demand for raw materials that was triggered by postwar reconstruction and rapid economic growth. A key issue, especially in Europe, was the problem of timber shortages, which became one of the first concerns of the newly established Food and Agriculture Organization of the United Nations. In 1947, the FAO organized the International Timber Conference to consider the problem of the supply of and availability of timber for reconstructing countries devastated by the war. The conference stressed the need for a satisfactory distribution of timber supplies and long-term measures to restore forests as part of the reconstruction of Europe and called upon governments to "take steps to control fellings . . . with the object of obtaining a sustained and, if possible, increased output."[12]

The first major and truly international initiative devoted to the status of world natural resources, however, was the United Nations Scientific Conference on the Conservation and Utilization of Resources, which convened in 1949 on the initiative of U.S. president Harry Truman. As a joint project of the United Nations and relevant specialized agencies, the conference was the first time that the United Nations brought together a large and representative group of scientists to address "the need for continuous development and widespread application of the techniques of resource conservation and utilization."[13] The primary goal of the conference was the exchange of ideas and experiences in the field of resource management and human use of resources. Discussions focused on the world resource situation, including the issues of resource depletion, critical shortages, use and conservation, and resource exploitation techniques suitable for less-developed countries. The conference devoted considerable time to assessing the adequacy of resources to meet growing demand. Most experts observed that the renewal capacity of the lands, forest, and inland waters of substantial areas had been impaired for years to come by errors that had been made years earlier but concluded that it was possible "through the less wasteful use of resources, the fuller application of existing techniques and the exploitation of new scientific developments, to support a far greater population than exists today, at a much higher level of living."[14] The conference thus underscored the relationship between the environment and development. Although it did not adopt any specific recommendations, the conference stated that "scientific knowledge can discover and husband better those already in use, so that a new era of prosperity awaited mankind," on the condition that war and the wasteful depletion of resources associated with it be eliminated.[15]

These proposals reflected the wartime problems of the Allied Powers in getting access to vital resources and properly managing scarce natural resources. Initially such proposals were made in an optimistic spirit of international cooperation. However, rivalry between the East and the West and the efforts of less-developed countries to control the management of their own natural resources soon came to dominate the scene. It proved impossible to develop international cooperation schemes for managing natural resources.

The Rise of Economic Nationalism

From the early 1950s various projects sought to reinforce national control over natural resources. First, in 1951 Poland introduced a draft resolution on integrated economic development in developing countries and long-term trade agreements.[16] The resolution invited member states to conclude long-term agreements "for supplying to the under-developed countries machinery and equipment essential for the fulfillment of the plans for economic development of these countries in exchange for raw materials exported by them." Poland pointed out that such agreements "must not contain any economic or political conditions violating the sovereign rights of the economically underdeveloped countries or conditions which are contrary to the aims of the plans for economic development of these countries." This document precipitated a vigorous debate that stimulated a flood of amendments and focused on the extent to which underdeveloped countries should take world economic interests into account in their natural resource policies. The Polish draft said that underdeveloped countries have the full right to determine freely how to use their natural resources and referred to the economic development plans and national interests of these countries. In contrast, the United States submitted amendments that proposed to insert a reference to "the interests of an expanding world economy," for example. The text that was adopted was based on a compromise proposal from Egypt. The scope of the final resolution was "the development of natural resources which can be utilized in the first instance for the domestic needs of the under-developed countries and also to further the expansion of the world economy."[17]

In 1951, the socialist government of Iran, led by Prime Minister Mohammed Mossadegh, announced the official decision to nationalize the property rights of the Anglo-Persian Oil Company and to terminate the concession agreement that had been concluded in 1933, whereby the company had the exclusive right to extract and process petroleum in a specified area in Iran up to 1993. The National Iranian Oil Company was established to take over the exploitation of the nationalized oil fields. Obviously, this jeopardized the free flow of oil to the United Kingdom. The Iranian government was unwilling to submit the dispute to arbitration. Subsequently, the United Kingdom instituted proceedings at the ICJ in The Hague, but the court decided in 1952 that it had no jurisdiction to adjudicate the case. The court found that the agreement was only a concessionary contract between a government and a foreign corporation and hence did not come within its purview.[18] An end to the dispute did not seem possible until 1957, when a new Iranian government took power under the leadership of General Fazlollah Zahebi after a coup d'état in which the British and U.S. secret services were allegedly involved. Subsequently, in 1954 an international consortium of oil companies was established that signed a new agreement with the new government.[19]

The case of Iran and other cases did not go unnoticed at the United Nations. In November 1952, Uruguay submitted a new draft resolution under the item "Economic Development of Under-Developed Countries."[20] It recognized the need to protect economically weak nations that tend to utilize and exploit their natural resources. It argued that as an essential element of independence, member states should recognize the right of each country to nationalize and freely exploit its natural wealth. This was in line with Article 1, paragraph 2 of the UN Charter, the draft resolution said, which refers to the principle of self-determination of peoples. Following strong protests from especially western countries, the explicit reference to the right to nationalize was replaced by language that spoke of the right of countries to use and exploit their natural wealth and resources. The draft resolution gave rise to heated debates that focused on the actual rights and obligations of states that were exploiting their natural resources. Last-minute amendments by India referring to "the need for the maintenance of mutual confidence and economic co-operation among nations" and "the need for maintaining the flow of capital in conditions of security" were adopted.

Even this language could not prevent the stigmatization of this project as "a nationalization resolution." Eventually the General Assembly adopted this draft resolution on the right to freely exploit natural wealth and resources as resolution 626 (VII), with 36 votes in favor, 4 against (New Zealand, South Africa, the United Kingdom, and the United States), and 20 abstentions.[21]

During this period, the issue of natural resource management began to play a role in the debates about the formulation of international covenants on human rights. In 1952, the General Assembly decided to include in the draft covenants an article on the right of peoples to political and economic self-determination. At an early stage, Chile's representative Carlos Valenzuela proposed that an additional paragraph be included in the article:

> The right of the peoples to self-determination shall also include permanent sovereignty over their natural wealth and resources. In no case may a people be deprived of its own means of subsistence on the grounds of any rights that may be claimed by other States.[22]

This proposal came under severe attack from western countries, which claimed that such a sovereignty provision would be out of place in an article on self-determination and human rights and that it could be interpreted as questioning the validity of treaties, contracts, and concession agreements. France stated that it could not accept a resolution to "legalize the autarchic practices of certain States which had a virtual monopoly of the raw materials indispensable to the international community." It argued that "some sovereignty would have to be surrendered to international organizations," listing as an example the 1950 Schuman Plan that placed the coal and steel industries of France and West Germany under a common High Authority. France maintained that "the Chilean proposal might impede international solutions and the execution of international treaties." In response to such strong opposition, a nine-member Working Party under the chairmanship of Miguel Rafael Urquía of El Salvador was established. The Working Party proposed a substantial change to the earlier text on sovereignty over natural resources.[23] This text was accepted and is part of what later became Article 1(2) of the two human rights covenants as they were at last adopted in 1966. It reads:

> The peoples may, for their own ends, freely dispose of their natural wealth and resources without prejudice to any obligations arising out of international economic co-operation, based upon the principle of mutual benefit, and international law. In no case may a people be deprived of its means of subsistence.

In 1966, the General Assembly's Third Committee decided, upon the proposal of African, Asian, and Latin American countries, to insert an additional article in both covenants that said that "nothing in the present Covenant shall be interpreted as impairing the inherent right of all peoples to enjoy and utilize fully and freely their natural wealth and resources."[24]

Deepening Resource Sovereignty: Protection for Newly Independent States

Following discussions in the Commission on Human Rights, ECOSOC, and the Third Committee of the General Assembly in 1954 and 1955, the General Assembly established a nine-member Commission on Permanent Sovereignty over Natural Resources. Its two main tasks were (1) to conduct a full survey of the right of peoples and nations to "permanent sovereignty over their natural wealth and resources" that they identified as a "basic constituent of the right to self-determination"; and (2) to make recommendations, where necessary, about strengthening this right.[25]

During the period 1958–1961, the commission held three sessions and as many as thirty-three meetings.[26] Members were chosen by the president of the General Assembly on the basis of geographical distribution and included representatives of Afghanistan, Chile, Guatemala, the Netherlands, the Philippines, Sweden, the Soviet Union, the United Arab Republic, and the United States. Persons who played a crucial role in these meetings included Hortencio J. Brillantes (Philippines), Oscar Schachter (on behalf of the UN Secretariat), Oscar Pinochet (Chile), V. J. Sapozhnikov (Soviet Union), and Sture Petren (Sweden). Though its deliberations were of a substantive nature, ideological divides soon dominated its proceedings. When Oscar Schachter presented the extensive Secretariat study in 1961, it was applauded by the Philippines and western delegations, whereas the delegates from the Soviet Union, United Arab Republic, and Afghanistan were less enthusiastic. The commission's final report was approved by 3 votes to 2, with 4 abstentions.[27]

Two alternative draft resolutions were proposed: one by the Soviet Union and one by Chile. The main thrust of the Soviet draft was its spelling out of discretionary regulatory rights of host states receiving foreign investment, including the right to exercise control over the distribution and transfer of profits and to carry out nationalization and expropriation measures "without let or hindrance." Chile's draft claimed to be better balanced. First, it stated that states had to have sovereignty over its resources to benefit its people. Second, it included some guarantees about protection of foreign capital once it was admitted into a country. Third, it promoted international economic cooperation through increased investment of foreign capital and greater exchange of information. Various amendments to Chile's draft were discussed and some were adopted, including those that focused on the modalities of compensation and dispute settlement in the event of expropriation or nationalization. Chile's final draft was adopted by 8 votes to 1, whereas the Soviet draft was rejected. In 1961, when the eighteen members of ECOSOC considered these issues,

Japan, France, and the United Kingdom figured prominently, as did Afghanistan, the United States, and the Soviet Union, which were also members of the Commission on Permanent Sovereignty over Natural Resources. Not surprisingly, the debate ended in a stalemate.[28]

In 1962, the Second Committee of the General Assembly extensively discussed the draft resolution,[29] notwithstanding the calls from Chile and the Netherlands to refrain from changing any part of the commission's draft since it constituted a careful compromise between developed and developing countries as well as between respect for national sovereignty and other rights and duties under international law (such as fair treatment of foreign investors). A host of amendments was submitted, the most far-reaching of which was a proposal by the Soviet Union that a new paragraph be inserted that confirmed "the inalienable right of peoples and nations to the unobstructed execution of nationalization, expropriation and other essential measures aimed at protecting and strengthening their sovereignty over their natural wealth and resources." During a breathtaking vote, this amendment was rejected since there was no majority: 30 votes to 30, with 33 abstentions.[30] However, emotions in the western camp ran very high when the General Assembly accepted another Soviet amendment that "unreservedly supports measures taken by peoples and States to re-establish or strengthen their sovereignty over natural wealth and resources, and considers inadmissible acts aimed at obstructing the creation, defense and strengthening of that sovereignty." As the representative from the United States stated: "It does not make sense, painstakingly to compose a draft resolution which sets forth the rights and obligations of States, which affirms the sovereignty, and, at the same time, declares unreserved support for measures to 're-establish' or strengthen their sovereignty over natural wealth and resources."[31] During the final round in the plenary General Assembly meeting, western states succeeded in eliminating this major stumbling block from the text of the draft resolution (by 41 votes to 38, with 15 abstentions).[32] Subsequently, the General Assembly adopted the Declaration on Permanent Sovereignty over Natural Resources on 14 December 1962 (General Assembly resolution 1803, XVII). This declaration is one of the landmark declarations of the United Nations: it has often been described as the economic pendant to the political decolonization declaration of 1960 ("Declaration on the Granting of Independence to Colonial Countries and Peoples," General Assembly resolution 1514, XV). The declaration recognizes the right of peoples and states to freely exercise permanent sovereignty over natural wealth and resources and stipulates that this right is exercised in the interest of their national development and of the well-being of the people. It makes special reference to the right to explore, exploit, and dispose freely of such resources as well as the right to regulate foreign investment.

Beginning in the 1960s, developing countries actively used the forum of the United Nations to pursue their goal of implementing the principle of permanent sovereignty over natural resources because they perceived this to be a major basis for their economic development and for a redistribution of wealth and power in their relations with the industrialized world. Initially, the political organs of the United Nations worked toward consolidating and elaborating the 1962 Declaration on Permanent Sovereignty over Natural Resources. UNCTAD I adopted General Principle Three on sovereignty over natural resources.[33] Developing countries also sought to establish a link between sovereignty over resources and development. The General Assembly's resolution on "Permanent Sovereignty over Natural Resources" (resolution 2158 [XXI], 1966) was especially instrumental in this effort. Elaborating on the provisions of the 1962 declaration related to foreign investment, it identifies some of the problems in the relationship and cooperation between foreign investors and host developing countries, such as share in the administration and profits of wholly or partly foreign-operated enterprises. The resolution emphasizes that it is essential that developing countries themselves exploit and market their natural resources.[34] The debate hence became increasingly about development and sought to legitimize efforts of developing countries to strengthen their own role and that of their nationals in resource exploitation, with the goal, of course, of maximizing the benefits of such activities both financially and in terms of employment, training, and technology transfer.

Broadening Resource Sovereignty: The Rush to Exploit Marine Resources

The reaffirmation and elaboration of permanent sovereignty over natural resources was paralleled by an increasing tendency to extend sovereignty over resources that were not under the control of states—that is, the living and nonliving resources of the seas. Bit by bit, the emphasis in policy considerations of states as well as UN discussions shifted from the sea as an avenue of transportation and communication to the sea as an important economic zone for exploiting natural resources.[35] The causes for this shift were twofold. In response to wartime concerns about the security of energy supplies, coastal states sought to gain access to oil and other mineral resources on the continental shelf (the natural prolongation of the coast that extends into the sea), which until the postwar years had been considered part of the high seas. At the same time, states realized the importance of fisheries resources for their national economic development and the importance of properly conserving these resources.

Both changes resulted in increased pressure to bring large portions of the sea under coastal state jurisdiction, especially from Latin American countries and newly independent countries in Asia and Africa and from countries that depended heavily upon fisheries resources, such as Iceland. Paradoxically, however, it was the United States that started this new rush for marine resources. In 1945, President Harry Truman issued two proclamations related to coastal resources—one extending access to and control over the natural resources (primarily gas and oil) of the continental shelf[36] and the other establishing conservation zones to improve the protection of fisheries resources.[37] Other coastal states soon followed the American example.[38] But while the Truman proclamations were carefully drafted so as to avoid any interference with the rights of navigation of other states, the same cannot be said for some bolder initiatives, such as the Declaration on the Maritime Zone of 1952, in which Chile, Ecuador, and Peru proclaimed "exclusive sovereignty and jurisdiction over the sea along the coasts of their respective countries to a minimum distance of 200 nautical miles" for the purpose of "conserv[ing] and safeguard[ing] for their respective peoples the natural resources of the maritime zones adjacent to their coasts."[39] The proclamations of these three Latin American states categorically asserted an extension of sovereignty not only over the continental shelf but also over the waters above that shelf, including the living resources of those waters.

While there was no dispute about the idea that a coastal state had sovereignty—and hence exclusive jurisdiction and control—over the territorial sea, including the seabed and subsoil thereof, there was no general agreement about the precise extent of this belt of waters. The limit of three nautical miles had widespread support but was not considered a universal rule, and in the 1950s various countries began to claim jurisdiction or sovereignty over resources in vast maritime areas. With the goal of finally settling this issue as well as concluding the unfinished business of the failed attempt of the League of Nations to create an international agreement about such issues, the newly established International Law Commission—a subsidiary organ of the General Assembly charged with promoting the development and codification of international law[40]—embarked upon the task of creating a comprehensive set of rules governing the use of the seas, including a definite limit of the territorial sea. Under the guidance of the Dutch rapporteur J. P. A. François, the ILC drafted a set of articles between 1950 and 1956 that included provisions that defined the continental shelf as a novel resource area and outlined principles for conserving and managing the living resources of the high seas.

However, because the ILC was comprised of a body of eminent jurists and its members did not possess the technical knowledge required to properly address the conservation and management aspects of these articles, the General Assembly decided to convene a conference "to study the problem of the international conservation of the living resources of the sea and to make appropriate scientific and technical recommendations."[41] The International Technical Conference on the Conservation of the Living Resources of the Sea was convened in 1955 under the auspices of the Food and Agriculture Organization, which then forwarded to the ILC a number of recommendations it had adopted. Among other things, the technical conference suggested that the principal objective of conservation was "to obtain the optimum sustainable yield so as to secure a maximum supply of food and other marine products."[42]

On the basis of the ILC's work, the United Nations convened the first United Nations Conference on the Law of the Sea, which took place in Geneva in 1958. The diplomatic conference resulted in the adoption of four treaties: the Convention on the Territorial Sea and the Contiguous Zone (1958), the Convention on the Continental Shelf (1958), the Convention on the High Seas (1958), and the Convention on Fishing and Conservation of Living Resources of the High Seas (1958).[43]

From the perspective of resource management, the Convention on the Continental Shelf was undoubtedly the greatest innovation, as it recognized the sovereign rights of coastal states to explore and exploit the natural resources of the continental shelf. It defined the continental shelf as "the sea-bed and subsoil of the submarine areas adjacent to the coast but outside of the area of the territorial sea, to a depth of 200 meters or, beyond that limit, to where the depth of the superjacent waters admits of the exploitation of the natural resources of the said areas."[44] Moreover, the convention clearly stated that the sovereign rights of coastal states "are exclusive in the sense that if the coastal State does not explore the continental shelf or exploit its natural resources, no one may undertake these activities."[45]

The Convention on Fishing and Conservation of Living Resources of the High Seas demonstrated the growing concern about the conservation and rational use of living resources of the seas. In its preamble, the convention noted that "the development of modern techniques for the exploitation of the living resources of the sea, including man's ability to meet the need of the world's expanding population for food, has exposed some of the resources to the danger of being overexploited."[46] The convention urged conservation measures, which it defined as "the aggregate of the measures rendering possible the optimum sustainable yield from those resources so as to secure a maximum supply of food and other marine products."[47] To that end, it recognized the competence of coastal states to impose unilateral conservation measures in certain circumstances, something that was not foreseen and probably not allowed under the traditional law of the sea.[48]

Yet the 1958 Geneva conference failed to reach agreement on one crucial question—the width of the territorial sea.[49] The Second United Nations Conference on the Law of the Sea, which was convened in 1960 for this purpose (and for setting fishery limits), did not lead to a breakthrough on that issue either.[50] This left the door open for states to continue to assert claims to an extensive territorial sea or (and this happened more and more often) to claim exclusive fisheries zones of various breadths in the waters adjacent to their territorial seas. A practice emerged of claiming a twelve-mile exclusive fishery zone beyond a twelve-mile territorial sea. However, coastal states did not stop at that. Iceland, for example, soon established a 50-mile exclusive fisheries zone in view of its specific dependence on fisheries. By the end of the 1960s, many states had claimed zones as vast as 200 nautical miles from their coastlines.[51]

The reasons for such extensive claims were primarily economic. Closing fishing grounds to foreign competition provided domestic fishing industries with a natural source of income. This was particularly appealing to developing countries, since industrialized countries owned many distant-water fishing fleets that had been fishing in waters that were included in the expanded claims. However, as technological developments in fisheries techniques and the increase of distant-water fishing fleets in the 1950s and 1960s brought many fish stocks under considerable pressure, there was growing concern about resource depletion and the need to take conservation measures. As early as 1968, the General Assembly expressed its concern that rapid progress in fisheries technology was contributing to the overexploitation and depletion of marine resources.[52] Gradually it became clear that the fisheries regime established by the 1958 Geneva conventions was not an adequate response to problems of overexploitation. Only a few states have acceded to the 1958 Convention on Fishing and Conservation of the Living Resources of the High Seas, thus making its far-reaching provisions to a large extent inapplicable to high-seas fisheries.[53] This compelled many coastal states to resort to unilateral acts, which eventually resulted in a new wave of extensive maritime claims in the 1960s, which in turn resulted in increasing uncertainty about the extent of the limits of national economic jurisdiction at sea.[54]

In response to these developments, the United States and the Soviet Union, which both had vast international shipping interests and were both champions of the freedom of the high seas, proposed that a new conference on the law of the sea be convened to settle the questions of the outer limits of the territorial sea and freedom of transit through international straits and to accommodate the "special interests" of coastal states in matters of conservation and fishing in the high seas. The proposal was welcomed by the majority of the newly independent states, since most of them had not participated in the formulation of the 1958 conventions and were thus in favor of reviewing the law of the sea. Moreover, between 1958 and 1967, the year when the discussion on a new law of the sea began, forty-one countries had joined the United Nations, where they soon challenged many of the principles and rules of the law of the sea that had been codified in the 1958 conventions.

Another main reason for seeking change in the existing law of the sea was related to regulation of the use of the deep seabed, where various interests were at stake. One important issue was implementing the principle of peaceful uses of the seas at a time when nuclear testing in maritime areas still took place and when serious consideration was given to using the seabed for the emplacement of weapons of mass destruction. During the 1960s, the United Nations served as the forum for discussing how to put a halt to this practice; the result was the Seabed Arms Control Treaty of 1967. In addition, the exploration and exploitation of the natural resources of the deep seabed emerged as a new issue. Before the middle of the 1960s, this question was hardly relevant, but owing to developments in technology, the exploitation of manganese and other polymetallic nodules was considered technically possible. Soon the question arose as to whether exploiting these resources would be considered a freedom of the high seas; the implication was that if such exploitation was included under this rubric, states would have equal access to those resources.[55] However, the problem was that if technologically advanced states began mining manganese nodule fields, developing countries would obviously not enjoy equal access to those resources in future. At the same time, the provisions of the Convention on the Continental Shelf, which defined the extent of the shelf by reference to the depth of 200 meters and the criterion for "exploitability," were somewhat open-ended, and developing countries legitimately feared that given the rapid advances in technology, industrialized countries would abuse this loophole to exploit marine mineral resources wherever they could.[56]

In 1967, Ambassador Arvid Pardo of Malta made a remarkable initiative. He proposed that the General Assembly declare that the seabed and the ocean floor beyond the limits of national jurisdiction was "the common heritage of mankind." Moreover, he put forward the idea that a United Nations organization be created to assure jurisdiction over this area as "a trustee for all countries" and that it establish an international regime and machinery for the exploration and exploitation of seabed resources. The notion of "common heritage" was not completely new. Earlier in the same year, the General Assembly had declared outer space, including the moon and other celestial bodies, to be "the province of all mankind,"[57] and the term "common heritage of mankind" had been used in these debates by Argentinean ambassador Aldo Armando Cocca. Similarly, Prince Wan Waithayakon of Thailand had stated in 1958 that the sea was "the common heritage of mankind" and that the law of the sea should ensure "the preservation of that heritage for the benefit of all."[58] But while in 1958 there was no support for such a proposal, in 1967, Pardo's request that the concept become a new legal principle in international law was quickly embraced by most of the developing countries, which saw in the internationalization of the seabed area the possibility that they could benefit from resources that would otherwise be available only to industrialized states and companies that possessed the technology to extract minerals.

Pardo's initiative met with approval in the General Assembly, which established in the same year the Committee on Peaceful Uses of the Sea-Bed and the Ocean Floor beyond the Limits of National Jurisdiction.[59] From then on, things moved rather quickly. Notwithstanding opposition from Western and Eastern European countries, the General Assembly adopted a moratorium resolution in 1969, recommending that states and corporations agree to refrain from mining the seabed until an international regime could be established to govern such activity.[60] This development culminated in the Declaration of Principles Governing the Seabed and the Ocean

Floor, and the Subsoil Thereof, beyond the Limits of National Jurisdiction (1970), in which the General Assembly proclaimed that "the sea-bed and ocean floor, and the subsoil thereof, beyond the limits of national jurisdiction, as well as the resources of the area, are the common heritage of mankind" and that "the exploration of the area and exploitation of its resources shall be carried out for the benefit of mankind as a whole, irrespective of the geographical location of states, whether land-locked or coastal."[61] The declaration was a clear follow-up to Pardo's proposals; it elevated the hitherto political principle of the common heritage into a norm of international law. On the same day, the General Assembly decided to convene a Third United Nations Conference on the Law of the Sea.[62]

The third law of the sea conference—which eventually started in 1973—was heavily influenced by two important developments that were taking place around that time: the growing concern about the natural environment and the debates on the establishment of a New International Economic Order. While the latter was a continuation of the discussion about resource sovereignty, the former marked the beginning of a development that would eventually lead to a more qualified view of resource sovereignty, one that entails obligations relating to the environment and other global concerns.

A Major Milestone:
The Stockholm Conference on the Human Environment

During the 1960s the extent of resource depletion and degradation of the environment around the world became a increasing matter of public concern.[63] Reports brought to the fore a variety of issues related to the environment, including the damaging long-term effects of pesticides on birds and other wildlife, especially DDT; excessive economic growth; tanker collisions and oil spills; contamination of water; discharges of harmful chemical waste; testing of nuclear weapons; the pressures of a growing world population; increased pollution; wasteful consumption patterns; and other forms of unrestricted use of the world's natural resources.[64] These issues provoked a new debate over some of the traditional paradigms of international relations, including freedom of action and noninterference in domestic affairs. Previously when pollution or the overexploitation of natural resources had been discussed at the international level, it was mainly because of a loss of important economic assets, not because of the damage to the natural environment. Yet during the 1960s, it was realized that the "human environment" was at stake. People began to see the world as one entity, as "spaceship earth." At the same time, it became apparent that the environmental problems of developing and industrialized countries differed in essential ways. Industrialized countries had to consider how making drastic changes in their production and consumption patterns could contribute to economic development that was more sound. In contrast, the standard of living in nearly all developing countries was low, as was their economic growth. In addition, developing countries' haphazard exploitation of their mineral and agricultural natural resources had led to unstable commodity prices.

In response to these problems, the General Assembly began to adopt resolutions that were relevant to the environment. Shortly after the 1962 Declaration on Permanent Sovereignty over Natural Resources, the General Assembly adopted a resolution called "Economic Development and the Conservation of Nature."[65] The resolution considered natural resources to be of fundamental importance to economic development and expressed an awareness of the need to preserve and rationally use natural resources. In 1968, upon the initiative of Sweden, the General Assembly addressed the accelerating impairment of the quality of the human environment and decided to convene a conference on the matter.[66] The result was the first intergovernmental global conference on environmental issues, the UN Conference on the Human Environment (UNCHE), which took place in Stockholm in June 1972. Although the conference was attended by 113 states, it was somewhat overshadowed by a traditional East-West conflict over the exclusion of the German Democratic Republic; most Eastern European countries stayed at home. On the other hand, the People's Republic of China, which had been granted the Chinese seat in the United Nations in 1971, participated very actively at the conference, particularly on the issue of the relationship between the environment and development.[67]

The most important result of the conference was undoubtedly the Stockholm Declaration on the Human Environment, which was adopted on 16 June 1972.[68] Achieving consensus on the final text of the declaration proved to be far from easy. When the work on a draft declaration began in 1969, it was agreed that the relationship between the environment and development was of crucial importance. Early drafts were severely criticized for dissociating environmental problems from development issues and for not putting "in the forefront the basic principle that each State has inalienable sovereignty over its environment and over its natural resources." In June 1971, Maurice Strong—who was to serve as the secretary-general of the Stockholm conference—convened an informal meeting of experts in Founex in Switzerland. This meeting produced substantive and balanced texts that emphasized that environmental issues should become an integral part of development strategy.[69] During the conference, however, these texts were subjected to substantive debate. China, in particular, submitted a series of amendments and was eventually successful in its efforts to link environmental issues more closely to development issues.[70]

In its final form, the Stockholm Declaration lays down twenty-six principles concerning the environment and development, many of which had an important bearing on the evolution of natural resource management. Principle 2 declares that careful planning and management are required for the safeguarding of the natural resources of the earth. Principle 3 stipulates that "the capacity of the earth to produce vital renewable resources must be maintained and, wherever practical, restored or improved." Principle 5 says that nonrenewable resources must be used in such a way "as to guard against the danger of their future exhaustion and to ensure that benefits of such employment are shared by all mankind." Principles 13 and 14 point out that an integrated and coordinated approach and rational planning are necessary in order to achieve a more rational management of resources and to ensure that development is compatible with preservation of the environment. It is Principle 21, however, that had perhaps the greatest impact on the further evolution of natural resource management. It placed sovereignty over natural resources in an international environmental context:

> States have, in accordance with the Charter of the United Nations and the principles of international law, the sovereign right to exploit their own resources pursuant to their own environmental policies, and the responsibility to ensure that activities within their jurisdiction or control do not cause damage to the environment of other States or of areas beyond the limits of national jurisdiction.

Principle 21 reflects the principles of the international law of good neighborliness and due diligence and care. However, the principle was exclusively concerned with preventing activities within one particular state from causing environmental damage in other countries or in areas outside national jurisdiction. Only in later years did the General Assembly begin to address the issue of the conservation and utilization of natural resources within states.

In addition to the declaration, the Stockholm conference adopted 109 specific recommendations that together constituted an "Action Plan for International Cooperation on the Environment."[71] Moreover, as an institutional follow-up to the conference, the General Assembly established the United Nations Environment Programme.[72] Originally, its role was to be that of a coordinator and catalyst in the field of environmental policy within the UN system. However, over time, UNEP has undertaken a variety of operational activities; for example, it serves as the secretariat for a number of multilateral environmental agreements for which it laid the groundwork. In many ways, UNEP's work has had an important bearing on the international as well as national management of natural resources.

Toward a New International Economic Order?

The Stockholm conference coincided with a number of major changes in the world economy that had a negative impact on the development prospects of developing countries. Since the early 1970s, many western countries had struggled with stagnating economies, high inflation, increasing unemployment, and international monetary instability. The political tensions between the East and the West as well as the Yom Kippur War in the Middle East in 1973 added to the gloomy international situation. In 1973, an oil crisis took place that resulted in a number of unprecedented price increases, partly owing to a successful cartel policy of the Organization of the Petroleum Exporting Countries (OPEC). OPEC used oil as a weapon in its temporary oil embargo against the United States and the Netherlands in response to their alleged pro-Israeli stands. The initial success of OPEC led to an assertive, if not militant, attitude of developing countries in international affairs, and consultations took place on establishing various producers' associations. Large-scale nationalizations of oil production took place in quite a number of developing countries, including Chile (1971), Iraq (1972), Peru (1974), Libya (1971 and 1973), and Venezuela (1976). These resulted in direct confrontations between transnational oil companies whose property had been taken and nationalizing host countries that often triggered the involvement of the home states of the oil corporations. The developing countries that carried out such nationalizations sought international support and legitimation for their policies in UN organs.

Various resolutions were adopted in 1972 and 1973 that introduced the prohibition of coercion—be it economic, political, or any other kind—into UN discussions on resource sovereignty.[73] The sovereign right to freely manage natural resources was even linked to maintaining international peace and security.[74] These resolutions questioned the limits international law placed on the right to nationalize foreign property as codified in the Declaration on Permanent Sovereignty over Natural Resources of 1962. The revolts related in particular to obtaining more discretion for a state in determining a legal justification for nationalization, the amount of (potential) compensation to be paid to the owner, and the primacy, if not the exclusiveness, of domestic dispute settlement procedures for settling resource conflicts.[75] In addition, the General Assembly endorsed the cooperative efforts of developing countries to protect their natural resources by coordinating pricing and production policies and improving access to markets.

In 1974, on the initiative of Algerian president Houari Boumédiene, a special session was convened that was devoted exclusively to the problems of raw materials and development for the first time in UN history. The session, formally the Sixth Special Session of the General Assembly, was well prepared by the Group of 77, which submitted two main draft documents: a Draft Declaration and a Draft Action Programme on the Establishment of a New International Economic Order.[76] The documents contained a series of provisions that raised very controversial topics in North-South relations. They extended permanent sovereignty over natural resources to all economic activities. They claimed that nationalization or even transfer of ownership to nationals, with very few qualifications, was a legitimate way of exercising such sovereignty "in order to safeguard these resources."[77] In a similar vein, the two documents claimed that restitution and full compensation was necessary when natural resources of states and peoples were exploited and depleted under foreign occupation, colonial domination, or apartheid. Furthermore, the documents reaffirmed the right to establish producers' associations and the need to link the prices of raw materials to the prices of industrialized products. Lastly, the draft resolutions contained far-reaching provisions on the control of the activities of transnational corporations.

Western countries opposed these draft resolutions and submitted various amendments that were not acceptable to the Group of 77. It is no wonder that negotiations on these texts reached an impasse time and again. In the eleventh hour, Iranian Fereydoun Hoveyda, chair of the Ad Hoc Committee (who had also distinguished himself as the chair of the Group of 77), the main negotiating forum during the Special Session, introduced in his own name a number of proposals on the understanding that the Group of 77 would not press for a vote. His proposals softened the Group of 77 texts to a certain extent without taking the gist out of them. Thereupon western states also decided to join the "consensus," in reality a "pseudo-consensus." As one of the few who spoke in public, U.S. ambassador John A. Scali made this very clear: "To label some of these highly controversial conclusions as 'agreed' is not only idle: it is self-deceiving. In this house, the steamroller is not the vehicle for solving vital, complex problems."[78] In the end, the Sixth Special Session adopted the Declaration and the Action Programme on the Establishment of a New International Order.[79]

Meanwhile, UN delegates were also working on a Charter of Economic Rights and Duties of States based on an initiative of Mexican president Luis Echeverría during UNCTAD III. The conference established a working group for this purpose, which met four times during 1973 and 1974.[80] The Sixth Special Session of the UN General Assembly had a major impact on its work. On the one hand, the substantive issues in international economic relations that divided the industrialized and the developing world were now well identified. On the other, the western countries were unwilling to hide their objections behind a pseudo-consensus again. In the course of the negotiations, the latter submitted a flood of amendments to the proposed charter. In the meantime, they also made efforts toward submitting a complete and generally acceptable draft charter to the Seventh Special Session of the UN General Assembly on Development and International Economic Co-operation, which was scheduled for September 1975. However, the Group of 77 was unwilling to agree to such a request and a confrontation between the two camps became unavoidable. In November–December 1974 as many as seventy-three separate votes on the draft charter took place in the General Assembly. In essence, all amendments were rejected. On 12 December 1974, the General Assembly adopted the Charter of Economic Rights and Duties of States by 120 votes to 6, with 10 abstentions.[81] The sixteen states that did not vote in favor were all OECD countries. The major source of offense was Article 2, which dealt with permanent resource sovereignty, regulation of foreign investment, expropriation and nationalization, and settlement of disputes.[82]

The charter contains a number of other resource-related provisions. The preamble and Article 16 include the principles of restitution and reparation ("making good injustices") where nations and oppressed peoples have been deprived of natural and other resources for their normal development. Article 1 emphasizes the sovereign right of every state to choose its economic and political system without outside interference. In more explicit terms, Article 32 spells out that "no State may use or encourage the use of economic, political or any other type of measures to coerce another State in order to obtain from it the subordination of the exercise of its sovereign rights." Article 3 addresses the topic of shared resources, an issue that traditionally divides developing countries deeply. The article states that "each State must co-operate" in the exploitation of natural resources shared by two or more countries "on the basis of a system of information and prior consultation in order to achieve optimum use of such resources without causing damage to the legitimate interests of others."[83] Article 5 proclaims that all states have the right to associate in organizations of primary commodity producers such as OPEC in order to develop and achieve stable development financing and asserts that all states have a duty to refrain from applying economic and political pressures that would limit that right. From a rather different angle, Article 6 deals with the duty of states to contribute to the development of international trade, particularly by concluding long-term multilateral commodity agreements. Article 31 records the duty of each state to contribute to the balanced expansion of the world economy. Finally, Article 30 calls upon all states to be responsible for preserving the environment.

It is worth noting that in subsequent years the basic conceptual differences between industrialized and developing countries have narrowed considerably. Echoes of the NIEO resolutions could be heard during the United Nations Industrial Development Organization (UNIDO) Second General Conference in Lima (1975), in the UN negotiations on a Draft Code of Conduct on Transnational Corporations (1976–1990), and in occasional debates in the General Assembly. But overall a new spirit of constructive cooperation emerged in 1975, as reflected in the unanimously adopted final document of the Seventh Special Session of the General Assembly on Development and International Economic Co-operation (1975), the UNCTAD IV Integrated Programme for Commodities (1976), and the Third United Nations Conference on the Law of the Sea (1973–1982). UNCTAD's aim of establishing a global commodity policy through the conclusion of individual commodity agreements and the establishment of an umbrella Common Fund for Commodities was realized in 1980.[84] In the discussion about resource sovereignty, the emphasis gradually shifted from setting the parameters of foreign participation in the exploitation of natural resources (including participation in management and profits and the training of national personnel) toward the question of what international cooperation could contribute to the exploration, exploitation, processing, and marketing of the natural resources of developing countries.

A New Constitution for the Seas and the Oceans

The NIEO discussions influenced the negotiations at the Third UN Conference on the Law of the Sea in important ways. The conference began in 1973 and lasted for nine years, culminating in the adoption of the United Nations Convention on the Law of the Sea (UNCLOS) in 1982.[85] The final outcome, unlike that of the Geneva conference of 1958, was one comprehensive convention that is an all-inclusive arrangement that determines the breadth and nature of various maritime resource zones and regulates the various uses of the seas and oceans. UNCLOS created "a legal order for the seas and oceans which will facilitate international communication, and will promote the peaceful uses of the seas and oceans, the equitable and efficient utilization of their resources, the conservation of their living resources, and the study, protection and preservation of the marine environment."[86] No doubt it was because of its comprehensiveness that the second president of the third conference, Ambassador Tommy Koh (Singapore), called UNCLOS "a Constitution for the Oceans."[87]

The negotiations were often protracted, as the 150 nations participating in the conference had to deal with many issues. Agreement about a legal regime for exploiting deep seabed resources was the most difficult to secure. Building on the 1970 Declaration of Principles, UNCLOS declared that the principle of common heritage of humankind applied to the natural resources of the seabed and ocean floor (including the subsoil thereof) beyond the limits of national jurisdiction. This is followed by detailed provisions on the establishment of an international machinery for exploiting these resources (which will be presented in greater detail in the next chapter), including various arrangements for providing financial assistance and transferring technology to developing countries wherein the influence of NIEO discussions was most visible.[88]

Agreement was more easily achieved about the idea that the states would enjoy extensive rights over the living resources adjacent to their coasts. This is perhaps attributable to the fact that in the preparation for the conference, various groups of states had sought to consolidate their claims and had adopted a number of declarations for that purpose.[89] Conceptually, these proposals were a somewhat unclear mixture of claims based on the "territorial sea" and "functional jurisdiction." At the conference, there was a tendency toward the latter, as was reflected, for example, in the proposal of the Caribbean countries regarding the "patrimonial sea," according to which a coastal state would enjoy sovereign rights over the renewable and nonrenewable natural resources up to a distance of 200 nautical miles.[90] Similarly, the concept of an exclusive economic zone—presented for the first time in 1972 by

Kenyan representative Frank X. Njenga in the Asian-African Legal Consultative Committee—was also based on the idea of functional rights.[91] In general, however, the proposals demonstrated that it was not possible to put a halt to the claims of coastal states of their right to control, exploit, and conserve the living resources of maritime areas adjacent to their coasts. Hence, at the first substantive session of the conference in Caracas in 1974, more than 100 delegates spoke in favor of some form of extended maritime jurisdiction.[92]

The final agreement on the limits of various maritime zones was a fine compromise. Article 3 of UNCLOS now provides that the territorial sea may not exceed twelve nautical miles. However, UNCLOS introduced the concept of exclusive economic zones (EEZs) and extended the continental shelf, considerably extending the economic jurisdiction of coastal states beyond their territorial waters. From a resource management perspective, the EEZs are one of the most important innovations of UNCLOS. With them, the coastal states acquired sovereign rights to explore, exploit, conserve, and manage natural resources, whether living or nonliving, in a zone that extends as far out as 200 nautical miles from the shore. These sovereign rights also extend to other economic activities, such as generating electricity from the water, currents, and winds.[93]

UNCLOS also introduced changes regarding the breadth of the continental shelf. This is no longer dependent upon the criterion of "exploitability" but extends, as a general rule, to a fixed distance of 200 nautical miles. Moreover, UNCLOS provides exceptions for states with broad continental margins, such as Brazil and In-

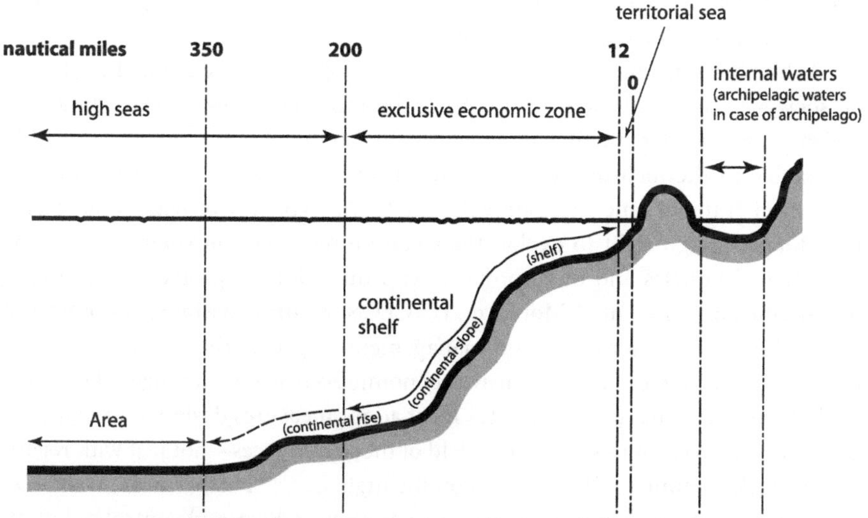

FIGURE 2.1. Natural Resource Regimes in Maritime Areas

dia. These states may extend their continental shelves to a maximum of 350 nautical miles from the territorial baselines.[94] However, by way of compromise, those coastal states are under an obligation to pay royalties for exploiting the nonliving resources of their extended continental shelves beyond 200 nautical miles. This innovative international tax is to be paid to the International Seabed Authority, the organization established by UNCLOS to regulate and administer deep seabed mining.[95]

UNCLOS also introduced the concept of archipelagic states—states whose islands, waters, and other natural features are so interrelated that they "form an intrinsic social, economic and political entity, or which historically have been regarded as such."[96] Such states obtained the right to draw baselines around the edges or fringes of their outermost islands and to consider the waters within these baselines as archipelagic waters over which they enjoy full sovereignty, including over marine natural resources. Beyond these baselines, archipelagic states may still claim a territorial sea and other maritime spaces. The chief beneficiaries of this new archipelagic regime are Indonesia, the Philippines, and a number of South Pacific island states.

UNCLOS brought about a major change in the distribution of the wealth of the oceans. With the establishment of EEZs, almost 30 percent of the ocean surface came under the control of coastal states. This includes around 90 percent of the commercially exploitable fishery resources whose life cycle is confined to the belt of 200 nautical miles from the shore.[97] Those that benefited most were countries with long coasts (paradoxically, the greatest EEZ could be established by the United States), but small island states also benefited. What remained beyond national jurisdiction was a much-reduced area of the high seas, where the traditional freedoms, including the freedom to fish, were preserved. The management of these remaining global commons will be presented in the next chapter.

While the introduction of the concept of EEZs and the extended continental shelves undoubtedly was a triumph of the movement toward extending sovereignty over resources, the influence of the Stockholm conference is readily observable in the inclusion of a comprehensive set of provisions regarding the protection of the marine environment.[98] UNCLOS explicitly provides that "States have the sovereign right to exploit their natural resources pursuant to their environmental policies and in accordance with their duty to protect and preserve the marine environment."[99] Moreover, UNCLOS requires coastal states to ensure "through proper conservation and management measures that the maintenance of the living resources in the exclusive economic zone is not endangered by over-exploitation." For that purpose, states must adopt measures designed to maintain or restore the maximum sustainable yield of those resources—not just with regard to fish stocks within an EEZ but also on the high seas.[100] Furthermore, UNCLOS obligates states to take specific measures to prevent, reduce, and control pollution of the marine environment.[101]

UNEP Guidelines and the Management of Shared Natural Resources

In the years following the UN Conference on the Human Environment, environmental concerns began to permeate the debate about natural resource management. General Assembly resolutions have gradually elaborated guidelines for the conservation and use of natural resources within states while at the same time recognizing permanent sovereignty over natural resources. Symptomatic of this new trend was General Assembly resolution 35/7 (1980), which invited member states "in the exercise of their permanent sovereignty over their natural resources, to conduct their activities in recognition of the supreme importance of protecting natural systems, maintaining the balance and quality of nature and conserving natural resources, in the interests of present and future generations."[102] Similar wording was repeated in resolution 37/7 (1982), in which the General Assembly adopted and proclaimed the World Charter for Nature.[103] The charter, which had been prepared by the International Union for Conservation of Nature (IUCN) with the support of UNEP, the FAO, and UNESCO,[104] was introduced to the UN agenda by President Mobutu Sese Seko of Zaire. It proclaimed five principles of conservation "by which all human conduct affecting nature is to be guided and judged," although its scope is generally limited to the conservation and better management of living resources. The charter expressed the conviction that competition for scarce resources can create conflicts, whereas the conservation of nature and natural resources contributes to justice and the maintenance of peace.

Another issue that came on the agenda of the General Assembly in the early 1970s was the question of shared natural resources. For a long time efforts to establish schemes for consultation and cooperation in the management of shared resources had been unsuccessful. Even at the Stockholm conference, it proved to be impossible to include a substantive paragraph on shared resources in the UN Declaration on the Human Environment. This was because of differences of opinion, for example between Argentina and Brazil on the use of the La Plata River Basin for a Brazilian hydroelectric project. In 1973, upon an initiative of the Non-Aligned Movement, the General Assembly mandated that UNEP formulate international standards for the conservation and harmonious exploitation of shared resources, including a system of information and prior consultation.[105]

UNEP began to deal intensively with the issue and in 1975 established an intergovernmental working group of experts to draft principles of conduct regarding shared resources.[106] Meanwhile, the General Assembly included a provision on shared resources in its 1974 Charter of Economic Rights and Duties of States: "In the exploitation of natural resources shared by two or more countries, each State must co-operate on the basis of a system of information and prior consultation in order to achieve optimum use of such resources without causing damage to the legitimate interests of others." This article was adopted by 100 votes to 8 (the countries opposing included Afghanistan, Bolivia, Brazil, Ecuador, Ethiopia, Paraguay, and Turkey), with 28 abstentions; the high number of abstentions illustrates the controversy involved.[107] Based on the work of the group of experts, UNEP's Governing Council presented a set of Draft Principles of Conduct in the Field of the Environment for the Guidance of States in the Conservation and Harmonious Utilization of Natural Resources Shared by Two or More States in 1978.[108]

The Draft Principles, commonly known as the "UNEP Guidelines on Shared Resources,"[109] contain fifteen principles intended to encourage states that share resources to cooperate for the purpose of conserving and harmoniously using those resources and with a view "to controlling, preventing, reducing or eliminating adverse environmental effects which may result from the utilization of such resources." These principles seek to intensify cooperation between states and to prevent or contain conflict by encouraging exchange of information, notification of plans, consultations, immediate information-sharing in emergency situations, mutual assistance, responsibility and liability, international dispute settlement, equal access to administrative and judicial proceedings, and equal treatment for persons affected in other states. A formal adoption of the guidelines by the General Assembly proved to be impossible, owing to continued differences of opinion. However, the assembly requested that all states use the principles as guidelines in the formulation of bilateral and multilateral conventions regarding shared resources.[110] UNEP, for example, managed to incorporate them in its own successful regional seas programs and international river cooperation projects such as those for the Nile, the Zambezi, and the Mekong.[111]

In the 1970s, a number of multilateral conservation treaties were negotiated in the trail of the Stockholm conference. Following Recommendation 99.3 of the Stockholm Action Plan, a conference was convened in 1973 that culminated in the Convention on International Trade in Endangered Species of Wild Fauna and Flora.[112] The convention—for which the IUCN had made numerous calls since the 1960s—seeks to protect endangered species of flora and fauna from overexploitation by prohibiting or otherwise regulating their international trade and reducing their economic value. On the basis of the Stockholm Action Plan, the Convention on the Conservation of Migratory Species of Wild Animals (also known as the Bonn Convention) was also adopted in 1979.[113] Concluded under the aegis of UNEP, the convention provides for a number of measures to conserve and effectively manage migratory species; these measures are not only aimed at protecting these animals but also at conserving or restoring the places where they live, mitigating obstacles to migration, and controlling other factors that might endanger them.

The two conventions imposed concrete obligations that affected the use of natural resources. Both were expressions of the need for international cooperation in safeguarding certain species from overexploitation and reflected the growing concerns about the sustainable use of natural resources. The conventions also stipulate that these concerns had to be taken into account in natural resource policies at the national level as well.

The 1992 Earth Summit

The issue of sustainability also came to the fore along another trajectory. In 1983, the General Assembly appointed the World Commission on Environment and Development—which quickly became known as the Brundtland Commission after its chair, Gro Harlem Brundtland—and gave it the mandate of proposing long-term strategies to achieve sustainable development in the year 2000 and thereafter. It was also mandated to recommend ways that greater cooperation could be achieved among developing countries and between developing countries and developed countries that would lead to "the achievement of common and mutually supportive objectives which take account of the interrelationship between people, resources, environment and development."[114] In 1987, the Brundtland commission published its report, *Our Common Future.*[115] Central to its work was the concept of "sustainable development," which the commission described as "development that meets the needs of the present without compromising the ability of future generations to meet their own needs." Initially, the General Assembly welcomed the Brundtland report without committing itself to its contents,[116] but in 1989 it decided to convene a "second Stockholm Conference" in view of "the continuing deterioration of the state of the environment and the serious degradation of the global life-support systems." The General Assembly warned that if such trends continued, the global ecological balance could be disrupted, resulting in "an ecological catastrophe."[117]

In 1992, after several years of preparation, the UN Conference on Environment and Development (UNCED) convened in Rio de Janeiro, gathering together representatives from 176 UN member states. More than fifty intergovernmental organizations participated, as did thousands of nongovernmental organizations in a separate gathering in Flamingo Park, located near Rio. One of the most notable outcomes of the Earth Summit, as it was called, was the adoption of the Rio Declaration on Environment and Development.[118] Unlike its predecessors—the Stockholm Declaration and the World Charter of Nature—the Rio Declaration is less specific about the management of natural resources and the conservation of nature. Instead, it seeks to strike a delicate balance between protecting the environment and promoting economic growth in developing countries. While the declaration emphasizes that "human beings are at the centre of concern for sustainable development" (Principle 1), it underlines that "in order to achieve sustainable development, environmental protection shall constitute an integral part of the development process and cannot be considered in isolation from it" (Principle 4). It states that the right to development must "be fulfilled so as to equitably meet developmental and environmental needs of present and future generations" (Principle 3). In order to satisfy the view of developing countries that environmental policy should not obstruct development policy, the declaration repeats Principle 21 of the Stockholm Declaration, albeit with a slight alteration: states have "the sovereign right to exploit their own resources pursuant to their own environmental *and developmental* policies" (Principle 2).[119] Moreover, the declaration links preservation of the environment more closely to the eradication of poverty (Principle 5) and calls for special priority for the needs of developing countries, particularly the least developed and those that are most environmentally vulnerable (Principle 6). Finally, the declaration emphasizes the importance of a number of principles of international law that were already in existence or were in the course of being developed, including the principle of common but differentiated responsibilities (Principle 7), responsibility of states for environmental damage (Principle 14), and timely notification "on activities that may have a significant adverse transboundary environmental effect" (Principle 19). It also calls for the wide application of the precautionary approach: "Where there are threats of serious or irreversible damage, lack of full scientific certainty shall not be used as a reason for postponing cost-effective measures to prevent environmental degradation" (Principle 15).

UNCED also adopted an international action program called Agenda 21. This comprehensive document outlined concrete measures for implementing its platform in the years following the conference. Many measures are of special relevance for natural resource management, in particular those under the heading "Conservation and Management of Resources for Development," which include measures on protecting the atmosphere; managing land resources; combating deforestation, desertification, and drought; promoting sustainable agriculture and rural development; conserving biological diversity; protecting, using, and developing the living resources of the oceans; and developing, using, and managing water resources.[120] In addition to the adoption of the Rio Declaration and Agenda 21, two important multilateral environmental treaties were opened for signature at the conference: the United Nations Framework Convention on Climate Change (1992)[121] and the Convention on Biological Diversity (1992).[122] The former—which will be examined in greater detail in the next chapter—provided the framework for addressing global warming by reducing carbon dioxide emissions, although it did not set any specific targets. The latter outlined a comprehensive framework for conserving biological diversity (that is, "the variability among living organisms from all sources including, *inter alia,* terrestrial, marine and other aquatic ecosystems and the ecological complexes of which they are part; this includes diversity within species, between species and of ecosystems"[123]), sustainably using these living organisms and ecosystems, and sharing the benefits arising from the use of genetic resources fairly and equitably.[124] Among other provisions, the convention outlined number of general and specific measures for conserving biodiversity, including establishing protected areas and facilitating access to genetic resources.[125] Both the climate change convention and the biodiversity convention also incorporated several of the Rio principles, in particular the precautionary principle and the principle of common but differentiated responsibilities.

Yet at Rio it proved impossible to reach consensus on a global forest convention because of the opposition of some developing countries, in particular Brazil and Malaysia. Instead, the summit adopted the "Non-Legally Binding Authoritative Statement of Principles for a Global Consensus on the Management, Conservation and Sustainable Development of All Types of Forests," while a chapter on "Combating Deforestation" was included in Agenda 21. The proposal of the United States that the concept of "common heritage of mankind" be incorporated in the management of tropical rain forests was rejected out of fear that such management would be internationalized.[126] The concept was rejected in the context of the climate change convention and biodiversity convention as well. By way of a compromise, the notion of "common concern of humankind" was instead inserted into these instruments.

Post-Rio Developments

Endorsing the outcomes of the Rio conference and following a proposal in Agenda 21, the General Assembly requested that ECOSOC establish a new UN Commission on Sustainable Development to monitor and review the implementation of Agenda 21. This took place in 1993, reflecting the belief that an institutional follow-up to the conference would maintain momentum for action, as the establishment of UNEP did after the Stockholm conference. In the field of international treaty-making, the momentum was indeed maintained, and a number of important treaties were negotiated and adopted in the trail of Rio. One of them was the United Nations Convention to Combat Desertification, which was adopted in 1994 with the objective of combating desertification and mitigating the effects of drought in countries experiencing these problems, particularly in Africa, through "long-term integrated strategies that focus simultaneously, in affected areas, on improved productivity of land, and the rehabilitation, conservation and sustainable management of land and water resources, leading to improved living conditions, in particular at the community level."[127] The convention is a prime example of an instrument that implements an integrated approach to environmental conservation and development, and it constitutes an important framework for managing natural resources in arid and semi-arid regions.

A number of other conventions and treaties that were concluded in the years following the Rio conference had an important bearing on the conservation and management of natural resources, including water resources, fisheries, and atmospheric resources. Notable accomplishments include the Convention on the Protection and Use of Transboundary Watercourses and International Lakes (1992),[128] the Agreement on the Cooperation for the Sustainable Development of the Mekong River Basin (1995),[129] and (after years of preparation by the International Law Commission) the Convention on the Law of the Non-Navigational Uses of International Watercourses (1997).[130] An important milestone was the adoption of the United Nations Fish Stocks Agreement (1995),[131] which seeks to improve the conservation and management of straddling and highly migratory fish stocks on the high seas. Under the auspices of the FAO, the Agreement to Promote Compliance with International Conservation and Management Measures by Fishing Vessels on the High Seas (1993)[132] and the Code of Conduct for Responsible Fisheries (1995) were adopted;[133] the former sought to strengthen control over fishing on the high seas, the latter sought to create an effective framework to ensure that aquatic living resources will be harvested sustainably. A particularly important event was the negotiation and adoption of the Kyoto Protocol to the United Nations Framework Convention on Climate Change (1997),[134] which laid down the specific obligations of states to reduce their emission of greenhouse gases. (These instruments will be presented in greater detail in the next chapters.) Although not much progress has been achieved toward a general treaty on forests because of a lack of political will, new institutional processes were established under the auspices of the United Nations Commission on Sustainable Development to provide a forum on international forest policymaking. Together, the Intergovernmental Panel on Forests (1995–1997) and the Intergovernmental Forum on Forests (1997–2000) examined a wide range of forest-related topics and produced more than 270 proposals for action toward sustainable forest management.[135]

In spite of these treaty-making and institutional activities, the radical changes to which states had committed at Rio did not really take place. In order to review progress achieved over the years that had passed since the Rio conference in 1992, a Special Session of the General Assembly took place in 1997 that was popularly known as Rio +5. The Special Session adopted by consensus (albeit with quite a number of reservations and declarations), a brief Statement of Commitment and a lengthy Programme for the Further Implementation of Agenda 21. These had been prepared by an ad hoc working group under the chairmanship of former UNEP director Mostafa Tolba. The statement acknowledges a number of positive results since 1992 but expresses deep concern that "the overall trends for sustainable development are worse today than they were in 1992."[136] Progress had indeed been made through the entry into force of the climate change, biological diversity, and anti-desertification conventions and UNCLOS. Furthermore, the working group found that conclusion of the Kyoto Protocol and the establishment in 1991 of a Global Environment Facility had also been positive steps. However, it was also quite obvious that many objectives and targets of the Earth Summit had not been met: an international forestry convention was not within reach; the level of official development assistance had decreased rather than increased toward the target of 0.7 percent of gross domestic product; and emissions of greenhouse gases had continued to increase and thus climate change could not be curbed.

Hence, the Rio+5 session of 1997 emphasized that the implementation of Agenda 21 remained "vitally important" and stated that "time is of the essence to meet the challenge of sustainable development."[137] The final document of the 1997 Special Session served as the program for the further implementation of Agenda 21. This contained programs for better international and national policies with respect to freshwater, oceans and seas, forests, energy, production and consumption patterns, the atmosphere, sustainable agriculture, and biodiversity. Implementing these programs required an increased flow of financial resources to developing countries at concessionary terms, the transfer of environmentally sound technology, education for sustainable development, and improved access to information and greater public participation in decision making.[138] On the last issue, the Convention on Access to Information, Public Participation in Decision-Making, and Access to Justice in Environmental Matters (1997), which was prepared at Aarhus under the auspices of the UN Economic Commission for Europe (ECE), was a notable step forward, at least in the European region.

At the dawn of the new millennium, a number of summits and gatherings of the world's leaders took place that chartered new directions for United Nations action. While none was exclusively devoted to natural resources, many of these activities have had a bearing on natural resource management.

In September 2000, the heads of state and government gathered at United Nations headquarters at what became known as the UN Millennium Summit. The outcome was the UN Millennium Declaration,[139] in which the world's leaders committed their nations to a new global partnership to respond to the world's main development challenges and specified a number of actions and targets, commonly known as the Millennium Development Goals. These are:

(1) to eradicate extreme poverty and hunger
(2) to achieve universal primary education
(3) to promote gender equality and empower women
(4) to reduce child mortality
(5) to improve maternal health
(6) to combat HIV/AIDS, malaria, and other diseases
(7) to ensure environmental sustainability
(8) to develop a global partnership for development[140]

The eight MDGs—which now form a blueprint for the activities of states, the UN, and its various specialized agencies—are based on a series of measurable targets and indicators for monitoring progress. The deadline for achieving nearly every goal is 2015. From the perspective of natural resource management, MDG 7 is of particular importance, inasmuch as three out of four targets that are linked to this goal directly relate to natural resources: integrating the principles of sustainable development into country policies and programs and reversing the loss of environmental resources (Target 1); achieving, by 2010, a significant reduction in the rate of biodiversity loss (Target 2); and halving, by 2015, the proportion of the population without sustainable access to safe drinking water and basic sanitation (Target 3).

Also in 2000, the General Assembly decided to organize a ten-year review of progress achieved in the implementation of the outcome of UNCED in order to "reinvigorate the global commitment to sustainable development."[141] The World Summit on Sustainable Development, which was held in Johannesburg in August and September 2002, did not have the goal of setting new norms; instead, it sought to review compliance with agreed policy and better integrate environmental, economic, and social development policies. The integration issue was important in light of the Millennium Development Goals, particularly MDG 8. At the instigation of Secretary-General Kofi Annan, the Johannesburg summit concentrated on five specific subjects known by the acronym WEHAB: water and sanitation, energy, health care, agriculture, and biological diversity. The summit gathered diplomats and politicians from the 189 UN member states and officials from international organizations as well as a colorful array of representatives from nongovernmental, scientific, women's, youth, environmental organizations, and development organizations; indigenous peoples; and the corporate world.

The summit adopted two policy documents. First, a political declaration—the Johannesburg Declaration on Sustainable Development (2002)—confirmed again the collective responsibility of the international community for a good living environment and the welfare of all people, now and in the future. It describes the challenges facing humanity, including bridging the enormous gap between poor and rich and slowing down or halting overfishing, climate change, desertification, and the loss of biological diversity. According to the declaration, the answer to all these problems lies in a clear link to efforts aimed at sustainable development, such as those relating to production and consumption patterns and decision making regarding concrete goals, timetables, and new public-private cooperation. In sum, the declaration advocates a multilateral approach and states that more effective and more democratically functioning international organizations are needed to achieve this link. Second, a comprehensive international action program—the Johannesburg Plan of Implementation (2002)—outlined the main points of international and national policy to be implemented, including reducing poverty, implementing sustainable food production strategies, changing unsustainable consumption and production patterns, protecting and managing natural resources (including sustainable fishing) as the basis for economic and social development, ensuring sustainable development in a globalizing world, achieving better standards of health, and implementing an institutional framework for sustainable development.[142]

However, the Johannesburg documents papered over many differences of opinion. For example, the European Union (EU) had wanted to make more quantitative and deadline-related agreements on many issues. This did occur with regard to subjects such as drinking water and sanitation, using chemicals, replenishing fish stocks, and sustainable fishing but not in others, such as the use of sustainable energy. It is striking that in the Johannesburg documents principles of international law related to the environment or development were barely touched upon, human rights were only briefly mentioned, and only lip service was given to the role of law in the implementation and monitoring of compliance with the agreements. Compared with Rio in 1992, Johannesburg in 2002 made little substantive progress.

During 12–16 September 2005, on the occasion of the sixtieth anniversary of the UN, the General Assembly convened a World Summit at the level of heads of state and prime ministers. In the words of UN Secretary-General Kofi Annan, this was "a once-in-a-generation opportunity"[143] to identify the momentum of and set the stage for reform of the United Nations.[144] Preparations for this summit had begun several years before: the High-level Panel on Threats, Challenges and Change had prepared a report on reform proposals, *A More Secure World: Our Shared Responsibility,* which was followed by a report of the Secretary-General, *In Larger Freedom.* Dominating the debate were issues such as Security Council reform, guidelines for the use of force, the establishment of a new UN Peacebuilding Commission, and the establishment of a new Human Rights Council to replace the UN Commission on Human Rights. The result was the World Summit Outcome document, officially (and somewhat serpentinely) called "Integrated and Coordinated Implementation of and Follow-Up of the Major United Nations Conferences and Summits in the Economic, Social and Related Fields. Follow-Up to the Outcome of the Millennium Summit."[145] This included an extensive section on development, which, however, largely repeated the Millennium Declaration of 2000, the Johannesburg Programme of Implementation of 2002, and the results of the Group of 8 Gleneagles Summit held in Perthshire, Scotland, in 2005. The document thus mainly summarized and updated UN development ideology on the occasion of the sixtieth anniversary of the world organization.

It is interesting to note that at the 2005 World Summit, world leaders stated that their efforts regarding sustainable development would include promoting

> the integration of the three components of sustainable development—economic development, social development and environmental protection—as interdependent and mutually reinforcing pillars. Poverty eradication, changing unsustainable patterns of production and consumption and protecting and managing the natural resource base of economic and social development are overarching objectives of and essential requirements for sustainable development.[146]

The question of integrating these three components of sustainable development is, indeed, the greatest challenge in the entire project of sustainable development policies. How should the various and quite different lines of standard-setting and policies in the three relevant areas (development, environment, and human rights) be linked to each other, adjusted to each other, and formed into the coherent whole that is required for achieving sustainable development?

Indigenous Sovereignty over Natural Resources

Following protracted negotiations for many years, the UN General Assembly at last adopted the Declaration on the Rights of Indigenous Peoples in 2007.[147] This 46-article declaration deals in a comprehensive way with the identity, position, and rights of indigenous peoples. It addresses their rights to self-determination, nondiscrimination, life and integrity, cultural identity and heritage, an educational system, and health services as well as their rights to their lands and their resources. With regard to the latter, it obliges states to consult and to cooperate with indigenous peoples in decision making regarding resource management. In several places the UN declaration explicitly uses the term self-determination, especially in Article 3. However, the declaration endorses a limited form of self-government within the framework of a state rather than political independence for indigenous peoples. Article 4 of the declaration specifies that the autonomy or self-government of indigenous peoples relates to "their internal and local affairs," and the final provision in Article 46(1) states that "nothing in this Declaration may be . . . construed as authorizing or encouraging any action which would dismember or impair, totally or in part, the territorial integrity or political unity of sovereign and independent States." Unfortunately, the declaration does not contain a definition of indigenous peoples. Equally striking is the fact that it refers only once to the concept of "sustainable development." Nevertheless, in many respects the declaration is quite a far-reaching and ambitious document.

The declaration touches in many of its provisions on the economic rights of indigenous peoples and their entitlement to their lands, territories, and resources. For example, Article 26 states that "indigenous peoples have the right to the lands, territories and resources which they have traditionally owned, occupied or otherwise used or acquired" and imposes an obligation upon states to "give legal recognition and protection to these lands, territories and resources. Such recognition shall be conducted with due respect to the customs, traditions and land tenure systems of the indigenous peoples concerned." Article 25 determines that indigenous peoples should be able to uphold their responsibilities to future generations in this regard. In a formulation reminiscent of the phrase in Article 1 of the two human rights covenants that states that "in no case may a people be deprived of its own means of subsistence," Article 10 states that indigenous peoples deprived of their means of subsistence are entitled to just and fair redress. Article 10 stipulates that "indigenous peoples shall not be forcibly removed from their lands or territories. No relocation shall take place without the free, prior and informed consent of the indigenous peoples concerned and after agreement on just and fair compensation and, where possible, with the option of return." In a similar vein, Article 28 adds: "Indigenous peoples have the right to redress, by means that can include restitution or, when that is not possible, just, fair and equitable compensation, for the lands, territories and resources which they have traditionally owned or otherwise occupied or used, and which have been confiscated, taken, occupied, used or damaged without their free, prior and informed consent." While these rights are certainly far-reaching, it should be noted that none of these provisions vests indigenous peoples *expressis verbis* with permanent sovereignty over their natural wealth and resources or includes exclusive rights for indigenous peoples over the natural resources within their territories. Rather they vest indigenous peoples with clear-cut rights in consultation and decision making and in benefit sharing. This interpretation is confirmed by Article 32 of the declaration, which specifies that states have an obligation to consult and cooperate in good faith with the indigenous peoples concerned before engaging in any project that will affect their lands and territories and other resources, particularly in connection with the development, utilization, or exploitation of mineral, water, or other resources.

TABLE 2.1. Milestones in the Evolution of UN Concepts Regarding Natural Resource Management at the National Level

Resolution, Declaration, or Multilateral Convention	*Significant Features*
"Integrated Economic Development and Commercial Agreements," General Assembly resolution 523 (VI), 12 January 1952	Early recognition of: • the right of underdeveloped countries to freely determine the use of their natural resources • the duty of such countries to utilize such resources to further their economic development and the expansion of the world economy
"Right to Exploit Freely Natural Wealth and Resources," General Assembly resolution 626 (VII), 21 December 1952	General recognition of: • the right of countries to use and exploit their natural resources • the duty of states, in the exercise of their right to freely use and exploit their natural wealth and resources, to have due regard to the need to maintain the flow of capital in conditions of security, mutual confidence, and economic cooperation among nations

(table continued on next page)

TABLE 2.1. *(continued)*

Resolution, Declaration, or Multilateral Convention	*Significant Features*
Convention on the Continental Shelf, 29 April 1958	• Recognition of the sovereign rights of coastal states over the continental shelf for the purpose of exploring and exploiting its natural resources
Convention on Fishing and Conservation of the Living Resources of the High Seas, 29 April 1958	• Achieving the "optimum sustainable yield" through conservation and rational use so as to secure a maximum supply of food and other marine products
"Permanent Sovereignty over Natural Resources," General Assembly resolution 1803 (XVII), 14 December 1962	Recognition of: • the right of peoples and nations to permanent sovereignty over their natural wealth and resources • the duty to exercise resource sovereignty in the interest of their national development and of the well-being of the people • modalities for the exercise of nationalization and expropriation, including payment of appropriate compensation • observance of foreign investment agreements in good faith
"Economic Development and the Conservation of Nature," General Assembly resolution 1831 (XVII), 18 December 1962	• First resolution to recognize that economic development of developing countries may jeopardize their natural resources and their flora and fauna if such development takes place without due attention to conservation and restoration
"Permanent Sovereignty over Natural Resources," General Assembly resolution 2158 (XXI), 25 November 1966	• Recognition that natural resources are limited and in many cases exhaustible and that their proper exploitation determines the conditions of the present and future economic development of the developing countries • Recognition of the right of all countries to secure and increase their share in the administration of foreign enterprises and to have a greater share in the profits
"International Covenant on Economic, Social and Cultural Rights and International Covenant on Civil and Political Rights," General Assembly resolution 2200 (XXI), 16 December 1966	• Recognition of the right of all peoples to freely dispose of their natural wealth and resources and to not be deprived of their own means of subsistence in identical articles 1 of both covenants

Resolution, Declaration, or Multilateral Convention	*Significant Features*
"Exploitation and Conservation of Living Marine Resources," General Assembly resolution 2413 (XXXIII), 17 December 1968	• Broadens resource management to include fishery resources • Recognition of the increasing importance of maximizing the sustainable yield of living marine resources through conservation and rational development • Awareness of the grave danger of the overexploitation and depletion of living marine resources
"Declaration of Principles Governing the Sea-Bed and the Ocean Floor, and the Subsoil Thereof, beyond the Limits of National Jurisdiction," General Assembly resolution 2749 (XXV), 17 December 1970	• Proclamation that the deep seabed area and its resources are the common heritage of mankind • Statement that the exploitation of these resources shall be carried out for the benefit of mankind as a whole
Declaration on the Human Environment (Stockholm Declaration), 16 June 1972	• Statement that careful planning and management are required for safeguarding the natural resources of the earth • Statement that the capacity of the earth to produce vital renewable resources must be maintained • Statement that nonrenewable resources must be used in a way that does not lead to exhaustion • Qualification of the sovereign right of states to exploit their own resources pursuant to their own environmental policies by establishing the responsibility to ensure that activities within their jurisdiction or control do not cause damage to the environment of other states or of areas beyond the limits of national jurisdiction (Principle 21)
"Declaration on the Establishment of a New International Economic Order," General Assembly resolution 3201 (S-VI), 1 May 1974	Expression of the need to establish a New International Economic Order based on: • Full permanent sovereignty over natural resources and all economic activities • Right of states not to be subjected to economic, political, or any other type of coercion • The right of all subjugated states, territories, and peoples to restitution and full compensation for the exploitation and depletion of natural resources • Just and equitable relationship between the prices of raw materials and (semi-) manufactured goods developing countries export and the prices of manufactures, capital goods, and equipment they imported • The need for all states to put an end to the waste of natural resources • The need for developing countries to concentrate all their resources for the cause of development

(table continued on next page)

TABLE 2.1. *(continued)*

Resolution, Declaration, or Multilateral Convention	*Significant Features*
"Charter of Economic Rights and Duties of States," General Assembly resolution 3281 (XXIX), 12 December 1974	• Proclaims the right of states to regulate and exercise authority over foreign investment, including the right to nationalize or expropriate foreign property • Requires states to cooperate in the exploitation of shared natural resources in order to achieve optimum use • Proclaims that every state has the primary responsibility to promote the economic, social, and cultural development of its people • Proclaims the protection of the environment for present and future generations to be the responsibility of all states; states that environmental policies should enhance and not adversely affect the present and future development potential of developing countries
UNEP Principles of Conservation and Harmonious Utilization of Natural Resources Shared by Two or More States, UNEP GC Dec. No. 6/14, 19 May 1978	• Requires states to cooperate in the conservation and harmonious utilization of shared natural resources • Requires states to avoid adverse environmental effects in areas beyond their jurisdiction of the use of a shared natural resource • Provides principles intended to increase cooperation and to prevent or contain conflict with regard to shared resources
UNCTAD IV Integrated Programme for Commodities, 31 May 1976	• Comprehensive action program for exploitation, processing, marketing, and distribution of commodities
"World Charter for Nature," General Assembly resolution A/RES/37/7, 28 October 1982	• Extensive set of principles of conservation and management of nature and natural resources • Urgency of achieving and maintaining "optimum sustainable productivity" of natural resources without endangering the integrity of ecosystems of species
United Nations Convention on the Law of the Sea, 10 December 1982	• Establishes maritime areas with specific natural resource regimes: territorial sea, archipelagic sea, exclusive economic zone, extended continental shelf, high seas, and the deep seabed area • Proclaims the deep seabed and its resources to be the common heritage of mankind and lays down a complex international regime regulating future deep seabed mining • Proclaims the sovereign right of states to exploit their marine resources pursuant to their environmental policies and in accordance with their duty to protect and preserve the marine environment • Establishes the duty of states to adopt measures to obtain the maximum sustainable yield of the living resources within the EEZ and on the high seas

Resolution, Declaration, or Multilateral Convention	*Significant Features*
UNCLOS (continued)	• Outlines obligations of states to take specific measures to prevent, reduce, and control pollution of the marine environment • Provides a comprehensive scheme for the peaceful settlement of international disputes
Rio Declaration on Environment and Development (Rio Declaration), 14 June 1992	• States that environmental protection constitutes an integral part of the development process and should not be considered in isolation from that process • Alters the wording of Principle 21 of the Stockholm Declaration (1972) by stipulating that states have "the sovereign right to exploit their own resources pursuant to their own environmental *and developmental* policies" • Proclaims that the right to development has to be fulfilled in order to equitably meet developmental and environmental needs of present and future generations
Convention on Biological Diversity, 5 June 1992	• A comprehensive framework for the conservation of biological diversity, the sustainable use of living organisms and ecosystems, and the fair and equitable sharing of the benefits arising from the use of genetic resources
United Nations Convention to Combat Desertification, 17 June 1994	• A framework for combating desertification and mitigating the effects of drought in arid and semi-arid regions through long-term integrated strategies that focus on improved productivity of land and the rehabilitation, conservation, and sustainable management of land and water resources
"United Nations Millennium Declaration," General Assembly resolution A/RES/55/2, 18 September 2000	• Establishes eight Millennium Development Goals to guide the activities of states, the UN, and its specialized agencies • MDG 7 aims at ensuring environmental sustainability through: —integration of the principles of sustainable development into policies and reversing the loss of environmental resources (Target 1) —achieving by 2010 a significant reduction in the rate of biodiversity loss (Target 2) —halving by 2015 the proportion of the population without sustainable access to safe drinking water and basic sanitation (Target 3)

(table continued on next page)

TABLE 2.1. *(continued)*

Resolution, Declaration, or Multilateral Convention	*Significant Features*
Johannesburg Declaration on Sustainable Development, 4 September 2002	• Confirms the collective responsibility of the international community for a good living environment and for the welfare of present and future generations • Calls for slowing down or halting overfishing, climate change, desertification, and the loss of biological diversity
"2005 World Summit Outcome," General Assembly resolution A/RES/60/1, 16 September 2005	• Explicitly endorses the need to integrate the three components of sustainable development—economic development, social development, and environmental protection—as interdependent and mutually reinforcing pillars • Recognizes that eradicating poverty, changing unsustainable patterns of production and consumption, and protecting and managing the natural resource base of economic and social development are essential for sustainable development
Declaration on the Rights of Indigenous Peoples, 13 September 2007	• States must consult and cooperate with indigenous peoples when making decisions regarding resource management • Indigenous peoples shall be protected from forcible removal from their lands or territories: no relocation can take place without their free, prior, and informed consent and after agreement on just and fair compensation and with the option of return • Indigenous peoples have the right to lands, territories, and resources that they have traditionally owned • Indigenous peoples have the right to redress and to just, fair, and equitable compensation for their lands, territories, and resources when these have been taken without their free, prior, and informed consent

Assessment

The UN debate on the management of natural resources began with postwar concerns about resource scarcity and focused initially on the extent to which states should take into account the interests of other states and of the world economy as a whole in their natural resource policy. This is reflected in the setup of the Bretton Woods order and UN Charter responsibilities in the social and economic field as well as in early UN General Assembly and ECOSOC resolutions.

Since 1952, however, the debate on natural resource management has taken quite a different course. In that year, Chile proposed that the UN include resource sovereignty in an article on the right of peoples to self-determination. Soon after that, Chile took the initiative for drafting a Declaration on Permanent Sovereignty over Natural Resources, a project that came to a successful conclusion in 1962. Resource sovereignty came to be viewed as an important aspect of the decolonization process and of the debate on the causes of underdevelopment and the conditions for development. Emphasis was increasingly placed on state sovereignty, in particular of developing countries, while the link to resource rights of peoples and to human rights became looser. During the 1950s through the 1970s, resource sovereignty became the subject of much politicized debate that was attributable to competing ideologies. On the one hand, western states promoted the idea of natural resource development through the increased flow of foreign investment and enhanced international economic cooperation for economic development. On the other hand, newly independent states and developing countries advocated the termination of the "unequal" treaties and contracts of the past, permanent sovereignty, and full national control over natural resources, if necessary by rescinding foreign property rights "without let or hindrance." Actual nationalizations—for example, those of the Suez Canal Company (1956), Dutch property in Indonesia (1958), French investments in Algeria (1961), copper mines in Chile (1971), or oil fields in Libya (1973)—brought the debate into high relief.

For a long time, the debate has tended to focus on the formulation of rights of non-self-governing peoples and newly independent states. Developing countries assembled in the Group of 77 attempted to broaden and strengthen their rights. They sought to broaden them by claiming sovereignty over marine resources in substantially extended sea areas and over all resource-related activities, including the processing, marketing, and distribution of raw materials. Most western states strongly opposed these extensions. In addition, the Group of 77 sought to strengthen resource sovereignty by claiming as many rights as possible, including the right to share in the administration and profits of foreign companies, the right to terminate concession agreements from the past, the right to determine freely the amount of "possible" compensation, and the right to settle disputes solely on the basis of national law and by national remedies.

During various periods controversy escalated, especially during the NIEO period of the 1970s. However, frequently it was the case that some of the rough edges could be removed and a return could be made to a strategy of compromise and cooperation. Landmark documents in this respect include the Declaration on Permanent Sovereignty over Natural Resources (1962), the UN Convention on the Law of the Sea (1982), the Declaration of the United Nations Conference on the Human Environment (1972), the Rio Declaration on Environment and Development (1992), the United Nations Millennium Declaration (2000), and the Johannesburg Declaration on Sustainable Development (2002). In summary, in adopting these resolutions, the member states of the United Nations attempted to balance rights and duties in natural resource management by establishing the following principles:

- natural resources be properly and prudently managed, based on the principle of sustainable use of natural resources;
- natural resources be employed for national development and the well-being of the people;
- the rights of indigenous peoples to their habitat and its natural resources be protected;
- policies related to nationalization and marine resources be implemented in accordance with international law;
- due care for the environment be made in ways that do not compromise the rights of future generations;
- states should cooperate for worldwide sustainable development.[148]

3

Management of the Global Commons

- **Resources of the High Seas and the Deep Seabed**
- **Resources of Outer Space and Celestial Bodies**
- **The Two Polar Regions**
- **The Atmosphere**
- **Assessment**

This chapter addresses the management of the areas and resources beyond the limits of national jurisdiction, often referred to as the global commons. The chapter presents the regime for deep seabed exploitation and the regulation of the exploitation and conservation of the living resources of the high seas—fisheries as well as whales and seals. It next presents the management regime applicable to the resources of outer space, particularly the moon and perhaps other celestial bodies. It then addresses the management of the natural resources in the two polar regions. Lastly, it examines the problems involved with managing atmospheric resources, in particular the ozone layer and the climate system. Some of these resource management regimes have been set up within the framework of the United Nations or with the participation of its organs and agencies. Others—namely the regime to manage Antarctica and the Arctic—have deliberately been kept outside the UN context, but the lessons learned from these management regimes might provide important insights on management techniques, principles, and processes that could be useful for improving the management of natural resources by the United Nations.

Resources of the High Seas and the Deep Seabed

The United Nations Convention on the Law of the Sea (1982) created a comprehensive legal framework for governing the exploitation and conservation of marine natural resources in areas beyond national jurisdiction—the deep seabed and the high seas. Considering that an account of the UN's involvement in the creation of UNCLOS was already given in preceding chapters, this section presents the management of the marine global commons, beginning with the convention's complex provisions on exploiting the resources of the deep seabed beyond national jurisdiction, followed by the regime for managing the living resources of the high seas. The section also describes agreements that built on the framework of UNCLOS and created additional rules for managing specific marine resources.

The Natural Resources of the Ocean Floor beyond National Jurisdiction

That the great ocean depths contain valuable resources was discovered as early as 1873, when the expedition of *HMS Challenger* revealed the presence of polymetallic (manganese) nodules on the deep seabed.[1] These potato-shaped, dark-colored, rock-like formations, which are rich in valuable metals such as nickel, manganese, copper, and cobalt, were the subject of increased interest, especially in the 1960s and 1970s, when great economic advantages were expected to be gained from their extensive deposits. By some estimates, these resources were on order of thousands of millions of tons and in concentrations richer than in many land-based deposits. Since the end of the 1970s, two other types of resources have been discovered on the deep seabed: polymetallic sulfides and cobalt-rich ferromanganese crusts, the latter particularly rich in such minerals as copper, iron, zinc, silver, gold, and cobalt. Polymetallic nodules are scattered across the vast abyssal plains of the seabed; the most promising deposits are in the Clarion-Clipperton Fracture Zone in the Pacific Ocean and in the central Indian Ocean. Polymetallic sulfides and cobalt crusts are concentrated in specific locations and are fused to the seabed. The former are found around hot springs in active volcanic areas (the greatest concentrations have so far been found beyond the continental shelves of the island nations of the western Pacific) while the latter occur on oceanic ridges and seamounts at several locations around the world.[2] In spite of these differences, all three types of resources are now subject to the complex and detailed provisions of UNCLOS.

Building on the Declaration of Principles Governing the Seabed and the Ocean Floor, and the Subsoil Thereof, beyond the Limits of National Jurisdiction (1970), UNCLOS proclaimed "the Area" (as "the sea-bed and ocean floor and the subsoil thereof, beyond the limits of national jurisdiction" was called) and its resources to be the common heritage of mankind and created a complex international regime to regulate future mining in the deep seabed and an appropriate international machinery.[3] Yet many provisions of this new regime had become controversial by the time UNCLOS was adopted. Although it soon became clear that commercial deep seabed mining was not likely to take place soon, controversies lingered that industrializing states used as justification for not ratifying the convention.[4] Owing to fierce ideological resistance, particularly from the United States (under President Ronald Reagan), the United Kingdom (under Prime Minister Margaret Thatcher), and Germany (under Chancellor Helmut Schmidt), the political fate of the convention remained uncertain for a long time.

For these reasons, UN under-secretary-general and special representative of the secretary-general for the law of the sea Satya Nandan (from Fiji) initiated a series of informal consultations aimed at achieving a universally acceptable regime. It was not until 1994 that an agreement was finally reached on various adjustments to UNCLOS that substantially accommodated the objections of the United States and other western nations to the deep seabed mining regime.[5] Although it was called a supplementary agreement, it de facto amounted to a substantive amendment of Part XI of UNCLOS, thereby watering down its controversial provisions on compulsory transfer of technology and compensation to countries that produce minerals from mines and significantly restraining the role of the envisaged supranational mining company, the UN Enterprise.[6] After the agreement was adopted, the convention quickly came into force.

The international regime that was created in Part XI of the convention and modified by the 1994 agreement governs all resource-related activities in the international seabed area.[7] In spite of the amendments to the convention, the guiding principles of the system of exploitation remain the same. First, UNCLOS states that the resources of the international seabed area shall be the common heritage of humankind and are not subject to appropriation by any state.[8] Second, it states that all rights in these resources shall be vested in humankind as a whole and the economic benefits from deep seabed mining are to be shared on a nondiscriminatory basis for the benefit all of humankind.[9] Third, the International Seabed Authority (ISA), which came into existence in 1994 with the entry into force of the convention and the members of which are all state parties to the convention, organizes and controls the activities in the Area. This entails not only administering the resources of the Area but also promoting and encouraging the conduct of marine scientific research in the international area.[10]

The ISA plays a central role in the functioning of the international regime of the Area. First, exploration and mining in the Area can be carried out only under a contract it has issued. These contracts may be issued to companies as well as to states. Second, the authority also devises regulations regarding exploration and exploitation of the seabed. In 2000, the ISA Assembly adopted Regulations on Prospecting and Exploration for Polymetallic Nodules in the Area;[11] this made it possible for the ISA to issue the first contracts. Since 2002, the ISA has been preparing similar regulations covering polymetallic sulfides and cobalt-rich ferromanganese crusts. Third, once mining becomes profitable, the contractors will pay royalties to the authority, which is then required to distribute those receipts equitably. In doing so, the authority has to take into account the interests and needs of developing countries.[12] Last but not least, the convention established a commercial arm of the authority, which is called the Enterprise. This is to come into operation only when seabed mining becomes feasible on a commercial scale. Until then, the functions of the Enterprise are to be carried out by the secretariat of the authority, which is headquartered in Jamaica.[13]

The seabed regime became operational in 2001, when the ISA signed the first contracts for exploring polymetallic nodules in the international seabed area. At the time of present writing, the number of contractors has risen to eight and include the following entities and governments: the China Ocean Mineral Resources Research and Development Association (2001), Japan's Deep Ocean Resources Development Company (2001), the government of India (2002), the government of the Republic of Korea (2001), the Institut français de recherche pour l'exploitation de la mer (2001), the Interoceanmetal Joint Organization (2001), the State Enterprise Yuzhmorgeologiya of the Russian Federation (2001), and the Federal Institute for Geosciences and Natural Resources of the Federal Republic of Germany (2006).[14] These contracts, which allow contractors to search for polymetallic nodules in specified parts of the deep oceans outside national jurisdiction, are valid for fifteen years. Nevertheless, it is still quite uncertain whether the exploitation of nodules will ever take place on a commercial basis. The existing contractors have so far concentrated most of their efforts on research and development activities and long-term environmental studies. A number of factors have inhibited progress toward commercial exploitation. Some of these are attributable to technical difficulties related to retrieving and lifting nodules from great ocean depths, and others are connected with the high costs of technological research and development. Yet as world markets experience increased demand for most metals that could be derived from seabed resources, the economic conditions for seabed mining are becoming increasingly promising. At the same time, the increased awareness of the fragility of the fauna and flora of the deep seabed and the marine environment in general has led many states to have second thoughts on the wisdom of the UN authorizing deep seabed mining.

A number of new activities that have already begun to take place in the Area or are likely to do so in the coming years will soon require appropriate regulation. These include nonmining activities such as ecotourism and bottom trawling for fish, which have begun to threaten vulnerable marine ecosystems in the Area. Of potentially even greater economic significance are activities known as bioprospecting, which entail the search for and exploitation of valuable compounds from genetic resources of the deep seabed, particularly those around hydrothermal vents and seamounts, which have proved to be major reservoirs of biodiversity. These marine genetic resources have potential applications in the food, industrial, and pharmaceutical sectors, among other usages.[15]

Living Resources of the High Seas

In contrast to the principle of the common heritage of humankind that governs the international regime for managing the resources of the Area, the principle of open access is the starting point of the regime that UNCLOS devised for the management of the *living* resources of the high seas.[16] These include stocks living permanently in the high seas, stocks that migrate across large portions of the oceans (highly migratory stocks), or high seas portions or life stages of stocks that straddle the boundaries of coastal states' EEZs and the high seas (straddling stocks). This essentially means that high seas resources can be exploited on a basis of first come, first served unless states establish a different regime for managing them on the basis of an international agreement. But while UNCLOS maintained the traditional freedoms of the high seas for all states, whether they are coastal or landlocked, including the freedom of fishing, it subjected these freedoms to the general proviso that they "shall be exercised by all States with due regard for the interests of other States in their exercise of the freedom of the high seas."[17] In this regard, UNCLOS builds on the dictum of the International Court of Justice in the 1974 fisheries jurisdiction cases between the United Kingdom and Germany and Iceland, which noted that "the former *laissez faire* treatment of the living resources of the sea in the high seas has been replaced by a recognition of a duty to have due regard to the rights of other States and the needs of conservation for the benefit of all."[18]

Furthermore, UNCLOS subjected the freedom of fishing to its provisions regarding the conservation and management of the living resources of the high seas. These are spelled out in Part VII of the convention and are a considerable step forward from the provisions of the 1958 Convention on the High Seas. UNCLOS now provides that "all States have the right for their nationals to engage in fishing on the high seas" but counterbalances this right by imposing on states the duty to take such measures for their nationals as may be necessary for the conservation of the living resources of the high seas and to cooperate with other states on that matter by establishing fisheries organizations if appropriate.[19] The right to fish is also subject to other treaty obligations and to the rights, duties, and interests of coastal states with regard to straddling, highly-migratory, anadromous, and catadromous stocks and marine mammals occurring in their EEZs.[20] UNCLOS supplements this general framework by stating the general objectives of fisheries management on the high seas. It stipulates that in determining the allowable catch and establishing other conservation measures for the living resources in the high seas, states shall

> take measures which are designed, on the best scientific evidence available to the States concerned, to maintain or restore populations of harvested species at levels which can produce the maximum sustainable yield, as qualified by relevant environmental and economic factors, including the special requirements of developing States, and taking into account fishing patterns, the interdependence of stocks and any generally recommended international minimum standards, whether subregional, regional or global.[21]

In addition, states shall also consider the effects of fishing on associated or dependent species.

UNCLOS thus provided important rules for managing the living resources of the high seas. Interested states can draw upon these principles in cases of dispute through the convention's compulsory dispute settlement mechanism.[22] However, this management regime has not prevented a large number of the living resources of the high seas from becoming overexploited and depleted. Among the first issues that attracted international attention was the problem of large-scale driftnet fishing and its negative impacts on the living marine resources of the high seas. After Pacific states took the first steps in addressing the problem,[23] the question was eventually considered by the General Assembly, which in 1989 adopted a resolution that imposed a moratorium on large-scale pelagic driftnet fishing.[24] Considerable problems also remained with the management of straddling and highly migratory fish stocks; in some cases these led to serious disputes.[25] In the 1990s, various measures were taken to address these problems, particularly in view of the commitments made at the Rio Summit on Environment and Development in 1992. As a result, the post-Rio period was marked by a considerable progress in the field of conservation and management of marine fisheries.

Soon after the 1992 Rio conference, an intergovernmental conference was convened under the auspices of the UN on the issue of straddling and highly migratory fish stocks. This resulted in the adoption in 1995 of the United Nations Agreement for the Implementation of the Provisions of the United Nations Convention on the Law of the Sea of 10 December 1982 relating to the Conservation and Management of Straddling Fish Stocks and Highly Migratory Fish Stocks (known as the Fish Stocks Agreement, FSA),[26] an implementing agreement of UNCLOS, which aims to improve the regime for conserving and managing straddling and highly migratory fish stocks on the high seas and to a certain extent within the areas under national jurisdiction.[27] The FSA includes a broad range of measures intended to ensure the long-term sustainability of these stocks. Among other novel provisions, it requires states to use the precautionary approach in adopting conservation measures and to consider the ecosystem when assessing the impact of fishing and other human activities on target stocks and other species. It also calls upon coastal states and states fishing on the high seas to cooperate for the purpose of achieving compatible conservation and management measures in EEZs and the high seas.[28] It also calls upon flag states (the states under whose flag and jurisdiction a ship sails), port states, and coastal states to more effectively enforce the conservation and management measures adopted for fish stocks.

In facilitating cooperation between states in developing and enforcing conservation and management measures, the FSA envisages a significant role for various regional fisheries management organizations and institutionalized arrangements (RFMO/As).[29] The tasks of these organizations and institutionalized arrangements range from collecting fishery statistics, assessing the state of resources, analyzing management options, and providing scientific advice for management to making management decisions and monitoring. The FSA also calls for the creation of new organizations in areas where none exist as yet. As a result, the number of RFMO/As has expanded considerably in the last decade. Table 3.1 depicts various fishery bodies, roughly distinguishing between RFMO/As that have a broad mandate and those vested with more limited and often only advisory functions.[30]

Some of these RFMO/As have been established under the auspices of the FAO, while others have retained their institutional independence. While the FAO plays no role in the actual management of fish stocks (most management decisions are made by the fishery bodies), it retains an important role in global fisheries governance by serving as a center for the coordination of activities of various RFMO/As.[31] This role has been performed by the FAO's Committee on Fisheries (COFI), a global intergovernmental forum for examining and discussing major problems with international fisheries and aquaculture that occasionally negotiates global agreements and nonbinding instruments. It was under the auspices of the COFI that the Agreement to Promote Compliance with International Conservation and Management Measures

Table 3.1. Regional Fisheries Management Organizations

Organizations with a Broad Management Mandate

Commission for the Conservation of Antarctic Marine Living Resources
Commission on the Conservation and Management of Pollock Resources in the Central Bering Sea
Commission for the Conservation of Southern Bluefin Tuna
General Fisheries Commission for the Mediterranean
Inter-American Tropical Tuna Commission
International Commission for the Conservation of Atlantic Tunas
Indian Ocean Tuna Commission
International Pacific Halibut Commission
Northwest Atlantic Fisheries Organization
North Atlantic Salmon Conservation Organization
North East Atlantic Fisheries Commission
North Pacific Anadromous Fish Commission
Pacific Salmon Commission
Southeast Atlantic Fisheries Organisation
Western and Central Pacific Fisheries Commission
Commission under the South Indian Ocean Fisheries Agreement
South Pacific Regional Fisheries Management Organisation

Organizations with an Advisory Mandate on Scientific and/or Management Matters

Asia-Pacific Fishery Commission
Southwest Indian Ocean Fisheries Commission
Permanent Commission for the South Pacific
Fishery Committee for the Eastern Central Atlantic
Western Central Atlantic Fishery Commission

by Fishing Vessels on the High Seas was negotiated and adopted in 1993, which, as the name suggests, imposes the duty upon states to effectively exercise their jurisdiction and control over fishing vessels flying their flags.[32] It was also within the framework of COFI that the Code of Conduct for Responsible Fisheries was adopted in 1995, which establishes principles and standards applicable to the conservation, management, and development of all fisheries, which are to be observed by states; fishing entities; regional, subregional, and global organizations; and all persons concerned in any way with the conservation of fishery resources and the management and development of fisheries. The comprehensive code covers processing and trade in fish and fishery products, fishing operations, aquaculture, fisheries research, and the integration of fisheries into the management of coastal areas. The code endorses the long-term conservation and sustainable use of fishery resources as the general and overriding objectives of fishery management and states that fishery management should promote the maintenance of the quality, diversity, and availability of fishery resources in sufficient quantities for present and future generations, paying particular attention to the issues of food security, poverty alleviation, and sustainable development. While it is voluntary, the code is global in scope and provides a necessary framework for national and international efforts to ensure sustainable exploitation of aquatic living resources in harmony with the environment.[33]

In spite of the considerable progress in fishery governance that took place in the 1990s, a number of problems related to fishery management remain. These include especially overfishing; illegal, unregulated, and unreported fishing; and destructive fishing practices that continue in many areas of the high seas. While restrictions to open access are essential for combating these problems, they are not always sufficient for effective fishery governance. Incentives need to be created to encourage limiting fishing to a level that is consistent with the long-term sustainable productivity of fishery resources, particularly by addressing the problem of fishing overcapacity.[34] Those incentives must be coupled with effective monitoring, control, and surveillance mechanisms. Part of these concerns might be addressed by improving the functioning of current RFMO/As. In his recent report, the UN Secretary-General recognized the need to update, strengthen, and modernize the mandates and competencies of RFMO/As by addressing gaps in the geographic coverage beyond areas of national jurisdiction, by extending them to cover discrete stocks of certain high-seas bottom fisheries, by strengthening their compliance and enforcement mechanisms, and by implementing in their work modern fishery management tools, in particular the precautionary and ecosystem approaches to management and the requirement that decisions be based on the best scientific information available.[35] Apart from improving the functioning of the RFMO/As, the management of high seas fisheries will have to address broader issues, such as the conservation of biodiversity. In this respect, discussions have already been taking place about the need to adopt a new global instrument regulating the establishment of marine protected areas in the high seas. The UN General Assembly and particularly the United Nations Open-ended Informal Consultative Process on Oceans and the Law of the Sea have been playing a central role in these efforts.[36]

The Management of Marine Mammals

While marine mammals fall under the broad category of marine living resources—a category that includes cetaceans (whales, dolphins), sirenians (manatees, dugongs), pinnipeds (seals, walruses), and sea otters—they are subject to a different management regime than that of high seas fisheries. This has to do partly with the fact that marine mammals have much slower reproduction rates than do most fish stocks, which makes them particularly vulnerable to overexploitation. Moreover, because they are examples of "charismatic megafauna," protecting and conserving them has been a matter of increased public concern, which explains why most of these species are now protected from overt commercial exploitation. UNCLOS envisaged separate treatment of marine mammals by explicitly providing that their exploitation might be prohibited, limited, or regulated more strictly than the exploitation of other living resources, not only in the EEZs of coastal states, but also on the high seas.[37] Moreover, UNCLOS subjected states to the duty to "cooperate with a view to the conservation of marine mammals and in the case of cetaceans . . . in particular work through the appropriate international organizations for their conservation, management and study."[38]

In the case of cetaceans, the most relevant international organization is the International Whaling Commission (IWC),[39] a natural resource regime that exists outside of but has links to the UN system. Created by the International Convention for the Regulation of Whaling (ICRW) in 1946[40]—long before the adoption of the various UN law of the sea conventions—the IWC was seen as the main body for regulating the whaling activities of signatory states.[41] The goal of the ICRW was "to establish a system of international regulation for the whale fisheries to ensure proper and effective conservation and development of whale stocks."[42] But while the convention recognized "the interest of the nations of the world in safeguarding for future generations the great natural resources represented by the whale stocks,"[43] it was also clear that its aim was "to provide for the proper conservation of whale stocks and thus make possible the orderly development of the whaling industry,"[44] a development that was desirable at that time in view of the need to provide sufficient raw materials during the postwar recovery period. With its current membership at eighty-two states,[45] the IWC is now seen as the principal body through which states cooperate in the management of cetaceans as required by UNCLOS,[46] although the emphasis of this cooperation has shifted from a combination of conservation and orderly exploitation to primarily conservation.

Regulations regarding the conservation and use of whale resources are included in the schedule that forms an integral part of the ICRW and can be added to or amended annually by a three-quarters majority vote of the IWC. The regulatory measures need to be "necessary to carry out the objectives and purposes" of the convention, must "take into consideration the interests of the consumers of whale products and the whaling industry," and must "be based on scientific findings." These might include determinations about which species are to be protected, when seasons should close and open, when waters should be closed and open (including designating which waters are to be sanctuary areas), and what type of whaling gear is to be used.[47] Moreover, the IWC can establish whale sanctuaries—as it did in 1979 for the Indian Ocean and in 1994 for the Southern Ocean—in which all commercial whaling is prohibited irrespective of the status of whale stocks. The species regulated in the schedule have been confined to the thirteen great whales that were historically targeted by the whaling industry.[48] As the convention does not provide a definition of "whale," however, differences of opinion have existed as to whether the IWC is competent to regulate small cetaceans, which have become subject of protection by other conservation agreements, as described below.

Regulatory measures are binding upon all members of the IWC unless a state objects to a specific amendment to the schedule, thereby exempting itself from the provisions of that amendment. This "objection procedure" has the potential to severely weaken conservation measures, as it allows members to opt out of a quota or moratorium. Furthermore, the IWC has no authority to enforce or means of enforcing these measures, although an international observer scheme was established in 1971 that granted it limited powers of observation. This perhaps explains why the early history of the IWC's management of whaling resources was not really one of great success.

Before 1972, the IWC regulated the total allowable catch of whales by reference to Blue Whale Units (BWU), a value used to measure yields of whale oil that blue, fin, sei, and humpback whales contributed to in a specific ratio. After bringing the Antarctic whale fishery close to extinction in the 1960s, the BWU system was replaced by a system of quotas for individual whale species. In 1976, the IWC introduced the so-called New Management Procedure, which divided each species into stocks and established a quota for each of them. This led the IWC to ban the whaling of overexploited stocks but not commercial whaling as such, which remained permissible for stocks considered to be in abundance. However, at the Stockholm conference in 1972, some called for a ten-year moratorium on all commercial whaling, while others insisted that the IWC needed to be strengthened and that scientific research regarding the global status of whale stocks needed to increase.[49] By 1982, the membership of the IWC had grown, and a number of the new members were nonwhaling nations. This enabled it to impose a moratorium on commercial whaling by setting catch limits at zero, although this change was made without supportive findings by its Scientific Committee. The moratorium appeared to be the only way to reverse the IWC's previously ineffective management, which had allowed the whaling industry excessive quotas for many years, resulting in continued overexploitation and depletion of whale stocks. The moratorium took effect fully in 1986 and remains in effect for the time being.

Pro-whaling states, such as Japan, Iceland, Norway, and the Soviet Union, lodged objections to the moratorium, but most of them removed their objections under threat of potential trade sanctions.[50] However, regardless of the moratorium, limited whaling operations have continued under the exemptions provided for noncommercial whaling intended to satisfy "aboriginal subsistence needs"[51] (that is, whaling conducted on a small scale using traditional methods of capture) and for whaling conducted for scientific purposes. While scientific whaling is explicitly allowed under the ICRW,[52] it continues to generate great public criticism and condemnation, particularly from environmentalist groups. These scientific programs are often seen simply as a way to circumvent the IWC's moratorium, and in the past whaling countries often resorted to them. Recently, they have been maintained mainly by Japan, which by some estimates has killed almost 10,000 whales in its Antarctic and North Pacific scientific whaling programs since 1987.[53] In the meanwhile, other pro-whaling states, such as Canada and Iceland, sought to circumvent the moratorium by leaving the IWC, although Iceland re-acceded in 2002, attaching a reservation to the moratorium.[54] Norway is the only remaining pro-whaling state that has preserved its original objection to the moratorium.

Today, the IWC remains a battleground between a large anti-whaling coalition of like-minded states that insist on the moratorium and a considerably smaller group of pro-whaling states and their supporters that advocate for sustainable whaling subject to regulation based on scientific findings. Proponents of whaling continue to argue that the purpose of the convention was not to prohibit whaling but to provide for its "orderly development"[55] and that certain stocks have now recovered enough to allow the moratorium to be lifted. They also contend that the ICRW was never intended to be a conservation treaty but is rather an agreement to regulate whaling interests. They point out that this was its form as it was concluded in 1946 among the fifteen main whaling nations of the day. Yet the danger remains that lifting the moratorium will once again lead to overharvesting unless an effective management regime is put into place. The IWC has been working on such a regime since the beginning of the 1990s. For that purpose, the so-called Revised Management Procedure (RMP) was devised in 1992 by the IWC's Scientific Committee—a new system that introduces an algorithm for catch limits by calculating quotas on the basis of a precautionary approach that is intended for the regulation of any future commercial whaling. Although the RMP was accepted by the commission in 1994, it has not been implemented because of the IWC's inability to reach agreement on the Revised Management Scheme (RMS), a compliance mechanism intended to supplement the RMP with an inspection and observation system.[56]

The fate of the IWC is unclear, as is the proposal that commercial whaling resume.[57] Since 2006, pro-whaling nations have been actively pushing for a "normalization" of the IWC, which they have long perceived as dysfunctional.[58] Talks have been conducted since then in an attempt to modernize the IWC. For that purpose, a small Working Group on the Future of the IWC has been recently established.[59] However, it remains to be seen whether any progress will be made in achieving a reconciliation between the anti-whaling members who see the prohibition of whaling as a moral and ethical question and the pro-whaling members who view whaling primarily through the lenses of traditional food customs and as a question of cultural relativism. What looms large, however, is the inherent danger that totally uncontrolled whaling might develop if the IWC breaks down completely.

Apart from the IWC, the only other organization involved in the management of marine mammals is the North Atlantic Marine Mammal Commission (NAMMCO). Established in 1992 by the Faroe Islands, Greenland, Iceland, and Norway, its objective is "to contribute through regional consultation and cooperation to the conservation, rational management and study of marine mammals in the North Atlantic."[60] While it is regional in scope, NAMMCO is the only organization that covers all marine mammals generally, although its powers are more of an advisory and scientific nature. Its founding agreement states that its council shall "provide a forum for the study, analysis and exchange of information among the Parties on matters concerning marine mammals." However, the agreement states that its management committees shall merely "propose . . . measures for conservation and management" and "make recommendations . . . concerning scientific research."[61] It is evident that NAMMCO was established out of dissatisfaction with and as a counterbalance to the IWC. In fact, its very existence has been seen as a threat to the IWC, in spite of the NAMMCO agreement's general provision that it is "without prejudice to obligations of the Parties under other international agreements."[62] NAMMCO has been carefully designed to prevent shifts in membership and interests akin to those the IWC has experienced, which is now dominated by anti-whaling states.[63] Yet it remains to be seen whether it will be an alternative, an antidote, or merely a complement to the IWC.[64] It also remains to be seen whether Japan's project of establishing a similar regional organization to regulate commercial whaling in the northwestern Pacific Ocean will ever be realized.

While no other international organizations are in place for managing marine mammals, a number of multilateral agreements have established specific regional regimes for conserving them. An example is the 1992 Agreement on the Conservation of Small Cetaceans of the Baltic and North Seas (ASCOBANS), which requires parties to "cooperate closely in order to achieve and maintain a favourable conservation status for small cetaceans"[65] in the agreement area (which was recently extended to include the northeast Atlantic Ocean and the Irish Sea).[66] ASCOBANS focuses on issues such as by-catch (species caught in a fishery intended to catch another species), habitat deterioration, and other anthropogenic disturbances that may adversely affect small cetaceans. The agreement also establishes a Conservation and Management Plan that obliges parties to conserve and manage habitat, participate in surveys and research, mitigate pollution, and provide public information. Another example is the 1996 Agreement on the Conservation of the Cetaceans of the Black Sea, Mediterranean Sea and Contiguous Atlantic Area (ACCOBAMS), which requires parties to "take co-ordinated measures to achieve and maintain a favourable conservation status for cetaceans," in particular to "prohibit and take all necessary measures to eliminate, where this is not already done, any deliberate taking of cetaceans and shall co-operate to create and maintain a network of specially protected areas."[67] The agreement requires states to implement a detailed conservation plan that seeks to outlaw any deliberate capture of cetaceans by the flag vessels of state parties and minimize their incidental capture. For that purpose, an amendment has been recently adopted that bans the use of driftnets in the agreement's area.[68] Other examples of multilateral agreements include the Multilateral Conservation of Polar Bears Agreement (1973) and the Convention for the Conservation of Antarctic Seals (1972), both of which will be presented in the section on the polar regions.

ASCOBANS and ACCOBAMS were both concluded in the framework of the Convention on the Conservation of Migratory Species of Wild Animals (1979), which seeks conservation and effective management of migratory species—that is, species for which a significant portion of members "cyclically and predictably cross one or more national jurisdictional boundaries."[69] As typical examples of migratory species, marine mammals are included in both the convention's endangered species list (Appendix I)—for which states "shall endeavour to provide immediate protection"—and the list of migratory species with an "unfavorable conservation status" (Appendix II)—the conservation and management of which require international agreements. Furthermore, agreements and memorandums of understanding of this kind were adopted for the conservation and management of seals,[70] turtles,[71] and other sirenians and cetaceans.[72] Marine mammals enjoy protection in other global conservation treaties, such as the Convention on International Trade in Endangered Species of Wild Fauna and Flora (1973),[73] which imposes restrictions on trade in certain species of marine mammals, and the Convention on Biological Diversity (1992). Coupled with regional conservation treaties that are either general in scope[74] or are directed at the protection of specific species (e.g., dolphins, turtles),[75] these agreements complement the general framework provided by UNCLOS for the protection of marine mammals in important ways. In addition, they strengthen the management regime provided by the ICRW.[76] UNEP has played an important role in the development and functioning of these instruments by providing the secretariats for the Convention on the Conservation of Migratory Species of Wild Animals, the Convention on International Trade in Endangered Species of Wild Fauna and Flora, and the Convention on Biological Diversity. In addition, some UN specialized agencies have begun to address the problems related to the conservation and management of marine mammals; one example is the Guidelines to Reduce Sea Turtle Mortality in Fishing Operations that the FAO recently developed.[77]

Resources of Outer Space and Celestial Bodies

Soon after the Soviet Union's successful launch of *Sputnik* in 1957 inaugurated actual space exploration, the "Question of the Peaceful Use of Outer Space" was included on the agenda of the General Assembly.[78] Shortly thereafter the first steps were taken in UN organs to regulate activities in outer space. In 1959, the General Assembly established the Committee on the Peaceful Uses of Outer Space, recognizing thereby "the great importance of international cooperation in the exploration and exploitation of outer space for peaceful purposes."[79] In the years that followed, the committee became very influential in elaborating basic legal principles governing the activities of states in the exploration and use of outer space. Its work culminated in the "Declaration of Legal Principles Governing the Activities of States in the Exploration and Use of Outer Space," which was unanimously adopted in resolution 1962 (XVIII) in the General Assembly in 1963.[80]

These principles were subsequently incorporated in the Treaty on Principles Governing the Activities of States in the Exploration and Use of Outer Space, Including the Moon and Other Celestial Bodies (also known as the Outer Space Treaty), which was adopted in 1967, a remarkable achievement considering that this was the period of the Cold War. While the treaty does not contain any provisions on the exploitation of natural resources, it lays down principles that are applicable to the management of natural resources of outer space. The treaty states, among other things, that the "exploration and use of outer space, including the moon and other celestial bodies, shall be carried out for the benefit and in the interests of all countries, irrespective of their degree of economic or scientific development, and shall be the province of all mankind." Furthermore, it stipulates that "outer space, including the moon and other celestial bodies, is not subject to national appropriation by claim of sovereignty, by means of use or occupation, or by any other means."[81]

However, the Agreement Governing the Activities of States on the Moon and Other Celestial Bodies of 1979 (also known as the Moon Agreement) is of much greater importance for the management and regulation of uses of the natural resources of outer space. It was drafted by the Committee on the Peaceful Uses of Outer

Space and was subsequently adopted by the General Assembly. So far, the agreement has been ratified by only thirteen states, none of which are capable of space exploitation.[82] This is a serious handicap for the moon regime that erodes its status and general acceptance, although its essential feature of nonappropriation has not been openly contested by space-faring nations. The agreement closes any legal gaps that could arise with regard to the appropriation of natural resources, unequivocally stating that "the moon and its natural resources are the common heritage of mankind." The agreement reaffirms that the moon is "not subject to national appropriation by any claim of sovereignty, by means of use or occupation, or by any other means" and states that "neither the surface nor the subsurface of the Moon, nor any part thereof or natural resources in place, shall become property of any State, international intergovernmental or non-governmental organization, national organization or non-governmental entity or of any natural person."[83] These provisions also apply "to other celestial bodies within the solar system, other than the Earth" but not "to extraterrestrial materials which reach the surface of the Earth by natural means."[84]

The Moon Agreement stipulates that the exploration and use of the moon and other celestial bodies shall be "the province of all mankind" and shall be "carried out for the benefit and in the interests of all countries, irrespective of their degree of economic or scientific development." It also stipulates that due regard shall be paid to "the interests of present and future generations as well as to the need to promote higher standards of living and conditions of economic and social progress and development."[85] Therefore, states have "the right to exploration and use of the moon without discrimination of any kind" and on an equal basis.[86] But while the agreement proclaims that the natural resources of the moon and other celestial bodies are the common heritage of mankind, it does not lay down a specific institutional structure to govern the exploitation of these resources akin to the provisions of UNCLOS. The Moon Agreement provides for the establishment of an international regime to govern the exploitation of the moon's natural resources only "as such exploitation is about to become feasible," and to that end it outlines the main purposes of such an international regime. These are:

(a) The orderly and safe development of the natural resources of the moon
(b) The rational management of the moon's natural resources
(c) The expansion of access to and opportunities to exploit those resources
(d) An equitable sharing by all states parties in the benefits derived from the moon's natural resources that gives special consideration to the interests and needs of developing countries and to the efforts of countries that have contributed directly or indirectly to the exploration of the moon[87]

In order to facilitate the establishment of such an international regime, the agreement also provides that states shall inform the UN Secretary-General, the public, and the international scientific community of any natural resources they may discover on the moon.[88] Finally, the agreement clearly states that all activities with respect to the natural resources of the moon shall be carried out in a manner compatible with the purposes of the international regime.[89] Exceptions to this rule are to be allowed only with regard to collecting and removing mineral and other substances for scientific research.[90]

The role of the United Nations in the management of the commons of outer space has been enormous. The international regime that is envisaged for exploiting and managing the natural resources of the moon and other celestial bodies has been fully the creation of UN organs, particularly of the Committee on the Peaceful Uses of Outer Space. Exploitation of the resources of outer space has yet to begin, and therefore the international regime has not yet been put in place. Notwithstanding this fact and the small number of ratifications, the 1979 Moon Agreement is important because it delegitimizes any unilateral action by interested states. During the last decade a renewed interest in outer space and its natural resources has emerged, in part generated by the recent exploration of Mars. The increased awareness of the fragility of the ozone layer and of major ecological functions in general has also stimulated an interest in the proper governance of outer space.

The Two Polar Regions

The natural resources of the two polar regions are governed by different international regimes that accommodate the different physical and political conditions of Antarctica and the Arctic. Antarctica is a continent with a huge landmass and part of it is claimed by states, whereas the Arctic region consists mainly of ice-covered sea. They have in common that their governance takes place principally outside the United Nations system, although proposals have frequently been put forward to bring Antarctica under the aegis of the United Nations. Similarly, it has been advocated that Antarctica and its natural resources be proclaimed a common heritage of humankind, but in recent years these attempts have faded away and a more practical modus vivendi between the Antarctic system and the United Nations has emerged. It can be expected that with the melting of the ice caps in the Arctic region, a new discussion on the management of the area and its resources will soon emerge. This discussion is linked to the wider issues of sustainable development and climate change in view of the vital ecological functions of the Arctic region for the world as a whole.

Antarctica

The Antarctic Treaty of 1959 created an international regime for the area below the latitude of 60° south that designated Antarctica as an area that shall be used only for peaceful purposes, including scientific investigation.[91] This treaty "froze" the existing claims of states to sovereignty over parts of the continent,[92] thereby placing the natural resources of the South Pole in a special position. All activities relating to natural resource management now must be agreed upon by the parties that have consultative status under the treaty.[93] While the treaty did not prescribe substantive rules relating to the natural resources of Antarctica, it established a procedural framework in the form of Antarctic Treaty Consultative Meetings, through which a number of legally binding recommendations have been adopted that include questions of natural resource management.[94] As early as 1964 the governments participating in the Third Consultative Meeting adopted the Agreed Measures for the Conservation of Antarctic Fauna and Flora,[95] which prohibited the killing, wounding, capturing, or molesting of any native mammal or native bird in Antarctica (except in accordance with permits issued for limited purposes) and established a system of "Special Protected Areas." It also declared Antarctica a "Special Conservation Area."

The Antarctic Treaty created the initial framework for an international regime that was further developed with the adoption of special conventions. The first to be added to the Antarctic treaty framework was the Convention for the Conservation of Antarctic Seals (1972), which was a response to the need for a more unified approach to the conservation of seals.[96] The convention addressed the defects of the measures agreed to in 1964, which protected seals while they were on land but not while they were on ice or in the sea. The 1972 convention—which applies to the whole sea area regulated by the Antarctic Treaty—defines permissible catches for certain seal species and prohibits catches of other seal species. It also establishes closed seasons, sealing zones, and sealing reserves and specifies obligations regarding exchange of information.

In response to concerns that an increase in krill catches in the Southern Ocean could have a serious effect on populations of krill and other marine life, the Convention on the Conservation of Antarctic Marine Living Resources (CCAMLR) was adopted in 1980.[97] The aim of the convention is to conserve marine life in the Antarctic south of the latitude 60° south and in the area between that latitude and the Antarctic Convergence.[98] This does not exclude harvesting and associated activities as long as such harvesting is carried out in a rational manner and does not lead to a decrease in the size of any population to levels below those that would ensure its sustainable use. The CCAMLR also mandates that the ecological relationships between harvested, dependent, and related populations be maintained and that depleted populations be restored to appropriate levels. Moreover, changes or risks of changes in the marine ecosystem that cannot be reversed over two or three decades must be prevented or at least minimized, taking into account the state of available knowledge of the direct and indirect impacts of harvesting, the effect of the introduction of alien species, the effects of associated activities on the marine ecosystem, and the effects of environmental changes. Each of these stipulations seeks to make the sustained conservation of Antarctic marine living resources possible.[99] The convention is thus one of the first instruments to have adopted an "ecosystem approach" to natural resource management and has thus served as an example that was subsequently relied upon by other environmental agreements. The commission and the Scientific Committee established by the convention played a pioneering role in the development and application in practice of the ecosystem approach. The CCAMLR established a system of observation and inspection, including boarding procedures, to ensure compliance with the convention.

A third instrument that further developed the 1959 Antarctic Treaty framework was the Convention on the Regulation of Antarctic Mineral Resource Activities (CRAMRA), which was adopted in 1988.[100] It was the result of a New Zealand initiative led by Ambassador Christopher Beeby. The convention provides a legal basis for assessing the possible impact on the environment of Antarctic mineral resource activities (i.e., prospecting, exploration, or development, but not scientific research activities), determining whether such activities were acceptable, and eventually governing the conduct of such activities.[101] The CRAMRA created a number of measures to ensure environmental protection and required decisions on mineral resource activities to be based on adequate information and the precautionary approach. The convention also outlined a comprehensive environmental impact assessment procedure and incorporated novel provisions on compliance, liability, and dispute settlement.[102] Despite these provisions, the convention attracted worldwide protest from many environmental NGOs, which saw the convention as an instrument for plundering Antarctica's mineral resources and destroying its fragile environment.

It is unlikely that the convention will ever be brought into force. Instead, a 50-year moratorium on Antarctic mineral resource activities was established with the adoption in Madrid of the Protocol on Environmental Protection to the Antarctic Treaty of 1991, which prohibits "any activity relating to mineral resources, other than scientific research."[103] The objective of the protocol is to achieve "comprehensive protection of the Antarctic environment and dependent and associated ecosystems." To that end, it sets out an elaborate list of principles and measures for planning and conducting all activities in the Antarctic treaty area, including provisions requiring

TABLE 3.2. The Antarctic Treaty System

- Antarctic Treaty (1959)
- Convention for the Conservation of Antarctic Seals (1972)
- Convention on the Conservation of Antarctic Marine Living Resources (1980)
- Convention on the Regulation of Antarctic Mineral Resource Activities (1988)*
- Antarctic Environmental Protocol (1991)

* not in force

environmental impact assessments. The protocol thus established one of the most comprehensive environmental protection regimes and designated Antarctica as "a natural reserve, devoted to peace and science."[104]

Apart from the conventions that form the Antarctic Treaty System, other global conventions contain specific provisions on the Antarctic region or otherwise are relevant to the management of the natural resources of the South Pole. One such treaty is the ICRW; the conservation measures adopted under its framework apply to the Antarctic area. In fact, the moratorium on commercial whaling adopted by the IWC provided an important component of the regime for managing Antarctic marine mammals, which is additionally strengthened by the whale sanctuary established for the Southern Ocean in 1994.[105] The positive impact of these conservation measures has recently been demonstrated by the evidence of increases in the number of blue and right whales in the southern hemisphere, although they are still far from their pre-whaling levels.[106] Besides the ICRW, other important treaties include UNCLOS and various marine protection treaties, such as the Convention on the Prevention of Marine Pollution by Dumping of Wastes and Other Matter (1972) and the International Convention for the Prevention of Pollution from Ships (1973) as Modified by the Protocol of 1978 Relating Thereto, all of which have a bearing on the management of natural resources of the Antarctic and therefore constitute (together with the specific Antarctic Treaty System) a comprehensive legal regime.

The Antarctic Treaty System was not a creation of the United Nations, and the world organization's involvement in issues pertaining to Antarctica has always been indirect, mostly through the work of the UN's specialized agencies and much less by the organization itself. This is not to say that no attempts were made to grant the United Nations a role in the governance of Antarctica. In 1958, India asked to put on the General Assembly's agenda the "Question of Antarctica," drawing attention to Antarctica's strategic, climatic, and geophysical significance to the world as a whole, but in the end it did not press for consideration and the question was not discussed.[107] The "Question of Antarctica" was not included on the agenda of the General Assembly until 1983, when Antigua, Barbuda, and Malaysia requested that it be added. They felt it was necessary to examine the possibility for a more positive and wider international concert to ensure that activities carried out in Antarctica were for the benefit of humankind as a whole. The initiative was met with strong reservations from the parties to the Antarctic Treaty of 1959. They noted that the treaty was open to all countries and of unlimited duration and claimed it had served the international community well and had averted international strife and disputes over sovereignty in Antarctica. Consequently, they warned against any attempt to revise or replace the 1959 treaty system.[108]

In the years that followed, the General Assembly continued to monitor the question of Antarctica. The fact that negotiations about the mineral resource exploitation treaty were made within the closed club of the consultative parties to the Antarctic Treaty became a source of contention within the General Assembly. While an initiative of the Organization of African Unity to have the General Assembly declare Antarctica a common heritage of humankind failed to receive sufficient support,[109] most of the developing countries that were not privy to the negotiations on CRAMRA managed to achieve the adoption in 1985 of an important General Assembly resolution that affirmed that "any exploitation of the resources of Antarctica should ensure the maintenance of international peace and security in Antarctica, the protection of its environment, the non-appropriation and conservation of its resources and the international management and equitable sharing of the benefits of such exploitation."[110] Similar appeals were made in resolutions in 1986 and 1987, which called upon the consultative parties to the Antarctic Treaty "to impose a moratorium on the negotiations to establish a mineral regime until such time as all members of the international community can participate fully in such negotiations."[111] Moreover, these resolutions asked that the United Nations be fully informed of developments regarding Antarctica and calls were made to invite the UN Secretary-General to attend the Antarctic Treaty Consultative Meetings, which so far, however, has not happened.[112] Instead, the UNEP executive director was invited beginning in the mid-1990s. The General Assembly responded to the subsequent adoption of CRAMRA in 1988 by the consultative parties with "deep regret"; the assembly felt that "any minerals régime on Antarctica, in order to be of benefit to all mankind, should be negotiated with the full participation of all members of the international community."[113] In subsequent resolutions, the assembly again urged "all members of the international community to support all efforts to ban prospecting and mining in and around Antarctica."[114]

The damaging oil spill from the Argentine supply ship *Bahia Paraiso* in 1989 off the western coast of the Antarctic raised the question in the General Assembly whether the regime for Antarctica was appropriate for managing the fragile and vulnerable ecosystem of the continent.[115] In resolution 44/124 (B) of 1989, the General Assembly expressed the conviction that "the establishment, through negotiations with the full participation of all members of the international community, of Antarctica as a nature reserve or a world park would ensure the protection and conservation of its environment and its dependent and associated ecosystems for the benefit of all mankind."[116] The assembly therefore welcomed the adoption in 1991 of the Protocol on Environmental Protection to the Antarctic Treaty, especially the ban on prospecting and mining, albeit with certain reservations.[117]

Because the contentious issues were resolved with the adoption of the 1991 protocol, the question of Antarctica received less attention in subsequent years, appearing on the agenda of the General Assembly only every three years. Since the early 1990s, the consultative parties to the Antarctic Treaty have begun to regularly provide the Secretary-General with information on their consultative meetings and on their activities in Antarctica. The General Assembly has also welcomed the commitments made by the consultative parties under Chapter 17 of Agenda 21 to ensure that information from scientific research activities conducted in Antarctica will be freely available.[118]

In contrast to the General Assembly's somewhat sporadic role, the involvement of UN specialized agencies in matters relating to Antarctica has been consistent since the time of the conclusion of the Antarctic Treaty.[119] The first to develop a cooperative relationship with the Antarctic Treaty System was the World Meteorological Organization, which has been closely involved in meteorological and related geophysical activities in the Antarctic. The International Maritime Organization has also conducted activities relating to Antarctica, particularly through its work on maritime safety and on preventing and controlling marine pollution from ships. The FAO has also been involved with this work and has been attending the meetings of the CCAMLR Commission and its Scientific Committee as an observer. The Intergovernmental Oceanographic Commission of UNESCO also has links with the Antarctic Treaty System. UNEP has played a particularly important role. Through its various programs, UNEP addresses assessment, management, and policy aspects of global and regional environmental issues, many of which are relevant to Antarctica. Moreover, it administers the secretariats of various global conventions dealing with subjects directly relevant to Antarctica.[120] In recent times, UNEP's executive director has been invited to attend consultative meetings, and UNEP now also prepares the reports on Antarctica on behalf of the UN Secretary-General.[121]

The Arctic Region

A great portion of the Arctic region is subject to the undisputed jurisdiction of eight states neighboring the area: Canada, Denmark (via Greenland), Finland, Iceland, Norway, Sweden, Russia, and United States. The region forms part of either the land territory or maritime area of these states. The rest of the area consists of the Arctic Ocean, a sea that is still largely covered with ice year-round. In contrast to Antarctica, which is a continent surrounded by oceans, the Arctic region consists of an ocean surrounded by continents, which partly explains why there is no special international legal regime in place for the North Pole and its surrounding area like the one for Antarctica.

The lack of a specialized international legal regime, however, does not mean that there is no legal framework to regulate the activities of states in the Arctic region. Because a large part of the area consists of the Arctic Ocean, a comprehensive set of rules is provided by the UN's Convention on the Law of the Sea (1982), which lays down important rights and obligations concerning the exploration, exploitation, conservation, and management of natural resources; the delineation of the maritime limits in the area; the protection of the marine environment (including ice-covered areas);[122] freedom of navigation; scientific marine research; and other uses of the sea. The resources of the Arctic Ocean are thus subject to public authority because they form part of the territorial seas, exclusive economic zones, or continental shelves of neighboring coastal states or they belong to the high seas or the deep seabed area, the natural resources of which are the common heritage of humankind.

Other multilateral treaties are relevant for the Arctic area. For example, the Convention on International Trade in Endangered Species of Wild Fauna and Flora of 1973 and the Convention on the Conservation of Migratory Species of Wild Animals of 1979 specifically protect some arctic species. Likewise, the Convention Concerning the Protection of World Cultural and Natural Heritage (1972), the Convention on Wetlands of International Importance Especially as Waterfowl Habitat (1971), and UNESCO's Programme on Man and the Biosphere (a biosphere reserve system) contain important provisions for the Arctic region. Many of the sites protected by these instruments are located in the Arctic region. The ICRW has played an important role since 1946 in the management of whales in the Arctic, and a role could also be accorded in future to NAMMCO. Last but not least, provisions of more general multilateral treaties are applicable to the Arctic, such as those of the Convention on Biological Biodiversity (1992) and of various treaties that protect the marine environment.

The only multilateral agreement specifically adopted for the Arctic region is the Agreement on the Conservation of Polar Bears (1973).[123] Signatories have agreed to manage polar bear populations in accordance with sound conservation practices. The agreement prohibits the hunting, killing, and capturing of polar bears except for limited purposes (e.g., exceptions are provided for aboriginal hunting) and by limited methods[124] and commits all parties to protect the ecosystems of polar bears, especially denning and feeding areas and migration corridors. The Agreement between the Government of the United States of America and the Government of Canada on the Conservation of the Porcupine Caribou Herd (1987) is one of the few bilateral agreements that regulates the use of an arctic natural resource.[125]

The international regime for the Arctic region has also been developed on the basis of soft law instruments. An important step in this regard was the adoption in 1991 of the Arctic Environmental Protection Strategy,[126] which seeks to protect the Arctic ecosystem, including human populations, and to protect, enhance, and restore the quality of the environment and the sustainable use of natural resources, including their use by local populations and indigenous peoples in the Arctic.[127] The next major step in the development of the Arctic regime was the creation in 1996 of the Arctic Council, a high-level forum intended to provide "a means for promoting cooperation, coordination and interaction among the Arctic States, with the involvement of the Arctic indigenous communities and other Arctic inhabitants on common arctic issues, in particular issues of sustainable development and environmental protection in the Arctic."[128] While the primary focus of the Arctic Environmental Protection Strategy was environmental protection, the Arctic Council's objectives include achieving sustainable development in the Arctic region. Among the important achievements of the council in this regard was the development of the Arctic Offshore Oil and Gas Guidelines.[129] The guidelines build on the precautionary approach and define a set of recommended practices for those who regulate the planning, exploration, and development of offshore oil and gas activities in the Arctic (including transportation and related onshore activities).

The Arctic Council is the most important intergovernmental initiative in the Arctic area and will likely continue to be so in the future. It remains to be seen, however, to what extent it will be possible to maintain such a loose institutional structure and how long it will be possible to avoid creating a comprehensive legal framework. Climate change and the melting of polar ice will have an impact on vulnerable ecosystems, the livelihoods of local inhabitants and indigenous communities, and the exploitation of the natural resources of the Arctic area. These impacts may be negative—as, for example, with the likely changes in the distribution of fish stocks, which will potentially have significant effects on commercial fisheries—as well as positive—inasmuch as global warming may also bring new economic opportunities through the opening of new Arctic sea routes. All of these challenges will need to be addressed, although the necessity of developing an Arctic treaty system has not yet materialized. In the recently adopted Ilulissat Declaration of 2008, five Arctic states recognized that the Arctic Ocean stands at the threshold of significant changes but reaffirmed their commitment to the legal framework of UNCLOS, seeing "no need to develop a new comprehensive international legal regime to govern the Arctic Ocean."[130] In this indirect way, the Arctic states have indicated their willingness to operate within a multilateral framework. At the same time, they have shown little appetite for having the United Nations directly involved in discussing and meeting the challenges that currently confront the Arctic region.

The Atmosphere

The term atmospheric resources refers to the resources of the air mass surrounding planet Earth, extending up to 150 kilometers or so. These consist of gases and aerosol (both solid or liquid) that fluctuate in the lower (troposphere) and upper (stratosphere) layers of the atmosphere, mostly nitrogen and oxygen but also argon, water vapor, carbon dioxide, nitrous oxide, ozone, sulfur dioxide, nitrogen dioxide, and other gases. Wind and solar radiation should also be considered as an atmospheric resource, although the analysis here will be limited mostly to gases as a natural wealth. Atmospheric resources should not be equated with the resources of outer space, although no definite boundary exists between outer space and the atmosphere.

While atmospheric resources share many characteristics with natural resources in international areas, they are not global commons in the strict legal sense. When they are located above areas beyond national jurisdiction of states and above exclusive economic zones,[131] atmospheric resources can be treated as common property, or *res communis.* When they are located above land territory, however, they are subject to the sovereignty of states. This does not mean that states can restrict access to atmospheric resources (after all, breathing is still free) but rather that states can regulate the exploitation of these resources, particularly by imposing measures to protect them. Until relatively recently the atmosphere provided a completely free waste disposal system for a whole range of anthropogenic pollutants, and it has been often abused as a "common sink."

Considering that the air mass does not remain confined to a certain territory but crosses state boundaries and fluctuates freely in the atmosphere, the natural resources of the atmosphere in practice do function like true global commons and managing them entails problems similar to the challenges of managing other global commons, particularly with regard to the problems of collective action and "free-riding." States that do not participate in the management of atmospheric resources undermine the measures of those states that participate in a collective management regime. Free-riding occurs when these nonparticipating states nevertheless benefit without contributing to the responsible management of resources. This is most evident in the case of air pollution, which is usually not limited to the contributing state but affects other states as well.[132]

In certain situations, as in the case of transboundary air pollution, it would be enough to treat atmospheric resources as shared resources, thereby implying the duty of states to cooperate in conserving and using them harmoniously on an equal basis.[133] Such a regime would require action on a bilateral or regional level. But in other situations, such as with regard to ozone depletion or global warming, atmospheric resources need to be treated as a global resource that requires joint action by all states. In these latter situations, atmospheric resources have come to be regarded as the common concern of humankind. In spite of the interconnectedness of these problems and the unity of atmospheric resources, the protection of the atmosphere is not governed by a comprehensive legal regime. Instead, rules have gradually been put in place for preventing and controlling transboundary air pollution, for eliminating ozone-depleting substances, and, most recently, for reducing emissions of gases that contribute to global warming. The United Nations and its organs have played a key role in creating the rules that now form an emerging international regime governing atmospheric commons.

Transboundary Air Pollution

Air pollution that traverses the territory of more than one state has been a clearly recognized problem since the mid-twentieth century. Pollution from a source in one country that affected the environment of another country lay at the core of the seminal arbitration of the Trail Smelter case between the United States and Canada in 1938 and 1941 that was presented in chapter 1. However, the first multilateral steps to protect atmospheric resources were not taken until the 1970s, in response to the problem of acid rain and its underlying cause, long-range transboundary air pollution. The problem of acid rain, or more precisely acid deposition deriving from gases that are released into the atmosphere and cause damage to the environment hundreds of miles from their emitting source, became most acute in Europe, which is the only region that has a comprehensive regime in place to deal with the problem.[134] The first to develop a strategy for dealing with transboundary air pollution was the OECD, which established a monitoring program as early as 1972. In that same year, the United Nations Conference on the Human Environment in Stockholm acknowledged the need to implement control programs for "pollutants distributed beyond the national jurisdiction from which they are released" and the need "to acquire knowledge for the assessment of pollutant sources, pathways, exposures and risks."[135]

However, it was under the auspices of the United Nations Economic Commission for Europe that the first multilateral agreement to address the problem of transboundary air pollution was adopted. This was because the ECE provided a suitable forum for discussing "low politics" (to which environmental problems belonged at that time) and to thereby further the détente in East-West relations that the Conference on Security and Co-Operation in Europe (1973) was facilitating. Negotiations between the members of the ECE, including Canada and the United States, soon led to the establishment in 1976 of the Co-operative Programme for Monitoring and Evaluation of the Long-Range Transmission of Air Pollutants in Europe (called EMEP for European Monitoring and Evaluation Programme). Three years later, in 1979, the members of the ECE adopted the Convention on Long-Range Transboundary Air Pollution (CLRTAP).[136] It acknowledged the problem of long-range transboundary air pollution (defined as pollution for which "it is not generally possible to distinguish the contribution of individual emission sources or groups of sources")[137] and laid down vague obligations to limit and as far as possible gradually reduce and prevent transboundary air pollution. It also outlined specific obligations regarding information-sharing, collaborative research, and the continued monitoring of pollutants and rainfall. Although it did not set any binding commitments regarding the limitation of emissions, the convention created an important framework within which actual commitments on pollution control could be negotiated.

Such commitments were subsequently achieved through the adoption of protocols that regulated the emissions of specific pollutants. The first protocol to which the parties to CLRTAP agreed was the Helsinki Protocol on the Reduction of Sulphur Emissions in 1985,[138] which required parties to reduce "their national annual sulphur emissions or their transboundary fluxes by at least 30 per cent as soon as possible and at the latest by 1993, using 1980 levels as the basis for calculation of reductions."[139] While the Helsinki protocol was an important first step in reducing the emissions of one pollutant, the equal-percentage approach it adopted failed to take into account differences in responsibility for acid rain, in the resources available to reduce acid rain, and in gains to be had from abatement measures. In contrast, the Protocol Concerning the Control of Emissions of Nitrogen Oxides or Their Transboundary Fluxes (1988)[140] and Protocol on Further Reductions of Sulphur Emissions (1994)[141] adopted differentiated emission targets for each party; the timing and levels of targets were specified in the annexes to the protocols. Moreover, the actual targets were based on the critical-loads approach,[142] which allocated abatement obligations based on how vulnerable each country's ecosystem was to acid deposition in order to maximize the environmental impact and value of the obligations on a regional scale.[143] In subsequent years, protocols that limited the emissions of other pollutants were added to the CLRTAP framework,[144] such as the Protocol Concerning the Control of Emissions of Volatile Organic Compounds or Their Transboundary Fluxes (1991),[145] the Aarhus Protocol on Persistent Organic Pollutants (1998),[146] the Protocol on Heavy Metals (1998),[147] and, most recently, the multipurpose Protocol to Abate Acidification, Eutrophication and Ground-Level Ozone (1999, also known as the Gothenburg Protocol), which covers multiple pollutants.[148]

The ECE continues to play a key role in the CLRTAP framework, not only by providing the secretariat for the convention and its protocols but also by supporting the scientific machinery established under EMEP. This scientific machinery has been crucial in developing protocols with differing targets. These targets are based on the critical-loads approach, which developed only after the emergence of a far-reaching consensus based on a long history of scientific cooperation in the context of EMEP.[149] Today EMEP continues to provide data on emissions and distribution of a wide range of substances that provides the basis for further action.

Many ECE member states participate in CLRTAP and its protocols, which has led to the successful reduction of many transboundary air pollutants, although some have questioned to what extent the reductions were actually attributable to the convention and its protocols and to what extent the reductions can be attributed to the economic decline of the former socialist economies of the countries of Eastern Europe. Be that as it may, CLRTAP so far remains the only major multilateral instrument aimed at controlling transboundary air pollution in a specific region. North American responses to the same problem are still limited to bilateral approaches to transfrontier pollution, and regional responses akin to that developed in the ECE area have not been developed in other areas of the world. One exception to this generalization could have been the Association of Southeast Asian Nations (ASEAN) Agreement on Transboundary Haze Pollution (2002),[150] which seeks to prevent and monitor transboundary haze pollution caused by fires, mainly in Indonesia. While the agreement was signed by all ASEAN states, it has proved to be of limited effectiveness, since Indonesia, the major source of transboundary haze pollution in the area, has so far failed to ratify the agreement.

The Ozone Layer

The protection of the ozone layer is the second element of the emerging international regime to protect the atmospheric commons. The thin layer of ozone—a gas with a molecular structure of three oxygen atoms (O_3) that is located in the upper part of the atmosphere of the lower stratosphere (about twenty to thirty kilometers up)—is essential to life on the planet. It shields the earth from most of the harmful ultraviolet-B radiation and from essentially all of the even more harmful ultraviolet-C radiation from the sun. Scientific concern about the thinning of the ozone layer started in 1970 when scientist Paul J. Crutzen suggested that nitrogen oxides from fertilizers and supersonic aircraft could catalyze the destruction of ozone.[151] Soon thereafter, chemists Frank Sherwood Rowland and Mario Molina discovered that the molecules of chlorofluorocarbons (CFCs)—a group of chemicals that until then had been widely used for refrigeration, foams, and industrial cleaning—remained in the atmosphere and could eventually reach the lower stratosphere, where they were broken apart by ultraviolet radiation and in turn broke down large amounts of stratospheric ozone.[152] These findings, which were confirmed by subsequent scientific observations that detected a steady thinning of the ozone layer, became the subject of increased international concern as it became clear that the depletion of the ozone layer would lead to increased ultraviolet radiation at the surface of the earth. This in turn would have harmful effects on human health (including damage to the eyes, skin cancers, and suppression of the immune system), animals, plants, microorganisms, and materials—effects that would not affect just one country but possibly all of them.

In 1976, the Governing Council of UNEP was the first to discuss the issue of ozone depletion, and soon thereafter UNEP and the WMO established the Coordinating Committee of the Ozone Layer to periodically assess ozone depletion. However, it was not until 1980–1981 that negotiations on a treaty to protect the ozone layer actually started.[153] And while it was expected that the first step of a framework agreement would be relatively easy to achieve, differences between countries advocating measures to control the use of CFCs in various sectors and countries supporting caps on existing production capacity led to four years of arduous negotiations. However, the negotiations eventually led to the adoption of a framework convention in March 1985. The resulting Vienna Convention for the Protection of the Ozone Layer[154] spelled out a general commitment to take "appropriate measures . . . to protect human health and the environment against adverse effects resulting or likely to result from human activities which modify or are likely to modify the ozone layer."[155] However, the convention did not outline concrete commitments to take action to reduce the production or consumption of ozone-depleting substances; it merely included provisions that encouraged intergovernmental cooperation on scientific research (specifying in an annex what the major scientific issues were), systematic observation of the ozone layer, monitoring of CFC production and emissions, and the exchange of information. Nevertheless, the convention was an important first response to the thinning of the ozone layer, in particular because it recognized "the potentially harmful impact on human health and the environment through modification of the ozone layer." It also acknowledged that "measures to protect the ozone layer from modifications . . . require international co-operation and action, and should be based on relevant scientific and technical considerations" and recognized "the need for further research and systematic observations to further develop scientific knowledge of the ozone layer and possible adverse effects resulting from its modification."[156] The convention thus quite remarkably defined certain general commitments even before the effects of the thinning of the ozone layer were definitely felt and the process was conclusively proven by science.

Soon after adoption of the 1985 convention, UNEP convened negotiations on a protocol that would include measures to control ozone-depleting substances. Concrete commitments were not made until the mid-1980s, when the British Antarctic Survey found that a hole existed in the ozone layer in the Antarctic stratosphere that was far larger than anyone had anticipated and a scientific consensus was reached that action was necessary to stop the deterioration of the ozone. As Mostafa Tolba, former UNEP executive director, recalls, "Only six months after the scientists spoke with one voice, we managed to get a legally binding treaty."[157] The result was the Montreal Protocol on Substances that Deplete the Ozone Layer (1987), which set forth a reduction formula based upon a gradual phase-down of global emissions. The protocol initially required parties to make 50 percent cuts from 1986 levels in the production and consumption (the latter meaning "production plus imports minus exports")[158] of a number of CFCs by 1999 and to freeze the production and consumption of the three main halons at 1986 levels by 1993.[159] At the same time, the protocol allowed developing countries to delay their compliance with the reduction schedule by ten years. While it outlined a timetable with interim targets, the protocol provided for the possibility that phase-out schedules could be revised on the basis of periodic scientific and technological assessments. On the basis of such assessments, the protocol was adjusted and amended at UN conferences several times: in London (1990), in Copenhagen (1992), in Vienna (1995), in Montreal (1997), in Beijing (1999), and again in Montreal (2007). These adjustments accelerated and further reduced the production and consumption of controlled substances, introduced other kinds of control measures, and brought additional substances under control (including carbon tetrachloride, methyl chloroform, methyl bromide, and hydroclorofluorocarbons). Presently, the Montreal Protocol controls ninety-six chemicals and sets forth a detailed schedule for phasing them out with differing deadlines for developed[160] and developing countries.[161]

By 2006, the Montreal Protocol had resulted in the phasing out of over 96 percent of all ozone-depleting substances (ODS) globally and the total consumption of CFCs worldwide had fallen to 3.2 percent of 1986 levels.[162] There is also strong evidence that the total combined levels of ODS are now declining in both the troposphere and the stratosphere. The recent report of the assessment panel to evaluate scientific information under the protocol has confirmed that the ozone layer shows some initial signs of recovery, while the decline of stratospheric ozone that was observed in the 1990s has not continued. It has been estimated that without the protocol, ozone depletion would have risen to at least 50 percent in the northern hemisphere's middle latitudes and to 70 percent in the southern hemisphere's middle latitudes by the year 2050, about ten times worse than current levels. But while the report concludes that "the Montreal Protocol is working," it emphasizes that the adverse impacts of stratospheric ozone depletion are expected to persist during at least the next decade. Moreover, polar ozone loss will generally remain large and highly variable in the coming decades, and the Antarctic ozone hole is persisting longer than previously estimated. The overall effectiveness of the protocol will therefore have to be assessed on a longer timescale. With continued compliance with current control measures, the ozone layer is generally not expected to recover earlier than 2050 (and in the case of the Antarctic ozone not earlier than 2060–2075) because of the long atmospheric lifetimes of various ODS, which range from 50 to 100 years in some cases. Furthermore, expected recovery might be disturbed by the transport, sinks, and future emissions of ODS; by future levels of greenhouse gasses; by climate changes; and by various natural occurrences, such as volcanic eruptions.[163]

Failure to continue to comply with the 1987 Montreal Protocol as amended would seriously delay or could even prevent recovery of the ozone layer. For this reason, it is rather discomforting that ratification of the more recent amendments of the protocol, including their stronger control measures, has been seriously lagging.[164] On the other hand, there are good reasons to introduce further adjustments to the protocol by accelerating the phase-out periods of various ODS. As the 2006 report of UNEP's Technology and Economic Assessment Panel points out, it is possible to return to the 1980 ozone levels more quickly through an accelerated phase-out of hydroclorofluorocarbons (HCFCs), tighter control of methyl bromide applications, and the collection and destruction of existing halons, CFCs, and HCFCs. This should not pose too big a problem, considering that technically and economically feasible substitutes are available for almost all ODS applications, including those that use HCFCs and methyl bromide.[165] The 2007 amendment to the protocol to accelerate the phase-out of HCFCs has been an important step in this direction. Yet the momentum needs to be sustained for the total global phase-out of all ODS as soon as possible, not only to ensure protection of the ozone layer but also as an additional way to combat climate change, inasmuch as most ODS are also potent greenhouse gases that contribute to global warming.

The 1987 Montreal Protocol has been hailed as an example of exceptional international cooperation. Former UN Secretary-General Kofi Annan described it as "perhaps the single most successful international agreement to date."[166] Part of its success might be attributable to the innovative trade measures the protocol introduced, such as the ban on imports of controlled substances, provisions to discourage the export of technology for producing or using ODS, and detailed reporting requirements and noncompliance procedures.[167] Widespread support of the protocol has also been secured by the differing obligations for developing countries, which were granted various grace periods in view of their lack of financial and technological resources for adopting ODS replacements and of the responsibility of the developed countries for the bulk of total emissions into the atmosphere. But the success of the protocol has also been possible because the opposition to the phasing out of ODS largely collapsed in the face of convincing scientific evidence of the linkage between ozone depletion and CFCs, which led the industry to start concentrating on the development and commercialization of alternatives to CFCs that do not deplete ozone.

United Nations organs have played an important role in this success, particularly UNEP, which has been concerned since its establishment with the problem of ozone depletion and has played a key role in the creation of the Vienna-Montreal regime. By serving as the secretariat for the convention and its protocol, UNEP carries out important tasks for their functioning. The Global Environment Facility has also played an important role. Together with the Multilateral Fund of the Montreal Protocol and the technical assistance of the UN Development Programme (UNDP), UNIDO, and the World Bank, the GEF finances and supports projects to phase out the consumption and production of ODS in developing countries and in economies in transition.

Climate Change

Instruments that address climate change constitute the third element of the international regime to protect the atmospheric commons. As is evident from observations of increases in global average air and ocean temperatures, of widespread melting of snow and ice, and of a rising global average sea level, the warming of the climate system is now unequivocal. Most of the observed increase in global average temperatures since the mid-twentieth century is very likely attributable to the observed increases in anthropogenic greenhouse gas concentrations, particularly of carbon dioxide (CO_2), methane (CH_4), and nitrous oxide (N_2O), which have increased markedly as a result of human activities since about 1850, exceeding now by far the preindustrial values determined from ice cores spanning many thousands of years. Merely between 1970 and 2004, global greenhouse gas emissions attributable to human activities increased by 70 percent. This is attributable mostly to the burning of fossil fuels but also to the manufacturing of cement and changes in land use, particularly the clearing of tropical forests.[168]

Scientific evidence of human interference with the climate was publicized for the first time at the First World Climate Conference, which was organized by the WMO in 1979. The conference, the first major international meeting on climate change, spurred increased public awareness and governmental concern about climate issues in the years that followed. The General Assembly articulated this concern for the first time in resolution 43/53 of 1988, in which it noted "that the emerging evidence indicates that continued growth in atmospheric concentrations of 'greenhouse' gases could produce global warming with an eventual rise in sea levels, the effects of which could be disastrous for mankind if timely steps are not taken at all levels" and recognized "that climate change is a common concern of mankind, since climate is an essential condition which sustains life on earth."[169] In the same year, the WMO and UNEP established the Intergovernmental Panel on Climate Change (IPCC), a body that since has been providing decision makers and the interested public with an objective source of information about climate change.[170] In its first assessment report, which was published in 1990, the IPCC confirmed that the threat of climate change was real. This eventually led the General Assembly to launch negotiations on a convention on climate change.[171] After just fifteen months of negotiations, the United Nations Framework Convention on Climate Change (UNFCCC)[172] was adopted and opened for signature at the Earth Summit in Rio (1992).

The UNFCCC defines climate change as "a change of climate which is attributed directly or indirectly to human activity that alters the composition of the global atmosphere and which is in addition to natural climate variability observed over comparable time periods."[173] It sets as its "ultimate objective" the stabilization of greenhouse gases "at a level that would prevent dangerous anthropogenic interference with the climate system" with the proviso that such stabilization "should be achieved within a time-frame sufficient to allow ecosystems to adapt naturally to climate change, to ensure that food production is not threatened and to enable economic development to proceed in a sustainable manner."[174] While all the parties "should protect the climate system for the benefit of present and future generations of humankind, on the basis of equity and in accordance with their common but differentiated responsibilities and respective capabilities," developed countries "should take the lead in combating climate change and the adverse effects thereof,"[175] considering that "the largest share of historical and current global emissions of greenhouse gases has originated in developed countries."[176]

All parties to the convention have agreed to respond to climate change. Taking into account their common but differentiated responsibilities and their specific development priorities, all parties have agreed to compile national inventories of anthropogenic emissions of greenhouse gases; prepare programs on measures to mitigate climate change; promote and cooperate in the development and transfer of environmentally friendly technologies; promote sustainable management and conservation of carbon sinks and reservoirs; prepare for adaptation to the impacts of climate change; integrate climate change considerations in their relevant social, economic, and environmental policies and actions; and cooperate in conducting research and observation and exchanging data on the climate system and in education, training, and raising public awareness related to climate change.[177] In addition to this, the convention imposes specific commitments on two groups of countries. The Annex I parties, which consist of industrialized countries (that is, the twenty-four original members of the OECD and the members of the European Union) and countries with economies in transition, are required to "adopt national policies and take corresponding measures on the mitigation of climate change, by limiting its anthropogenic emissions of greenhouse gases and protecting and enhancing its greenhouse gas sinks and reservoirs," thereby demonstrating that they "are taking the lead in modifying longer-term trends in anthropogenic emissions."[178] The Annex II parties, which consist only of the original twenty-four OECD member states and the members of the European Union, are required to "provide new and additional financial resources" to enable developing countries to undertake emission reduction activities and to "assist the developing country Parties that are particularly vulnerable to the adverse effects of climate change in meeting costs of adaptation to those adverse effects." The Annex II parties shall also take "all practicable steps to promote, facilitate and finance, as appropriate, the transfer of, or access to, environmentally sound technologies and know-how to other Parties, particularly developing country Parties."[179] The remaining parties to the convention, who are mostly developing countries, are not encumbered with special obligations. Rather, certain groups of developing countries are recognized as being especially vulnerable to the adverse impacts of climate change, including countries with low-lying coastal areas and those prone to desertification and drought.

There can be little doubt that the 1992 climate change convention is one of the prime legal instruments in the field of sustainable development. The core principles of sustainable development are amply reflected and further developed in the convention. Among its fundamental principles, the convention proclaims that "the Parties have a right to, and should, promote sustainable development,"[180] thus enunciating the right to development as well as the duty to eliminate unsustainable patterns of production and consumption. Other key principles include common but differentiated responsibilities, resources that are a common concern of humankind, and the precautionary principle.[181]

The convention entered into force soon after its adoption in 1994 and obtained almost universal participation.[182] However, by the time the convention was adopted it was already evident that its provisions would not be sufficient to tackle climate change in all its aspects. Following the approach that had already been successfully used to devise the legal regimes to combat transboundary air pollution and ozone depletion, a new round of negotiations was launched in 1995 at the Conference of the Parties (known informally as the COP), which was the first meeting to arrive at more detailed commitments for industrialized countries. After more than two years of intensive negotiations, a legally binding protocol was adopted in December 1997 at the third COP in Kyoto.

The Kyoto Protocol of 1997,[183] which shares the convention's ultimate objective of stabilizing atmospheric concentrations of greenhouse gases at a level that will prevent dangerous interference with the climate system, stipulates binding commitments to limit or reduce greenhouse gas emissions. It requires industrialized countries (as listed in Annex I of the UNFCCC) to reduce their collective emissions of carbon dioxide, methane, nitrous oxide, hydrofluorocarbons, perfluorocarbons, and sulphur hexafluoride from sources and sectors listed in Annex A of the protocol by at least 5 percent[184] by the period 2008–2012 compared to their 1990 emission levels.[185] The commitment period stretches over five years, which allows for more flexibility in reaching the targets than if a single target year were provided, particularly for countries with variable annual emission levels. In contrast to other multilateral environmental agreements, however, the protocol allows developed countries to change the level of their allowed emissions over the commitment period through participation in special mechanisms and through the enhancement of carbon sinks.[186]

The Kyoto Protocol requires parties to implement and/or further elaborate policies and measures aimed at increasing energy efficiency, protecting and enhancing sinks and reservoirs of greenhouse gases (through, for example, promoting sustainable forest management practices and reforestation), promoting sustainable forms of agriculture, promoting new and renewable forms of energy, and promoting technologies aimed at carbon dioxide sequestration. It also requires parties to implement policies and measures that address market, fiscal, and other imperfections in sectors that emit greenhouse gases and that reduce or limit greenhouse gases in the transport sector, in waste management, and in the production, transport, and distribution of energy. To enhance the individual and combined effectiveness of their policies and measures, the parties are also to cooperate with each other.[187]

The protocol introduces a number of mechanisms that allow for a greater degree of flexibility in achieving the agreed targets and boost the cost effectiveness of climate change mitigation. First, it allows states to make use of carbon sinks produced by human-induced changes in land use and forestry activities (although such activity has been limited to establishing forests or reforestation since 1990).[188] Second, it gives parties the option of taking joint action to fulfill their emission reduction targets, for example by allowing member states of the European Union to redistribute their reduction targets among themselves (known as the "EU bubble").[189] Third, it allows developed countries to pursue joint projects that reduce emissions or increase removals using sinks (joint implementation). Fourth, it establishes the clean development mechanism, which allows developed countries to invest in emission reduction projects or afforestation or reforestation projects in developing countries and receive credit for the emission reductions or removals achieved.[190] Finally, it endorses the establishment of an emission trading system, which allows Annex I countries to transfer to (or acquire from) other Annex I parties emission reduction units and thereby pursue cheaper opportunities for curbing emissions or increasing removals wherever those opportunities exist.[191] In any event, the use of these mechanisms must be "supplemental to domestic action," meaning that domestic policies and measures of the industrialized states must constitute "a significant element" of efforts to meet their commitments.[192]

The provisions of the protocol are also advanced with regard to the monitoring of compliance with its provisions. The parties are subject to regular and ongoing reporting requirements, and the reports are subject to enhanced review procedures. Moreover, the protocol established a special committee to facilitate, promote, and enforce the compliance of the parties (the Compliance Committee). Monitoring of compliance and implementation also takes place more generally at the conferences of the parties to the convention, which also serves as the meeting of the Parties to the Kyoto Protocol (CMP).[193] The successive decisions taken by the COP and CMP constitute a detailed set of rules for the practical and effective implementation of the convention and the protocol that includes issues such as finance and technology transfer.

Because the protocol introduces legally binding emission limitations, its adoption is an important step in reducing the potentially devastating impact of climate change. However, support of and participation in the protocol has been much lower than for the convention, as is evident from the much longer time it took for the protocol to enter into force. Ratification required at least fifty-five parties to the convention, including enough industrialized (Annex I) countries to account in total "for at least 55 per cent of the total carbon dioxide emissions for 1990 of the Parties included in Annex I."[194] The protocol did not enter into force until 16 February 2005, after the Russian Federation ratified in 2004. In subsequent years, Japan (2005) and Australia (2008) also joined. Even today, its effectiveness remains undermined by the fact that it still it does not have on board the largest emitter of carbon dioxide, the United States. This may change with the Obama administration.

The most notable achievements of the UNFCCC and its Kyoto Protocol are "the establishment of a global response to climate change, stimulation of an array of national policies, and the creation of an international carbon market and new institutional mechanisms that may provide the foundation for future mitigation efforts," as the IPCC recently noted in its fourth assessment report. However, this is far from enough. As the IPCC suggests, there is much evidence and high levels of agreement that current climate change mitigation policies and related sustainable development practices will not be enough to reverse the trend; global emissions of greenhouse gases will continue to grow over the next few decades. This will cause more warming and induce many changes in the global climate system, much larger than those observed during the twentieth century, which included changes in wind patterns, changes in precipitation patterns and levels, the loss of sea ice, and some aspects of weather extremes. Changes in the frequency and intensity of extreme weather events combined with rises in the sea level are expected to have highly adverse effects on natural and human systems. What is most worrisome is that even if greenhouse gas concentrations are stabilized, anthropogenic warming and rises in the sea level will continue for centuries because of the time scales associated with climate processes and feedbacks.[195] In view of this, it is regrettable that no further steps were taken at the thirteenth COP at Bali (2007), which produced only an Action Plan with a mandate, a road map, and a timetable for negotiating a post-Kyoto regime.[196]

Nor was any considerable breakthrough achieved at the conference in Copenhagen in December 2009. But despite all the negative assessments in the media, the outcome of the conference—the legally non-binding Copenhagen Accord, as it is called—might be considered a step forward, as it officially recognized "the scientific view that the increase in global temperature should be below 2 degrees Celsius" and because it brought about a number of important financial and institutional developments. These include the pledge of developed countries to provide additional US$30 billion short-term funding for immediate action until 2012 and US$100 billion annually by 2020 in long-term financing, and the establishment of a Copenhagen Green Climate Fund (to support projects, programs, policies, and other activities in developing countries related to mitigation, adaptation, capacity-building, and technology development and transfer) and of a Technology Mechanism (to accelerate technology development and transfer in support of action on adaptation and mitigation). But while the accord acknowledges that climate change is "one of the greatest challenges of our time" and emphasizes the "strong political will to urgently combat" this challenge, it does not lay down any legally-binding commitments on further emission reductions, even though states agreed ". . . that deep cuts in global emissions are required according to science." Developed states are merely asked to submit to the UNFCCC secretariat by the end of January 2010 information on quantified economy-wide emissions targets for 2020 and developing countries information on their mitigation actions for that same period.[197]

Another positive result was the full return of the United States to the UN as the principal forum of negotiations on climate change. President Obama demonstrated his own commitment to achieving progress by engaging directly in the climate change negotiations. Together with the Chinese prime minister Wen Jiabao and the leaders of India, Brazil, and South Africa, joined later by those of France, Germany, the United Kingdom, and some developing countries, he brokered the accord as described above. At the last moment the conference of the parties merely decided "to take note of" the Copenhagen accord, as a result of last minute opposition by a small group of countries, including Sudan, Venezuela, Bolivia, Cuba, and Nicaragua. Nevertheless, the traditional "fire-wall" between the developed countries and the developing countries had been broken.[198]

The "sealing" of a legally-binding deal on quantified emission reductions has thus once again been unduly postponed until the next meeting of the parties in Mexico. Yet, the accord reflects a political consensus of what needs to be done on the long-term global response to climate change. As UN Secretary-General Ban Ki-moon stated: "This accord cannot be everything that everyone hoped for, but it is an essential beginning."[199]

As with the regime for addressing the ozone layer problem, the regime for addressing global climate change has been a "UN child" since its inception. Many UN organs have played an important role in its creation, starting with the General Assembly, which was crucial in fostering consensus on the need to combat climate change and the need to translate this into appropriate political action. Various other UN specialized agencies and organs, particularly the WMO and UNEP, often provided crucial technical and scientific support. However, the role of the IPCC was particularly prominent in this process, inasmuch as its findings were crucial to the launching of a serious response to global warming. The IPCC's first assessment report (1990) provided the crucial scientific input that triggered the negotiations on the UNFCCC, while its second assessment report (1995) provided key input for the negotiations of the Kyoto Protocol. Its third report (2001) improved the climate for negotiations at the seventh COP held in Marrakesh, Morocco, which led to a broad package of decisions regarding further implementation of the convention and the protocol. It is hoped that its fourth assessment report (2007) will trigger a new round of commitments. The best affirmation of the IPCC's outstanding role is the fact that it was awarded the 2007 Nobel Peace Prize, which it shared with former U.S. vice-president Al Gore. The IPCC will likely continue to play an important role in the further elaboration of the climate change regime. Determining what constitutes "dangerous anthropogenic interference with the climate system," the prevention of which is the ultimate goal of the UNFCC, involves value judgments for which science can provide crucial support.[200]

Assessment

During the twentieth century an enormous expansion of state economic sovereignty took place over maritime areas and to a lesser extent over air space. This resulted in "nationalizing" natural resource management in areas that hitherto had been international areas. This is not to say that states can do whatever they like with "their" natural resources. In modern international law, sovereignty over natural resources has come to entail a considerable number of duties, including the duty to preserve the natural environment and to take world interests into account. Such duties emanate in particular from the law of the sea, international environmental law, human rights law (including with respect to indigenous peoples), and general international law.

The twentieth century also witnessed the emergence of international regimes for areas and natural resources that remained beyond the limits of national jurisdiction. These global commons include the high seas and their living resources; the deep seabed; outer space, including the moon and other celestial bodies; the two polar regions; and the atmosphere in general and the ozone layer and the climate system in particular. The principle of freedom of access to the high seas remained intact, although it was qualified by obligations to manage fish stocks properly and not deplete them. Marine mammals as examples of "charismatic megafauna" enjoy particular protection under various instruments. The deep seabed and its mineral resources have been proclaimed as the common heritage of humankind, a relatively new and potentially far-reaching principle that also applies to the moon and its natural resources. The international regimes for the two polar regions are very different, reflecting the very different geophysical and political conditions of Antarctica and the Arctic region. But they have in common the facts that both regions are crucial to the global environment, are fragile, and are increasingly the object of specific international regulation aimed at cooperation for nature conservation. Both the ozone layer and the climate system have been declared a common concern of humankind. Obviously this new concept is much more vague and has fewer legal connotations than the concept of a common heritage of humankind, but it still implies a strong international dimension and the taking into consideration of the interests of future generations.

These international regimes are subject to different principles of management and have put in place different institutional structures and various systems for monitoring compliance. Some regimes provide for institutionalized consultation and cooperation, such as the meetings of the consultative parties under the 1959 Antarctic Treaty, the conference of the state parties to the 1982 law of the sea convention, the conferences or meetings of parties under the conventions on the ozone and climate change regime, and more recently the meetings of the Arctic Council. In some situations, new standing international institutions were established, such as the International Whaling Commission, the International Seabed Authority, or the various fishery management organizations. Some of these institutions have wide regulatory competences—the IWC and the ISA are the best examples. A number of these international regimes have put in place far-reaching mechanisms for enforcement (even through penalties) and settling disputes, such the Implementation Committee of the 1987 Montreal Protocol and the Compliance Committee of the 1997 Kyoto Protocol or the International Tribunal for the Law of the Sea under the 1982 UN Convention on the Law of the Sea. This varied situation illustrates the fragmented and inchoate structure of global natural resource management.

The general regimes of important multilateral treaties such as the 1982 UN Convention on the Law of the Sea, the 1992 Convention on Biological Diversity, and the 1992 UN Framework Convention on Climate Change apply to these global commons. The period following the 1992 Earth Summit was marked by considerable progress in the field of international law-making with respect to conservation and sustainable use of natural wealth and resources, both through treaty-making and through soft law instruments such as the 1995 Code of Conduct for Responsible Fisheries. United Nations organs (including UNEP, the IPCC, and the Committee on the Peaceful Uses of Outer Space) and various specialized agencies of the UN system (the WMO, the FAO, and others) have been playing a central role in the creation of the principles and rules that now form distinct international regimes governing the global commons, although they are still emerging, fragmented, and incomplete. This means that a host of relatively new principles and concepts of contemporary international law apply to the global commons. In addition to the principles of the common heritage of humankind and the common concern of humankind, these principles include the precautionary principle, the sustainable use of natural resources, intergenerational equity, common but differentiated responsibilities, and the principle of interrelatedness and integration.[201] The specific rights and duties derived from many of these principles have still not fully crystallized, but this does not affect their now firm status in modern international law.

To a certain extent the global commons are used as the laboratories for the testing of these new principles and the rights and corollary duties emanating from them. The international regimes that have emerged for the management of the global commons created different institutional structures and various systems for monitoring compliance. Some provide for institutionalized consultation, others established standing international organizations. In some cases, groundbreaking regulatory innovations were introduced, such as the imposition of a moratorium on whaling or penalties on the production and use of ozone-depleting substances. Furthermore, novel solutions were devised for resolving and avoiding conflicts, for example by freezing the claims to sovereignty over Antarctica. These varied situations and examples illustrate the fragmented and inchoate structure of global resource management. But, the freedom of access to and exploitation of global commons that for a long time prevailed under the Grotian doctrine of the freedom of the seas all too often resulted in a "first come, first served" advantage for industrialized states. This regime is now supplemented by new schemes of international cooperation and protection of natural wealth and resources beyond the limits of national jurisdiction, in the creation of which the United Nations has often played a pioneering role.

4

The International Architecture for Environmental Governance and Global Resource Management

- **The United Nations Environment Programme**
- **The Commission on Sustainable Development**
- **The Specialized Agencies**
- **Other Institutions within the UN System**
- **Treaty Secretariats and Commodity Organizations**
- **Alternative Ideas**
- **Assessment**

As the previous chapters have demonstrated, consultation and decision making regarding environmental affairs and natural resource management is scattered over a number of institutions. No single world environmental organization or world sustainable development organization exists. UNEP, established in 1972, comes close to this only in some respects, since it was designed for a much more limited purpose and suffers from many limitations and shortcomings. A number of other UN organs deal with environmental issues, most notably the Commission on Sustainable Development and the United Nations Development Programme. Outside the UN system, various international commodity agreements exist as well as treaty secretariats of multilateral environmental agreements. The work of a number of specialized agencies has a bearing on global resource management and environmental governance. Notwithstanding all these institutions and initiatives, it is widely felt among both academics and various states that a single more powerful institution is needed to govern environmental conservation and global resource management.[1]

The United Nations Environment Programme

As a follow-up to the 1972 United Nations Conference on the Human Environment, the United Nations Environment Programme was established as a subsidiary organ of the General Assembly.[2] Initially located in Nairobi (but later moved to its outskirts), UNEP became the first UN organ whose head office was situated in a developing country. This was the result of a political bargain with developing countries, which were initially skeptical about the establishment of a special environmental program. Originally its role was to be that of a coordinator and catalyst in the field of environmental policy within the UN system rather than an agency for operational action. Nonetheless, UNEP has also undertaken a variety of operational activities. As formulated in General Assembly resolution 2997 (XXVII), UNEP has been endowed with the following mandates:

- Promote international cooperation in the field of the environment
- Provide general policy guidance for the direction and coordination of environmental programs within the UN system
- Review the implementation of these environmental programs
- Keep under review the world environmental situation and ensure appropriate and adequate consideration by governments
- Promote the development, exchange, and application of technical knowledge and information
- Review the impact of national and international environmental policies and measures on developing countries and ensure that such programs and projects are compatible with the development plans and priorities of those countries[3]

Beyond this formal mandate, UNEP has also undertaken activities relating to the environmental consequences of warfare, the relationship between human rights and the environment, the relationship between the environment and peace, and the drafting of guidelines on specific issues such as the management of transboundary or shared resources, as was discussed in chapter 2.

Governance of UNEP

UNEP has a 58-member intergovernmental Governing Council, a secretariat in Nairobi with five regional offices in the world, and an environment fund. The Governing Council sets general policy and reports annually to the mother organ, the UN General Assembly, through ECOSOC. The Committee of Permanent Representatives, composed of all member states, provides leadership on a regular basis. The Governing Council meets in regular and special sessions. Once a year it meets at the ministerial level in the form of the Global Environmental Forum.

The executive director has a broad mandate to manage UNEP, to provide advisory services, and to bring to the attention of the Governing Council any environmental matter that he feels requires its consideration. Maurice Strong, secretary-general of the 1972 Stockholm conference, served as its first executive director (1972–1975) and was very instrumental in setting a new and ambitious environmental agenda for the UN. The executive director has wide discretion in setting the agenda and pro-

Table 4.1. UNEP Executive Directors

Maurice Strong (1972–1975)
Mostafa Kamal Tolba (1975–1992)
Elizabeth Dowdeswell (1992–1998)
Klaus Töpfer (1998–2006)
Achim Steiner (2006–)

vides early warning to the international community about environmental damage. He or she also provides guidance for the operation of environmental programs in the UN system and organizes reviews of the implementation of these programs. Following the effective work of Maurice Strong in building up UNEP, Mostafa K. Tolba (1975–1992) provided dynamic leadership. His most direct result was the creation of an effective regime to protect the ozone layer through the 1985 Vienna Convention and the 1987 protocol to it.

Activities of UNEP

UNEP has established a number of useful mechanisms for monitoring and reporting on the state of the environment, including an "Earthwatch" with the following arms:

- The Global Environmental Monitoring System (GEMS)
- The Global Resource Information Data Base (GRID)
- The International Environmental Information System (Infoterra)
- The International Register of Potentially Toxic Chemicals (IRPTC)
- The International Programme on Chemical Safety (IPCS)

UNEP has also developed an active role in sponsoring international environmental negotiations and drafting multilateral environmental agreements. In practice, it has been a leading force for the sound management of hazardous chemicals, pesticides, and organic pollutants. For example, UNEP played a key role in supporting the negotiations for the Basel Convention on the Control of Transboundary Movements of Hazardous Wastes and Their Disposal (1989) and it now administers the secretariat of that convention. It played a key role in developing the Vienna Convention for the Protection of the Ozone Layer (1985) and its Montreal Protocol on Substances that Deplete the Ozone Layer (1987); many view these as examples of rather effective multilateral agreements. UNEP not only served as the driving force toward the conclusions of these instruments but also continues to have operational responsibilities for both. In spite of UNEP's successful involvement in the creation of regimes for the ozone layer and hazardous waste, it is interesting to note that it has not played a central role in the genesis of what became the United Nations Framework Convention on Climate Change (1992). While this could have been partly attributable to interinstitutional jealousy and skirmishes, a more accurate view would be that as an environmental agency, UNEP was considered to have a too narrow mandate. Most of the developing countries saw climate change not merely as an environmental problem but as an important developmental issue as well and thus preferred that the negotiating process be conducted under the auspices of the General Assembly.[4]

Since 1977 UNEP has coordinated the anti-desertification work of UN agencies. In this connection, it sponsors activities related to upgrading rangeland, irrigation, soil conservation, seed banks for dryland trees, and reforestation. Its efforts resulted in the UN Convention to Combat Desertification in Those Countries Experiencing Serious Drought and/or Desertification, Particularly in Africa, which was adopted on 17 June 1994. UNEP also laid the groundwork for the 1992 Convention on Biological Diversity.

The environmentally sound management of water is also a main concern of UNEP. Three particular aspects of its activities can be mentioned. First, UNEP's Regional Seas Programme, which involves more than 120 countries in ten regions, seeks to bring countries together to take scientific, economic, and legal action to protect their shared seas by combating and reducing pollution.[5] The Mediterranean Programme is one of the largest among them. Second, UNEP also started a program for the environmentally sound management of inland waters and integrated environment and development programs for the catchment areas of large river systems.[6] These programs draw together experts on forests, soils, wildlife, energy, human settlements, and industry. The first result was an agreement by the eight countries of the Zambezi River Basin to cooperate in conserving its resources and planning their future use.[7] Similar programs followed, including one for the Mekong River. Third, UNEP launched a program for the protection of the environment of the oceans, which includes a global plan of action for the protection of marine mammals.[8] Its coral reef unit is another marine activity.

Cooperation with Others

UNEP also works closely with a number of specialized agencies and UN organs. Since 1979, UNEP has managed the World Climate Impact Studies Programme (now the World Climate Impact Assessment and Response Strategies Program) as part of the WMO's World Climate Programme. UNEP has been working with the WMO and the International Council of Scientific Unions on assessments of and responses to climate change. It co-sponsors with the WMO the IPCC, which was awarded the Nobel Peace Prize in 2007 along with former U.S. vice-president Al Gore. The Vienna Convention for the Protection of the Ozone Layer and the 1987 Montreal Protocol on Substances that Deplete the Ozone Layer are also examples of successful activities in this field. In addition, UNEP works closely with UNESCO and the FAO to conserve the earth's tropical rain forest belt, which is seriously shrinking as a result of timber exploitation, forest fires, construction of roads, and land cultivation. UNEP has been instrumental in including environmental considerations in the International Tropical Timber Agreement (1983), which includes a paragraph emphasizing "the importance of, and the need for, proper and effective conservation and development of tropical timber forests with a view of ensuring their optimum utilization while maintaining the ecological balance of the regions concerned and of the biosphere."[9]

At the regional and national levels, UNEP promotes integrated forest management as a way to make forest conservation economically efficient and environmentally sound. Finally, UNEP and UNESCO work together with a number of nongovernmental organizations (NGOs), such as the International Union for Conservation of Nature, in monitoring the implementation of multilateral conservation treaties and in strengthening their implementation strategies. Reference should also be made to UNEP's ongoing efforts to develop international environmental law through the adoption of multilateral environmental agreements and soft legal instruments such as guidelines or principles of conduct.[10]

Unfortunately, UNEP has not been spared from serious North-South confrontations. These conflicts escalated in 1997 when Spain, the United Kingdom, and the United States threatened to withhold funds until reforms were made to strengthen the role of member states in determining UNEP's policy, thereby seeking to erode the role of UNEP's executive director and his staff. In the view of these industrial states, UNEP had come to serve the interests of developing countries too one-sidedly. Apart from financial difficulties and management problems, UNEP's structural challenges include a changed international environmental agenda and a changed organizational structure in international environmental affairs. These changed contexts have created a loss of clear focus at UNEP.[11]

As mandated, UNEP tries hard to inject environmental issues in policy making at all levels and with regard to all relevant fields, including international trade, development financing, and adjustment programs. However, UNEP is seriously handicapped by its very limited powers to impose regulation and environmental action on specialized agencies, regional institutions, and national governments other than through persuasion and providing funds. Moreover, UNEP has only some 400 staff members and a budget of only $285 million, more or less the same amount that the average medium-sized western city spends for the maintenance of its public parks. Under these restraints, at best, UNEP can serve as the world's environmental conscience but not as the planetary cleanup office.

The Commission on Sustainable Development

In the best tradition of major summits that create new institutions, the Commission on Sustainable Development was established as an offspring of the Rio Conference

TABLE 4.2. Mandate of the UN Commission on Sustainable Development

The mandate of the CSD includes: • Monitoring progress in the implementation of Agenda 21 and activities related to integrating environmental and developmental goals throughout the UN system • Considering information provided by governments regarding the activities they undertake to implement Agenda 21, the problems they face, and other relevant environment and development issues • Reviewing progress in the implementation of the commitments set forth in Agenda 21 • Reviewing and regularly monitoring progress toward the UN target of 0.7 per cent of the gross national product of developed countries for official development assistance • Reviewing the adequacy of funding and mechanisms • Receiving and analyzing relevant input from competent nongovernmental organizations and enhancing the dialogue within the UN framework with nongovernmental organizations and organizations in the independent sector as well as other entities outside the UN system • Considering information regarding the progress made in the implementation of environmental conventions • Providing appropriate recommendations to UN organs • Promoting the incorporation of the principles of the Rio Declaration and other nonbinding documents into the implementation of Agenda 21 • Monitoring progress in promoting, facilitating, and financing access to and transfer of environmentally sound technologies and corresponding know-how • Considering issues related to the provision of financial resources from all available funding sources and mechanisms

Source: "Institutional Arrangements to Follow Up the United Nations Conference on Environment and Development," General Assembly resolution A/RES/47/191, 22 December 1992.

on Environment and Development of 1992. The Rio summit, which endorsed the concept of sustainable development as presented by the Brundtland Commission in 1987, wanted the UN to create a special body to promote and monitor implementation of Agenda 21, the international action program for the twenty-first century.[12] Following endorsement of these recommendations by the General Assembly, the Commission on Sustainable Development was established as a functional commission of ECOSOC. It is composed of fifty-three members elected from among UN member states and members of the specialized agencies.[13]

The CSD is mandated to review reports from member states, coordinate sustainable development activities within the UN system, and enhance policy dialogue among member states and within the UN system. The CSD's brief also includes encouraging technical cooperation and capacity building at the international, regional, and national levels. An important task for the CSD became the strengthening of the participation of nongovernmental organizations and other societal groups such as indigenous peoples, cities, workers, businesses, women, and youth in environmental consultations. The CSD's location in New York is conducive to this role, and it has been suggested that this is one of the reasons why UNEP could not take on this new mission of pursuing sustainable development since its secretariat in Nairobi cannot easily interact with the secretariats of the principal UN organs or the staff of the missions of the member states in New York. In addition, the CSD took on some new areas of concern such as the problems of small island developing states.[14] This resulted in the Barbados Programme of Action (1994)[15] and the Mauritius Strategy for the Further Implementation of the Programme of Action for the Sustainable Development of Small Island Developing States (2005).[16] The CSD also addressed tourism and sustainable consumption patterns as new items on the UN agenda.

The CSD was also responsible for organizing the first major review of the Rio summit, the Rio+5 conference of 1997. At that time it was concluded that the environmental situation had actually deteriorated instead of improving since 1992. The CSD also prepared the World Summit on Sustainable Development, which was held in Johannesburg from 26 August to 4 September 2002. At the summit, it was decided that the commission should continue its role as a high-level forum within the UN for discussing sustainable development issues but that it needed to place more emphasis on implementation. In response, the commission organized its work on the basis a multiyear work program that consisted of seven two-year programs organized around thematic clusters of issues. For example, the issues for 2008–2009 are agriculture, rural development, land, drought, desertification, and Africa; those for 2010–2011 are transport, chemicals, waste management, mining, and sustainable consumption and production patterns. The CSD has been active in designing formats for reports and monitoring the progress of national states and international organizations. This CSD reporting process has been instrumental in generating data collection and coordination within states and international organizations.[17] However, like UNEP, the CSD lacks the power to make binding decisions, to mainstream sustainable development in all the policies of the UN system, or to finance major projects aimed at sustainable development. The perception quickly arose that the CSD could not provide the fresh impetus and serve as the driving force for sustainable development that was envisaged for it at the Rio summit in 1992.[18]

The Specialized Agencies

A number of UN specialized agencies have been involved, directly or indirectly, in the management of natural resources because they have been dealing in the course of their work with various environmental questions. These include the FAO, the International Fund for Agricultural Development (IFAD), the WMO, the World Bank and the IMO, and UNESCO.

Food and Agriculture Organization

The FAO was founded in 1945 (eight days before the United Nations itself) as a specialized agency of the United Nations with the goal of promoting common welfare by "raising levels of nutrition and standards of living of the peoples," "securing improvements in the efficiency of the production and distribution of all food and agricultural products," "bettering the condition of rural populations," and "contributing towards an expanding world economy and ensuring humanity's freedom from hunger."[19] For these purposes, the organization has been given the task of collecting, analyzing, interpreting, and disseminating information relating to nutrition, food, and agricultural production (the latter including fisheries, marine products, forestry, and primary forestry products). It has also been charged with the task of promoting and recommending national and international actions regarding "the conservation of natural resources."[20]

Throughout its history, action against hunger and malnutrition has been the center of the FAO's concerns. This was manifested, for example, in the creation in 1961 of the World Food Programme (which was jointly established by the FAO and the UN General Assembly), which has become the world's largest humanitarian organization mandated to combat global hunger.[21] In this context, the FAO is also involved in the management and utilization of natural living resources, particularly in the context of providing assistance to developing countries in modernizing and improving agriculture, forestry, and fishery practices as well as more generally in fields such as commodity trade, rural development, and food security. The FAO has carried out important work in establishing norms and standards, strategies, policies, and studies and in providing technical assistance to member countries.

The management of fishery resources was one of the early areas where the FAO had an effect on the development of international treaties and the creation of management institutions. In the immediate postwar years, a number of regional fishery commissions were established under the FAO's framework, such as the Asia-Pacific Fishery Commission (1948) and the General Fisheries Commission for the Mediterranean (1949). Others followed in subsequent years. Some were established directly under the FAO and others were established outside its framework but with the FAO functioning as a depositary.[22] In 1965, the FAO's Committee on Fisheries was created, which presently constitutes the only global intergovernmental forum where major international fishery and aquaculture problems and issues are discussed and (if necessary) global agreements and nonbinding instruments are negotiated. Meeting biannually, COFI reviews the FAO's programs of work in the field of fisheries and aquaculture and the implementation of these programs and conducts periodic general reviews of fishery and aquaculture problems.[23]

FAO's early postwar concerns focused primarily on the development of fishery resources, and in this context it focused on conservation measures. It was under the auspices of the FAO that the International Technical Conference on the Conservation of the Living Resources of the Sea was convened in 1955 to study the problem of the international conservation of marine living resources and to make appropriate scientific and technical recommendations to the UN International Law Commission, which was at that time involved in the codification of the law of the sea.[24] This resulted, among other things, in the incorporation of the concept of "maximum sustainable yield" in the 1958 Convention on Fishing and Conservation of Living Resources of the High Seas. After the adoption of UNCLOS in 1982, the FAO's activities focused on adapting fishery management policies to the new framework of that convention and on improving the capacity of states (particularly developing states) to develop fisheries within their exclusive economic zones. It was for that purpose, for example, that the FAO launched an EEZ program in 1982. Another important event was the World Conference on Fisheries Management and Development, which the FAO convened in 1984. While initially envisaged to consider the technical aspects of implementing the convention's provisions about fisheries, the conference eventually also discussed the far-reaching changes brought about by the extension of fisheries jurisdictions. It endorsed a Strategy for Fisheries Management and Development, which provided a set of principles and guidelines for managing and developing fisheries. The major focus of the strategy was the rational management and optimum use of fishery resources within the EEZs; very little attention was paid to environmental issues.[25]

In response to the rapid increase in global marine catches that occurred in the 1980s and the rising overexploitation of fish stocks, the FAO has increasingly focused on the sustainable use of fishery resources. A number of important new instruments were adopted with this goal in the post-Rio era under the auspices of COFI. In 1993, the Agreement to Promote Compliance with International Conservation and Management Measures by Fishing Vessels on the High Seas was adopted to create a detailed framework of responsibilities for fishing vessels on the high seas.[26] An important achievement was the adoption in 1995 of the voluntary Code of Conduct for Responsible Fisheries, which specified principles and standards for the conservation, management, and development of all fisheries and provided a global framework for national and international efforts to ensure sustainable exploitation of aquatic living resources.[27] In the following years, voluntary international plans of action were also adopted to reduce incidental catches of seabirds in longline fisheries, to conserve sharks, and to manage fishing capacity (all in 1999) and to prevent, deter, and eliminate illegal, unreported, and unregulated fishing (in 2001).

The FAO's activities have also led to the adoption of important instruments for protecting plants and plant resources. As early as 1951, the International Plant Protection Convention was adopted under FAO auspices; its purpose is to prevent the spread and introduction of pests that attack plants and plant products and to promote appropriate measures for controlling these products.[28] This was followed by the Plant Protection Agreement for the Asia and Pacific Region in 1955. More recently, the FAO has been involved in regulating the use of genetic plant resources. In 2001, the International Treaty on Plant Genetic Resources for Food and Agriculture was concluded under FAO auspices, which focuses on the conservation and sustainable use of plant genetic resources for food and agriculture and the fair and equitable sharing of the benefits arising out of their use for sustainable agriculture and food security.[29]

The FAO also provides direct technical support to countries to help them conserve and manage their forests. Every two years, the heads of national forest services meet under the auspices of FAO's Committee on Forestry to identify emerging policy and technical issues, seek solutions, and advise the FAO and others on appropriate action.[30] The FAO has established six regional forestry commissions that address the most important issues pertaining to forestry in their specific region. The FAO also regularly publishes statistics regarding types of forests, land mass devoted to forests, and forest products on a country basis.[31]

The FAO often works in partnership with other institutions of the UN system, including the UNDP, the World Bank, UNEP, the GEF, the WMO, and IFAD.

International Fund for Agricultural Development

As a follow-up to the 1974 World Food Conference, the International Fund for Agricultural Development was established as a specialized agency of the United Nations in 1977 for the purpose of financing agricultural development projects in developing countries, primarily for food production. IFAD is headquartered in Rome and seeks to helps 75 percent of the world's poorest people who live in rural areas and depend on agriculture and related activities for their livelihoods—small farmers, artisanal fishermen, poor rural women, landless workers, rural artisans, nomadic herdsmen, and indigenous populations—by empowering them to increase their food production, raise their incomes, and improve their health, nutrition, education standards, and general well-being on a sustainable basis. It also works in close cooperation with the other two Rome-based agencies—the FAO and the WFP—to address growing hunger, malnutrition, and poverty. As part of its current Strategic Framework (2007–2010), IFAD is focusing on the following issues: increasing and improving rural poor peoples' access to natural resources and the skills and organization they need to take advantage of those resources (especially secure access to land and water); improved agricultural technologies and effective production facilities; various financial services; transparent and competitive markets for agricultural inputs and produce; opportunities for rural off-farm employment and enterprise development; and local and national policy and programming processes.[32]

As an international financial institution, IFAD provides loans to the governments of developing countries for programs and projects that enable rural poor people to overcome poverty. It also provides grants to institutions and organizations to support activities that strengthen technical and institutional capacities linked to agricultural and rural development. Since the start of its operations in 1978, IFAD has invested US$10.6 billion in 796 projects and programs. During this same period, governments and other financing sources in recipient countries have contributed US$15.3 billion and multilateral, bilateral, and other donors have provided approximately US$9.5 billion in co-financing.[33] Apart from providing loans and grants, IFAD also functions as a global platform for discussing policy issues that influence the lives of rural poor people.

World Bank Group and the Global Environment Facility

The inception of the World Bank dates back to the 1944 conference in Bretton Woods, where the International Bank for Reconstruction and Development (IBRD) was established as one of the two principal pillars of the postwar economic order, alongside the International Monetary Fund.[34] Initially, the mission of the IBRD—which subsequently became a specialized agency of the United Nations—was to assist in the reconstruction and development of war-torn territories and to "promote the long-range balanced growth of international trade and the maintenance of equilibrium in balances of payments by encouraging international investment for the development of the productive resources of members."[35] With time, however, this mission evolved into the IBRD's present-day mandate of worldwide poverty alleviation through inclusive and sustainable globalization.[36]

Since its establishment in 1944, the IBRD has expanded from a single institution into an associated group of five development agencies. The IBRD now works in close coordination with its affiliate, the International Development Association (IDA); together they form what is commonly known as the World Bank. The IBRD focuses on middle-income and creditworthy poor countries, and the IDA focuses on the poorest countries in the world. They both provide low-interest loans, interest-free credits, and grants for a wide array of purposes, including for investment in education, health, public administration, infrastructure, financial- and private-sector development, agriculture, and environmental and natural resource management. The International Finance Corporation, the Multilateral Investment Guarantee Agency, and the International Centre for Settlement of Investment Disputes are the other three agencies of the World Bank Group.

Since it officially started its operations in 1947, the World Bank has financed a large number of projects, some of which have a direct bearing on natural resource management, such as various water management projects, pollution management projects, and land administration and management projects. Table 4.3 depicts the

TABLE 4.3. World Bank Projects Relating to Environment and Natural Resource Management, 1947–March 2009

Projects by Theme	***Number***
Biodiversity	468
Climate Change	495
Environmental Policies and Institutions	823
Land Administration and Management	472
Other Environment and Natural Resources Management	331
Pollution Management and Environmental Health	857
Water Resource Management	644
All projects under major theme "Environment and Natural Resources Management"	2,132[1]

1. All World Bank projects are classified in a variety of categories that are associated with the goals and priorities of the Bank. The total number of projects is 2,132 even though the number of individual projects adds up to 4,090 because individual projects are each listed in one or more categories.

Source: World Bank, "Projects & Operations," available at http://go.worldbank.org/0FRO32VEI0.

approximate number of World Bank projects that have been approved in the fields of environment and natural resource management from 1947 through March 2009. The table includes projects financed through investment and adjustment loans/credits, full-sized and medium-sized GEF projects, and projects relating to the 1987 Montreal Protocol. It also includes projects involving carbon offsets, the debt servicing facility, guarantees, the rainforest, and special financing projects. The total number of projects classified under the rubric "Environment and Natural Resources Management" is 2,132. However, the figures under each theme are partly inflated because the themes are not mutually exclusive; because of the Bank's methodology, a project may be classified under numerous themes.

The involvement of the World Bank in financing projects related to environmental and natural resources has increased since the establishment of the Global Environment Facility in October 1991. Initially conceived as a $1 billion pilot project of the World Bank to assist in the protection of the global environment and to promote sustainable development, the GEF was subsequently restructured into a permanent and separate institution outside the World Bank system. It is "a global partnership among 178 countries, international institutions, nongovernmental organizations, and the private sector."[37] The three main partners for implementing GEF projects are the UNDP, UNEP, and the World Bank. The World Bank also serves as the trustee of the GEF trust fund and provides administrative services for it. Other agencies now participate in GEF projects, including the FAO, IFAD, and UNIDO. In this respect, the GEF provides a rather striking example of cooperation between institutions for environmental projects.

The GEF provides new and additional grants and concessional funding to cover the incremental or additional costs associated with transforming a project with national benefits into one with global environmental benefits. It is also the designated financial mechanism for a number of multilateral environmental agreements, including the Convention on Biological Diversity, the United Nations Framework Convention on Climate Change, the Convention to Combat Desertification, and the Stockholm Convention on Persistent Organic Pollutants (1998). Moreover, it is associated with number of global and regional agreements that deal with international waters or transboundary water systems. The GEF helps fund initiatives that help developing countries meet the objectives of these conventions and agreements.

Since 1991, the GEF has provided $8.26 billion in grants and leveraged $33.7 billion in co-financing for over 2,200 projects in over 165 countries. Through its Small Grants Programme, it has also made more than 7,000 small grants directly to nongovernmental and community organizations.[38] Today it is the largest funder of projects related to biodiversity, climate change, international waters, land degradation, the ozone layer, and persistent organic pollutants. Projects related to biodiversity constitute the largest percentage of its portfolio. In particular, the GEF is the largest funding mechanism for protected areas worldwide, having provided more than $1.56 billion to fund protected areas and leveraged an additional $4.15 billion in co-financing from project partners.[39] Table 4.4 depicts the number and volume of GEF-funded projects from 1991 through March 2009. The size and types of projects vary, ranging from the GEF's Small Grants Programme to enabling activities, medi-

TABLE 4.4. GEF Projects, 1991–March 2009

Focal Area	*Number of Projects*	*GEF Grants (in US$ million)*	*Co-Financing (in US$ million)*
Biodiversity	872	2,529,459	6,558,585
Climate Change	669	2,497,963	15,313,416
International Waters	158	1,074,111	4,617,110
Ozone Depletion	27	183,472	187,632
Multiple Focal Areas	295	1,058,265	3,257,364
Land Degradation	59	360,081	2,237,394
Persistent Organic Pollutants	182	312,816	419,627
Total	2,262	8,016,167	32,591,128

Source: Compiled from "The GEF Project Database," available at http://gefonline.org/home.cfm.

um-sized projects, and full-sized projects, including the Project Preparation Grants that are used to prepare them.

As the UN system's most important source of financing, the World Bank has often been accused by critics of being more interested in development than the environment.[40] Over time, the World Bank has become more sensitive to environmental concerns, in part as a result of major failures in this area. Examples include the significant environmental harm and negative social effects resulting from the construction of huge hydroelectric dam projects in India and China that the World Bank co-financed. The Bank's increasing attention to the environmental impact of projects—no project is approved until it is cleared by the environmental department—is itself an important factor of progress, and has stimulated cooperation with UNEP and other UN organs. In addition, in response to rather strong international criticism, the Board of Executive Directors established the World Bank Inspection Panel in 1994.[41] As an independent investigatory body, the panel receives and reviews complaints from communities, organizations, or other groups residing in the borrowing country whose rights or interests have been adversely affected by the Bank's failure to comply with its own policies and procedures in designing, assessing, and implementing a project financed by the IBRD or the IDA. These complaints can also relate to the harmful impact of such projects on the environment and natural resources. The three-member panel may investigate complaints, and the process can result in a remedial action plan requiring management to take actions in response to bank failures. By 2009, the panel had received fifty-two requests, a large number of which concerned complaints about compliance with the World Bank's operational directive on proper environmental assessment.[42] Similarly, the International Finance Corporation and the Multilateral Investment Guarantee Agency have jointly established the Office of the Compliance Advisor/Ombudsman to respond to complaints about the environmental or social impact of their projects.[43]

United Nations Educational, Scientific and Cultural Organization

The United Nations Educational, Scientific and Cultural Organization was founded in 1945 as a specialized agency of the United Nations. Its goal is "to contribute to peace and security by promoting collaboration among the nations through education, science and culture in order to further universal respect for justice, for the rule of law and for the human rights and fundamental freedoms which are affirmed for the peoples of the world, without distinction of race, sex, language or religion, by the Charter of the United Nations."[44] UNESCO has often functioned as a laboratory for ideas and as a forum for discussing and setting standards on important ethical issues. It has also served as a clearinghouse for the dissemination and sharing of information and knowledge and helps member states build human and institutional capacities in diverse fields. In that respect, it has been useful in providing essential scientific information for policy makers, informing them on environmental and developmental issues and issues related to the management of natural resources.

Since its early days, UNESCO has initiated programs and activities that focus on diversity, natural resources, humans' impacts on biodiversity, and how biodiversity affects human activities. The Programme on Man and the Biosphere (MAB) has been of special importance in managing natural resources. Launched in 1971, the program promotes interdisciplinary research, training, and communications in the field of ecosystem conservation and the rational use of natural resources. Central to the MAB program is the establishment of "biosphere reserves"—that is, internationally recognized areas of terrestrial and coastal marine ecosystems. These biosphere reserves—currently there are 531 in 105 countries[45]—are designed to promote and demonstrate a balanced relationship between people and nature and to encourage innovative approaches to conservation and sustainable development. Thus, they are much more than merely protected areas. Biosphere reserves are nominated by states themselves and remain under the state's sovereign jurisdiction. Yet states share their experiences through the World Network of Biosphere Reserves, which promotes cooperative research, monitoring, and exchanges of information. The network provides an effective scientific support structure that features worldwide coverage of representative ecosystems and agreed objectives for carrying out research and monitoring.[46] When two biosphere reserves in two neighboring states are contiguous they often cooperate closely and coordinate their research and other activities.

A second aspect of UNESCO's involvement in natural resource management has been through the work of its International Oceanographic Commission (IOC). Since its establishment in 1960, the commission has worked to promote international cooperation and coordinate programs in research, services, and capacity-building in order to learn more about the nature and resources of the ocean and coastal areas and to apply that knowledge to sustainable development, protection of the marine environment, the improvement of management, and decisionmaking. In this function, the IOC has been working with UNEP in establishing a process for global reporting and assessment of the state of the marine environment, the "Assessment of Assessments."[47] Moreover, it has collaborated with the WMO and UNEP in monitoring the oceans through the Global Ocean Observing System, which works to monitor, understand, and predict weather and climate; report and forecast the state of the oceans (including their living resources); improve management of marine and coastal ecosystems and resources; and mitigate damage from pollution and natural hazards.[48] Finally, the IOC functions as the focal point for ocean matters in the UN system. It hosts the implementing secretariat of UN-Oceans (formerly the Oceans and Coastal Areas Network), a mechanism that is responsible for effective, transparent, and regular interagency coordination on ocean and coastal issues within the United Nations system.[49]

The IOC's work has also had important implications for the management of marine resources, which will likely continue in the future. As part of its current midterm objectives, the IOC will work on preventing and reducing the impacts of natural hazards, mitigating the impacts of climate change and adapting to variability, safeguarding the health of ocean ecosystems, and formulating management procedures and policies that will lead to the sustainability of the coastal and ocean environment and resources.[50]

A third area of UNESCO's involvement in natural resource management has been its work in the field of freshwater resources through its International Hydrological Programme, which was established as a scientific cooperative program in water research, water resource management, education, and capacity-building. Its primary objectives are improving knowledge of the water cycle and thereby increasing the capacity of states to better manage and develop their water resources, improving local and global water management, and assessing the sustainable development of vulnerable water resources.[51] UNESCO also houses the World Water Assessment Programme, founded in 2000 under the UN-Water mechanism.[52] The program monitors freshwater issues so it can provide recommendations, develop case studies, enhance assessment capacity at a national level, and inform the decision-making process. It periodically provides comprehensive reviews of the state of the world's freshwater resources.[53]

World Meteorological Organization

Established in 1950, the World Meteorological Organization is a specialized agency of the United Nations for meteorology, operational hydrology, and related geophysical sciences. One of its primary purposes is to organize and support international research and cooperation between national meteorological and hydrological services, particularly by facilitating the establishment of networks for making observations about weather, climate, water, and the environment. It also promotes the exchange, processing, and standardization of related data and assists in technology transfer, training, and research.[54] The WMO has acted as facilitator and catalyst in improving our understanding of the state and behavior of the earth's atmosphere, how the atmosphere interacts with the oceans, the climate the atmosphere produces in interaction with the oceans, and the resulting distribution of water resources. Through facilitating the exchange of data and information, it has thus contributed to policy formation at national and international levels, including with regard to the management of natural resources.

Since its establishment, the WMO has been supporting national hydrological services, river basin authorities, and other institutions responsible for water management in a wide range of activities. Presently, the WMO maintains the Hydrology and Water Resources Programme, which is concerned with assessing the quantity and quality of water resources, both surface and groundwater, in order to meet the needs of society; mitigation of water-related hazards; and maintaining or enhancing the condition of the global environment.

The WMO has also been instrumental in bringing the problem of the ozone layer to international attention and generating awareness of the need for more meteorological research and research about the ozone layer in light of pollution of the atmosphere and climate change. This started as early as 1957, when the WMO declared an International Geophysical Year (1957–1958) and established under its auspices the Global Ozone Observing System.[55] Subsequently, the WMO became increasingly involved in ozone layer research and in 1976 conducted the first international assessment of the state of the global ozone. The findings of this assessment helped generate momentum for international action, which eventually resulted in the creation of the Vienna-Montreal ozone layer regime. The WMO now coordinates the global ozone observing network and since 1985 has been providing scientific assessments of ozone depletion in collaboration with UNEP.

The WMO has also been prominent in the study of global climate change. The information national meteorological and hydrological services have gathered, managed, and analyzed under the aegis of the WMO has contributed significantly to monitoring and detecting climate change, attributing causes, and projecting the magnitude and rate of human-induced climate change, regional variations, and increases in sea levels. One of the most important milestones in this respect was the establishment with UNEP of the Intergovernmental Panel on Climate Change in 1988. The cooperation between the WMO and the IPCC is close: not only does the WMO host the panel's headquarters but it has also been the principal provider of the scientific and technical information that underpins IPCC assessments, particularly through its World Climate Programme.[56] Moreover, observation programs, such as the Global Climate Observing System and the Global Ocean Observing System (which the WMO maintains in cooperation with UNEP and other agencies), have played a major role in improving the collection of data needed to develop climate forecasts and detect climate change.[57]

The WMO also participates in the work of subsidiary bodies on scientific and technical advice under a number of multilateral environmental agreements, including the International Convention to Combat Desertification (1994), the ECE Convention on Long-Range Transboundary Air Pollution (1979), the Convention on Biological Diversity (1992), and the Convention for the Protection of Marine Environment and the Coastal Region of the Mediterranean (1976/1995). By providing data collected from its networks of ground- and space-based systems, scientific knowledge, and computing technology, the WMO has played an important role in the formulation of policy decisions and has significantly contributed to international environmental governance.

International Maritime Organization

The International Maritime Organization (IMO) is a specialized agency of the United Nations devoted exclusively to maritime matters. Established in 1948 as the Inter-Governmental Maritime Consultative Organization (its name changed to the current one in 1982), the IMO was intended to provide the machinery for cooperation in technical matters affecting international shipping and to promote the "adoption of the highest practicable standards in matters concerning maritime safety and efficiency in navigation."[58] It became operational in 1959; its main concern was initially how to improve safety at sea. In 1960, the IMO convened a conference that led to the adoption of the International Convention on Safety of Life at Sea, which represented a major advance in updating commercial shipping regulations. However, the organization soon took up the broader task of developing and maintaining a comprehensive regulatory framework for shipping in general. In addition to maritime safety, the organization has been dealing with a broad range of issues, including technical cooperation, maritime security, legal matters, efficiency of shipping, and environmental concerns.[59]

Since its establishment, the IMO has promoted the adoption of many conventions and protocols as well as numerous codes and recommendations to protect the marine environment from human activities, particularly pollution. Soon after it came into existence, the IMO took responsibility for administering and promoting the 1954 International Convention for Prevention of Pollution by Oil—one of the first major conventions designed to curb the impact of oil pollution on the marine environment. In the following years, the IMO produced a number of new and updated instruments to deal with this problem, often in response to major accidents. A series of conventions was, for example, adopted in the wake of the Torrey Canyon accident of 1967, when a supertanker ran aground on rocks off the western coast of Cornwall, spilling its entire cargo of 120,000 tons of crude oil in the sea and causing an environmental disaster of unprecedented scale. The IMO responded with the 1969 International Convention Relating to Intervention on the High Seas in Cases of Oil Pollution Casualties (which granted coastal states the right to take such measures as may be necessary to prevent, mitigate, or eliminate a grave and imminent danger to its coastline in cases of incidents on the high seas that could potentially result in oil pollution), the 1969 International Convention on Civil Liability for Oil Pollution Damage (which established the liability of the owner of the ship or cargo for damage arising from an oil pollution incident), and the 1971 Convention on the Establishment of an International Fund for Compensation for Oil Pollution Damage (which provided the victims of pollution damage with additional compensation).

These conventions—many of which were then further refined by amendments and protocols in subsequent years—are a typical example of how disasters prompt the adoption of new law.[60]

However, the focus of IMO's work was certainly not limited to the legal aspects of oil pollution. In the early 1970s, the organization also began to deal with the problem of marine pollution generally. The major result of such activities was the adoption of the International Convention for the Prevention of Pollution from Ships in 1973. As modified by the Protocol of 1978 (known by the acronym MARPOL 73/78), the convention now constitutes the most important and most comprehensive instrument that regulates and prevents marine pollution by ships, as it governs not only accidental and operational oil pollution but also pollution by chemicals, goods in packaged form, sewage, garbage, and air pollution. The regulations dealing with each of these pollutants are laid down in complex and detailed annexes to the convention, which have been revised and amended many times throughout the years. Gradually, new annexes were also added to the convention, further expanding its legal framework.[61] In general, MARPOL 73/78 has been hailed as very effective in combating marine pollution as it led to substantial decreases in the amount of oil and other pollutants entering the sea. Yet noncompliance with its provisions remains a problem due to limitations in enforcement measures.[62]

Another important achievement in this period was the adoption of the Convention on the Prevention of Marine Pollution by Dumping of Wastes and Other Matter in 1972, for which the IMO provides secretariat support. The convention eliminated the dumping of certain hazardous materials (in particular industrial and radioactive wastes) and identified a number of wastes for which a special dumping permit was required. Through various amendments, the convention also gradually banned the incineration of wastes and other matter at sea. In 1996, a new protocol was adopted that will gradually replace the convention. The protocol now prohibits all dumping at sea with the exception of waste on an approved list that includes dredged material; sewage sludge; fish waste; vessels, platforms, or other manmade structures at sea; geological material; organic material of natural origin; bulky items primarily comprising iron, steel and concrete; and carbon dioxide streams.[63]

In the 1990s and early 2000s, the IMO adopted a number of new conventions and additional protocols in response to a broader range of environmental concerns, such as air and ballast water pollution. These include the 1990 International Convention on Oil Pollution Preparedness, Response and Co-operation (which provides a global framework for international cooperation in combating major incidents or threats of marine pollution, such as tanker incidents), the 1996 International Convention on Liability and Compensation for Damage in Connection with the Carriage of Hazardous and Noxious Substances by Sea (which provides for a system of compensation for damage arising from pollution and from fires and explosions), the

2001 International Convention on Civil Liability for Bunker Oil Pollution Damage (which provides a system of compensation for damage caused by oil spills), the 2001 International Convention on the Control of Harmful Antifouling Systems on Ships (which bans the use of certain harmful compounds in anti-fouling paints on ships), and the 2004 International Convention for the Control and Management of Ships' Ballast Water and Sediments (which seeks to prevent, minimize, and ultimately eliminate the transfer of harmful aquatic organisms and pathogens that are found in ships' ballast water and sediments).[64]

In addition to these conventions, the IMO has also prepared numerous codes, recommendations, and guidelines on important environmental matters not considered suitable for regulation by formal treaty instruments. Responsibility for the preparation of these regulations has been in the hands of the Maritime Safety Committee, the Legal Committee, and the Marine Environment Protection Committee (the IMO's senior technical body responsible for coordinating the organization's activities in the prevention and control of pollution of the marine environment).[65] Apart from developing and adopting new regulations, however, these bodies also play a significant role in updating existing legislation. It has been a particular feature of IMO conventions that the principal rules and standards are not found in their main text but in their annexes, which can be easily amended and if necessary supplemented by a decision of the Maritime Safety Committee or the Marine Environment Protection Committee. This has made it possible for the IMO to quickly adapt to the requirements of the industry and to respond to changes in technology and environmental concerns. At the same time, the organization has often been criticized for focusing only on rule-making while devoting too little attention to the actual implementation of and compliance with these instruments.[66] Nonetheless, the IMO has played and continues to play a particularly important role in its own specific area of global environmental governance, often with the assistance and in close cooperation with other UN bodies and specialized agencies.

Other Specialized Agencies

While it is mostly the FAO, IFAD, the WMO, the World Bank, UNESCO, and the IMO that exercise some measure of competence over environmental matters, the work of a few other specialized agencies should briefly be mentioned here, either because they contribute an important element to the patchwork of global environmental governance or because they respond to specific problems that have their origin in the degradation of the global environment.

One of them is the International Atomic Energy Agency (IAEA). Established in 1957 in response to fears and expectations about the discovery of nuclear energy, the IAEA is strictly speaking not a specialized agency but an independent intergovernmental organization brought under the aegis of the UN by special agreement.[67]

Its objective is to "accelerate and enlarge the contribution of atomic energy to peace, health and prosperity throughout the world" and to prevent the proliferation of nuclear weapons.[68] The activities of the IAEA can generally be grouped into three categories: verification, safety, and technology. It is probably through its verification activities that the IAEA has attracted most attention in world public opinion, especially when it comes to contentious issues such as the Iraqi, Iranian, and North Korean nuclear programs. Yet it is perhaps somehow forgotten that the IAEA also plays a particular role in global environmental governance. This is because of its important role in the development and maintenance of a global nuclear safety regime. The IAEA's role in this field includes not only fostering the exchange of scientific and technical information and the training of scientists and experts but also establishing nuclear safety standards that are then used as a basis for national standards and rules. The aim of these standards is to provide for protection of people and the environment from the effects of ionizing radiation, minimize the likelihood of accidents that could endanger life and the environment, and effectively mitigate the effects of any such events in case they happen. This includes standards for the safety of nuclear installations and radioactive sources, the safe transport of radioactive material, and the management of radioactive waste. The IAEA has also provided a forum for the negotiation of conventions on nuclear safety, radioactive waste, liability for nuclear accidents, and emergency notification and cooperation.[69]

Second, one could also mention the work of the United Nations Industrial Development Organization, which was established in 1966 and became a specialized agency of the UN in 1985.[70] Its primary objective has been the promotion and acceleration of industrial development in developing countries and of global industrial cooperation generally. In the context of this mandate, the organization has focused in recent years specifically on poverty reduction, inclusive globalization, and environmental sustainability.[71] UNIDO does not provide its activities on a stand-alone basis but integrates them into comprehensive and integrated packages of services that combine the organization's normative functions with its operational activities. Its normative functions include mostly producing and disseminating knowledge relating to industrial development. As the central international body responsible for collecting international industrial statistics, UNIDO can serve as an important source of industrial policy advice. UNIDO's operational activities, on the other hand, mostly involve technical cooperation projects with developing countries and countries with economies in transition. Such projects have focused on three thematic priority areas: poverty reduction through productive activities, building capacity for trade, and energy and the environment. In the field of energy, UNIDO is an important provider of services for improved industrial energy efficiency and the promotion of renewable sources of energy. In the area of the environment, UNIDO promotes sustainable patterns of industrial consumption and production as well as water management projects. Moreover, it helps developing countries meet their commitments under multilateral environmental agreements. For example, UNIDO is one of the implementing agencies of the Montreal Protocol. In all these activities, UNIDO closely cooperates with the UNDP and UNEP. With the latter, for example, it has established several national cleaner production centers and programs.[72] Moreover, UNIDO often partners with other UN agencies, including the FAO, IFAD, UNESCO, and the World Bank.

Finally, one should briefly mention the work of the World Health Organization (WHO). Established as a specialized agency of the UN in 1948, the WHO serves as the directing and coordinating authority on international health issues within the UN system. Through the production of health guidelines and standards, assistance to countries in addressing public health issues, and support and promotion of health research, the WHO works toward its main objective: "the attainment by all peoples of the highest possible level of health."[73] Natural resource management, of course, does not feature among the WHO's competences and activities. Yet, environment-related issues started to feature among its programs as the organization began to respond, within its own field of competencies, to the negative consequences of pollution, resource degradation, or climate change. Its work on air pollution is an important example of such programs. Today, the WHO's Air Quality Guidelines represent the most widely agreed and up-to-date assessment of health effects of air pollution. They include recommended targets for air quality to diminish health risks.[74] Moreover, many WHO regional offices have increasingly begun to address specific environment-related health issues. The most active in this field is perhaps the WHO's Regional Office for Europe, which has action plans aimed at preventing and reducing respiratory disease caused by polluted air and at reducing ill health from water-related diseases resulting from bad sanitation. WHO/Europe also works to identify policy options to help prevent, prepare for, and respond to the health effects of climate change, stratospheric ozone depletion, and natural resource degradation, and it supports its member states in selecting and implementing the most suitable strategies for responding to these problems. Similarly, the WHO's Regional Office for the Western Pacific has established a working group to address climate change and health issues in the region, including heat stress and water- and food-borne diseases associated with extreme weather events and respiratory diseases due to air pollution.[75] The regional office for Africa, in turn, has concentrated on various programs that aim at supporting the countries in the region in their efforts to identify, control, and prevent environmental conditions that have adverse effects on human health. This includes a program to support countries in providing access to safe water and adequate sanitation.[76]

ECOSOC and Coordination

ECOSOC plays a specific role with regard to natural resource management issues. As provided for in Article 63 of the UN Charter, ECOSOC coordinates the activities of the seventeen UN specialized agencies, numerous functional commissions, and five regional commissions. It performs this work by consulting with and making recommendations to such agencies and by making recommendations to the General Assembly and to UN members.[77] It also receives regular reports from the specialized agencies and from eleven UN funds and programs.

However, ECOSOC has functioned rather minimally and has not been very successful in practice. Because western nations were initially overrepresented, ECOSOC quickly acquired a colonialist image, which led newly independent states to prefer the General Assembly for the discussion of economic questions.[78] Moreover, the powers of ECOSOC to coordinate activities were shown to be inefficient, thereby allowing other UN organs and specialized agencies to more or less ignore its discussions and recommendations. Yet the need for coordination, particularly in the field of environmental activities, became a concern. Upon the initiative of former Secretary-General Kurt Waldheim (1972–1981), the System-Wide Medium-Term Environment Programme was put in place in 1985 in order to integrate environmental concerns into the work of all UN organs and specialized agencies. This was very much an endeavor of UNEP's former executive director, Mostafa K. Tolba (1975–1992). The program proved to be an effective instrument for coordinating planning and programming activities, but it was discontinued in 1999. This led to an exacerbation of the duplication and overlapping of programs and resources in the following years.

In response to the fragmentation of environmental activities within the UN system, a number of initiatives have been recently put in motion. Following the 2005 World Summit, Secretary-General Kofi Annan established a High-level Panel on United Nations System-wide Coherence in the areas of development, humanitarian assistance, and the environment. In 2006, the panel presented a report with a series of recommendations for overcoming the fragmentation of the United Nations so that the system could "deliver as one."[79] Subsequently, the UN Joint Inspection Unit was commissioned to prepare an independent assessment of international environmental governance within the United Nations system and related reform. In a 2008 report, the Joint Inspection Unit concluded that the current framework of international environmental governance is weakened by institutional fragmentation and specialization and the absence of a holistic approach to environmental issues and sustainable development. It attributed these problems to the lack of a clear distinction among the work programs of UN system organizations regarding environmental protection and sustainable development and to the absence of a single strategic planning framework.[80]

Other Institutions within the UN System

Apart from UNEP, the CSD, and the specialized agencies, many other institutions in the United Nations system participate in natural resource management issues. Either as functional commissions, subsidiary organs of principal UN organs, or as treaty-based organs, these institutions perform important functions by providing forums for consultation and policy making, providing information and technical expertise, coordinating the activities of other institutions, and elaborating rules and principles of natural resource management.

UNCTAD

In 1964, the United Nations Conference on Trade and Development was established as an organ of the General Assembly. Its principal function is to promote international trade, especially trade between developing countries and between countries at different stages of development and with different systems of economic and social organization. For that purpose, it formulates principles and policies, makes practical proposals, and coordinates the activities of UN institutions in the field of international trade and trade development.[81] UNCTAD has functioned as a forum for intergovernmental deliberations and has undertaken research, policy analysis, and data collection for those debates and provided technical assistance tailored to the specific requirements of developing (especially the least developed) countries. UNCTAD quickly evolved into an autonomous body within the UN system and was used, especially in its early years, as a vehicle for promoting the idea of a New International Economic Order. It currently focuses on a wide range of activities that range from trade and commodities to investment and enterprise development; macroeconomic policies, debt, and development financing; technology; and logistics. This work focuses particularly on Africa, the least developed countries, landlocked developing countries, and small island developing states.[82]

These activities are relevant to natural resource management in a number of ways. UNCTAD has played an important role in the field of commodity diversification and development. Through its Commodities Branch, UNCTAD helps commodity-dependent developing countries respond to the challenges of commodity markets, in particular by supporting and promoting the efforts of these countries to restructure, diversify, and strengthen the competitiveness of their commodity sectors. It also helps governments formulate and implement diversification policies and encourages enterprises to adapt their business strategies to changes in commodity markets. The Commodities Branch has also played a role in contributing to the economically and ecologically sustainable management of natural resources, particularly in developing countries, by providing support in the formulation of economic policies and legislation in the mineral sector, offering advice and training in regional planning and participatory development in areas that depend on the exploitation of natural resources, and developing frameworks for regional planning. UNCTAD's role has also been visible in the field of trade and environment. Through its Trade and Sustainable Development Section, UNCTAD has assessed the trade and development impact of environmental requirements and relevant multilateral agreements and has offered capacity-building activities to developing countries.[83]

United Nations Development Programme

The UNDP was established in 1965, when the General Assembly decided to combine the Expanded Programme of Technical Assistance and the Special Fund into one program. The purpose was to provide a more solid basis for the future growth and evolution of the development assistance programs of the UN system.[84] Since its inception, the focus of the UNDP has been to assist developing countries in properly managing the human and natural resources required for their economic growth and human development, in particular by helping them to attract and effectively use development aid, training personnel, and modern technologies. Over the years, the UNDP has grown into the main body responsible for coordinating UN development work and has evolved into the largest provider of development grant assistance within the UN system, with an on-the-ground presence in as many as 166 countries. In view of this fact, UNDP now also coordinates global and national efforts to reach the Millennium Development Goals and helps countries build the institutional capacity, policies, and programs needed to achieve these goals.

From the beginning of its operations, the UNDP promoted initiatives that had a bearing on environmental conservation and natural resource management, for example through various projects that aimed at restoring soil fertility and water quality. In 1990, the environment and natural resource management was also selected as one of the six areas of focus in UNDP's programming cycle. Yet, it was the Rio Summit of 1992 that considerably strengthened the position of this UN organ in global environmental governance, as Agenda 21 emphasized specifically the crucial role of the UNDP in the implementation of international policy on sustainable development and earmarked it as the lead agency in organizing UN system efforts to build capacity at the local, national, and regional levels.[85] A particularly important part of these efforts has been the integration of an environmental component into all of the UNDP's operational activities.

In the current multiyear funding framework (2008–2011), "Environment and Energy" continue to figure among the five themes that are the focus of the UNDP's work. Six priority areas have been selected as particularly important:

- Frameworks and strategies for sustainable development, including capacity-building for the management of the environment and natural resources;

- Effective water governance, including the promotion of sustainable use of marine, coastal, and freshwater resources and of cooperation in transboundary waters management;
- Access to sustainable energy services, including the support for energy activities to reduce poverty and achieve sustainable development objectives;
- Sustainable land management to combat desertification and land degradation;
- Conservation and sustainable use of biodiversity, including the support of sustainable management of agriculture, fisheries, forests, and energy;
- National and sectoral policy and planning to control emissions of ozone-depleting substances and persistent organic pollutants, in particular through the Montreal Protocol and GEF programs of the UNDP[86]

In pursuing its objectives, the UNDP cooperates closely with the other organs and agencies of the UN system. Together with UNEP, it established a joint Poverty-Environment Initiative, which seeks to integrate environmental issues into poverty reduction strategies, and a Partnership Initiative for the Integration of Sound Management of Chemicals into Development Planning Processes.[87] Alongside with UNEP and the World Bank, the UNDP is also one of the main implementing agencies of the Global Environment Facility and the Multilateral Fund under the Montreal Protocol on Substances that Deplete the Ozone Layer. The UNDP is thus an important stone in the edifice of global environmental governance. Although it is always in some competition with the much larger World Bank, increasingly it works closely with that body now that the missions of the two bodies have become quite similar.[88]

The International Law Commission

The International Law Commission deserves special attention in the discussion of natural resource management because it has played a distinctive role in codifying, elaborating, and developing rules and principles for managing natural resources, including the living resources of the seas, international watercourses, and shared resources. The General Assembly established the ILC on 21 November 1947 as one of its subsidiary organs.[89] Its function is "the promotion of the progressive development of international law and its codification."[90] Progressive development in this context refers to "the preparation of draft conventions on subjects which have not yet been regulated by international law or in regard to which the law has not yet been sufficiently developed in the practice of States," while codification refers to "the more precise formulation and systematization of rules of international law in fields where there already has been extensive State practice, precedent and doctrine."[91] The ILC's work has often involved both of these functions; the balance between the two varies depending on the particular topic.

One of the earliest topics that the commission considered was the codification and development of the law of the sea. In the course of its work, the commission, and in particular its special rapporteur, J. P. A. François, who was preparing draft articles on the topic, touched upon natural resource management issues in many ways that included the limit of the territorial sea, the extent of fishing rights of coastal states, the extent of a state's rights on the continental shelf, and the conservation of marine resources on the high seas. With regard to the latter, it is interesting to note that as early as 1953 Special Rapporteur François felt that existing international law did not do enough to protect marine fauna from extinction and even went so far as to propose the establishment of an international organization that would be mandated to adopt conservation measures on the high seas.[92] These recommendations were not accepted by the General Assembly, and governments that favored the regulation of fisheries and the conservation of marine resources continued to be governed on the basis of international agreements between interested states. Nevertheless, the ILC drafts included many of the progressive provisions that were incorporated into the Convention on Fishing and Conservation of Living Resources of the High Seas in 1958.

In 1979, the General Assembly asked the ILC to study the regulation of the non-navigational uses of international watercourses. Under the guidance of a number of special rapporteurs, including Richard D. Kearney, Stephen Schwebel, Jens Evensen, Stephen C. McCaffrey, and Robert Rosenstock, the commission succeeded in preparing a draft convention on the topic by 1995. The work of the commission resulted in the adoption in 1997 of the Convention on the Law of the Non-Navigational Uses of International Watercourses, which applies to "the utilization, development, conservation, management and protection of international watercourses" and seeks "the promotion of the optimal and sustainable utilization thereof for present and future generations."[93] The convention specifies the obligations of parties, which include equitable and reasonable use of watercourses, prevention of harm to other watercourse states, cooperation on the basis of sovereign equality, and exchange of data and information about the conditions of the watercourse.[94] The convention also sets out a notification procedure for planned measures that could have adverse effects on other watercourse states and includes important provisions on the protection and preservation of ecosystems; the prevention, reduction, and control of pollution; the introduction of alien or new species; and the protection and preservation of the marine environment.[95]

Following the work on international watercourses, the commission decided in 2002 to include in its program of work the issue of "shared natural resources." Under the guidance of Special Rapporteur Chusei Yamada of Japan, the commission has since then begun to prepare a set of rules on the use of transboundary aquifers and shared deposits of oil and natural gas. The task of the commission on this topic has been far from easy, as its ambition is to universally regulate a subject matter that is highly technical and politically sensitive and encompasses diverse regional situations.

In view of these problems, the commission considered that it was more practical to split the topic and deal with aquifers separately from oil and gas. The decision bore fruit in 2008 when the ILC adopted the Draft Articles on the Law of Transboundary Aquifers, which provide a set of principles and rules that are to guide states in the use of transboundary aquifers or aquifer systems. The draft articles lay particular emphasis on the principle of equitable and reasonable utilization and list a number of factors that are to be taken into account by states in their efforts to achieve such utilization. These factors include the interests of the population dependent on the aquifer as well as the social and economic needs of the aquifer states. The draft clarifies a number of obligations that states have with regard to shared aquifers, such as the obligation not to cause significant harm, the general obligation to cooperate, and obligations regarding the regular exchange of data and information. Moreover, it proposes a number of measures for the protection and preservation of ecosystems that are within or are dependent upon transboundary aquifers; for the prevention, reduction, and control of pollution; and for the proper management of transboundary aquifers or aquifer systems, including through the establishment of joint management mechanisms.[96] The draft articles thus constitute an important step in the management of shared underground water resources. It would be desirable if a similar set of principles and rules could be developed for shared oil and gas deposits. In view of the political sensitivity of the topic, however, it remains uncertain whether the commission will ever proceed with this aspect of the topic as well.

In addition to codification and the progressive development of principles and rules for managing specific natural resources, the ILC's work on more general topics has also had a bearing on natural resource management. Examples include the articles on the Prevention of Transboundary Harm for Hazardous Activities (2001) and the Draft Principles on Allocation of Loss in the Case of Transboundary Harm Arising out of Hazardous Activities (2006), which refine international law on the protection and preservation of the environment in important ways. The former regulate activities that have the potential to cause significant transboundary harm even though they are not prohibited by transnational law, while the latter deal with transboundary damages (including damages to the environment) that result from such activities.[97]

UN Committee on Natural Resources

In 1970, convinced that the activities of the United Nations with regard to the development of natural resources should be "widened, accelerated and given more adequate intergovernmental leadership and guidance," ECOSOC established a standing Committee on Natural Resources to provide assistance to the council in planning, implementing, and coordinating activities to develop natural resources (particularly water, energy, and mineral resources) and to provide advisory services for planning, developing, and using the natural resources of UN member states within the framework of their overall development plans.[98] Primarily composed of experts in the field of natural resources, the committee discussed trends in investment legislation and in legal and economic arrangements between mineral-producing developing countries and transnational corporations, often reviewing the role that the latter had been playing in the mining sector. A central topic of these discussions was how to strengthen the capabilities of developing countries to make optimum economic use of their natural resources. The committee also focused on how to promote investments in line with the basic priorities of developing countries. Later, it also worked on new techniques for natural resource exploitation and assessment.[99]

In 1992, the committee was restructured and its mandate was restricted to minerals and water resources only, while a newly established Committee on New and Renewable Sources of Energy and on Energy for Development assumed the mandate of the previous committee with respect to energy.[100] In the new form, the Committee on Natural Resources focused its attention on how the integrated management of water, land, and minerals related to sustainable development, providing input to the work of the newly established Commission on Sustainable Development. In 1998, ECOSOC decided to merge both committees into a single expert body, the Committee on Energy and Natural Resources for Development. This was comprised of two subgroups, one dealing with issues relating to energy and the other with issues relating to water resources.[101] In 2002, however, ECOSOC decided to terminate the work of the Committee on Energy and Natural Resources for Development and transfer its work to the Commission on Sustainable Development.[102]

United Nations Forum on Forests

In the wake of the 1992 Rio Summit, two new institutional processes were established under the auspices of the Commission on Sustainable Development to provide a forum on international policy making related to forests—the Intergovernmental Panel on Forests and the Intergovernmental Forum on Forests—which together examined a wide range of forest-related topics and produced more than 270 proposals for action toward sustainable forest management.[103] In order to carry on the work of these two new institutions, the United Nations Forum on Forests (UNFF) was established in 2000 as a functional commission of ECOSOC. Its main objective is to promote "the management, conservation and sustainable development of all types of forests and to strengthen long-term political commitment to this end."[104] The forum is composed of all UN member states and specialized agencies, and its principal functions are to facilitate implementation of forest-related agreements; to foster a common understanding of sustainable forest management; to provide for continued policy development and dialogue; to address forest issues and emerging areas of concern in a holistic, comprehensive, and integrated manner; and to enhance cooperation and policy and program coordination on forest-related issues. In order to support the work of the UNFF and to foster increased cooperation and coordination on forests, the Collaborative Partnership on Forests (CPF) was established in April 2001 as a partnership of fourteen major forest-related international organizations, institutions, and convention secretariats with substantial programs on forests. These include the FAO, the International Tropical Timber Organization, the UNDP, and UNEP.[105]

In 2006, the UNFF managed to agree on four shared global objectives regarding forests that provide clear guidance for future work toward an international arrangement on forests.[106] Part of this work has already materialized in the landmark Non-Legally Binding Instrument on All Types of Forests, which the forum adopted after nearly three years of intense negotiations on 28 April 2007. The instrument, which was subsequently endorsed by the General Assembly on 17 December 2007 in resolution 62/98, is the first international instrument for sustainable forest management. Its purposes are to strengthen political commitment and action at all levels in order to implement the sustainable management of all types of forests, to achieve shared global objectives on forests, to enhance the contribution of forests to the achievement of internationally agreed development goals, and to provide a framework for national action and international cooperation.[107]

The work of the Intergovernmental Panel on Forests, the Intergovernmental Forum on Forests, and the United Nations Forum on Forests have thus made possible significant progress in developing coherent policies to promote the management, conservation, and sustainable development of all types of forests.

Law of the Sea Institutions within the United Nations

In addition to fisheries organizations and the International Whaling Commission discussed in chapter 3, several bodies exist in the context of the United Nations that have tasks relating to the management of marine resources: the International Seabed Authority, the International Tribunal for the Law of the Sea, and the Commission on the Limits of the Continental Shelf.

International Seabed Authority

The International Seabed Authority came into existence in 1994 following the entry into force of United Nations Convention on the Law of the Sea. Situated in Kingston, Jamaica, the ISA is an autonomous international organization that is closely related to the UN. Composed of all states parties to UNCLOS, the ISA is mandated to organize and control all resource-related activities on the deep ocean floor in areas beyond national jurisdiction. It is guided by the principal goals of the international seabed regime, which is to simultaneously encourage the development of seabed resources and safeguard the marine environment and to ensure the equitable sharing of economic benefits from those resources.[108]

In many respects, the ISA would resemble any other international organization were it not for a unique feature in its institutional design that distinguishes it from other institutions that are involved in natural resource management—namely, the Enterprise. As one of ISA's principal organs, the Enterprise is empowered to directly carry out mining activities in the deep seabed and to transport, process, and market minerals recovered from the deep seabed area. At present, the Enterprise is not yet operational and its functions are being temporarily carried out by ISA's secretariat until seabed mining becomes feasible on a commercial scale. Once functional, the Enterprise will be the commercial arm of the ISA—something akin to an international mining corporation—although it will initially operate only through joint ventures with mining companies or states belonging to the authority.[109]

The ISA plays a key role in managing the natural resources of the deep seabed; UNCLOS mandates that exploration and mining in the deep seabed can be carried out only under a contract issued by the authority. The ISA also devises and adopts regulations on prospecting and exploration, setting out the duties and obligations of the ISA and of contractors relative to their mining and other seabed activities. In 2000, the first set of regulations was adopted for polymetallic nodules, and since 2002 the council of the authority has been working on another set of regulations for polymetallic sulfides and cobalt-rich crusts. Once mining becomes profitable, the authority will collect royalties from contractors and distribute them equitably among states, particularly taking into account the needs of developing countries. The ISA has also extensive responsibilities regarding the protection of the marine environment. Not only is it obliged to establish environmental rules, regulations, and procedures to protect and preserve the marine environment, but in the event of serious harm to the marine environment, the ISA's secretary-general also has the power to take immediate temporary measures to prevent, contain, and minimize the harm. As such it is an interesting example of how global public responsibility has been vested in an international office.

International Tribunal for the Law of the Sea

UNCLOS also established the International Tribunal for the Law of the Sea (ITLOS) as one of the four mechanisms for binding third-party dispute settlement established under Part XV of the convention.[110] Similarly to the ISA, ITLOS is an independent organ—albeit one with direct links with the UN system[111]—intended to adjudicate disputes concerning the interpretation or application of the convention and, in specific cases, international agreements other than UNCLOS. Seated in Hamburg, the tribunal is open to states parties to the convention and in specific circumstances to other states and international organizations. In cases involving deep seabed exploitation, it is also open to disputes among nonstate actors, including mining corporations. ITLOS also has mandatory jurisdiction over all parties to UNCLOS with regard to disputes in the following areas: activities in the deep seabed, the prompt release of detained vessels and crews, and—and this is especially important from a natural resource management perspective—requests for provisional measures to preserve the rights of the parties to a dispute or to prevent serious harm to the marine environment.[112] Here, ITLOS functions as the general guardian of the marine environment—but only to a certain extent, since ITLOS can come into operation only when a state party submits a case. So far, ITLOS has had only few cases and these have mainly involved provisional measures. In these cases ITLOS demonstrated its utmost concern with the preservation of the marine environment in its provisional measures in the *Southern Bluefin Tuna Cases* (1999),[113] the *MOX Plant Case* (2001),[114] and the *Straits of Johor Case* (2003).[115]

The Commission on the Limits of the Continental Shelf

In addition to the ISA and ITLOS, UNCLOS also established the Commission on the Limits of the Continental Shelf (CLCS), the purpose of which is to make recommendations to coastal states on matters related to the establishment of the outer limits of their continental shelf—that is, the limits of those portions of the continental shelf that lie beyond 200 nautical miles from the coast. It is composed of experts in the fields of geology, geophysics, and hydrography who evaluate data submitted by coastal states. The limits of the shelf that a coastal state establishes on the basis of such recommendations are final and binding. Upon request, the CLCS can provide scientific and technical advice to coastal states during preparation of such data.[116]

Once concluded, the work of the CLCS will have an important impact on natural resource management, in that it will result in the final delineation of the extent of the sovereign rights of coastal states over the resources of the continental shelf. The commission is thus involved in a work with great geopolitical consequences, as it determines, in principle, the final boundaries that still need to be determined on the planet.

UN Regional Commissions

The five regional commissions of the United Nations—the United Nations Economic Commission for Europe, the Economic and Social Commission for Asia and the Pacific, the Economic Commission for Latin America and the Caribbean, the Economic Commission for Africa, and the Economic and Social Commission for Western Asia—have sometimes played an important role in various regional activities related to natural resource management, especially after the World Summit on Sustainable Development in 2002.[117]

The Economic Commission for Europe was created by ECOSOC in 1947 to "initiate and participate in measures for facilitating concerted action for the economic reconstruction of Europe," although "reconstruction" has since changed to "economic development and integration."[118] Today it brings together fifty-six countries from Europe, North America (quite notably), and the Commonwealth of Independent States and provides analysis, policy advice, and assistance to governments in such sectors as economic cooperation and integration, energy, the environment, housing and land management, population, statistics, timber, trade, and transport. The ECE also offers a regional framework for the elaboration and harmonization of conventions, norms, and standards. In that regard, it has been particularly active in the environmental field and has often played a pioneering role. Five environmental conventions were negotiated and concluded under its auspices, together with a number of additional protocols. They are listed in table 4.5.

A number of the commission's programs and divisions are directly involved with natural resource management issues. One of them is the Sustainable Energy Division, which promotes a sustainable energy development strategy for the ECE region. This work covers various intersectoral issues, especially regarding energy and environment. The ECE also has a Timber Committee, which works with the FAO's European Forestry Commission to promote sustainable forest management in the ECE region, specifically through monitoring and analyzing issues and trends. The ECE has also been playing an important role in preventing and reducing long-range transboundary air pollution by providing key technical support to the 1979 CLRTAP regime, as described in chapter 3.

ECOSOC established the Economic Commission for Asia and the Far East on the same day it established the ECE. Its mandate is similar to that of its European counterpart: to initiate and facilitate the "economic reconstruction of Asia and the Far East."[119] In 1974, the commission changed its name to the Economic and Social Commission for Asia and the Pacific (ESCAP) to reflect a greater attention to social issues related to the Pacific region (but also because the phrase "Far East" was too reminiscent of an Eurocentric colonial era). It now has sixty-two member governments and ranges in geographical scope from Turkey to Kiribati, making it the biggest of the UN's five regional commissions in terms of population served and area covered. ESCAP seeks to overcome some of the region's greatest challenges in the areas of poverty and development, trade and investment, transport and tourism, social development, and the environment and sustainable development. ESCAP has been involved in many issues that relate to natural resource management. It has, for instance, encouraged the establishment of several commodity bodies, including the Asian Coconut Community (1969), the Association of Natural Rubber Producing Countries (1970), and what became the International Pepper Community (1972). ESCAP has also been extensively involved in water management. The Bureau of Flood Control, which was established under its auspices as early as 1949, does important work regarding water management and flood control. One of the most significant outcomes of this work was the Mekong Project, which led to the estab-

TABLE 4.5. Environmental Treaties and Their Protocols Concluded under the Auspices of the ECE, 1979–2003

Convention (and Year)	***Protocols to Conventions (and Years)***
Convention on Long-Range Transboundary Air Pollution (1979)	Protocol on Long-term Financing of the Cooperative Programme for Monitoring and Evaluation of the Long-Range Transmission of Air Pollutants in Europe (1984)
	Protocol on the Reduction of Sulphur Emissions or Their Transboundary Fluxes by at Least 30 Per Cent (1985)
	Protocol Concerning the Control of Emissions of Nitrogen Oxides or Their Transboundary Fluxes (1988)
	Protocol Concerning the Control of Emissions of Volatile Organic Compounds or Their Transboundary Fluxes (1991)
	Protocol on Further Reduction of Sulphur Emissions (1994)
	Protocol on Heavy Metals (1998)
	Protocol on Persistent Organic Pollutants (1998)
	Protocol to Abate Acidification, Eutrophication and Ground-Level Ozone (1999)
Convention on Environmental Impact Assessment in a Transboundary Context (1991)	Protocol on Strategic Environmental Assessment (2003)
Convention on the Protection and Use of Transboundary Watercourses and International Lakes (1992)	Protocol on Water and Health (1999)
	Protocol on Civil Liability (2003)*
Convention on the Transboundary Effects of Industrial Accidents (1992)	Protocol on Civil Liability for Damage and Compensation for Damage Caused by Transboundary Effects of Industrial Accidents on Transboundary Waters (2003)*
Convention on Access to Information, Public Participation in Decision-Making and Access to Justice in Environmental Matters (1998)	

*Joint protocol to both the 1992 Convention on the Protection and Use of Transboundary Watercourses and International Lakes and the 1992 Convention on the Transboundary Effects of Industrial Accidents.

lishment of the Mekong River Commission in 1995. In 2006, ESCAP participated in the establishment of the Chu-Talas Rivers Commission, which promotes cooperative maintenance and use of the water infrastructure that Kazakhstan and Kyrgyzstan share. ESCAP has also been active in mineral extraction and energy supply, including the development of petroleum resources. During the 1950s, ESCAP was involved in preparing a geological map of the region and a comprehensive review of coal and iron resources. It also organized conferences on the development of mineral resources (1953) and petroleum resources (1958). In the 1960s, it actively helped countries with offshore prospecting for oil, gas, and metals. From the 1970s, ESCAP began to be increasingly used as a forum for discussing problems related to deforestation, pollution, and shortages of water. Nowadays most of these issues are discussed in ESCAP's Committee on Environment and Development, which addresses issues such as integrating environmental and developmental policies, policies and strategies for planning about using water resources sustainably, and regional cooperation for enhanced energy security and the sustainable use of energy resources.

Regional economic commissions were soon established for other parts of the world as well. The first to follow was the Economic Commission for Latin America, established in 1948 with the purpose of contributing to the economic development of Latin America, coordinating actions directed toward that end, and reinforcing economic ties among the countries in the region and with other nations of the world. Its scope of work was later broadened to include the countries of the Caribbean and its primary objectives were extended to include the promotion of the region's social development, leading ECOSOC in 1984 to rename it the Economic Commission for Latin America and the Caribbean (ECLAC).[120] It is now composed of forty-four member states, which include the countries of Latin America and the Caribbean and several North American, Asian, and European states that have historical, economic, and cultural ties with the region. Since its establishment, ECLAC has functioned as an important think tank for development issues that offers its own analytical and theoretical approach to the medium- and long-term economic and social development of the region of Latin America and the Caribbean. Under the influence of its executive secretaries, which included such energetic personalities as Raúl Prebisch, the commission has produced important studies for Latin American and Caribbean policy makers. These have included various studies and reports on natural resource management, in particular on water and mineral resources.[121] ECLAC's work in this field is now conducted by its Natural Resources and Infrastructure Division, which deals with various aspects of the conservation and sustainable use of water, mineral, and energy resources; efficiency and competitiveness of the mining and energy sectors; and international and regional legal aspects of natural resource management. The division concentrates on strengthening the technical capabilities of states to implement public policies aimed at development, protecting natural wealth, and achieving social justice on the basis of sustainable natural resource use, in particular by offering expert support regarding natural resource regulation and management.[122]

In 1958, after years of opposition from former colonial powers, ECOSOC finally established the Economic Commission for Africa (ECA) to promote the economic and social development of its member states, foster intraregional integration, and promote international cooperation for Africa's development.[123] It is composed of all African states. The ECA's program of work now focuses on two related and mutually supportive areas: promoting regional integration in support of the vision and priorities of the African Union and meeting Africa's special needs and emerging global challenges. The ECA's activities are predominantly focused on monitoring and reporting on Africa's progress in meeting global and continental commitments and on contributing to advocacy and consensus building, including developing common positions to give Africa a stronger voice in global forums. It supports member states by providing policy analysis and advocacy, enhancing partnerships, supplying technical assistance, facilitating communication and knowledge sharing, and supporting subregional activities. The ECA has been involved in natural resource management issues since its inception. For example, its first program of work referred to the need to study the problems involved with stabilizing commodity prices. Likewise, at one of the first conferences organized by the commission, a regional conference of African businessmen in 1961, cooperation through joint ventures to develop natural resources by private enterprise was discussed. Nowadays, the tasks of the ECA in the field of natural resource management are performed by its Food Security & Sustainable Development Division, which promotes awareness of the need to improve stewardship of the natural resource base and the environment by strengthening the capacity of member states to sustainably exploit those resources and manage and effectively use mineral, energy, and water resources. As part of a focus on WEHAB priority issues (water, energy, health, agriculture, and biodiversity), the ECA is particularly involved in strengthening strategies and programs for integrating water resource management and for improving land resource management.[124]

The Economic Commission for Western Asia was established in 1973 as the last of the UN regional commissions, succeeding the United Nations Economic and Social Office in Beirut.[125] In 1985, it was renamed the United Nations Economic and Social Commission for Western Asia (ESCWA). As the smallest of the regional commission in terms of membership—it members are thirteen Arab countries, including Palestine as a full-fledged member—ESCWA provides a framework for formulating and harmonizing sectoral policies for member countries, a forum for discussion and coordination, a center of expertise and knowledge, and an information repository. Some of its main objectives are supporting economic and social development in the countries of the region and promoting cooperation and encouraging interac-

Table 4.6. The Five Regional Commissions of the United Nations

Name	*Year of Establishment*	*Headquarters*
Economic Commission for Europe (ECE)	1947	Geneva
Economic and Social Commission for Asia and the Pacific (ESCAP); until 1974 Economic Commission for Asia and the Far East	1947	Bangkok
Economic Commission for Latin America and the Caribbean (ECLAC); until 1984 Economic Commission for Latin America	1948	Santiago
Economic Commission for Africa (ECA)	1958	Addis Ababa
Economic and Social Commission for Western Asia (ESCWA); until 1985 Economic Commission for Western Asia	1973	Beirut (previously located in Baghdad and Amman)

tion among those countries, particularly by promoting the exchange of experience, best practices, and lessons learned with a view to achieving regional integration. The activities of ESCWA have been particularly important with regard to the development of water resources. Since the commission was established, water security has been a priority issue because water scarcity in the region is among the highest in the world. ESCWA has been carrying out a wide variety of activities aimed at enhancing regional cooperation in the sustainable management of shared water resources. It has been actively helping member countries prepare and implement integrated water resource management, including preparing national policies and plans and developing the institutional and legal frameworks needed to integrate water management. It also played a leading role in establishing the Arab Countries Water Utilities Association in April 2007. In order to strengthen regional cooperation regarding water resources, ESCWA established in 1995 the Committee on Water Resources, which now provides a formal forum for discussing water-related issues.

Treaty Secretariats and Commodity Organizations

Among the institutions involved in the management of natural resources one should also count various treaty bodies and international organizations that have been established under multilateral environmental treaties and international commodity agreements—some of them under the auspices of the United Nations, others outside the UN system.

The secretariats of multilateral environmental treaties play an important role in global environmental governance and resource management.[126] Their tasks are mainly administrative. This often includes making practical arrangements for sessions of the Conference of the Parties, the Meeting of Parties, and/or subsidiary bodies established under those conventions.[127] Often secretariats are in charge of compiling reports from the parties and transmitting them to the other parties, facilitating implementation domestically, and ensuring that activities under a convention are coordinated with the secretariats of other relevant international bodies and conventions. They also serve as important sources of information needed for the functioning of a convention and conduct training and support for capacity-building. Their resource-rich Web sites often play an important role in disseminating information to the wider public.

Several United Nations organs, particularly UNEP and the ECE, and various specialized agencies, such as the FAO, UNESCO, and the WMO, host the secretariats of multilateral environmental agreements. For example, UNEP services the secretariats of the Convention on the Conservation of Migratory Species of Wild Animals (in Bonn), the Vienna Convention for the Protection of the Ozone Layer and its Montreal Protocol (in Nairobi), and the Basel Convention on the Control of Transboundary Movements of Hazardous Wastes and Their Disposal (in Geneva). The ECE also hosts a number of environmental treaty secretariats, including the Convention on Long-Range Transboundary Air Pollution, the Convention on Environmental Impact Assessment in a Transboundary Context, and the Convention on Access to Information, Public Participation in Decision-Making and Access to Justice in Environmental Matters. UNESCO administers the Convention Concerning the Protection of the World Cultural and Natural Heritage with the support of the IUCN. Several treaty secretariats operate autonomously, and some have become important institutions. Examples include the secretariat of the Convention on Wetlands of International Importance (in cooperation with the IUCN; Gland, Switzerland), the secretariat of the United Nations Framework Convention on Climate Change (Bonn), and the secretariat of the Convention on Biological Diversity (Montreal).

While the UN specialized agencies manage their conventions within their regular work programs, most multilateral environmental agreements that are administered by UNEP retain separate secretariats. This mosaic of agreements—each with their individual secretariats—has proven to be not very efficient and has attracted much criticism. Various attempts to create synergies and remove inconsistencies among multilateral environmental agreements have also turned out to be very costly. The Joint Inspection Unit's 2008 assessment emphasized the necessity of developing modalities by which multilateral environmental instruments could be better formulated and integrally managed without creating new independent secretariats.[128]

In contrast to the organs established by multilateral environmental treaties, a number of international commodity agreements have established international organizations, albeit with powers that are mostly limited to consultation, technical cooperation, and policy development. Examples of these individual commodity organizations include the Common Fund for Commodities, the International Tropical Timber Organization, the International Cotton Advisory Committee, the International Cocoa Organization, the International Coffee Organization, the International Copper Study Group, the International Grains Council, the International Jute Study Group, the International Lead and Zinc Study Group, the International Nickel Study Group, the International Olive Oil Council, the International Rubber Study Group, the International Sugar Organization, the International Network for Bamboo and Rattan, and the International Organisation of Vine and Wine.

The International Tropical Timber Organization (ITTO) is perhaps one of the most interesting examples among these, in that unlike many other commodity organizations it is as much concerned with trade and industry as it is with forest conservation and sustainable management of tropical timber resources. The ITTO was established under the auspices of the United Nations in 1986, following the adoption of the first International Tropical Timber Agreement in 1983.[129] Headquartered in Yokohama, Japan, the ITTO functions as a forum for discussion, consultation, and international cooperation between countries that produce and countries that consume tropical timber on issues relating to the international trade in tropical timber and the sustainable management of this resource base. It also helps its member states adapt policies appropriate to local circumstances and implement them in the field through projects; collects, analyzes, and disseminates data about the production and trade of tropical timber; and funds a range of projects and other actions aimed at developing industries at the community and industrial level.[130]

Another interesting institution is the Common Fund for Commodities, envisaged in UNCTAD IV's Integrated Programme for Commodities (which was brokered by Henry Kissinger) and established by the United Nations under an agreement negotiated by UNCTAD in 1979.[131] As an intergovernmental financial institution, the fund's main functions are to contribute (through its first account) to the financing of international buffer stocks, to finance (through its second account) the diversification of production in developing countries, and to expand the processing, marketing, and distribution of primary products by developing countries. Its goals are to promote industrialization in and increase the export earning of developing countries and promote coordination and consultation regarding actions taken in the field of commodities. Currently, however, the fund mainly concentrates on commodity development projects designed to enhance the socioeconomic development of commodity producers and contribute to the development of the societies of these producers. The fund thus finances projects for smallholder farmers as well as small- and medium-sized enterprises involved in commodity processing and production as well as projects involving trade in developing and least developed countries, thereby focusing on specific commodity problems or opportunities rather than on country-specific situations. By 31 December 2008, the fund had approved 283 projects (covering thirty-seven agricultural and three mineral commodities) with an overall cost of US$506.4 million, of which the fund financed US$259.6 million.[132]

International commodity organizations are headquartered in cities such as London, Amsterdam, or Washington and tend to operate rather independently of the UN system. Some of them have grown into large institutions, although most maintain secretariats that are not larger than those of treaty bodies under multilateral environmental treaties. Many of these commodity organizations have a peculiar institutional design that distinguishes between producing and consuming member states—usually via so-called caucuses. Within each caucus, the dues and votes of individual members are calculated based on the extent of commodity trade or commodity production within the country.

Alternative Ideas

Throughout the years several proposals have been made regarding establishing new organs and institutions for global resource management and environmental governance.

An Environmental Security Council

In his address to the forty-third session of the General Assembly on 27 September 1988, Soviet minister for foreign affairs Eduard Shevardnadze proposed a discussion on how to turn UNEP into an environmental council capable of taking effective decisions to ensure ecological security.[133] For this purpose the Soviet Union proposed a summit meeting under UN auspices in 1990 of the leaders of some fifteen or twenty states representing all continents and the Non-Aligned Movement. This proposal was part of the various General Assembly resolutions at the time on environmental aspects of a comprehensive system of international peace and security, which were put forward by countries that belonged to the Soviet bloc, especially by Bulgaria.[134] In the context of East-West tensions during the Cold War, the origins of the proposal meant that sufficient support could not be generated for this thought-provoking and interesting idea. With the demise of the Soviet Union and the Soviet bloc, these proposals withered away. However, they were not essentially different from what would many years later be the environmental dimension of the concept of comprehensive security advocated by Secretary-General Kofi Annan's High-level Panel on Threats, Challenges and Change.[135]

Similarly, various proposals have been put forward to change the existing Trusteeship Council into an environmental council. In 1945, the Trusteeship Council was established to supervise the administration of trust territories, mainly mandated territories from the period of the League of Nations. However, with the termination of the last trusteeship agreements, the Trusteeship Council has become obsolete. In addition to proposals to eliminate this council in accordance with Article 108 of the UN Charter, it has been suggested that the Trusteeship Council be reconstituted as an environmental council, since the natural wealth and resources of the planet can also be viewed as a trusteeship of humankind.[136] The last time this suggestion was put forward was in one of Kofi Annan's reform reports. It is no coincidence that major parts of this report were drafted by Maurice Strong, at that time undersecretary-general for UN reform. The advantage would be that because the Trusteeship Council is one of the six principal organs of the UN, a reconstituted council would continue to have this status. Secretary-General Kofi Annan felt that a collective trusteeship should be established to promote the integrity and sustainable use of the global environment and common areas, such as the high seas, outer space, and the atmosphere.[137] However, the present functions of the Trusteeship Council have nothing to do with environmental affairs and (at least in the view of many developing states) the Trusteeship Council is stigmatized by its colonial past. Moreover, notwithstanding its status as a principal organ, the Trusteeship Council does not have more powers than UNEP or the CSD currently do.

Green UN Police Forces

Another thought-provoking idea was green UN police forces. This idea was originally suggested in the 1980s in the context of the Ecoforum for Peace, a Sofia-based NGO in which international environmental experts participated. Such police forces might be charged with preventing illegal dumping (at sea or on land) and monitoring pollution problems and accidents. They might also supervise the implementation of international safety guidelines for constructing chemical factories, inspect the operation of such factories, and so forth. Under the current broad mandate of peacekeeping operations, the establishment of police forces for environmental purposes is theoretically possible, but in practice it would be very difficult to agree on their mandate, composition, and financing.

The International Environmental Commissioner (Ombudsman)

The office of the executive director of UNEP could gradually evolve into that of an international environmental commissioner or ombudsman. At present, as the only elected under-secretary-general in the UN system, the executive director is already invested with a broad mandate. This office could come to include receiving petitions of individuals and groups such as the World Wide Fund for Nature, Greenpeace, and other environmental nongovernmental organizations; and the right to ask questions of governments and boards of international organizations and transnational companies about environmental issues. The environmental commissioner could build on the experience of the World Bank Inspection Panel and the compliance advisor/ombudsman of the International Finance Corporation and the Multilateral Investment Guarantee Agency. The international environmental commissioner and UNEP could develop the ability to compose and send multilateral inspection teams (comparable to those of the International Atomic Energy Agency or the Organization for the Prohibition of Chemical Weapons) for the purposes of fact-finding and reporting on the illegal dumping of industrial waste at sea or on land. The annual report of UNEP's executive director or the international environmental commissioner could become an authoritative source on the state of the world's environment.

Upgrading UNEP to a Specialized Agency

As discussed above, UNEP has many functions but hardly any powers and inadequate financial resources. On various occasions, it has been suggested that UNEP be transformed from a General Assembly subsidiary organ into a full-fledged international organization. There is a precedent for this, namely the United Nations Industrial Development Organization, which was established in 1966 and became a specialized agency in 1986.[138] The status of UNEP could be similarly transformed.

Nonetheless, some possible drawbacks inherent in this option should be taken into account. At present, all member states are automatically represented in UNEP. If UNEP becomes a specialized agency, states will have to decide whether or not they will become members and pay their financial contributions. If they do not enthusiastically support the upgrading of UNEP, they may well decide not to become a member of the new specialized agency. If they become members, they will be free to withdraw if they are dissatisfied with UNEP's policy. (Mere reference to UNESCO may suffice to illustrate the problems associated with this kind of structure.)[139] Therefore, there is some wisdom in opting for an evolutionary approach by which member states first seek to strengthen UNEP through a number of improvements and a better use of existing mechanisms while keeping open the option of a future upgrading of UNEP into a United Nations environment organization. Proposals for strengthening include the expansion of the membership of UNEP's Governing Council to include all UN member states, a better-functioning Global Ministerial Environment Forum, and more stable, adequate, and predictable financing for UNEP.

A New UN World Environmental Organization

In addition to proposals to strengthen the position of UNEP, there has been considerable discussion about the advantages and disadvantages of setting up a new world environmental organization or a world organization for sustainable development, as the Brundtland Commission proposed in 1987.[140] There are many arguments against such a step. After all, there already are so many international organizations.[141] And would not the establishment of a new "specialized" organization contradict an integrated approach? The questions of environmental conservation and sustainable development must, after all, form an integral part of general financial, trade, and development policies. This would require a decisive political forum that could apply itself energetically to this task. It seems clear that ECOSOC, UNEP, and the UN Commission on Sustainable Development will never acquire the stature this mission demands. Only a full-fledged international organization can provide checks and balances against other powerful international organizations such as the World Trade Organization and the World Bank.

One Standing Treaty Body for Environmental Conventions

A less far-reaching but nonetheless bold step would be to establish a single standing treaty body for various environmental conventions. It is clear that an extensive treaty system of monitoring and reporting procedures exists within the United Nations. Compared with the pre-Stockholm period this is a major improvement. At the same time, all this could be done much better and more effectively. Currently there is overlap and hence duplication among the many treaty organizations. One single treaty body would have the merit of allowing environmental policies in a given country to be assessed in a coherent manner by reference to integrated reports. This would also make possible a consistent approach to interpreting existing treaty standards. If the members of the treaty body were appointed on a full-time basis, this would create a high-quality body that would always be available and could take action at any moment in the event of serious environmental problems. Making appointed members full time would also increase the body's visibility and authority and make it more accessible to various actors. This higher public profile would increase the chance of intensive dialogue among the members of the treaty body, the states parties, NGOs and other UN bodies. Such dialogue is necessary because cooperation is at present fragmented and relatively unstructured and inefficient.

However, there are quite a number of obstacles to establishing a single treaty body. The present treaty bodies are for the most part independent and autonomous in the exercise of their monitoring bodies. Their mandates are based on the specific treaties under which they were established. Not all treaties have the same number of states parties. The treaty committees are not subordinate to the United Nations but are independent. For all these reasons, it is doubtful whether there is legal scope or sufficient political will to introduce measures aimed at establishing one single treaty body.

Therefore, it may well be worth considering a number of less far-reaching amalgamation options that might be feasible and could be instrumental in fostering a coherent approach.[142] The present treaty bodies could intensify their efforts to harmonize, coordinate, and integrate the different aspects of their mandates while maintaining the specificity of their respective functions. This could be done first of all by harmonizing, wherever possible, the treaty procedures, such as the procedures for reporting, accepting input from expert bodies, dialogue with NGOs, investigation, and complaints. All of this should be discussed at regular chairpersons' meetings. This is not just a question of working methods but also one of coordinated and mutually inspired interpretations of standards of environmental conservation and sustainable use of natural resources. Such an approach could enhance the quality, coherence, effectiveness, and authority of the treaty system as a whole.

Assessment

As this chapter has demonstrated, the current institutional structure of environmental governance and global resource management is poorly organized in a mosaic of organizations, UN organs, funds, and programs dealing with circumscribed aspects. Coordination of these activities is often lacking. Taking everything into consideration and mindful of the weak international structure for environmental conservation and sustainable development, it may well be that the best course of action would be to establish a new world organization for sustainable development or a UN world environment organization, as has recently been proposed by France, Sweden, and other countries. This could place the whole question of sustainable development much more clearly on the international agenda and provide an efficient center for the coordination of international environmental and development policy and operational activities. UNCTAD, UNEP, and parts of the UNDP and the regional economic commissions could be integrated into such a new world organization.

5

Natural Resources and Armed Conflict

- **The Nexus between Natural Resources and Armed Conflict**
- **Protecting Natural Resources and the Environment during Armed Conflict**
- **The UN's Role in Natural Resource Conflicts**
- **Assessment**

Each state has a large appetite for natural resources, and the temptation for one state to appropriate resources of other states in border areas or in international areas beyond the jurisdiction of any state is sometimes irresistible. Not surprisingly, gaining access to natural resources has more than once been a casus belli, both between and within states. All too often, wars generate devastating impacts for civilian populations and wreak havoc on the environment, including its natural resources. At the same time, wars offer plenty of opportunities for rebellious groups or warlords (at times with the complicity of international companies) to loot and plunder natural resources. These problems raise fundamental questions about the relationship between natural resources and armed conflict. Does natural resource wealth increase the likelihood of violent conflict? Do specific natural resources fuel and prolong conflicts? What happens to natural resources during armed conflict? Does any UN organ and/or body of law protect them? And finally, what is the role of the United Nations with regard to these problems? Some of these questions are addressed in the first section of this chapter, which sketches the basic nexus between natural resources and armed conflict and presents a typology of resource conflicts. The second section outlines the rules of international humanitarian law that shield the environment and natural resources as well as humans during hostilities and briefly evaluates their effectiveness. Finally, the third section assesses the role of the United Nations in addressing the different aspects of the link between natural resources and conflict and evaluates the role of the Security Council and other United Nations organs in containing or resolving resource conflicts.

The Nexus between Natural Resources and Armed Conflict

Achieving or maintaining access to natural resources, particularly those that are in short supply, has always figured among the policy and strategic considerations of states. The very survival of a nation depends on vital natural resources, such as water or food crops. Therefore, it is not surprising that strategic considerations have sometimes led to forced annexations of neighboring land—particularly in cases of long-disputed borders that were a consequence of arbitrary partitioning by former colonial powers—and sometimes to the conquering of distant lands. Such strategic considerations have also figured among the primary motives for appropriating common resources not under the jurisdiction of other states, such as the resources in adjacent maritime areas.[1] This will likely not change in the future: gaining or maintaining access to natural resources will always be an important element of national foreign policy.

Apart from being of vital importance for the well-being of a nation, the presence of natural resources within a country is also seen as a blessing and a precondition to development. Many UN studies, reports, resolutions, and specific instruments are based upon this premise, especially those of the UN's Committee on Natural Resources and UNCTAD.[2] This premise also explains the desire of the newly independent nations of the 1950s and 1960s to regain control over their natural resources. In many of these countries practically all agricultural, mining, and industrial resources and the means of communication or transport were in foreign hands. Therefore, in order to fully realize their newborn independence, these countries often decided to nationalize the property of foreign companies, particularly those in the oil extracting and mining sectors, an action that brought them into conflict with the governments of the companies whose property had been nationalized. The nationalizations were primarily aimed at changing the existing distribution of economic resources, yet they also had a more symbolic meaning. The newly independent states clearly wanted to free themselves of the bonds of foreign capital—which represented to many of them the remnants of the colonialism and imperialism of former European powers—and demonstrate their ability to use their natural resources independently, without interference from other states.

However, the views about natural resources and their importance for economic development have gradually become more qualified. As it turned out, the success of none of the newly industrialized developing states, such as for example the "Asian Tigers," was attributable to their natural resources. Moreover, economists started to realize that natural resource abundance might have negative effects on economic performance. This was the case in the Netherlands following the discovery of large natural gas deposits in the North Sea in the 1960s. Owing to increases in revenues from gas extraction, Dutch currency became stronger and, in turn, the country's exports became less competitive. This had unexpectedly serious repercussions for important segments of the Dutch economy, particularly its manufacturing sector. The phenomenon, also known as the "Dutch disease," was later observed in many other resource-rich countries. It happened, for example, in Chile, following that nation's increased reliance on copper exports, and in Russia, after the boom in its oil and natural gas sectors.[3] For many years, this issue has occupied economic theorists who looked for possible causes for the poor economic performance (in terms of high inflation rates, growing public debt, slow economic growth, etc.) of oil- and commodity-exporting countries.[4]

But while economists focused on the relationship between an abundance of natural resources with economic performance, political scientists increasingly began to study natural resource wealth as a cause of political and socioeconomic instability. The basic assumption behind these propositions was that large levels of natural resource rents relative to income generate disproportionate levels of rent-seeking, which results in greater conflict about distribution and the militarization of politics, often with the involvement of foreign conspirators and adventurers.[5] With time, the relationship between natural resource wealth and development began to be considered more broadly, particularly after case studies demonstrated how a number of countries that relied heavily on natural resource exports suffered from high levels of corruption, increasing income inequality, growing poverty, and poor governance. The assumption was that states that earn a large proportion of their revenue from natural resource rents have less need to levy domestic taxes. As a result, leaders tend to be less accountable to individuals and groups within civil society. This line of research intensified after the end of the Cold War, when the proliferation of civil wars pointed to a conspicuous concentration of violent conflicts in countries rich in minerals and other resources, thereby reviving the idea that natural resource wealth might be more of a curse than a blessing.[6]

Since the 1990s, two lines of research have received increased attention from policy makers and social scientists. Many researchers (in particular in the field of conflict studies) began to explore the relationship between natural resource abundance and the pace, intensity, and duration of conflicts.[7] While they diverged considerably in their findings about whether, how, and which natural resources influence the onset and the duration of conflicts, these studies share common findings about the relationship between natural resource wealth and violent conflict. First, the availability of oil increases the likelihood of conflict, particular secessionist wars. Second, diamonds, gemstones, and other "lootable" commodities, including drugs such as cocaine and opium, do not necessarily contribute to the onset of conflicts, but they do tend to prolong the duration of conflicts. Apart from these similar conclusions, however, these studies did not confirm a clear link between conflict and primary commodities in general or any agricultural commodities in particular.[8]

A second line of social-scientific inquiry focused on environmental degradation and resource scarcity as possible causes of violent conflict. This line of research—often subsumed under the concept of "environmental security"[9]—has looked into the consequences of environmental scarcity—in particular scarcity of renewable resources such as forests, cropland, fresh water, and fish stocks—that can arise from the depletion or degradation of resources, increased demand for resources, and unequal distribution of resources. Proponents of this research have argued that a number of factors can lead to increased social stress within countries that has the potential to stimulate ethnic clashes, urban unrest, or civil strife (including insurgencies and coups d'etat). These factors can even lead to interstate wars or even broader North-South conflicts over scarce natural resources. They are:

- Pollution
- Deforestation
- Climate change
- Soil erosion
- Salinization of water
- Desertification
- Overuse of resources
- Rapid population growth
- Changes in consumption behavior
- Concentration of control over natural resources in the hands of powerful groups[10]

All these lines of research reveal the complexity of the nexus between natural resource exploitation and conflict. Natural resources might become a direct cause of conflict—due to disputes over the ownership of or the distribution of revenue from such resources or to conflicts that stem from scarce and depleted resources. The presence of natural resources might contribute to conflict in less direct ways. On average, countries with a high dependency on natural resources have been associated with an increased risk of weak governance and poor economic performance, both factors that contribute to conflict-prone environments. At the same time, natural resources might also serve as a means for pursuing conflict, in that they provide armed opposition groups with the revenue to finance their activities.[11] This explains why conflicts involving natural resources have taken various forms, depending on the

TABLE 5.1. Types of Natural Resource Conflicts

- Disputes over nationalization and expropriation of natural resources
- Interstate "resource wars" and conflicts over transboundary or shared natural resources
- Resource-related disputes within a state
- Conflicts over natural resources in international areas, including the polar regions

types of resources and actors involved in the disputes. Table 5.1 distinguishes four main categories of natural resource conflicts. Each of them is discussed below.

Nationalization and Expropriation Disputes

Few issues in international relations are as controversial as nationalization disputes, which often involve the taking of foreign property rights and hence foreign companies. The early debates in the United Nations on resource sovereignty took place when the memory of the Russian Bolshevist nationalizations of 1917 and the Mexican oil nationalizations of 1938 were still fresh, when the Anglo-Iranian Oil Company dispute (1950–1952) was a hot issue, and when nationalizations were taking place or were being seriously considered in Latin America. In 1951, Bolivia nationalized its tin mines and Guatemala launched a program of agrarian land reform under which it would take over United Fruit Company properties. A few years later, a very serious North-South dispute occurred when the government of Egypt led by President Gamal Abdel Nasser nationalized the Anglo-French Suez Canal Company in 1956, which gave rise to a dramatic chain of confrontations. Indonesia's nationalization of Dutch property in 1958 under President Sukarno was a further blow to the western world.

The countries that took such measures eagerly sought justification in UN debates and UN resolutions. The Latin American countries in particular linked the right of each country to nationalize and freely exploit their natural resources to the principle of self-determination of peoples as endorsed in Article 1(2) of the UN Charter and the principle of permanent sovereignty over natural resources, which was new at the time. While emotions ran high in UN debates on these issues, the elements of a compromise could also be found in the UN in special clauses in resolutions prepared by the General Assembly's Second and Third committees. This led to the compromise formula in draft Article 1 of the two 1966 human rights covenants and paragraph 4 of the Declaration on Permanent Sovereignty over Natural Resources of 1962.

A nine-member working party of the Third Committee consisting of Brazil, Costa Rica, El Salvador, Greece, India, Pakistan, Poland, Syria, and Venezuela reached a clear majority agreement on the following formulation, which features in the identical Article 1 of the two covenants that were finally adopted in 1966:

> The peoples may, for their own ends, freely dispose of their natural wealth and resources without prejudice to any obligations arising out of international economic co-operation, based upon the principle of mutual benefit, and international law. In no case may a people be deprived of its own means of subsistence.

The UN's special Commission on Permanent Sovereignty over Natural Resources, which was charged with drafting a declaration, also faced very difficult times in addressing the issue of the taking of foreign property as a key dimension of the exercise of resource sovereignty. Chile brokered the compromise, which was partly based on a UN Secretariat study prepared under the leadership of the director of the Office of Legal Affairs at the time, Oscar Schachter.[12] The paragraph on nationalization in the General Assembly's resolution on the issue reads as follows:

> Nationalization, expropriation or requisitioning shall be based on grounds or reasons of public utility, security or the national interest which are recognized as overriding purely individual or private interests, both domestic and foreign. In such cases, the owner shall be paid appropriate compensation, in accordance with the rules in force in the State taking such measures in the exercise of sovereignty and in accordance with international law.[13]

During the 1970s, various nationalizations took place, especially by oil-producing countries such as Libya, Saudi Arabia, and Kuwait. Occasionally, nationalizations took place in other sectors, such as Chile's nationalizations of copper mines in 1971 (which unfortunately led to the fall of President Salvador Allende and the coming into power of General Augusto Pinochet). The efforts of developing countries to extend the grounds and justification for nationalization beyond those painstakingly agreed to in the 1962 declaration caused considerable uncertainty for some years, but ultimately such attempts were unsuccessful. The basic compromise that had been brokered through the UN and resulted in the 1962 declaration survived.

In the early years of the twenty-first century, nationalization of natural resource sectors appeared to once again be in vogue, especially with leftist-oriented governments in Latin America, such as in Venezuela under President Hugo Chávez (oil and other assets in the energy sector) and in Bolivia (oil and gas) and Ecuador (oil). To date, these governments have rarely used the forum of the United Nations as a platform for advertising and seeking legitimization for their policies.

Expropriation of foreign property and nationalization of entire sectors of an economy are two of the most divisive issues in international politics and at times can escalate into serious international conflict. In 2008, the nationalization discourse suddenly took a new direction. In response to the credit crisis, some western governments nationalized individual banking and finance companies in an effort to protect economic stability in general and the interests of savers in particular.

Resource Management Conflicts and Interstate "Resource Wars"

Water, fisheries, rivers, lakes, forests, and oil and gas deposits often straddle state boundaries. Similarly, atmospheric resources and the climate cross boundaries. Therefore, consultation and cooperation are necessary to prevent disputes over concurrent national uses of internationally shared natural resources and to make an optimal use of those resources. When agreement on the joint management of transboundary resources cannot be reached, unilateral action by one of the states can spark serious conflict, in the worst case leading to war. It has been said, for example, that Iraq's invasion of Kuwait in August 1990 was partly induced by Iraq's perception that Kuwait was stealing oil from the transboundary Rumaila oil field.[14] Very often, however, disputes over straddling or transboundary resources have been disguised in more general disputes over interstate boundaries or disputes relating to sovereignty over coasts and adjacent maritime areas. In each of these situations, access to natural resources can play an important role in the development of the dispute. In the dispute over the sovereignty of the Bakasi Peninsula (which was submitted to the ICJ), for example, both Cameroon and Nigeria had an important interest in the oil reserves adjacent to the peninsula. Similarly, the dispute between Guyana and Suriname over their common maritime boundary was exacerbated by the possibility of exploiting offshore oil resources. In June 2000, Surinamese gunboats even forced a Canadian company that had erected an oil platform contracted by neighboring Guyana to leave the area immediately after Suriname claimed that the platform was in its waters and over its continental shelf. This prompted Guyana to invoke the dispute settlement procedure under the United Nations Convention on the Law of the Sea. Examples of this kind of conflict abound (some are presented in the next chapter on the judicial settlement of disputes).

Apart from disputes over transboundary and shared resources, interstate conflicts have also arisen when the scarcity of natural resources has triggered a country to seize the resources of another country. While this kind of "resource war" has not been a common feature of international relations, the desire to gain access to natural resources has been an important factor in many interstate disputes, albeit usually only one among many causes contributing to a conflict. Germany's desire to gain access to the iron-rich region of Lorraine (in France) and to resources in Africa were important factors in the beginning of World War I. Similarly, Germany's expansion into Eastern Europe and Japan's expansion into Asia during World War II were partly motivated by the desire to gain access to natural wealth. In both cases, though, natural resources were only a part of the broader considerations that drove these states.

Apart from the two great wars, a number of other interstate wars were driven by conflicts over natural resources. During the League of Nations period, Bolivia and Paraguay fought over access to the Gran Chaco wilderness area. The conflict degenerated into a full-fledged war, the Chaco War (1932–1935), during which the League of Nations failed to do anything but stand by idly. Although Paraguay succeeded in annexing part of the Gran Chaco, it turned out that the area contained no oil. Another example would be the Arab-Israeli war of 1967, which was attributable in part to increased tension between Israel and the Arab states over access to water. A major factor that led to the war was an Arab League plan (the Headwater Diversion Plan) to divert the Hasbani and Banias rivers, two of the three sources of the Jordan River, and prevent them from flowing into the Sea of Galilee in 1964. This plan would have thwarted Israel's plans to use these waters for its National Water Carrier irrigation project. In April 1967, Israeli air strikes targeted Syria's diversion works. Two months later the Six-Day War broke out, during which Israel conquered portions of the Sinai Peninsula in Egypt, the West Bank (then controlled by Jordan), and the Golan Heights in Syria. With the latter, Israel gained control over tributaries of the Hasbani and Banias rivers, thereby preventing the implementation of the Headwater Diversion Plan. At the same time, by occupying the Sinai Peninsula Israel also gained access to Egyptian oil fields. Until 1979, when the Egypt-Israel Peace Treaty was signed, the exploitation of those oil fields provided for two-thirds of Israeli oil needs.[15] Although the 1967 war was not about water, it must be seen in the broader context of the Arab-Israeli conflict in all its complexity.[16]

Other examples of conflicts where natural resources played a role include the occupation by Morocco and Mauritania of phosphate-rich Western Sahara in 1972 and the war between Argentina and the United Kingdom in 1982, which followed the unsuccessful attempt by the former to (re)claim the Falkland Islands/Islas Malvinas, including the rich fishery resources that surround the islands. More recently, the involvement of Burundi, Rwanda, and Uganda in the internal conflict in the Democratic Republic of the Congo was also related to natural resources and resulted in extensive plundering of the rich natural wealth of the DRC in the late 1990s. In all these cases, resource-related factors played a role in very complex disputes.

Intrastate Resource-Related Disputes

Access to natural resources constitutes an important factor in the dynamic of many internal disputes. Preserving access to natural resources, for example, played a background role in a number of wars of independence. France's reluctance to lose its colonial territory of Algeria was attributable in part to the fact that Algeria had rich deposits of oil and natural gas; this prolonged the Algerian war of independence (1954–1962). The Congo Civil War of 1960–1964 was precipitated by the unsuccessful attempt of Katanga Province to secede from the newly independent Republic of the Congo. Belgian troops and industrialists supported Katanga Province because they wanted to protect their investments there in copper and other minerals. Another example is the Nigerian Civil War of 1967–1970, which took place after Nigeria's southeastern region attempted to secede and proclaimed itself the independent republic of Biafra. This conflict was in large part attributable to the fact that the central government of Nigeria did not want to lose the rich deposits of oil located in the seceding provinces. During the immediate postcolonial period, former colonial powers or central governments invariably wanted to maintain their hold over natural resources, a political dynamic that inhibited many colonies or resource-rich regions from becoming independent.

When the regions with the resources embarked upon secessionist and independence movements, they often sought the support of one of the superpowers. However, when the Cold War and superpower rivalry ended in 1991, many secessionist movements and other rebel groups were left without the support that the United States or the Soviet Union had previously provided and had to turn to other sources of income to finance their activities. Revenue from natural resource extraction has become an important source of income that has financed many civil wars. In Angola, diamonds became a strategic resource for the União Nacional para a Independência Total de Angola movement (UNITA) in its struggle in the Angolan Civil War of 1975–2002. Led by Jonas Savimbi, the movement occupied important diamond-producing areas, particularly the Cuango Valley, in November 1992 and began extracting diamonds, which provided income for UNITA's rearmament process and helped defray the costs of war. The quantities were not negligible; according to some estimates, UNITA removed diamonds valued at US$3 billion during the period 1993–1998, which made it the world's largest diamond-smuggling operation.[17] In Cambodia, "conflict timber" provided important sources of revenue for the Khmer Rouge, which led an insurgent rebellion after being driven from power in 1979. By 1995, timber exports to Thailand were earning the Khmer Rouge approximately US$10–20 million per month.[18]

In Liberia, the armed insurrection that Charles Taylor and his National Patriotic Front of Liberia began in 1989 was in large part financed by the looting of diamonds, gold, iron ore, rubber, timber, marijuana, palm oil, coffee, and cocoa. In the early 1990s, mining, logging, and rubber revenue generated about US$75 million yearly.[19] In 1991, Taylor also helped organize and militarily supported the Revolutionary United Front (RUF)—an armed Sierra Leonean opposition group under the leadership of Foday Sankoh—which invaded Sierra Leone in an effort to gain control over the lucrative alluvial diamond fields situated in Sierra Leone less than 100 miles from the Liberian border. During the civil war that followed in Sierra Leone, the Revolutionary United Front used diamonds as the primary source of its income. It is estimated that the RUF looted diamonds worth between US$25 and 125 million in the second half of the 1990s.[20] In the Democratic Republic of the Congo, the civil war that began in 1996 involved armies and militias of as many as six different countries in addition to numerous rebel groups, all of which engaged in massive plundering and looting of the country's vast natural resources of diamonds, coltan (short for columbite-tantalite), gold, tin, and cobalt in order to fund their war efforts. And while the war officially ended in 2003, gaining access to or retaining control over natural resources has remained a key motivation of the warring factions and opposition groups that continue to undermine the stability of the country and the region.[21]

Reliance upon revenue generated by natural resource exploitation has also been characteristic of more recent conflicts. In Côte d'Ivoire, the rebel Forces Nouvelles, which began its armed opposition in 2002, has been relying heavily upon diamonds mined in areas under its control and on cocoa and cotton to fund its war effort. The revenues were also for the personal gain of its members.[22] In Somalia, warlords have been relying on charcoal extraction and fishery licensing for their funding.[23] And in Equatorial Guinea, the third largest oil exporter of Africa, the unsuccessful coup d'etat that was attempted in 2004 was motivated by the desire to gain access to the lucrative oil reserves of the country. Foreign adventurers were conspicuously involved in this conflict, including the son of Margaret Thatcher. In some of these cases, sanctions imposed by the Security Council banning the trade in "conflict goods" have helped undermine the revenue generated by the illicit exploitation of natural resources. Yet the lack of state control over natural resources in many of these states continues to be a source of instability. In Liberia, for example, cases have been reported of illegal occupation and exploitation of rubber plantations even after the conclusion of peace agreements by former combatants who were not successfully integrated into the demobilization scheme.[24]

These protracted civil wars caused considerable damage to natural resources, including food stocks, and in some situations left the population without viable prospects for the future. Resource depletion and scarcity will continue to be key sources of instability in the future. It is often argued, for example, that one of the driving forces behind the current crisis in Darfur in Sudan is the battle between ethnic groups over access to fertile lands for their cattle and other natural resources.[25] Similarly, the current increase in piracy around the coast of Somalia has been associated with the depletion of fishery resources in the area.

The effects of resource scarcity might be further exacerbated by the adverse impacts of global climate change. The reduction of arable land, increasing shortages of potable water, diminishing food and animal stocks, desertification, prolonged droughts, flooding, and altered rainfall patterns are all likely to influence potential disputes over rare and depleting natural resources, especially where access to those resources has been or will become politicized. Conflicts brought about by global climate change will most likely transcend specific regions, and intensified competition for energy resources will likely be observed on a global scale, particularly as developing countries continue to grow. The expected increase in sea levels and the probable increase in the occurrence of natural disasters are also likely sources of conflict. Receding coastlines and the submergence of coastal areas will lead to the loss of territory and potentially to the disappearance of some low-lying countries and island states. It is not too far-fetched to think in this connection of renewed territorial and maritime disputes arising from changing borders. Decreases in territory will increase demographic pressure on the remaining land. This pressure will likely be exacerbated by migration (both between and within countries) in response to environmental changes; such population movements will most likely be precipitated by or amplified by natural disasters and other adverse effects of climate change.[26]

Disputes over Natural Resources in International Areas

Disputes relating to the access to and exploitation of global commons have been less frequent, although not necessarily less violent. In the 1970s, Iceland adopted legislation extending jurisdiction over maritime areas that previously had been categorized as the high seas. The violent exchanges between Iceland's government vessels and British fishing trawlers that followed were not without reason given the name "cod wars." Similar disputes that resulted from the legislative amendments that extended Canada's jurisdiction over high seas areas in the 1990s (this time for the purpose of conserving highly migratory and straddling fish stocks) were only slightly less violent, as exemplified in the arrest of the crew of the Spanish vessel *Estai* by Canada's law enforcement vessels in 1995. However, disputes over global fishery commons (or better, over the conservation of these resources) were more commonly fought by less violent means—for example, by imposing trade sanctions or before judicial bodies. The dolphin-related dispute between the United States and various tuna-fishing states (including Mexico) or the dispute between Chile and the European Commission over the conservation of swordfish stocks in the Southern Pacific are typical examples.[27]

Fishery resources are not the only global commons that have given rise to conflicts. Prior to the negotiation of a new legal regime for the oceans at the Third United Nations Conference on the Law of the Sea (1973–1982), tensions were rising regarding the exploitation of the mineral resources of the deep seabed. By the late 1960s, a number of companies in the United States, Japan, and Europe had developed substantial interests and activities in commercial deep-sea mining. Special ships were designed and special dredging systems developed to mine nodules containing nickel, cobalt, copper, and other materials that were expected to be found in large quantities on the deep seabed. Developing countries were not very favorable to such developments, as they wanted to partake of the benefits from the exploitation of deep seabed nodules through revenue sharing or direct participation in exploitation. As a result of those tensions, the General Assembly passed a resolution in 1969 calling for a moratorium on the exploitation of the resources of seabed and subsoil areas beyond the limits of national jurisdiction pending establishment of an international regime for their equitable exploitation.[28] Developed states did not take favorably to the moratorium. The United States in particular did not "believe it is either necessary or desirable to try to halt exploration and exploitation of the seabeds . . . during the negotiating process" and called on other states to support its idea of an interim policy of regulated exploration and exploitation through a so-called mini-treaty.[29]

Tensions eventually receded with the adoption of UNCLOS, which granted coastal states sovereign rights over the continental shelves off their shores and established a special system for exploiting deep seabed resources, as described in the previous chapters. In the meanwhile, it had become clear that the exploitation of deep seabed nodules was far from commercially viable, which was an additional reason that tensions dissipated.

Conflicts over natural resources also arose in relation to the resources of the polar regions. In spite of its isolated location on the margin of maritime and trade routes, Antarctica has not escaped rivalries over its resources. Conflicts over natural resources more often were related to disputes about title to territory and effective occupation of the southern polar region, particularly those that emerged in the first half of the twentieth century. The dispute that emerged between the United Kingdom, Argentina, and Chile was a particularly bitter episode. During World War II, Argentina and Chile advanced sovereignty claims to the Antarctic continent and associated islands; these claims overlapped substantially with claims the United Kingdom had made in 1908 and 1917. An important consideration behind the claims of Argentina and Chile was their interest in developing commercial whaling.[30] In the 1950s, the conflict escalated after the usual diplomatic protests gave way to direct confrontations that involved reciprocal destruction of installations, harassment of personnel, and the intensification of naval movements of a military nature.[31] In 1955, the United Kingdom even instituted proceedings before the ICJ against Argentina and Chile, although the case was never pleaded.[32]

These tensions—together with other conflicts of this kind, such as a dispute that subsequently developed between Chile and Argentina regarding the delimitation of their respective areas on Antarctica or the dispute between the United Kingdom and France over the precise limits of Adélie Land—were eventually settled with the adoption of the Antarctic Treaty in 1959. As discussed in the previous chapter, the treaty froze the existing claims of states to sovereignty over parts of the continent (by carefully preserving the position of both claimant and nonclaimant states without resolving the status of individual claims)[33] and today remains the keystone of Antarctic cooperation. With sovereignty disputes temporarily set aside, the states parties to the Antarctic Treaty were able to develop a sophisticated regime for managing resource- and environment-related issues, including the question of mineral resource exploitation. It is to be hoped that the Antarctic Treaty will prove to be flexible enough to address current challenges to the Antarctic environment, particularly questions of whaling, fishing, and bioprospecting and those connected to the process for claiming the outer continental shelf.[34]

But while overt conflicts over natural resources have so far been more or less dormant in Antarctica, a new resource grab has recently begun in the Arctic region. In 2007, a Russian expedition reopened the quiet struggle over the Arctic by planting a titanium flag on the deep seabed beneath the North Pole, symbolically claiming that it had found proof of seabed continuity with the Russian continental shelf. Should this proof be accepted by the UN Commission on the Limits of the Continental Shelf—a body UNCLOS established "to consider the data and other material submitted by coastal States concerning the outer limits of the continental shelf in areas where those limits extend beyond 200 nautical miles"[35]—Russia would eventually be able to exercise sovereign rights for the purposes of exploring and exploiting the natural resources of the seabed and subsoil under the North Pole. Russian scientists are not the only ones interested in proving that the seabed below the North Pole is part of the Eurasian continental shelf, an area called the Lomonosov Ridge. Danish scientists are trying to prove that the Lomonosov Ridge is connected to Greenland, while Canadian scientists are looking for links between the ridge and Ellesmere Island, which forms part of Canadian territory. States are interested in these land masses because it is believed that rich reserves of natural resources lurk in the deep, including oil, diamonds, gold, silver, lead, copper, and zinc. As the ice fields melt as a result of global warming, these resources will become much more accessible than before and perhaps will be easily mined.

Protecting Natural Resources and the Environment during Armed Conflict

Having sketched the rather complex causal link between natural wealth and conflict, it is pertinent to examine another aspect of the resource-conflict nexus—the effects of warfare on natural resources. War has always left its mark on the natural environment, sometimes extremely long lasting. Even today some battlefields of the world wars cannot be cultivated or are dangerous to the population because unexploded mines and projectiles are still embedded in the soil. The destruction of the physical environment and natural resources has often been seen as merely "collateral damage" attributable to the inherently destructive nature of war, although such destruction has sometimes taken place as an end in itself, as a means of fighting the enemy or of blackmailing the world community.[36] As a result of the growth of environmental awareness, a greater appreciation has developed of the negative impacts of all forms of armed conflict on nature and the consequences these impacts might have for human well-being. This is well reflected in three key UN documents on this issue: the Stockholm Declaration of the United Nations Conference on the Human Environment (1972), the World Charter for Nature (1982), and the Rio Declaration on Environment and Development (1992). Principle 26 of the Stockholm declaration states, "Man and his environment must be spared the effects of nuclear weapons and all other means of mass destruction." Principle 5 of the World Charter for Nature proclaimed that "nature shall be secured against degradation caused by warfare or other hostile activities." Ten years later, the Rio Declaration even more explicitly asserted that "warfare is inherently destructive of sustainable development. States shall therefore respect international law providing protection for the environment in times of armed conflict and cooperate in its further development, as necessary."[37]

Since their inception, the laws and customs of war—a body of rules that govern the conduct of hostilities that in recent times has more often been referred to as international humanitarian law—have set limits on the right of belligerents to cause suffering and injury to people and to destroy objects. However, these laws have been slow to recognize that the environment requires protection by a set of rules specific to it. One would look in vain for the word "environment" in the traditional rules incorporated in Hague Convention IV of 1907[38] or the Geneva Conventions of 1949.[39] This is not to say that the older rules have no bearing on the protection of the environment and natural resources. A certain amount of protection is afforded by the general principles that govern the conduct of hostilities, such as military necessity, proportionality, distinguishing between combatants and civilians, and humanity. These principles build upon the fundamental tenet—codified in Hague Convention IV and elsewhere—that the right of belligerents to adopt a means of injuring the enemy is not unlimited but is confined to activities necessary to achieve military objectives.[40] Inasmuch as the environment and natural resources are *essentially* not a military objective but are civilian objects that enjoy protection, the application of these fundamental principles would warrant the following conclusions. First, no part of the natural environment may be attacked unless it is a military objective. Second, the destruction of any part of the natural environment is prohibited unless required by military necessity. And third, launching an attack against a military objective that can be expected to cause incidental damage to the environment that would be excessive in relation to the concrete and direct military advantage anticipated is prohibited. These rules and principles are clearly now part of customary international law.[41]

Minimum (albeit indirect) protection for the environment and natural resources is also provided by the provisions of Hague Convention IV that prohibit the destruction or seizure of enemy property not "imperatively demanded by the necessities of war"[42] and the similar provisions of the Fourth Geneva Convention that forbid the destruction of "real or personal property belonging individually or collectively to private persons, or to the State, or to other public authorities, or to social or cooperative organizations," unless "rendered absolutely necessary by military operations" during military occupation.[43] Natural resources are also protected by the rules that prohibit the pillaging of towns and places—that is, the systemic and violent appropriation by members of the armed forces of movable public or private property that belongs to the enemy state; to wounded, sick, or shipwrecked persons; or to prisoners of war.[44] These rules prohibit the willful destruction of the environment and the pillaging of natural resources, including forests and wildlife, in the same way that they protect other private or public property. At the same time, this does not mean that the parties engaged in an armed conflict are completely banned from using or otherwise exploiting natural resources. Hague Convention IV provides specific provisions that regulate the exploitation of natural resources of occupied territory:

> The occupying State shall be regarded only as administrator and usufructuary of public buildings, real estate, forests, and agricultural estates belonging to the hostile State, and situated in the occupied country. It must safeguard the capital of these properties, and administer them in accordance with the rules of usufruct.[45]

These rules must be read against the background of certain fundamental principles of the law of belligerent occupation. First, the occupant does not acquire sovereignty over the territory it occupies; it merely exercises de facto authority.[46] Second, occupation is a provisional situation, meaning that the rights of the occupant are transitory and are accompanied by an overriding obligation to respect the existing laws and rules of administration. Third, in exercising its powers, the occupant must be fulfilling its military needs and must respect the interests of the inhabitants. And fourth, the occupying power must not exercise its authority in order to further its own interests or to meet the demands of its own population.[47] This implies that the occupant cannot permit the exploitation of natural resources other than for the benefit of the occupied state.

Nevertheless, the rules of the Hague Convention and the Geneva Conventions offer only indirect protection to the environment and natural resources in times of armed conflict. Provisions specifically designed to protect the environment have made their way only into more recent instruments, mostly in response to the catastrophic environmental effects of the Vietnam War (1961–1975) brought about by the use of chemical herbicides and the bombardment of large areas of jungle forest.[48] The first of these instruments is the Convention on the Prohibition of Military or Any Other Hostile Use of Environmental Modification Techniques, popularly known as the Environmental Modification Convention (1976), which prohibits "military or any other hostile use of environmental modification techniques having widespread, long-lasting or severe effects as the means of destruction, damage or injury to any other State Party." This includes techniques that are used "for changing—through the deliberate manipulation of natural processes—the dynamics, composition or structure of the Earth, including its biota, lithosphere, hydrosphere and atmosphere, or of outer space."[49] The convention is therefore specifically intended to prevent the use of the environment as a means of warfare by prohibiting the deliberate manipulation of natural processes that could produce phenomena such as hurricanes, tidal waves, or changes in climate. It is also a response to the practice of the U.S. military in Vietnam of using cloud-seeding operations to extend the monsoon season in certain targeted areas of Laos in Operation Popeye.[50]

While the Environmental Modification Convention prohibits the hostile use of the environment as a means of warfare, the first additional protocol to the Geneva Conventions, which was adopted in 1977, explicitly prohibits the use of "methods or means of warfare which are intended, or may be expected, to cause widespread, long-term and severe damage to the natural environment."[51] This general rule, which is applicable to all acts of warfare, is further supplemented with specific provisions intended to protect the civilian population from the negative effects of warfare on the environment:

> Care shall be taken in warfare to protect the natural environment against widespread, long-term and severe damage. This protection includes a prohibition of the use of methods or means of warfare which are intended or may be expected to cause such damage to the natural environment and thereby to prejudice the health or survival of the population.[52]

Together with other rules of the protocol that have an indirect bearing on the matter, for example by prohibiting the destruction of "objects indispensable to the survival of the civilian population" or by prohibiting attacks on works or installations that contain dangerous forces, such as dams, dykes, and nuclear electrical generating stations,[53] these rules establish a clear and general obligation to protect the environment, including natural resources, during the conduct of hostilities. Furthermore, the provisions of the protocol are directly and indirectly supplemented by provisions in other international instruments that prohibit certain forms of weaponry and warfare that are particularly harmful to the environment[54] or that provide specific protection to designated areas.[55]

Taken together, however, many of the aforementioned provisions suffer from several limitations or setbacks. First, one wonders whether the fundamental principles of international humanitarian law are merely a bundle of very general principles that at best act as guidelines that do not protect the environment enough. Second, although many provisions of Hague Convention IV and the Geneva Conventions

TABLE 5.2. Main Instruments of International Humanitarian Law Relevant to Protecting the Environment and Natural Resources in Times of Armed Conflict

- Hague Regulations Concerning the Laws and Customs of War on Land (Annex to Convention IV of the Hague Conventions; 1907)
- Convention (IV) Relative to the Protection of Civilians in Time of War (Geneva Convention; 1949)
- Convention on the Prohibition of Military or Any Other Hostile Use of Environmental Modification Techniques (1976)
- Protocol Additional to the Geneva Conventions of 12 August 1949, and Relating to the Protection of Victims of Non-International Armed Conflicts (Protocol II, 1977)

protect property from destruction, they bow to the necessities of war and other limitations. This is not surprising considering that they were conceived in an era when concern about the environment and ecological awareness were almost nonexistent, particularly with respect to armed conflict. The provisions of Hague Convention IV and the fundamental principles of belligerent occupation do not always make it easy to discern the parameters of an occupant's legitimate powers over specific natural resources—for example, forests, wildlife, or mineral resources—in an occupied territory. This issue potentially impinges upon questions of private or public ownership, movable or immovable property, *munitions de guerre,* and (especially with nonrenewable resources) the limits of usufruct.[56]

In addition, the Environmental Modification Convention does not protect the environment as such, only its use as a weapon. And doubts have been raised about whether the first additional protocol to the Geneva Conventions offers significant protection to the natural environment except in the most serious cases. Its prohibition of damage that is "widespread, long-term and severe" is a cumulative requirement that imposes a very high (and somewhat nebulous) threshold, thereby making it absolutely clear that not all damage to the environment is outlawed. Moreover, as it focuses only on the protection of the territory of the enemy state, it does not protect the environment of one's own state, areas beyond national jurisdiction, and those parts of the environment that cannot be related to a single state, such as the ozone layer, the atmosphere, or the climate. In case of invasion, the protocol even entitles a state that is defending its national territory to destroy, remove, or render useless natural resources (e.g., foodstuffs, agricultural areas, or livestock) or natural resource–based works (e.g., irrigation works or installations that provide safe drinking water) where required by "imperative military necessity."[57]

Yet perhaps the most serious gap in the first additional protocol is that it does not afford direct protection to the environment in civil—that is, noninternational—armed conflicts, which are nowadays so prevalent. The protocol applies only when hostilities break out between two or more parties to it; it does not apply in cases of armed confrontations that occur within the territory of a single state. Common Article 3 of the Geneva Conventions of 1949, which protects the victims of internal armed conflicts, contains no provisions to protect specific objects or the environment during civil wars; it addresses only humanitarian issues in the strictest sense. The second additional protocol to the Geneva Conventions of 1977, which was devised to ensure better protection for the victims of internal armed conflicts and intended to develop and supplement Common Article 3, does not contain any express provisions about the protection of the environment, even though a number of its provisions might indirectly contribute to that end.[58]

The silence of Common Article 3 and both additional protocols on the rules that would afford direct protection to the environment in civil armed conflicts is partly mitigated by the fact that many provisions of international humanitarian law now function as customary law. They have not only become binding upon combating parties irrespective of their treaty obligations but in many cases have also become applicable to both international and internal armed conflicts. This is certainly the case with the fundamental principles that govern the conduct of hostilities.[59] A comprehensive study on customary international humanitarian law undertaken by the International Committee of the Red Cross suggests that even in situations of internal strife, methods and means of warfare must be employed with due regard to the protection and preservation of the natural environment.[60] Yet it is not clear whether the prohibition on the use of methods or means of warfare that are intended or may be expected to cause widespread, long-term, and severe damage to the natural environment has obtained the status of customary law in the case of internal conflicts.[61] Be that as it may, even in cases of civil armed conflicts, states must consider certain effects that hostilities might have on the environment. As the International Court of Justice pointed out in its advisory opinion on nuclear weapons, states are under the general obligation to ensure that activities within their jurisdiction and control respect the environment of other states or of areas beyond national control.[62]

In general, however, the protection afforded by international humanitarian law to the environment and natural resources has often been seen as insufficient. In response to the environmental consequences of the first Gulf War,[63] proposals were made to further develop the relevant rules in ways that lower the threshold of damage and provide greater protection to the natural environment in times of armed conflict. In response to that, the ICRC drafted the "Guidelines for Military Manuals and Instructions on the Protection of the Environment in Times of Armed Conflict" in 1993, which were subsequently endorsed by the General Assembly.[64] However, proposals that major treaties be revised or that new international instruments be adopted have generally been rejected. A number of scholars have therefore suggested that the defects of international humanitarian law could be considerably strengthened through the application of peacetime rules of international environmental law, which contain specific and precise provisions regulating the conduct of states with respect to certain activities and protect nearly all components of the environment without restriction to territorial borders.[65] Other scholars have raised doubts about whether these treaties are applicable in times of armed conflict. Yet as the ICJ pointed out in its advisory opinion on nuclear weapons in 1996:

> The issue is not whether the treaties relating to the protection of the environment are or are not applicable during an armed conflict, but rather whether the obligations stem-

> ming from these treaties were intended to be obligations of total restraint during military conflict.
>
> The Court does not consider that the treaties in question could have intended to deprive a State of the exercise of its right of self-defence under international law because of its obligations to protect the environment. Nonetheless, States must take environmental considerations into account when assessing what is necessary and proportionate in the pursuit of legitimate military objectives. Respect for the environment is one of the elements that go to assessing whether an action is in conformity with the principles of necessity and proportionality.[66]

With this, the court—which in its past jurisprudence had repeatedly clarified the rules of international humanitarian law—confirmed a long-standing belief that international humanitarian law neither can nor aims to prevent damage to the natural environment and resources altogether but rather seeks to minimize it to a level deemed tolerable.

On balance, the effectiveness of international law in protecting the environment and natural resources in times of armed hostilities has often been limited. Even in situations where it could have afforded protection (or kept damage at a "tolerable" level), its provisions have often not been effectively implemented or enforced. This has again been noted in UNEP's recent study, which generally concluded that the environment continues to lack effective protection during armed conflict.[67] According to UNEP, an important step would be to update the ICRC Guidelines on the Protection of the Environment during Armed Conflict (1994), particularly in view of the rapid transformations in the means and methods of warfare and the increase of civil conflicts. UNEP also proposed that the ILC examine the existing international law for protecting the environment during armed conflict and make recommendations about how it can be clarified, codified, and expanded. Moreover, UNEP advocated the drafting of a new legal instrument to protect vital natural resources and areas of ecological importance (e.g., important groundwater aquifers or habitats of endangered species) during armed conflicts and—at the institutional level—the establishment of a new permanent UN body to monitor legal infringements and address compensation claims for environmental damage resulting from armed conflicts. This new body—which should have powers to investigate and decide upon alleged violations of international law—would partly resemble the UN Compensation Commission that was established in the aftermath of the 1991 Gulf War (and will be presented in the next section). Last but not least, UNEP called for the strengthening of the ability of the Permanent Court of Arbitration to address disputes related to environmental damage during armed conflict.[68] However, it yet remains to be seen whether UNEP's calls will be heeded by the General Assembly and UN member states and whether something will be done to effectively protect the environment in times of armed conflict.

The UN's Role in Natural Resource Conflicts

While the principles and rules of international humanitarian law are intended to shield the environment and natural resources when armed hostilities break out, the UN Charter lays out strict rules for cases when resort to the use of force is permitted. Maintaining international peace and security was of utmost importance to the founding fathers of the United Nations, who—determined "to save succeeding generations from the scourge of war"—made it the primary purpose of the newly established organization. To that end, they pledged:

> to take effective collective measures for the prevention and removal of threats to the peace, and for the suppression of acts of aggression or other breaches of the peace, and to bring about by peaceful means, and in conformity with the principles of justice and international law, adjustment or settlement of international disputes or situations which might lead to a breach of the peace.[69]

The primary responsibility for maintaining or restoring peace and security was vested in the Security Council, which for that purpose was also equipped with a wide arsenal of powers. These are not limited to recommendations for the pacific settlement of disputes (Chapter VI), but in cases of a threat to peace, a breach of the peace, or an act of aggression, provide the council with the power to take mandatory action, including the use of force (Chapter VII). There can be little doubt that the founding fathers wanted to establish a principal organ with mandatory and supranational powers that would be different from the powerless Council of the League of Nations. In Article 25 of the Charter, all members agree "to accept and carry out" the decisions of the Security Council, which acts on their behalf in carrying out its duties.[70] Instead of the unanimity required in the decision making of the League's Council (which provided each League member with a de facto right of veto),[71] the drafters of the Charter introduced majority voting for the Security Council with a right of veto for five members only.[72]

Initially, the Security Council was primarily (if not exclusively) concerned with military threats to or breaches of the peace that would alter the status quo between states. Gradually, and under the influence of normative resolutions and political pressure from the General Assembly, the council expanded its interpretation of the concept of the threat to peace, acknowledging that such threats could also result from a refusal to change a status quo that was widely considered to be intolerable, as, for example, the denial of the right to self-determination in Southern Rhodesia and the mass and flagrant violations of human rights in apartheid South Africa.[73] At a meeting in Panama City in 1973—on one of the very rare occasions when a meeting took place outside UN headquarters in New

York—the council even recognized that the use of coercive measures, which affect the free exercise of permanent sovereignty over the natural resources of Latin American countries, may create situations that are likely to endanger peace and security.[74]

After the end of the Cold War in 1991, the council further expanded the concept of a threat to peace to include situations such as a massive flow of refugees across international frontiers,[75] acts of international terrorism, the proliferation of weapons of mass destruction,[76] and, most recently, piracy.[77] The council has also declared that "non-military sources of instability in the economic, social, humanitarian and ecological fields" can constitute threats to peace, although it has not yet made a determination of this kind in practice.[78]

The Security Council has also broadened its understanding of situations that constitute threats. These are no longer limited to specific countries or conflicts but can now include general situations, such as terrorist acts, the financing of terrorist acts, or the failure to deny terrorists access to certain weapons that constitute ongoing, open-ended threats to peace.[79] Moreover, since the end of the Cold War substantial changes have been made in the modus operandi of the council. It has begun to explore new avenues for discharging its special responsibilities for peace and security by creating the United Nations Compensation Commission in the aftermath of the Second Gulf War[80] and by establishing two ad hoc international criminal tribunals, one for the former Yugoslavia[81] and another for Rwanda.[82] The council has also drastically reshaped and refined its arsenal of coercive measures. In its recent practice, it has shifted away from imposing general economic sanctions on states and begun to target specific individuals by imposing selective travel bans and freezing financial assets.[83] Similarly, it has begun to target specific commodities that have fueled civil wars in African countries.[84]

While the Security Council has not been very successful so far in containing and resolving (let alone in preventing) resource-related conflicts, the council's past and more recent practices nevertheless reveal its potential for responding to various challenges that arise from the complex nexus between natural resources and violent conflict. Two instances are particularly significant in this regard: the establishment of the United Nations Compensation Commission and the imposition of various sanction regimes directed at specific natural resources. Whereas the former points to the council's potential role in addressing the externalities of armed conflict (i.e., the negative effects of hostilities on the environment and natural resources), the latter underlines the specific responsibilities of the council in addressing the causal linkages between natural resources and conflict (i.e., the ways that profits from plundering natural resources initiate, intensify, and sustain conflict). These two examples merit closer consideration.

The United Nations Compensation Commission

The Security Council's establishment in 1991 of the United Nations Compensation Commission (UNCC) in the aftermath of the Iraq's invasion of Kuwait in 1990 was one of its more unusual measures since the end of the Cold War. As a neutral, fact-finding, quasi-judicial body, the UNCC was to assess—and eventually award—claims for "any direct loss, damage, including environmental damage and the depletion of natural resources, or injury to foreign Governments, nationals and corporations, as a result of Iraq's unlawful invasion and occupation of Kuwait."[85] Established as a subsidiary body of the Security Council, the UNCC was governed by a Governing Council composed of the representatives of the current members of the Security Council at any given time and a secretariat. The claims for which Iraq was "liable under international law" were to be dealt with by commissioners, and claimants were to be compensated from the UN Compensation Fund.[86] The nature of the commission was rather unusual, although the process that the commissioners (sitting in three-member panels) were to administer was prima facie quite plainly judicial. However, as the UN Secretary-General observed:

> The Commission is not a court or an arbitral tribunal before which the parties appear; it is a political organ that performs an essentially fact-finding function of examining claims, verifying their validity, evaluating losses, assessing payments and resolving disputed claims. It is only in this last respect that a quasi-judicial function may be involved.[87]

In 1998, the UNCC Governing Council appointed the "F-4" Panel of Commissioners—composed of Thomas A. Mensah, José R. Allen, and Peter H. Sand—to review claims related to damage to or depletion of natural resources (including cultural heritage resources), claims related to damage to public health, and proposals for measures for cleaning up damage to the environment.[88] The panel reviewed approximately 170 claims that sought almost US$80 billion in compensation. Most were related to damage caused by pollutants from the oil well fires and damaged oil wells in Kuwait; oil spills into the Persian Gulf from pipelines, offshore terminals, and tankers; the influx of refugees into the territories of some of the claimant states; the operations of military personnel and of equipment, mines, and other tools of war; the exposure of the populations of the claimant states to pollutants from the oil well fires and oil spills in Kuwait and to hostilities and various acts of violence; and costs incurred by governments outside the region in providing assistance to alleviate the damage caused by the oil well fires, preventing and cleaning up pollution, and providing labor and supplies.[89] In June 2005, the commission issued its fifth and final report and made awards totaling approximately US$252 million to the governments of Kuwait, Iran, Jordan, and Saudi Arabia for the loss of various natural resources, crops, livestock, and water resources (including the cost of remediation) and damage to public health.[90] The claims-processing stage ended in 2005, and payments to claimants ended in 2007.[91]

From the perspective of environmental dispute settlement, the work of the commission has broken new ground, as it has established that there can be compensation for environmental damage resulting from international wars. It can well be expected that a similar body could be established for the compensation of war-related damage to the environment in the future.

Sanctions and Natural Resources

The Security Council's practice of imposing sanctions that target specific natural resources underlines its potential to directly address the nexus of instability and natural resources. In fact, as an organ vested with the primary responsibility for maintaining international peace and security, the council is the most appropriate institution for addressing this relationship. The Charter has endowed the council with broad discretion to decide what measures not involving the use of armed force are to be employed to maintain or restore international peace and security (Article 41) and, should these prove to be inadequate, with the possibility of taking "such action by air, sea, or land forces as may be necessary to maintain or restore international peace and security" (Article 42). This gives the council great flexibility to decide upon the most appropriate response for each particular case.

While Cold War politics for a long time prevented the Security Council from exercising its responsibilities as they had originally been envisioned, the 1990s brought a revival in council activity that is nowhere more apparent than with regard to coercive sanctions. These have taken various forms:

- **Economic sanctions** have been applied to prevent the flow of commodities or products to or from a target state or nonstate entity. Sometimes they were comprehensive (preventing the flow to and from a target of all commodities and products),[92] but more often they were limited to particular commodities or products, such as arms, petroleum, precious minerals, transport vehicles, or even luxury goods.
- **Specific financial sanctions** have been employed to prevent the flow of financial and other economic resources to or from a target, for example by freezing specific financial assets of the target.[93]
- **Non-economic sanctions** have been used to interrupt the target's relations with the external world in areas such as diplomatic relations, transportation, travel, aviation, and telecommunications and with regard to sporting, cultural, and scientific events.[94]

Sanctions regimes have rarely been static, and the council has expanded or reduced the extent and type of sanctions depending on the development of a specific situation. As a result, no two sanctions regimes have ever been exactly the same, except perhaps with some arms embargoes. The council's flexibility in choosing the most appropriate types of sanctions has been paired with considerable adaptability in selecting the targets of sanctions. While initially confined to states generally, sanctions have gradually begun to target rebel groups and, more recently, specific individuals and legal entities. With these "targeted sanctions," as the latter are called, the council considerably improved the effectiveness of coercive measures because it channeled the effects of sanctions to those who were directly undermining the maintenance or restoration of international peace and security.[95]

In a number of cases, the Security Council adopted sanctions regimes that prevented the flow of or affected the exploitation of natural resources. Initially, sanctions that banned or otherwise affected the exports or imports of natural resources formed part of broad sanctions regimes by which the council addressed a specific threat to peace or breach of the peace. These included sanctions to weaken a racist minority regime (Southern Rhodesia), to induce a government to extradite suspected terrorists (Libya),[96] to restore a democratically elected government to power (Haiti), or to bring an end to aggression (Iraq, Federal Republic of Yugoslavia). However, since the end of the 1990s, sanctions have increasingly been directed at specific commodities in order to suppress revenue from the illicit extraction and trafficking of "conflict goods," such as diamonds and timber, that have been used by armed groups to finance their activities during civil wars (for example, in Angola, Sierra Leone, Liberia, and Côte d'Ivoire). For similar reasons, sanctions have been applied to prevent the production of illegal commodities (such as the ban imposed on Afghanistan on chemicals used for the production of opium). Alternatively, resort has been made to sanctions that impose a selective travel ban on individuals who support illegal armed groups through illicit trade in natural resources and freeze the financial assets and economic resources of individuals and entities involved in such illicit trade.[97] By banning imports of selected natural resources or preventing the production of illicit commodities, these sanctions regimes have directly hit the main source of income of various armed groups or terrorists without severely affecting the whole population of those countries, as would have sometimes happened with "blunt" comprehensive economic sanctions. Not without reason, therefore, selected commodity sanctions and targeted sanctions that impose travel bans and freeze the assets of individuals have been termed "smart" sanctions.

Table 5.3 presents an overview of sanctions regimes that directly or indirectly included natural resources.

Table 5.3. UN Sanctions Regimes Related to Natural Resources

Country and Duration of Relevant Sanctions	*Type of Sanctions and Relevant Resolution Number and Date*
Southern Rhodesia (1966–1979)	• ban on supplying oil and oil products to Southern Rhodesia • ban on importing asbestos, iron ore, chrome, pig iron, sugar, tobacco, copper, meat and meat products, and hides, skins, and leather from Southern Rhodesia (S/RES/232, 16 December 1966)
Iraq (and occupied Kuwait) (1991–2003)	• ban on importing all commodities and products originating in Iraq or Kuwait, including any activities that facilitate exports or transshipment of any such commodities or products • ban on selling or supplying any commodities or products to any person or body in Iraq or Kuwait, including any activities that facilitate the sale or supply of any such commodities or products (S/RES/661, 6 August 1990)
Federal Republic of Yugoslavia (Serbia and Montenegro), in relation to Bosnia and Herzegovina (1992–1996)	• ban on importing all commodities and products originating in the Federal Republic of Yugoslavia, including any activities that facilitate exports or transshipment of any such commodities or products (with exceptions for transshipment through the Federal Republic of Yugoslavia of commodities and products that originate outside it) • ban on selling or supplying any commodities or products to any person or body in the Federal Republic of Yugoslavia, including any activities that facilitate the sale or supply of any such commodities or products (with exceptions for transshipment through the Federal Republic of Yugoslavia of commodities and products that originate outside it) (S/RES/757, 30 May 1992) • additional ban on transshipping crude oil, petroleum products, coal, energy-related equipment, iron, steel, other metals, chemicals, and rubber through the Federal Republic of Yugoslavia in order to ensure that these goods are not diverted (S/RES/787, 16 November 1992) • ban on unauthorized imports to, exports from, or transshipments through UN Protected Areas in Croatia and areas of Bosnia under the control of Bosnian Serb forces • ban on unauthorized transshipments of commodities and products through the Federal Republic of Yugoslavia on the Danube • ban on transporting all commodities and products across the land borders or to or from the ports of the Federal Republic of Yugoslavia (with exceptions) (S/RES/820, 17 April 1993)
Haiti (1993–1994)	• ban on selling or supplying petroleum or petroleum products to Haiti (S/RES/841, 16 June 1993)

Country and Duration of Relevant Sanctions	*Type of Sanctions and Relevant Resolution Number and Date*
Angola (UNITA) (1993–2002)	• ban on selling to or supplying UNITA with petroleum and petroleum products (S/RES/864, 15 September 1993) • ban on directly or indirectly importing all diamonds from Angola that are not controlled through the certificate of origin regime of Angola's Government of Unity and National Reconciliation (S/RES/1173, 12 June 1998)
Libya (1993–2003)	• ban on providing Libya with items used in refining and exporting petroleum and petroleum products (i.e., pumps, equipment designed for use in or that can possibly be used in exporting crude oil terminals, refinery equipment, and spare parts destined for any of those items), including providing any type of equipment, supplies, and grants of licensing arrangements for the manufacture or maintenance of such items (S/RES/883, 11 November 1993)
Sierra Leone (1997–2003)	• ban on selling or supplying petroleum and petroleum products to Sierra Leone (S/RES/1132, 8 October 1997) • ban on directly or indirectly importing all rough diamonds from Sierra Leone (S/RES/1306, 5 July 2000)
Afghanistan (Taliban/ Al Qaeda) (2000–ongoing)	• ban on selling, supplying, or transferring the chemical acetic anhydride (which is used in the production of opium) to any person in territory of Afghanistan under Taliban control or to any person for the purpose of any activity carried on in or operated from the territory under Taliban control (S/RES/1333, 19 December 2000)
Liberia (2001–2006, 2007)	• ban on directly or indirectly importing all rough diamonds from Liberia, whether or not such diamonds originated in Liberia (S/RES/1343, 7 March 2001, supplemented by S/RES/1521, 22 December 2003) • ban on importing all round logs and timber products originating in Liberia (S/RES/1478, 6 May 2003, supplemented by S/RES/1521, 22 December 2003)
Côte d'Ivoire (2005–ongoing)	• ban on importing all rough diamonds from Côte d'Ivoire (S/RES/1643, 15 December 2005)
Democratic Republic of the Congo (2008–ongoing)	• ban on travel and freezing of assets of individuals/entities supporting the illegal armed groups in the eastern part of the Democratic Republic of the Congo through illicit trade in natural resources (S/RES/1857, 22 December 2008)

In all the cases presented above, sanctions that imposed limitations on imports and/or exports of commodities or prevented the exploitation of natural resources were applied in conjunction with other forms of sanctions, which makes it difficult to isolate their separate effects. Undoubtedly, selected commodity sanctions have helped drain off the supply of funds to armed groups involved in resource-related conflicts, but one can only speculate about their individual contribution to the overall solution of these conflicts. Yet it cannot be denied that sanctions have been adopted sparingly rather than systematically, that they have required much time to be adopted, and that they have not always been successfully implemented, in spite of the efforts of various sanction committees, groups of experts, and peacekeeping operations that have assisted the Security Council in the monitoring and implementation of sanctions in practice.[98]

In the case of "blood diamonds," moreover, it is doubtful whether sanctions alone would have been enough to bring an end to their illicit trafficking. Illicit diamonds, which according to some estimates made up 20 percent of the value of the worldwide annual production of rough diamonds in 2000, were in fact not traded primarily in open markets but were sold directly to cutters and were stockpiled by buyers. Their origin was often disguised as they moved through tax havens or were sold through neighboring countries; these indirect routes made it almost impossible to track their trade. As a result, sanctions as such would not have been sufficient without addressing the question of diamond smuggling in general.[99] This was possible only through the creation of a diamond certification scheme, which was established (with the endorsement of the General Assembly)[100] as a joint effort by states, the private sector, and civil society on 5 November 2002. The Kimberley Process Certification Scheme, which came into force in 2003, created certificates of origin that now accompany most rough diamonds traded legitimately.[101] While strictly speaking not a UN creation, the scheme supplemented various UN sanctions regimes, and the Security Council encouraged participation in it and used it as a criterion for lifting embargoes on rough diamonds.

Similar certification schemes are now being considered for other precious minerals, such as copper, cobalt, cassiterite, wolframite, and coltan. For example, in 2006 the Group of Experts on the Democratic Republic of the Congo proposed that the Security Council start a pilot study that would lead to a certification scheme for mineral resources originating in the DRC on the basis of a "fingerprinting" system for precious materials. In a subsequent report, however, the group recorded broad disagreement among scientists as to the practical possibility of developing such a system.[102] Nonetheless, various governments funded studies to develop practical methods for tracing the origin of ore concentrates, in particular methods that rely upon the specific mineralogical and geochemical signatures of these ores. Some of these studies have already revealed promising results, although the methods are still costly and slow.[103] In the view of the Group of Experts, however, a solution could already be found in enhancing the DRC's capacity to properly process the administration of the exploitation and export of its natural resources. As a follow-up, the country announced in 2008 that it would set up, as a first step, a scheme to certify coltan, a mineral that is particularly valuable in many high-technology and medical applications. The creation of a "fingerprint" program for this ore was expected to be finalized in 2009, although the deadline proved to be too optimistic considering that researchers first had to map the country's coltan-producing areas and isolate unique characteristics of local ore samples. This and other initiatives—such as the recent introduction of the bipartisan Congo Conflict Minerals Act of 2009 in the U.S. Senate, which would require annual disclosure to the U.S. Securities and Exchange Commission of activities involving coltan, cassiterite, and wolframite from the DRC,[104] or the initiative for establishing a regional mechanism for certifying natural resources that is yet to be developed in the context of the International Conference on the Great Lakes Region[105]—should gradually lead to the creation of a global certification system for coltan as well as for other ores and thereby strengthen existing sanction regimes.

Whereas sanctions against selected commodities have contributed to bringing protracted violent conflicts to an end, the complexity of some situations makes it difficult if not impossible for the Security Council to effectively deploy its coercive measures. The clearest example of this is the situation in the Democratic Republic of the Congo. As early as 2003, the council condemned "categorically the illegal exploitation of the natural resources and other sources of wealth of the Democratic Republic of the Congo" and mandated a group of experts to report on illegal exploitation and on the link between such exploitation and the continuation of hostilities.[106] In 2006, that group presented extensive evidence proving the link between the mismanagement of mineral concessions and diversions of natural resources to finance violations of the UN arms embargo against the eastern DRC.[107] Upon the council's request that it prepare recommendations on feasible and effective measures,[108] the group presented a report in 2007 that noted that "urgent intervention against all forms of illegal natural resource exploitation is required" and recommended that the existing laws of the DRC, particularly the regulations governing natural resources and their orderly exploitation, be used as a baseline for a new sanctions regime. Moreover, the group was not opposed to imposing sanctions on the importation of specific commodities originating in the DRC, including petroleum.[109] Yet the Secretary-General cautioned against imposing any economic sanctions in the DRC in view of the negative impact that sanctions might have on artisanal miners who depend upon some of those commodities. In his view, the sanctions could perhaps cause inconvenience to their targets but their overall effect would be to only marginally diminish the general practices they were designed to curtail.[110] In a subsequent resolution, the Security Council urged the DRC "to strengthen its efforts . . . with a view to effectively extending the State's authority throughout its territory, establishing its control over the exploitation and export of natural resources, and improving the transparency of the management of the revenues from the exploitation of those natural resources."[111] Apparently the Security Council was receptive to the concerns of the Secretary-General that the imposition of sanctions would undermine the hard-won legitimacy of the country's first democratically elected president, who was sworn into power in 2006 after a lengthy election process.[112] Eventually, the Security Council responded to the problem of the linkage between the illegal exploitation of natural resources, illicit trade in such resources, and the proliferation and trafficking of arms in the DRC in another way. On 22 December 2008, the council decided to extend the travel ban and the freezing of assets (that had already been put in place in response to breaches of the arms embargo) to those individuals or entities "supporting the illegal armed groups in the eastern part of the Democratic Republic of the Congo through illicit trade of natural resources."[113] Meanwhile, the ICJ also addressed the exploitation of the DRC's natural resources; in a 2005 judgment, it pronounced upon the role of Uganda's forces in plundering the DRC's natural wealth.[114]

Most of the time, the attention of the Security Council has been focused on the exploitation of natural resources in the context of specific conflict situations. The council's response to the situation in the DRC was therefore ad hoc and tailored to those specific situations. Occasionally, however, the council has addressed the relationship between natural resources and conflict from a more general perspective. Thus, in its declaration adopted at a meeting of heads of state during the 2005 World Summit, the council expressed its determination to enhance the effectiveness of the United Nations in preventing armed conflicts and to monitor more closely situations of potential armed conflicts. It also reaffirmed "its determination to take action against illegal exploitation and trafficking of natural resources and high-value commodities in areas where it contributes to the outbreak, escalation or continuation of armed conflict."[115]

In 2007, on the initiative of Belgium, the Security Council also discussed the various roles that natural resources can play in armed conflict and postconflict situations.[116] In the presidential statement that ensued from those discussions, the council indicated the importance of improving the functioning of existing sanction committees and the various experts' groups and panels. In addition, it pointed to the role that UN missions and peacekeeping operations deployed in resource-endowed countries experiencing armed conflict could play in helping the governments concerned prevent the illegal exploitation of those resources from further fueling the conflict. Moreover, it recognized the importance of cooperation among source, transit, and destination countries in preventing and combating trafficking, illicit trade, and the illegal exploitation of natural resources and emphasized the important contribution of commodity monitoring and certification schemes. It also recognized the need for the private sector to contribute to good governance and to the avoidance of illegal exploitation of natural resources in countries in conflict. Finally, the council acknowledged the crucial role that the Peacebuilding Commission, together with other UN and non-UN actors, can play in postconflict situations in helping governments ensure that natural resources become an engine for sustainable development. The council emphasized that in such situations, lawful, transparent, and sustainable management and exploitation of natural resources are critical factors in maintaining stability and preventing a relapse into conflict and stressed in particular the important role of transparent and effective national security and customs structures for the effective control and management of natural resources.[117]

The presidential statement of 2007 indicates a growing realization that apart from negative measures in the form of sanctions, positive measures such as good governance assistance, international development cooperation, and human rights protection can also play a role both in preventing conflict and in postconflict peace building. Such measures, of course, will require the contribution of various UN organizations. As the Security Council stressed in the same statement, "the use, disposal and management of natural resources is a multi-faceted and cross sector issue that involves various UN organizations." Yet a crucial role will have to be played by the Security Council, which has the primary responsibility for all questions related to peace and security. Since the drafting of the UN Charter in 1945, the council's powers have expanded and extended to a degree probably not envisioned by its drafters. It was through innovation and adaptation that the council has been able to fulfill its tasks and responsibilities under the Charter in light of changing circumstances and new threats. The flexibility provided by the Charter in that respect will undoubtedly allow the council to continue to fulfill its primary responsibility for maintaining international peace and security and face the challenges of the twenty-first century.[118]

Assessment

This chapter demonstrates that for a variety of reasons there is a connection between natural resources and conflict. Gaining access to and securing a reliable supply of natural resources have for long been primary concerns in the policies of many states. This issue has received additional importance now that the demand for natural resources has become huge as a result of the increasing world population and the rapid development of a number of developing countries, most notably China and India. There is also an increasing awareness of the limits to growth owing to scarcity of resources. Furthermore, the proliferation of civil wars during the 1990s and the concentration of such conflicts in resource-abundant countries have called into question the relationship between natural resources and stability. The availability of natural resources is increasingly viewed as both a political and societal evil and an economic blessing. The conflicts in Angola, Liberia, and Sierra Leone, to mention just a few, were caused or fueled by access to natural resources. Furthermore, several interstate wars have been characterized if not sparked by rivalry over resources. For example, the invasion of Kuwait by Iraq in 1990 was sparked by a dispute over the transboundary Rumaila oil field, and a principal reason for the Rwandan and Ugandan aggression against the Democratic Republic of the Congo was to gain access to its extensive natural resources.

The growth of environmental awareness has been paralleled by a greater appreciation of the negative impacts of armed conflict on the physical environment. This is reflected in a comparison of the Stockholm Declaration of the United Nations Conference on the Human Environment of 1972 and the Rio Declaration on Environment and Development of 1992. Whereas Principle 26 of the UNCHE declaration states that "man and his environment must be spared the effects of nuclear weapons and all other means of mass destruction," the Rio Declaration is more explicit: "Warfare is inherently destructive of sustainable development. States shall therefore respect international law providing protection for the environment in times of armed conflict and cooperate in its further development, as necessary." Gradually, provisions specifically designed to protect the environment have been added to the regulations governing the conduct of hostilities. However, the effectiveness of international law in protecting the environment and natural resources in times of armed conflict has often been limited. Even in situations where it could have afforded protection, its provisions often have not been effectively implemented or enforced. So far, in the UN context such provisions have been applied only to those states that have lost wars, such as Iraq through the work of the United Nations Compensation Commission. Much more needs to be done in this regard. The solution is not only in clarifying and strengthening existing law, but especially in devising effective ways to monitor infringements and open up avenues to institute and enforce compensation claims for environmental damage resulting from armed conflicts.

The Security Council, too, has given its attention to the nexus of instability and natural resources and has worked to prevent the illicit trafficking of "conflict goods" such as diamonds and timber. A key aspect of the council's work in this area has been the establishment of various sanctions regimes. These put a stop on the illegal trade of valuable natural resources, thereby suppressing the revenues from which armed groups financed their activities during civil wars, or targeted individuals who supported such illegal trade. Sanctions regimes successfully addressed some of the causes that for many years had been central to the perpetuation of conflicts in western and eastern Africa. Yet, all too often, the imposition of sanctions came much too late. Also a key part of the council's work has been the establishment of a regime to certify the origin of certain precious natural resources. This regime has sought to ban the trade in "blood diamonds" that has been central to the perpetuation of conflict in western and eastern Africa.[119] In general terms, it can be concluded that the Security Council has not always been instrumental in containing and resolving (let alone preventing) resource-related conflicts. The ICJ has proven to be more useful in this respect, as is elaborated in some detail in the next chapter.

6

The Role of the International Court of Justice in the Settlement of Natural Resource Disputes

- **Maritime Delimitation and Fishery Disputes**
- **Natural Resources in the Settlement of Territorial Disputes**
- **Disputes over Water Management**
- **Natural Resources and Armed Conflict**
- **Aborted Cases on Natural Resource Disputes**
- **Assessment**

Not every dispute over natural resources leads to violent conflict. A number of conflicts have been resolved by peaceful means through negotiation, mediation, or judicial processes. As a complement to the previous chapter, this chapter examines the role natural resources have played in the decisions of the International Court of Justice, the principal judicial organ of the United Nations. The main functions of the court are to adjudicate disputes between states (so-called contentious cases) and to give advisory opinions requested by other principal organs of the UN or specialized agencies. As is demonstrated in this chapter, natural resources play a distinctive role in the jurisprudence of the ICJ. Sometimes they are treated as factors that could influence the outcome of maritime delimitation, sometimes as features that have a bearing on the course of land boundaries. In other cases they implicitly determine questions of title to territory or are explicitly part of the subject matter of the dispute. Thus, one thing is certain: natural resources have often determined the outcome of the court's decisions.

Maritime Delimitation and Fishery Disputes

The question of access to natural resources has figured most prominently in maritime delimitation cases or in cases where the court had to pronounce upon the legality of unilaterally established maritime boundaries. Access to natural resources played a role in one of the earliest cases on the docket of the court, the *Fisheries* case (1951), where the court was asked to determine whether the method Norway used to delimit its fishery zone was in accordance with international law at that time. The proceedings were instituted by the United Kingdom, which protested Norway's method of delimitation because it impinged upon the interests of the British trawlers fishing in the area. In assessing the legality of Norway's method of delimitation, the court took account of the importance of access to natural resources. In view of the court, "there is one consideration not to be overlooked, the scope of which extends beyond purely geographical factors: that of certain economic interests peculiar to a region, the reality and importance of which are clearly evidenced by a long usage."[1] The court had in mind especially the fishery resources on which the Norwegian coastal population depended. In the end, the court concluded that the method Norway used to delimit its fishery zone was not contrary to international law.

Access to marine resources played an even stronger role in a similar dispute that emerged two decades later, in 1972: the *Fisheries Jurisdiction Cases,* in which the United Kingdom and Germany asked the court to determine the legality of Iceland's zone of exclusive fisheries jurisdiction that extended fifty nautical miles from the shore. The United Kingdom and Germany, whose trawlers were most seriously affected by Iceland's unilateral extension of its fishery jurisdiction, asked the court to declare that Iceland's actions had no foundation in international law. In 1974, the court delivered its judgments on the merits, in which it observed that in order to reach an equitable solution of the dispute it was necessary that the preferential fishing rights of Iceland, as a state specially dependent on coastal fisheries, be reconciled with the traditional fishing rights of the United Kingdom and Germany.[2] In the view of the court, neither right was absolute: The preferential rights of coastal states were limited by the extent of their special dependence on the fisheries and by their obligation to take account of the rights of other states and conservation principles, whereas the established rights of other fishing states were limited by the special dependence of coastal states on fisheries and their obligation to take account of the rights of other states as well as conservation principles.[3]

According to the court, this meant that all three states had an obligation to take full account of each other's rights and of any fishery conservation measures, the need for which was shown to exist in those waters. The court particularly noted that:

> It is one of the advances in maritime international law, resulting from the intensification of fishing, that the former *laissez faire* treatment of the living resources of the sea in the high seas has been replaced by a recognition of a duty to have due regard to the rights of other States and *the needs of conservation for the benefit of all.* Consequently, both Parties have the obligation to keep under review the fishery resources in the disputed waters and to examine together, in the light of scientific and other available information, the

> measures required for the conservation and development, and equitable exploitation, of those resources, taking into account any international agreement in force between them . . . as well as such other agreements as may be reached in the matter in the course of further negotiation.[4]

The court consequently found that Iceland's unilateral extension of its exclusive fishing rights to fifty nautical miles from the shore could not be imposed upon the United Kingdom and Germany and that Iceland therefore could not unilaterally exclude British and German fishing vessels from its fishery zone or otherwise impose restrictions on the activities of those vessels. Moreover, it instructed all three countries to undertake negotiations in order to reach an equitable solution of their differences concerning their respective fishery rights.

The judgment thus represented an attempt to balance the interests of the states involved and to find a compromise regarding access to the fishery resources of the high seas. It also pointed to the need for conservation and can hence be interpreted as one of the early judgments predating the later principle of sustainable use of natural resources. However, Iceland not only refused to appear before the court throughout the proceedings but subsequently also refused to implement the judgment. A year after the court delivered its final judgment, Iceland actually extended its fisheries jurisdiction to 200 nautical miles from the shore, in line with the trend that was emerging at the third United Nations Conference on the Law of the Sea, which began in 1973.[5]

The court frequently treated natural resources as a factor that could influence the outcome of maritime delimitation. This point was emphasized early on in the *North Sea Continental Shelf* cases (Federal Republic of Germany v. Denmark; Federal Republic of Germany v. Netherlands, both 1969), where the court was asked to determine the principles and rules of international law and outline the factors that should be taken into account by the Netherlands, Germany, and Denmark in the delimitation of their continental shelves. The court initially noted that "the question of natural resources is less one of delimitation than of eventual exploitation."[6] Nevertheless, it stated that one of the factors states should take into consideration in the delimitation of areas of the continental shelf was the "unity" (i.e., the fact that they lay along several national boundaries) of any mineral deposits. The court was guided by considerations of equity:

> It frequently occurs that the same deposit lies on both sides of the line dividing a continental shelf between two States, and since it is possible to exploit such a deposit from either side, a problem immediately arises on account of the risk of prejudicial or wasteful exploitation by one or other of the States concerned.[7]

In the course of their negotiations regarding delimitation, therefore, the three states had to consider "the physical and geological structure, and natural resources, of the continental shelf areas involved" so far as they were "known or readily ascertainable."[8]

In the court's subsequent jurisprudence, natural resources have on occasion been invoked as a general consideration that should influence the outcome of maritime delimitation. In the *Continental Shelf* case of 1982, where the court was asked to pronounce upon the principles and rules of international law to be employed in delimiting the continental shelf areas of Tunisia and Libya, both parties invoked various economic factors that should be taken into account in the delimitation process. Tunisia drew attention to its relative poverty vis-à-vis Libya regarding natural resources such as agriculture and minerals. In contrast, Libya had an abundance of oil and gas wealth as well as agricultural resources. Tunisia also pointed out that the fishing resources of its coastal areas should be taken into account as a supplement to its national economy in the nation's efforts to eke out a living and survive as a country. Libya argued that the presence or absence of oil or gas in the oil wells in the continental shelf areas of either party should play an important part in the delimitation process.[9]

The court was not keen on accepting general economic considerations as a factor that should be taken into account in the delimitation of the continental shelf areas. In view of the court:

> They [economic considerations] are virtually extraneous factors since they are variables which unpredictable national fortune or calamity, as the case may be, might at any time cause to tilt the scale one way or the other. A country might be poor today and become rich tomorrow as a result of an event such as the discovery of a valuable economic resource.[10]

Nevertheless, the court felt that the presence of oil wells in an area to be delimited might be an element to be taken into account in the process of weighing all relevant factors to achieve an equitable result.

Economic factors were again invoked in the delimitation process in the *Continental Shelf* case of 1985, where the court had to spell out the principles and rules of international law to be applied in delimiting the continental shelf areas of Libya and Malta. Malta contended that its lack of energy resources, its requirements as an island developing country, and the range of its established fishing activity were all relevant considerations that should be used not to dictate the delimitation but to contribute to an assessment of the equitableness of the delimitation. The court, however, did not consider that delimitation should be influenced by the relative economic position of the two states in question

> in such a way that the area of continental shelf regarded as appertaining to the less rich of the two States would be somewhat increased in order to compensate for its inferiority in economic resources. Such considerations are totally unrelated to the underlying intention of the applicable rules of international law.[11]

The court repeated its earlier position that the natural resources of the continental shelf under delimitation "so far as known or readily ascertainable" might well constitute relevant circumstances that the delimitation should take into account, inasmuch as those resources were also the essential objective envisaged by states when they put forward claims to seabed areas containing them. As a practical matter, however, the parties had not furnished the court with any indications of the size and nature of the natural resource deposits on the continental shelf.[12]

In subsequent cases where the court had to draw a boundary line that divided not only the continental shelf but also other maritime areas, the role of natural resources in the delimitation process gradually changed. Natural resources became less a factor that influenced the drawing of a boundary line and more a yardstick to check the equitableness of the outcome of a delimitation. In the *Delimitation of the Maritime Boundary in the Gulf of Maine Area* (Canada v. United States of America, 1984), a chamber of the court was for the first time asked to describe the course of a single maritime boundary to divide the continental shelf and fishery zones simultaneously. The chamber observed that such a delimitation could be carried out only by applying a criterion or combination of criteria that did not give preferential treatment to either the continental shelf (and its nonliving resources) or the fishery zone. The court chamber had to give preference, therefore, to more neutral criteria that were better suited for use in a multipurpose delimitation.[13]

When it drew the actual delimitation lines, the chamber did not take into account various economic factors the parties had invoked (particularly, the importance to the economy of the neighboring areas of the fishing resources of the area to be delimited or to the economic dependence on those resources of the populations of the adjoining coastal areas[14]). However, in the final instance, it considered them relevant for assessing the equitable character of the delimitation line.[15] As the chamber explained,

> The respective scale of activities connected with fishing—or navigation, defence or, for that matter, petroleum exploration and exploitation—cannot be taken into account as a relevant circumstance or . . . as an equitable criterion to be applied in determining the delimitation line. What the Chamber would regard as a legitimate scruple lies rather in concern lest the overall result, even though achieved through the application of equitable criteria and the use of appropriate methods for giving them concrete effect, should unexpectedly be revealed as radically inequitable, that is to say, as likely to entail catastrophic repercussions for the livelihood and economic well-being of the population of the countries concerned.[16]

After careful assessment, the chamber concluded that there was no reason to fear that any such danger would arise on account of its choice of delimitation line, since it left on the Canadian side the part of the Georges Bank where the greatest concentrations of the sedentary species exploited by Canadian fishermen were to be found (particularly scallops) and it left entirely to the United States those parts where the same sedentary species had been traditionally fished by the United States. The same line more or less neatly divided other fishery areas. Moreover, the delimitation line divided the main areas where the subsoil was being explored for its mineral resources, leaving on either side broad expanses in which prospecting had been undertaken in the past and might be resumed to the extent desired by the parties.[17] In sum, because the delimitation line did not entail serious economic repercussions for either of the parties, the court did not find it necessary to correct it.

Availability of and access to natural resources did serve an important corrective function in another maritime delimitation case that involved the drawing of a single delimitation line. This was the case concerning the *Maritime Delimitation in the Area between Greenland and Jan Mayen* (Denmark v. Norway; 1993), where the court was asked to delimit the fishing zone and continental shelf area in the waters between Greenland and the Norwegian island of Jan Mayen. In the first place, the court considered whether the natural resources of the continental shelf that had to be delimited "so far as known or readily ascertainable" could constitute relevant circumstances to be taken into account in the delimitation, but eventually it found that little information had been given to it in that respect, although reference had been made to the possibility that there were deposits of polymetallic sulfides and hydrocarbons in the area.[18]

Of much greater importance in this case, however, were the fishery resources of the waters in the sea area that had to be delimited. These were an important fishing ground for summer capelin, a migratory fish that fishermen of both states exploited commercially. The court stated that the parties were essentially in conflict over access to fishery resources and deemed it appropriate, therefore, "to consider whether any shifting or adjustment of the median line, as fishery zone boundary, would be required to ensure equitable access to the capelin fishery resources for the vulnerable fishing communities concerned."[19] As the seasonal migration of the capelin presented a pattern that centered on the southern part of the area of overlapping claims, the delimitation of the fishery zone had to reflect this fact. While the court thought that "no delimitation in the area could guarantee to each Party the presence in every year of fishable quantities of capelin in the zone allotted to it by the line," it found it appropriate to adjust and shift eastward the median line between Greenland and Jan Mayen in order to assure Denmark equitable access to the capelin stock.[20]

Natural resources have not played this kind of significant role in subsequent court rulings on maritime delimitation questions. In the case concerning *Maritime Delimitation and Territorial Questions between Qatar and Bahrain* (2001), the court had to determine the single maritime boundary between the maritime areas of the seabed, the subsoil, and the superjacent waters appertaining to Qatar and Bahrain.

The contending states invoked fishery resources as factors that could have a bearing on the delimitation. Bahrain claimed that there were a significant number of pearling banks in one of the areas to be delimited that constituted a special circumstance to be taken into consideration. Qatar denied that Bahrain had ever had exclusive rights to exploit the pearling banks, as those fisheries had always been considered as common to all tribes along the shores of the gulf. The court, however, did not consider the existence of pearling banks as a circumstance that would justify an eastward shifting of the equidistance line as requested by Bahrain, in part because of the fact that the pearling industry had effectively ceased to exist a considerable time before the case came to the court.[21]

The location of natural resources is not the only factor that has played a role in maritime delimitation cases. Patterns of exploitation, particularly as reflected in the granting of oil concessions, have also played a significant role. In the *Continental Shelf* case between Tunisia and Libya (1982), the court examined the question of the significance of oil concessions for maritime delimitation. While it did not take into consideration the line that Libya asserted was the boundary of its petroleum zones, it nevertheless found that close to the coasts the concessions of the parties showed and confirmed the existence of a modus vivendi.[22] Therefore, the court—which had not been asked to itself draw the line of delimitation but merely to specify the principles and rules of international law to be applied by the parties when negotiating the delimitation agreement—considered that this delimitation was to be effected in accordance with equitable principles and taking account of all relevant circumstances, including "the land frontier between the Parties, and their conduct prior to 1974 in the grant of petroleum concessions, resulting in the employment of a line seawards from Ras Ajdir at an angle of approximately 26° east of the meridian."[23]

The question of oil concessions was more systematically addressed in the case concerning the *Land and Maritime Boundary between Cameroon and Nigeria* (2002), where the court was asked, among other issues, to extend Cameroon's maritime boundary with Nigeria up to the limit of the maritime zones that international law places under their respective jurisdictions (i.e., the territorial sea, the continental shelf, and exclusive economic zones). The court had to address the question of whether the practices of the parties in extracting oil provided helpful indications for purposes of delimiting their respective maritime areas. Nigeria contended that a state's practice with regard to oil concessions was a decisive factor in the establishment of maritime boundaries and argued that the court could not redistribute such oil concessions between the states by adjusting the delimitation line.[24] The court noted that it had already had occasion to deal with the issue of oil concessions in maritime delimitation disputes:

> Overall, it follows from the jurisprudence that, although the existence of an express or tacit agreement between the parties on the sitting of their respective oil concessions may

> indicate a consensus on the maritime areas to which they are entitled, oil concessions and oil wells are not in themselves to be considered as relevant circumstances justifying the adjustment or shifting of the provisional delimitation line. Only if they are based on express or tacit agreement between the parties may they be taken into account.[25]

However, in this case there was no agreement between the parties regarding oil concessions and thus the court ruled that the oil situation did not matter for the maritime delimitation.[26]

Practice regarding natural resource exploitation has also been invoked in more recent cases. In the *Territorial and Maritime Dispute between Nicaragua and Honduras in the Caribbean Sea* (2007), where the court ruled on a dispute relating to the delimitation of the maritime areas, the question arose of whether the practice of the two states and third parties confirmed the existence of a tacitly agreed boundary along the fifteenth parallel. Honduras argued that its oil concession practice coincided with the fifteenth parallel. Moreover, Honduras produced sworn statements by a number of fishermen attesting to their belief that the fifteenth parallel had always been the maritime boundary.[27] However, the court did not find the evidence put forward before it sufficiently compelling to presume the existence of a tacit agreement.

In the case concerning *Maritime Delimitation in the Black Sea* (2009), the court determined the maritime boundary dividing the continental shelf and the exclusive economic zones of Romania and Ukraine. Ukraine invoked a number of licensing activities relating to the exploration of oil and gas deposits within the disputed area, claiming that its oil-related activities constituted relevant circumstances that warranted changing a provisional equidistance line. It also argued that the boundary it claimed corresponded generally to the limit of the exclusive fishing zones of both states, alleging that its coastguard had been actively policing a part of the delimitation area and had assumed the sole responsibility of intercepting illegal fishing vessels.[28] However, upon weighing the evidence, the court considered the resource-related activities of the two states had no particular role in its deliberations. Moreover, the court noted that resource-related criteria had been treated very cautiously in decisions of international courts and tribunals.[29] With respect to fisheries, the court concluded that there was no evidence that any delimitation line other than the one claimed by Ukraine would be "likely to entail catastrophic repercussions for the livelihood and economic well-being of the population," referring thereby to the test developed by one of the court's chambers in the Gulf of Maine case (1984).[30]

Natural Resources in the Settlement of Territorial Disputes

Natural resources also played a role in cases where the court had to determine land boundaries or otherwise decide upon questions of sovereignty over parts of territory. In some cases, natural resources were features that influenced the course of the boundary line; in other cases, they determined the location of the boundary line. One such case was the *Frontier Dispute* of 1986, where a chamber of the court decided on the location of the frontier between Burkina Faso and Mali. In determining the line of the common boundary, the chamber was twice faced with a situation where natural resources straddled the frontier. Guided by considerations of equity, it divided these resources between the parties. With regard to the frontier pool of Soum, the chamber was of the opinion that in the absence of any precise indication in the texts of the position of the frontier line, the line should divide the pool in two in an equitable manner.[31] When similarly faced with a lack of more precise and reliable information concerning the relationship between the frontier line and the pool of In Abao, it concluded that the boundary had to run through the pool in such a way as to divide it between the two parties (previously the frontier line had located it solely within the territory of Burkina Faso).[32]

Equitable access to natural resources was again one of the concerns of the court in the *Case Concerning Kasikili/Sedudu Island* (1999), where the court pronounced upon the boundary between Botswana and Namibia around the island known in Namibia as Kasikili and in Botswana as Sedudu and to determine the legal status of the island in inland waters. In that instance, the court thought it important to maintain the shared nature of the channels that constituted the boundary between the two states. While it attributed the island to Botswana, it also unanimously resolved that in the two channels around Kasikili/Sedudu Island, the nationals of Botswana and Namibia and the vessels flying the flags of each state should enjoy equal national treatment.[33]

A state's endowment with natural resources has been advanced among the considerations that should influence the course of a land boundary, as is the case in maritime delimitation cases. This was the case in the *Land, Island and Maritime Frontier Dispute* of 1992, where a chamber of the court determined the course of the land boundary between El Salvador and Honduras. It also had to determine the legal situation of the islands and maritime spaces in the Gulf of Fonseca. El Salvador put forward a body of arguments referred to as "arguments of a human nature," contending that the international legal principle of *uti possidetis juris* was not the only one to be taken into consideration in determining the land boundary. These arguments stated that population pressures in El Salvador had created a need for territory and that Honduras was relatively sparsely populated. El Salvador claimed that Honduras also enjoyed superior natural resources (e.g., water for agriculture and hydroelectric power). The chamber recalled the view of the court in the 1982 Continental Shelf case that "economic considerations of this kind could not be taken into account for the delimitation of the continental shelf areas appertaining to two States" and from that concluded that "still less can they be relevant for the determination of a land frontier which came into existence on independence."[34]

Natural resources also played a distinctive role in cases where the court decided upon questions of sovereignty over disputed territory. In such situations, the court has taken into account activities relating to the exploitation or preservation of natural resources as evidence of acts of administration, the so-called *effectivités*. In the *Case Concerning Sovereignty over Pulau Ligitan and Pulau Sipadan* (2002), where the court decided whether the islands of Ligitan and Sipadan belonged to Malaysia or Indonesia, it took account of Malaysia's activities to regulate the collection of turtle eggs and the establishment of bird sanctuaries on the two disputed islands and on that basis eventually decided that Ligitan and Sipadan belong to Malaysia. In absence of other clear proof of title over the two islands, the court was of the opinion that Malaysia's actions to protect turtles and birds "must be seen as regulatory and administrative assertions of authority over territory which is specified by name."[35] So far, this has been the only case in history in which a natural resource—the laying of eggs by turtles!—played such a determining role in a judgment.

The *Frontier Dispute* case of 2005 was another instance where acts of administration regarding natural resources were important. In that case, the court decided on the course of the land boundary between Benin and Niger. Both parties relied on their authorization of the felling of palm trees as regulatory and administrative assertions of authority over territory, but the court did not weigh this evidence as heavily as it did the fact that Niger had created game reserves and national parks in the disputed area. The court used the boundaries of these in determining the course of the boundary.[36]

Activities relating to the exploitation of natural resources were also decisive in the *Territorial and Maritime Dispute between Nicaragua and Honduras in the Caribbean Sea* (2007), where in the course of maritime delimitation between the two states, the court determined which of the parties had sovereignty over four cays in the Caribbean Sea. Having established that neither of the states had clear title to the coral islands in question, the court had to weigh which of the two parties had shown more convincing evidence about some actual exercise or display of authority over the disputed islands. The court noted that fishing activities took place under Honduran authorization in the waters around the islands, which in the view of the court showed that the Honduran authorities issued fishing permits with the belief that Honduras had a legal entitlement to the maritime areas around the islands derived from that nation's title over the islands. The court also considered that the permits issued by the Honduran authorities allowing the construction of houses and the storage of fishing equipment on one of the cays could also be regarded as a display, albeit a modest one, of the exercise of authority.[37] At the same time, the court found the evidence relating to the offshore oil exploration activities of both parties to have no bearing on the islands in dispute, although it took into account, under the category of public works, the authorization to construct an antenna in the context of authorized oil exploration activities.[38] Having weighed the arguments and evidence put forward before it, the court eventually decided that the disputed islands belonged to Honduras, as the activities invoked by Honduras evidenced an intention and will to act as sovereign and constituted a modest but real display of authority over the four islands.

In other disputes regarding the legal status of a territory, natural resources have played a less central role, although they have determined the general circumstances in the context of which the court had to reach a decision. This was the case in *Western Sahara* (1975), where the General Assembly asked the court to give an advisory opinion on the question of whether Western Sahara was at the time of colonization by Spain a territory belonging to no one (*terra nullius*) and, if that was not the case, on the question of what the legal ties were between the territory and the Kingdom of Morocco and the Islamic Republic of Mauritania. The court's opinion was intended to assist the General Assembly in properly exercising its functions concerning the decolonization of Western Sahara.

Before answering the questions posed to it, the court observed that the legal regime of Western Sahara, including its legal relations with neighboring territories, could not properly be appreciated without reference to the special characteristics of the territory, which, at the time of colonization by Spain, largely determined the way of life and social and political organization of the peoples inhabiting it. In this regard, the court observed, among other characteristics, that "the area of this desert . . . was being exploited, because of its low and spasmodic rainfall, almost exclusively by nomads, pasturing their animals or growing crops as and where conditions were favourable" and that "the territory . . . had a sparse population that, for the most part, consisted of nomadic tribes the members of which traversed the desert on more or less regular routes dictated by the seasons and the wells or water-holes available to them." From this, the court adduced:

> These various points of attraction of a tribe to particular localities were reflected in its nomadic routes. But what is important for present purposes is the fact that the sparsity of the resources and the spasmodic character of the rainfall compelled all those nomadic tribes to traverse very wide areas of the desert. In consequence, the nomadic routes of none of them were confined to Western Sahara; some passed also through areas of southern Morocco, or of present-day Mauritania or Algeria, and some even through further countries.[39]

In view of the court, it was for the court to examine the question of the "legal ties" between Western Sahara and Morocco and Mauritania at the time of colonization by Spain in the context of this kind of territory and this kind of social and political organization of the population.

Disputes over Water Management

In the jurisprudence of the court, one case stands out for the way the court dealt with water as a natural resource. In *Gabčíkovo-Nagymaros Project* (1997), the court ruled in a dispute between Hungary and Slovakia that arose out of the construction of two series of locks on the Danube that had been designed under the joint Gabčíkovo-Nagymaros Project between the two countries to develop the water resources of the river and to develop the energy, transport, and agricultural sectors of both Hungary and Slovakia. The project, which was essentially aimed at the production of hydroelectricity, the improvement of navigation on the Danube, and the protection of the areas along the banks against flooding, was suspended because of environmental concerns and subsequently abandoned by Hungary. In turn, Slovakia put the project into operation by a provisional solution, which among other things entailed a unilateral diversion of the Danube onto the territory of Slovakia. In addressing whether Slovakia was entitled to proceed to the provisional solution and to put it subsequently into operation, the court observed that the operation of the provisional solution led Slovakia

> to appropriate, essentially for its use and benefit, between 80 and 90 per cent of the waters of the Danube before returning them to the main bed of the river, despite the fact that the Danube is not only a shared international watercourse but also an international boundary river.[40]

Although Hungary's decision not to implement its obligations arising out of the project constituted a violation of its legal obligations, the court was of the opinion that that "cannot mean that Hungary forfeited its basic right to an equitable and reasonable sharing of the resources of an international watercourse."[41] In the opinion of the court, therefore, Slovakia's action of putting the provisional variant into operation was illegal. The court also rejected the argument that the provisional variant could be justified as a countermeasure against Hungary's failure to comply with its treaty obligations because Slovakia's action was not proportionate. Considering that the effects of a countermeasure must be commensurate with the injury, the court held that Slovakia,

> by unilaterally assuming control of a shared resource, and thereby depriving Hungary of its right to an equitable and reasonable share of the natural resources of the Danube—with the continuing effects of the diversion of these waters on the ecology of the riparian area of the Szigetkoz—failed to respect the proportionality which is required by international law.[42]

In view of the court, Hungary was thus entitled to compensation for the damage sustained as a result of the diversion of the Danube, as "Slovakia deprived Hungary of its rightful part in the shared water resources, and exploited those resources essentially for their own benefit."[43]

The court eventually established that the treaty governing the project had not ceased and that Hungary and Slovakia both were still under a legal obligation to consider how the multiple objectives of the treaty could best be served. The court observed that the project's impact on the environment was a key issue in that respect. According to the court, current norms and standards were to be taken into consideration and given proper weight, not only when states contemplated new activities but also when continuing with activities begun in the past. In this regard, the court recalled, in what has become a well-known comment, that "the need to reconcile economic development with protection of the environment is aptly expressed in the concept of sustainable development."[44] For the purposes of the case, this meant that the parties together should look afresh at the effects on the environment of the operation of the project.

A recent addition to the case law on water management disputes is the court's judgment in the *Dispute regarding Navigational and Related Rights* (Costa Rica v. Nicaragua, 2009). The case concerned a dispute between Costa Rica and Nicaragua regarding the precise extent of Costa Rica's right of free navigation on the San Juan River and the concomitant right of Nicaragua to regulate such navigation, as stipulated by the terms of the 1858 Treaty of Limits between the two states. This treaty fixed their common boundary along the right bank of the San Juan River, thereby establishing Nicaragua's sovereignty over the entire river, while at the same time affirming Costa Rica's navigational rights on the lower course of the river and establishing other rights and obligations for both parties. Among other issues the court had to decide whether Costa Rica's right to free navigation extended to certain modern-day activities, such as transport of passengers and tourism, as well as to navigation of its official vessels, and whether or not Nicaragua had the right to impose specific requirements on Costa Rican vessels and passengers traveling on those vessels.

By adopting a rather evolutionary approach to treaty interpretation, the court decided that Costa Rica's 1858 treaty right of free navigation nowadays included the transport of passengers and tourists, which were, for that purpose, not required to obtain Nicaraguan visas or to purchase Nicaraguan tourist cards. It also held that the inhabitants of the Costa Rican bank of the San Juan River have the right to navigate on the river between the riparian communities for the purposes of meeting the essential needs of everyday life that require expeditious transportation. At the same time, the court denied that navigational rights applied to Costa Rican vessels carrying out police functions (except in those specific situations when they are used to provide essential services for the inhabitants of the riparian areas) or those used for the exchange of police personnel on border posts along the river bank and of the resupply of these posts. On the other hand, the court considered that Nicaragua has the right to require Costa Rican vessels and their passengers to stop at the first and last Nicaraguan posts on their route along the San Juan River and to require persons traveling on the San Juan River to carry a passport or an identity document. Moreover, the court considered that Nicaragua has the right to issue departure clearance certificates to Costa Rican vessels, to impose timetables for navigation of these vessels, and to require them to display the Nicaraguan flag.

The court also had to decide whether Nicaragua could impose certain regulations for the purpose of environmental protection—an issue that was clearly not covered by the 1858 treaty. While Costa Rica considered those regulations to be a pretext to imposing other requirements, Nicaragua insisted that the San Juan River and the Nicaraguan shore adjacent to it were extremely important and gravely threatened natural reserves that are covered by a number of international treaties for environmental protection.[45] The court eventually agreed with Nicaragua, considering that "over the course of the century and a half since the 1858 Treaty was concluded, the interests which are to be protected through regulation in the public interest may well have changed in ways that could never have been anticipated by the Parties at the time: protecting the environment is a notable example."[46] In view of the court, therefore, in adopting certain measures of environmental protection, Nicaragua was "pursuing the legitimate purpose of protecting the environment."[47]

Lastly, in addition to navigational and related rights, the court had to separately address the issue of subsistence fishing. Costa Rica submitted that there had long been a practice allowing the inhabitants of the Costa Rican bank of the San Juan to fish in that river for subsistence purposes—a practice that had survived the Treaty of 1858 and that had evolved into a customary right that according to Costa Rica, Nicaragua was now bound to observe. Considering that Nicaragua had usually tolerated the limited use of the San Juan for noncommercial fishing by Costa Rican riparians and that subsistence fishing had without doubt occurred over a very long period, the court had no problem in concluding that "fishing by the inhabitants of the Costa Rican bank of the San Juan river for subsistence purposes from that bank is to be respected by Nicaragua as a customary right."[48] What led the court to such conclusion was the fact that "the practice, by its very nature, especially given the remoteness of the area and the small, thinly spread population, is not likely to be documented in any formal way in any official record." What was particularly significant was "the failure of Nicaragua to deny the existence of a right arising from the practice which had continued undisturbed and unquestioned over a very long period."[49] At the same time, the court considered that this right "would be subject to any Nicaraguan regulatory measures relating to fishing adopted for proper purposes, particularly for the protection of resources and the environment."[50] And furthermore, it would not extend to fishing from vessels on the river.[51]

Pulp Mills on the River Uruguay, currently on the docket of the court, is another case where the importance of water as a natural resource will be central to the deliberations of the court. In this case, the court was asked in 2006 to decide in a dispute between Argentina and Uruguay arising out of Uruguay's authorization, construction, and commissioning of two pulp mills on the River Uruguay. Argentina was especially concerned about the effects of such activities on the quality of the waters of the River Uruguay and on the areas affected by the river. While the case has not yet been decided on its merits, environmental concerns about the River Uruguay, a shared natural resource, have already been highlighted in the early phase of court proceedings. In deciding on the provisional measures Argentina requested in 2006, the court considered that

> the present case highlights the importance of the need to ensure environmental protection of shared natural resources while allowing for sustainable economic development; whereas it is in particular necessary to bear in mind the reliance of the Parties on the quality of the water of the River Uruguay for their livelihood and economic development; whereas from this point of view account must be taken of the need to safeguard the continued conservation of the river environment and the rights of economic development of the riparian States.[52]

Natural Resources and Armed Conflict

A number of cases the court has decided have dealt with situations involving natural resources in times of armed conflict. Thus, in *Armed Activities on the Territory of the Congo* (2005), the court determined whether Uganda engaged in the illegal exploitation of natural resources on the territory of the Democratic Republic of the Congo and in the pillaging of that state's assets and wealth and whether it failed to take adequate measures to prevent the illegal exploitation of the DRC's resources by persons under its control or failed to punish those persons. For this purpose, the DRC relied on several relevant General Assembly resolutions, including the Declaration on Permanent Sovereignty over Natural Resources of 1962, which—in the view of the DRC—continued to apply at all times, including during armed conflict and occupation.

On the basis of evidence submitted to it, the court concluded that officers and soldiers of the Uganda Peoples' Defence Forces (UPDF), for the conduct of which Uganda was considered responsible (including the most high-ranking officers), were involved in the looting, plundering, and exploitation of the DRC's natural resources and that the military authorities had not taken any measures to put an end to those acts.[53] In the view of the court, Uganda could in all circumstances be held responsible for the acts of members of its military forces in the DRC whether or not it was an occupying power in particular regions. Thus, whenever members of the UPDF were involved in the looting, plundering, and exploitation of natural resources in the territory of the DRC, they acted in violation of the law applicable in armed conflict (*jus in bello*), which prohibits the commission of pillage and similar acts by a foreign army in the territory where it is present.[54] The court also found that Uganda violated its duty of vigilance by not taking adequate measures to ensure that its military forces did not engage in the looting, plundering, and exploitation of the DRC's natural resources.[55] Yet the court did not uphold the DRC's contention that Uganda violated the principle of permanent sovereignty over natural resources, as "there is nothing in these General Assembly resolutions[56] which suggests that they are applicable to the specific situation of looting, pillage and exploitation of certain natural resources by members of the army of a State militarily intervening in another State." The court, in fact, did "not believe that this principle is applicable to this type of situation."[57]

It is not clear from this judgment whether the ICJ is of the opinion that the principle of sovereignty over natural resources is not applicable at all in times of armed conflict under *jus in bello* or whether its inapplicability relates to the particular circumstances of this case—that is, the actions committed by individual members of the Ugandan army while the court had no credible evidence at its disposal "to prove that there was a governmental policy of Uganda directed at the exploitation of natural resources of the DRC or that Uganda's military intervention was carried out in order to obtain access to Congolese resources."[58] The issue was discussed by various judges of the court. In the view of Judge Abdul G. Koroma in a separate opinion, the court's acknowledgment of the customary international law character of the 1962 declaration implies that the rights and interests formulated therein "remain in effect at all times, *including during armed conflict and occupation.*"[59] In contrast, ad hoc Judge James L. Kateka (who had been nominated by Uganda) argued in his dissenting opinion that the concept of permanent sovereignty over natural resources as embodied in General Assembly Resolution 1803 (XVII) "was adopted in the era of decolonization and the assertion of the rights of newly independent States."[60] In his view it would be inappropriate to invoke this concept in a case involving two African countries.

The role of natural resources in times of armed conflict has occasionally also featured in the court's advisory opinions. In *Legality of the Threat or Use of Nuclear Weapons* (1996), the court was requested to give an advisory opinion to the General Assembly on the question of whether the threat or use of nuclear weapons is in any circumstance permissible under international law. For that purpose, the court had to address the arguments advanced by some states that any use of nuclear weapons would be unlawful according to the existing norms relating to the safeguarding and protection of the environment. The court recognized that the environment is under daily threat and that the use of nuclear weapons could constitute a catastrophe for the environment, adding that

> the environment is not an abstraction but represents the living space, the quality of life and the very health of human beings, including generations unborn. The existence of the general obligation of States to ensure that activities within their jurisdiction and control respect the environment of other States or of areas beyond national control is now part of the corpus of international law relating to the environment.[61]

However, the court did not believe that the treaties relating to the protection of the environment contained obligations of total restraint during military conflict that were intended to deprive a state of the exercise of its right of self-defense under international law, although it stated that states had to take environmental considerations into account when they assess what is necessary and proportionate in the pursuit of legitimate military objectives. In view of the court, these provisions embody a general obligation to protect the natural environment against widespread, long-term, and severe environmental damage. The court stated that international law, by which it meant specifically Articles 35 and 55 of Additional Protocol I to the Geneva Conventions, prohibits methods and means of warfare that are intended, or may be expected, to cause such damage and prohibits attacks against the natural environment by way of reprisals. In view of the court, these are powerful constraints for all the states that have subscribed to those provisions. In sum, while existing international law relating to the protection and safeguarding of the environment did not specifically prohibit the use of nuclear weapons, it indicated important environmental factors that were to be taken into account in the context of implementing principles and rules of the law applicable in armed conflict.[62]

Natural resources also played an important role in the advisory opinion in *Legal Consequences of the Construction of a Wall in the Occupied Palestinian Territory* (2004), where the General Assembly asked the court to determine what the legal consequences were of the construction of the wall that Israel, the occupying power, was building in the Occupied Palestinian Territory.

In determining, first of all, whether the construction of the wall violated the relevant principles and rules of international law (including the human rights instruments the court found to be applicable to the Occupied Palestinian Territory), the court took into account the fact that the construction of the wall had led to serious repercussions for agricultural production. Relying on a number of sources, the court noted that approximately 10,000 hectares of the West Bank's most fertile agricultural land that the Israeli Occupation Forces had confiscated had been destroyed during the first phase of the wall construction and that this involved the disappearance of vast amounts of property, notably private agricultural land and olive trees, wells, citrus groves, and hothouses upon which tens of thousands of Palestinians relied for their survival. The court further noted that the construction had led to increasing difficulties for the population of the occupied territories regarding access to primary sources of water, since by constructing the wall Israel was in a position to effectively annex most of the aquifer system of West Gaza.[63] These findings led the court to conclude that the construction of the wall and its associated regime impeded the inhabitants of the Occupied Palestinian Territory from exercising the right to an adequate standard of living as proclaimed in the 1966 International Covenant on Economic, Social and Cultural Rights and in the 1989 United Nations Convention on the Rights of the Child. The destruction of personal property Israel had carried out as it was building the wall were, in view of the court, not absolutely necessary for military operations.[64]

The court determined that Israel had the obligation to cease constructing the wall. Moreover, given that the construction entailed the requisition and destruction of homes, businesses, and agricultural holdings, the court further found that Israel had the obligation to make reparations for the damage caused to all the natural or legal persons concerned and hence to return the land, orchards, olive groves, and other immovable property seized from any natural or legal persons. In cases where such restitution proved to be materially impossible, Israel had to compensate the persons in question for the damage suffered.[65] However, these and other recommendations in the Wall Opinion have not been implemented.

Aborted Cases on Natural Resource Disputes

Besides the variety of cases where natural resources in one way or another have played a role in the decisions of the court, there have been several cases where natural resources lay at the very heart of the disputes brought before the court but owing to jurisdictional or other issues could not be decided on their merits. One of those was the *Anglo-Iranian Oil Company* case mentioned in chapter 2, where the court, had it not lacked jurisdiction, would have had to pronounce upon the United Kingdom's claim that the socialist government of Iran, led by Prime Minister Mohammad Mossadegh, had unlawfully terminated petroleum concessions held by the Anglo-Iranian Oil Company.[66] In a provisional order of 5 July 1951, the court prescribed a number of interim measures that parties should observe in order to prevent an aggravation of the dispute. These included permission for the Anglo-Iranian Oil Company to continue operating pending settlement of the dispute.[67] Iran refused to comply with this order, and the United Kingdom subsequently submitted the issue to the Security Council. After an extensive debate the Security Council decided to await the outcome of the court's deliberations regarding its jurisdiction on the matter. On 2 July 1952, the court decided, by nine votes to five, that it was not competent to decide the case on its merits because a concessionary contract cannot be considered an international treaty on the interpretation and application of which the court would have jurisdiction.[68] Although oil resources were central to the dispute, they did not feature in the court's decision.

In *Aegean Sea Continental Shelf* of 1978, the court was similarly without jurisdiction to decide a dispute between Greece and Turkey regarding disputed islands and their appertaining continental shelf in the Aegean Sea. Greece asked the court to adjudge that certain islands belonged to its territory and were entitled to a portion of the continental shelf and to decide the course of the boundary between the portions of the continental shelf appertaining to Greece and Turkey. Greece also asked the court to declare that it was entitled to exercise sovereign and exclusive rights over its continental shelf for the purpose of researching and exploring it and exploiting its natural resources and that Turkey was not entitled to undertake any activities on the Greek continental shelf without its consent.[69] But the court found itself without jurisdiction to entertain Greece's application.

In *Certain Phosphate Lands in Nauru* (1992), the International Court of Justice was asked to decide a dispute brought by Nauru against Australia concerning the rehabilitation of phosphate lands on the Island of Nauru. Nauru's claims related to the phosphate lands that had been mined until 1967 by a board known as the British Phosphate Commissioners, under whose control and management approximately one-third of the island's phosphates had been extracted to meet the agricultural requirements of the United Kingdom, Australia, and New Zealand. After Nauru became independent in 1968, it demanded that the United Kingdom, Australia, and New Zealand rehabilitate mined-out lands but without success. Nauru thus turned to the court for the settlement of the dispute. The court found itself competent to decide the case on its merits, in spite of Australia's preliminary objections to its jurisdiction.[70] At the merits stage, the court would have had to address the principles of permanent sovereignty over natural resources and questions regarding international responsibility for environmental harm, and perhaps to determine the amount of reparation Australia should pay. However, before a decision on the merits could be delivered, Australia and Nauru reached a friendly settlement of the case. This entailed a cash settlement and development cooperation assistance, although Australia stipulated that these payments were being made without prejudice to its position in the case and that it bore no responsibility for the rehabilitation of the phosphate lands.

In another case that touched on questions of permanent sovereignty over natural resources, *East Timor* (1995), the court found that it had no jurisdiction to entertain the claims Portugal had brought against Australia. The claims concerned an agreement that Australia had negotiated and concluded with Indonesia—which was occupying East Timor at that time—concerning the delimitation and the exploration and exploitation of the continental shelf in the area of the Timor Gap. The court considered that it could not decide the case in the absence of Indonesia from the proceedings, but had it found that it had jurisdiction in the case, it would have had to decide whether Australia had infringed or was infringing on the right of the people of East Timor to self-determination, to territorial integrity and unity, and to permanent sovereignty over East Timor's natural wealth and resources.[71]

Finally, the court found it had no jurisdiction to entertain Spain's application in the 1998 *Fisheries Jurisdiction* case, in which it was asked to pronounce upon the legality of Canada's amendments to its Coastal Fisheries Protection Act and related regulations and upon the specific actions Canada had taken on the basis of the amended act and regulations that included its pursuit, boarding, and seizure on the high seas on 9 March 1995 of the *Estai,* a fishing vessel that was flying the Spanish flag. As a result of the wording of Canada's declaration, by which it otherwise accepted the compulsory jurisdiction of the court, the court could not adjudicate upon a dispute that in principle revolved around the legality of fishery conservation measures that Canada had imposed outside its exclusive economic zone.[72]

Assessment

The ICJ is often a somewhat underestimated part of the UN system. However, this chapter demonstrates that the court has played an important role in settling a good number of conflicts related to natural resources (as summarized in table 6.1) and has thus contributed to the maintenance of international peace and security. The chapter also highlights the important role of the court in consolidating, clarifying, and further developing new principles and concepts relating to maritime delimitation, fishery management, transboundary resources, and people's right to resources. This applies in particular to new concepts, such as the application of the principle of equity in maritime delimitation, the establishment of fishery zones, the duty to cooperate in the management of transboundary resources, and the concept of sustainable development. Third, while a judicial body ought to function independently, there is reason to note that a better use could be made of the court to achieve the overall goals of the United Nations. In general terms, the knowledge of members of the other principal UN organs about the role, the jurisprudence, and the potential contribution of the court to stability and peaceful settlement of international disputes is strikingly poor.

TABLE 6.1. Overview of International Court of Justice Cases Involving Natural Resource Issues

Name of Case	Parties	Year of Application	Year of Judgment	Natural Resource Issue at Stake
Fisheries	United Kingdom v. Norway	1949	1951	Fisheries (marine living resources)
Anglo-Iranian Oil Co. (aborted)	United Kingdom v. Iran	1951	1952 (jurisdiction)	Termination of petroleum concessions
North Sea Continental Shelf	Federal Republic of Germany/Netherlands; Federal Republic of Germany/Denmark	1967	1969	Natural resources of continental shelf (mineral deposits)
North Sea Continental Shelf	Federal Republic of Germany/Denmark	1967	1969	Natural resources of continental shelf (mineral deposits)
Fisheries Jurisdiction	United Kingdom v. Iceland; Germany v. Iceland	1972	1974	Fisheries (marine living resources)
Western Sahara	Advisory Opinion	1974	1975	Scarcity of resources
Aegean Sea Continental Shelf (aborted)	Greece v. Turkey	1976	1978 (jurisdiction)	Natural resources of continental shelf
Continental Shelf	Tunisia/Libya	1978	1982	Endowment with natural resources, oil wells, oil concessions
Delimitation of the Maritime Boundary in the Gulf of Maine Area	Canada/United States	1981	1984	Natural resources of continental shelf, fisheries
Continental Shelf	Libya/Malta	1982	1985	Natural resources of continental shelf
Frontier Dispute	Burkina Faso/Mali	1983	1986	Frontier pools

(continued on next page)

Table 6.1. Overview of International Court of Justice Cases Involving Natural Resource Issues *(continued)*

Name of Case	Parties	Year of Application	Year of Judgment	Natural Resource Issue at Stake
Certain Phosphate Lands in Nauru (aborted)	Nauru v. Australia	1989	1992 (preliminary objections)	Phosphates
Land, Island and Maritime Frontier Dispute	El Salvador/Honduras; Nicaragua intervening	1986	1992	Endowment with natural resources
Maritime Delimitation in the Area between Greenland and Jan Mayen	Denmark v. Norway	1988	1993	Fisheries (predominantly)
East Timor (aborted)	Portugal v. Australia	1991	1995 (jurisdiction)	Natural resources of continental shelf
Legality of the Threat or Use of Nuclear Weapons	Advisory Opinion	1994	1996	Protection of environment and use of nuclear weapons
Gabčíkovo-Nagymaros Project	Hungary/Slovakia	1993	1997	International watercourse/water/river
Fisheries Jurisdiction (aborted)	Spain v. Canada	1995	1998 (jurisdiction)	Fishery conservation measures
Kasikili/Sedudu Island	Botswana/Namibia	1996	1999	Shared watercourse
Maritime Delimitation and Territorial Questions between Qatar and Bahrain	Qatar v. Bahrain	1991	2001	Fisheries
Land and Maritime Boundary between Cameroon and Nigeria	Cameroon v. Nigeria; Equatorial Guinea intervening	1994	2002	Oil concessions

Sovereignty over Pulau Ligitan and Pulau Sipadan	Indonesia/Malaysia	1998	2002	Regulation of natural resource use (collection of turtle eggs, bird sanctuaries)
Legal Consequences of the Construction of a Wall in the Occupied Palestinian Territory	Advisory Opinion	2003	2004	Destruction of natural resources in occupied territory
Frontier Dispute	Benin/Niger	2002	2005	Regulation of natural resource use (establishment of game reserves and national parks)
Armed Activities on the Territory of the Congo	Democratic Republic of the Congo v. Uganda	1999	2005	Looting, plundering, illegal exploitation of natural resources in armed conflict
Territorial and Maritime Dispute between Nicaragua and Honduras in the Caribbean Sea	Nicaragua v. Honduras	1999	2007	Oil concessions, fishing activities
Maritime Delimitation in the Black Sea	Romania v. Ukraine	2004	2009	Oil concessions, fishing activities
Dispute regarding Navigational and Related Rights	Costa Rica v. Nicaragua	2005	2009	Shared watercourse; river; fishery resources
Pulp Mills on the River Uruguay	Argentina v. Uruguay	2006	pending	Shared watercourse

Note: In Contentious Proceedings, when a dispute is brought before the court by a unilateral application filed by one state against another state, the names of parties in the official title of the case are separated by the abbreviation v. (for the Latin *versus*). When a dispute is submitted to the court on the basis of a special agreement between two states, the names of the parties are separated by a forward slash (/).

Source: Data drawn from International Court of Justice, "List of All Cases Referred to the Court since 1946 by Date of Introduction," available at http://www.icj-cij.org/docket/index.php?p1=3&p2=2.

7

The UN's Conceptual Contribution: Conclusions and Challenges

- **Main Roots of UN Involvement in Natural Resource Management**
- **Principal Actors in UN Involvement in Natural Resource Management**
- **Conceptual Contributions and Implications**
- **Assessment**

The debate on natural resource policies within the United Nations spans a period of nearly sixty-five years. The United Nations has been instrumental in generating widespread interest in rational resource management, taking into account developmental, environmental, and social dimensions. UN organs as well as its specialized agencies have made significant intellectual contributions and undertaken numerous standard-setting and operational activities to foster the economic development and sustainable use of natural resources. By way of conclusion, this chapter identifies the main roots of the UN's involvement with natural resource management. Second, it discusses the principal actors and persons within the UN system engaged in the formation of natural resource policies. Third, it demonstrates how the political debates in various UN forums and conferences have resulted in new concepts for resource management and regimes based on those concepts. These include resource sovereignty (on land and at sea), the global commons, shared resources, and sustainable development. This chapter summarizes these intellectual contributions and reflects on their implications for the future. Lastly, the chapter identifies a number of key functions the United Nations has performed during these sixty-five years of debate on natural resource management and highlights some shortcomings.

Main Roots of UN Involvement with Natural Resource Management

Four roots of the United Nations involvement with natural resources can be distinguished. Shortly after its establishment, the world organization began to deal with the management of natural resources in response to wartime concerns of the Allied Powers, particularly the United States, about "security of supply and access to natural resources." Early projects of the UN system sought to reconstruct the natural resource bases destroyed during the war (e.g., forestry projects by the FAO), to promote the development of and spread knowledge about the effective use of natural resources (e.g., by ECOSOC), to discuss how to take world economic interests into account in the exploitation of natural resources (e.g., by the General Assembly), to avoid depletion of fish stocks, and to achieve "maximum sustainable yield" (e.g., by the law of the sea conferences).

Soon, however, colonial peoples and representatives of newly independent states began to argue that they should benefit fully from the exploitation of "their own" natural resources. The UN became the central arena for their claims. Consequently, they asked UN bodies to review, if appropriate, "inequitable" legal arrangements from the past with other states or foreign companies. The central proposition of the claimants was that the natural resources had always been theirs (their "birthright"). Hence, permanent sovereignty is the second root of the UN's involvement with natural resource management.

A third root emerged in the 1960s that developed more fully after the Conference on the Human Environment in Stockholm in 1972. Gradually environmental concerns entered the debate on resource management in response to alarming information about pollution, scarcity of natural resources, and resource depletion. This gave rise to new concepts, such as rational use, optimal use, and ultimately the notion of "sustainable use of natural resources." It took until the 1990s, however, for this concept to crystallize into a principle of international law, as exemplified by the incorporation of sustainable development into treaties[1] and international jurisprudence[2] after the Conference on Environment and Development in Rio in 1992. Subsequent global conferences have also been instrumental in developing and consolidating this particular root of UN involvement with natural resource management.

The devastating effects of armed conflict on natural resource management gave rise to a fourth root. The prevailing view had been that the possession of natural resources was a blessing for a country as well as for the people living in resource-rich areas. However, especially in the last decade of the twentieth century, possessing natural resources and controlling the exploitation of those resources increasingly seemed to fuel armed conflict, sometimes between states (e.g., Iraq and Kuwait, Israel and Palestine), but all too often within states (e.g., Cambodia, Democratic Republic of Congo, Liberia, Sierra Leone, Somalia). Internal conflicts frequently take root in rivalry for access to natural resources, such as oil, gas, diamonds, timber, and fresh water. In fragile states with various groups struggling for power, the possession of areas rich in natural resources is often the key to power. This new awareness of the relationship between natural resources and armed conflict is now sometimes called the "resource curse."

Principal Actors in UN Involvement with Natural Resource Management

The debate on natural resource policies within the United Nations has involved all six principal organs: ECOSOC, the General Assembly, the Security Council, the Trusteeship Council, the International Court of Justice, and the Secretariat.

Initially, ECOSOC and the General Assembly played pivotal roles. ECOSOC was the first to address the postwar concerns about scarcity of natural resources and the effective use of natural resources. For this purpose, it organized conferences and was instrumental in collecting data and disseminating that data to relevant specialized agencies such as the FAO and the World Bank. In doing so, it performed the role Article 62 of the UN Charter envisaged for it as the coordinating agency within the UN system. ECOSOC also established the ad hoc Committee on the Survey Programme for the Development of Natural Resources, a forerunner of the Standing Committee on Natural Resources established in 1970. This committee was supposed to help ECOSOC plan and coordinate activities within the UN system to manage natural resources and make recommendations to governments and UN bodies—such as the UNDP—about appropriate priorities for exploration and exploitation.

The Standing Committee on Natural Resources analyzed the implementation of the principle of permanent sovereignty over natural resources and tracked trends in national legislation, joint ventures, service agreements, government ownership of natural resource ventures, transfer of technology, and technical cooperation in developing countries. However, despite the solid information generated by its work, the committee's status has remained marginal during its existence.

The institutional profile of the Standing Committee contrasts with the political profile of one of ECOSOC's main functional commissions, the Commission for Human Rights—replaced in 2006 by the Human Rights Council.[3] During the 1950s, the rights of colonial peoples to economic self-determination and permanent sovereignty over natural resources were hotly debated in this body. However, as the decolonization period ended, the General Assembly became the preferred body for debate on these issues. The assembly has approved a considerable number of resolutions and declarations that stress the right of developing countries to exercise control over their natural resources and the need to enhance developing countries' role in the processing, marketing, and distribution of natural resources. In a later phase the General Assembly initiated the global conferences on environment and development. Furthermore, some of its subsidiary organs such as the United Nations Conference on Trade and Development, the United Nations Environment Programme, and the United Nations Development Programme have evolved as major think tanks on natural resource policies and environmental conservation.

The Security Council has also addressed issues relating to natural resource management. For example, in 1991 the council held Iraq liable for the environmental damage and depletion of natural resources caused by its invasion and occupation of Kuwait.[4] The Security Council has also occasionally used Chapter VII of the UN Charter to impose trade embargoes on states where natural resources have fueled or sustained violence and has empowered expert panels to look into specific situations. An example of such a panel is the Group of Experts that investigated the plundering of natural resources in the Democratic Republic of Congo.[5] In September 2005, the council, resolving to strengthen its effectiveness in conflict prevention, particularly in Africa, affirmed in resolution 1625 "its determination to take action against illegal exploitation and trafficking of natural resources and high-value commodities in areas where it contributes to the outbreak, escalation or continuation of armed conflict." In 2006, the council reaffirmed this policy with resolution 1653 about the Great Lakes Region.[6]

In more general terms, the International Court of Justice has settled various land boundary and maritime delimitation disputes in which natural resources were at stake.[7] Maritime delimitation disputes have come more frequently before the court, and several of these cases have involved access to marine resources.[8] Its advisory opinion on *Legality of the Threat or Use of Nuclear Weapons* (1996) declared that states have "the responsibility to ensure that activities within their jurisdiction or control do not cause damage to the environment of other States or of areas beyond the limits of national jurisdiction." It went on to argue that this obligation was "now part of the corpus of international law relating to the environment."[9] In *Gabčíkovo-Nagymaros Project (Hungary v. Slovakia)*, the court recognized that the "need to reconcile economic development with protection of the environment is aptly expressed in the concept of sustainable development."[10] More recently, the ICJ has taken up the issue of the relationship between natural resources and armed conflict. In the specific context of armed conflict, the ICJ pronounced in *Armed Activities on the Territory of the Congo (Democratic Republic of the Congo v. Uganda)* that the looting, plundering, and exploitation of natural resources by Ugandan military forces was a violation of the laws and customs of war.[11]

Apart from these principal UN organs, special mention should be made of the United Nations Conference on Trade and Development and the United Nations Environment Programme. UNCTAD originally focused on articulating the specific interests of developing countries in obtaining higher (and more just) prices for their raw materials as well as increasing their share in the processing, marketing, and distribution of those resources. More recently, UNCTAD has worked on regulating the activities of multinational enterprises and on the special interests of developing countries in climate change policies. UNEP is another UN organ that has focused on issues related to natural resources. Important examples include the Regional Seas Programme (which now involves ten regions and 120 countries), integrated environment and development programs for the catchment areas of large river systems (such as the Zambezi and the Mekong), and UNEP's work to lay the groundwork for various multilateral and regional environmental treaties, including those relating to the ozone layer (1985), dangerous waste products (1989), and biological diversity (1992).

As the main body responsible for coordinating UN development work, the UNDP has played an important role in the UN's involvement in natural resource management, especially through its operational activities in the field. It has frequently provided developing countries assistance in properly managing the human and natural resources required for their economic growth and human development. The UNDP's importance has increased as a result of the Rio conference. At this conference member states identified the UNDP as an entity that would play a "crucial role" in the implementation of international policy on sustainable development and earmarked it as the "lead agency" in organizing UN system efforts toward capacity-building for sustainable development at all levels.

Persons—like institutions—do matter in the initiation of ideas and projects. The UN debate on global resource management testifies to this. In chapter 1 we discussed the significant conceptual contribution made by the Argentinean José León Suárez with respect to the exploitation of the natural resources of the seas and the general interests of mankind. In the succeeding chapters, many other persons were mentioned and should perhaps be briefly recalled here. For example, the Chilean delegate Carlos Valenzuela played an important role during the 1950s in conceiving the principle of permanent sovereignty over natural resources and generating political support for it, as exemplified by the incorporation in the identical articles 1 of the draft covenants on human rights in 1955 and the adoption of the declaration on this principle in 1962.

American president Harry Truman gave the starting shot for coastal states' rush to the resources of the sea with his proclamations related to control over the minerals of the continental shelf and over fishery resources. The opposite movement of internationalization of maritime resource regimes was inaugurated by Prince Wan Waithayakon of Thailand, who stated as early as 1958 at the law of the sea conference that the sea was the common heritage of mankind and that the law of the sea should ensure the preservation of that heritage for the benefit of all.[12] It was the Maltese Arvid Pardo who elaborated these ideas and presented forward-looking proposals on a new law of the sea in a four-hour speech in the General Assembly in 1967. With respect to outer space, the Argentinean Aldo Armando Cocca launched similar ideas of applying the notion of the common heritage of mankind to outer space and the natural resources of the celestial bodies in 1967.

Meanwhile, resource management became intrinsically linked to efforts to promote development. Here the work of the Argentinean Raúl Prebisch, first the president of ECLA and later the first secretary-general of UNCTAD, has been truly pioneering. Others who followed in his tracks include the Sri Lankan Gamani Corea and the Dutchman Jan Pronk. Both of them played key roles in the debate on a New International Economic Order in the 1970s and subsequently served with UNCTAD. In this context, mention should also be made of the instrumental role the American secretary of state Henry Kissinger played in adopting the Integrated Programme for Commodities at UNCTAD IV in Nairobi.

Meanwhile, as a follow-up to the proposal of Arvid Pardo, a new law of the sea conference was convened in 1973, which eventually lasted until 1982. As examined in this book, this conference served as the laboratory for many new ideas, ranging from extended coastal jurisdiction over natural resources through protection of the marine environment to rather revolutionary ideas on deep seabed mining, including the establishment of a UN Enterprise, compulsory transfer of deep seabed mining technology, and protection of the interests of nations that produced land-based minerals. Many persons played a key role at this conference and often acted from a general public interest point of view rather than just serving their own nation's interest. Such persons include Jens Evensen from Norway (who later served as judge on the ICJ), José Luis Jesus from Cape Verde, L. Dolliver M. Nelson from Grenada, Christopher Pinto from Sri Lanka, P. Chandrasekhara Rao from India, Alexander Yankov from Bulgaria, and Joseph Sinde Warioba from Tanzania. President Hamilton Amerasinghe from Sri Lanka and his successor Tommy Koh from Singapore have been very instrumental in orchestrating this large undertaking and bringing it to a successful conclusion with the adoption of a book-length new multilateral treaty that regulates nearly all the conceivable uses of the seas and oceans at that time and establishes various zones of maritime jurisdiction. Frank Njenga from Kenya coined the concept of the Exclusive Economic Zone, which became the convenient compromise between those who advocated extensive jurisdiction by coastal states and those who pled for a truly international regime.

Obviously, persons within secretariats also count. In the 1950s, Oscar Schachter wrote the first extensive studies of sovereignty over natural resources; negotiations on the text of the 1962 Declaration on Permanent Sovereignty over Natural Resources were based on his work. Reportedly for the entire period of its existence, the excellent UN reports of ECOSOC's Standing Committee on Natural Resources were written by an American who was a former priest. Maurice Strong and Mostafa Tolba as executive directors shaped UNEP into a global environmental agency of considerable repute. Assistant Secretary-General Satya Nandan of Fiji served as the soft-spoken steering man who skillfully maneuvered—in close cooperation with UN legal counsel Carl-August Fleischhauer—the informal negotiations on a supplementary agreement to the law of the sea convention in 1994.

Conceptual Contributions and Implications

Multilateral processes at the United Nations have generated a number of new concepts that have had important and lasting implications for international law and international relations, and that, in turn, have influenced trends in natural resource management. First and foremost among these innovations is the principle of resource sovereignty. While sovereignty over natural resources seems like a corollary of the traditional concepts of territorial jurisdiction and national sovereignty, state practice during the colonial era and the immediate postcolonial years suggested different dimensions and new interpretations.

The initial emphasis in attempts to define resource sovereignty was on strengthening the potential application of the principle, both by claiming as many resource-related rights as possible (including the right to regulate foreign investment and the right to establish producers' associations) and by extending the principle to cover natural wealth (forests, fauna and flora, and biological diversity) and marine resources. After a nine-year conference, the UN succeeded in adopting a new "Constitution for the Oceans" that not only regulated nearly all uses of the seas and oceans (navigation, fishing, overflight, marine scientific research, etc.) but also established distinct zones of jurisdiction for managing natural resources. These include internal waters, a twelve-nautical-mile territorial sea, a 200-nautical-mile exclusive economic zone, an extended continental shelf, the high seas, and the deep seabed.

Gradually, the rights conferred by resource sovereignty have become qualified by formulations of accompanying duties and obligations. These include the duty to use natural resources for national economic development and the well-being of the entire population; the obligation to respect the rights and interests of indigenous peoples; the duty to grant foreign investors fair treatment and to ensure due process of law; and the responsibility to conserve the environment.[13] The last responsibility, more commonly known as the sustainable use of natural resources, is the hallmark of the concept of sustainable development.

Sustainability is closely related to two other key concepts that were generated during negotiations and deliberations at the UN: the common heritage of humankind and the common concern of humankind. The former concept emerged in the context of the natural resource regimes for outer space and the celestial bodies (see in particular the Agreement Governing the Activities of States on the Moon and Other Celestial Bodies of 1979) and for the deep seabed and its mineral resources (the United Nations Convention on the Law of the Sea of 1982). These remote areas functioned as the laboratory for the new principle of common heritage, a principle that implies not only nonappropriation but also the distribution of benefits across countries and the obligation to preserve the environment and reserve natural resources for future generations.[14]

The watered-down principle of the common concern of humankind emerged as a compromise in light of apprehension over the internationalization of national resource management and the environmental regime. The common concern of humankind thus informs the conventions on climate change, biological diversity, and anti-desertification. This concept avoids the creation of an international regime yet still conveys the global scope of the problems at stake and takes into account the rights of future generations.

It is interesting to note that these conceptual contributions found practical implementation in regimes that were established for the management of global commons—that is, the natural resources beyond the limits of national economic jurisdiction, which hence belong to everyone and yet are from no one. The UN now also participates in these regimes with various degrees of involvement. The concepts of sustainable use, the common heritage of humankind, and the common concern of humankind now inform the management regimes for the resources of the high seas (e.g., straddling and highly migratory fish stocks), the deep seabed (e.g., manganese nodules), outer space and particularly the resources of the moon, atmospheric resources (e.g., the air mass and the ozone layer), and the climate system. The latter two are, of course, not global commons in the strict sense because they may sometimes also be located within the national jurisdiction of states, but in practice they do function like true global commons.

In contrast, the conceptual contributions of the UN have found much less acceptance with respect to transboundary resources, also called shared resources. The management of these resources has proved to be most difficult. Fervent nationalism was never far below the surface. UNEP's Guidelines on Shared Natural Resources of 1978 remained mere guidelines and have no compliance mechanisms. The Brundtland Commission's set of principles, rights, and obligations concerning transboundary natural resources and environmental interferences of 1987 received no endorsement at the UN (not even by the commission itself). The 1992 Rio Declaration calls merely for "prior and timely notification and relevant information to potentially affected States." Nevertheless, the UN has put the issue of cooperation in managing transboundary resources firmly on the international agenda and has been instrumental in generating practical schemes of cooperation, such as the Zambezi

River Action Plan of 1987, the Agreement on the Cooperation for the Sustainable Development of the Mekong River Basin of 1995, and UNEP's rather successful Regional Seas Programme that was launched as early as 1974.[15]

Another conceptual contribution of the UN has been to identify the nexus between armed conflict and natural resource exploitation and help formulate policies to address it. This was in particular the case with respect to "blood diamonds," which fueled the bloody conflicts in Angola, the Democratic Republic of the Congo, Liberia, Sierra Leone, and Côte d'Ivoire. The Security Council's response to this, namely imposing sanctions and subsequently endorsing a certification regime requiring diamonds to be traceable to the country of origin, shed light on the interface between international economic activity and instability. The issue also brought urgency to the need to formulate responsible, accountable strategies for natural resource management so that a country's natural wealth is harnessed to benefit its development instead of being a tool that is used to inflict violence on its people.

At first glance considerable tensions, if not contradictions, exist among these various concepts. However, the UN has arguably been able to help interested parties strike a viable balance among interests. The concept of national resource sovereignty has been complemented with duties concerning proper resource management, while environmental and developmental issues have been joined within the comprehensive concept of sustainable development. Furthermore, functional rather than strictly territorial arrangements have been negotiated that facilitate the sharing of the world's resources through cooperative regimes for managing natural resources prudently, combating climate change, preserving biological diversity, and promoting sustainable fisheries and forestry.[16]

Assessment

The United Nations has performed a number of key functions during the sixty-five years of debate on natural resource management. These include the following:

- It is a place where problems are identified and relevant data are presented.
- It is a place where countries can seek approval or disapproval of certain policies.
- It is a place where policies can be formulated.
- It is a place where international cooperation is envisaged and programs and operational activities are designed.
- It is a place where norms gradually emerge and can be drawn up in nonbinding resolutions that pave the way for national legislation and multilateral treaties.
- It is a place where the policies of international organizations and national governments are reviewed and compliance with international standards and performance are monitored.

- It is a place where new problems can be identified and new policy directions can be indicated.
- It is a place where mechanisms are provided to contain and resolve international disputes.[17]

As in various other fields of international politics, the performance of these functions has created impressive results in terms of standard-setting at the international and national levels. These are indeed considerable achievements, but much still waits to be achieved. The international architecture for environmental conservation and global resource management needs to be strengthened substantially. Furthermore, current concepts and institutions are incomplete and are not sufficiently equipped to curb the current alarming rates of resource degradation and to provide functional rather than territorial regimes. More bold steps have to be taken to create an integrated ecosystem approach to sustainably using natural resources and healing the earth's fragile environment.

Notes

Series Editors' Foreword

1. Richard Jolly, Louis Emmerij, and Thomas G. Weiss, *UN Ideas That Changed the World* (Bloomington: Indiana University Press, 2009).

2. Craig N. Murphy, *The United Nations Development Programme: A Better Way?* (Cambridge: Cambridge University Press, 2005); and D. John Shaw, *The UN World Food Programme and the Development of Food Aid* (Basingstoke, UK: Palgrave Macmillan, 2001). For further information see, the Routledge Global Institutions Series, ed. Thomas G. Weiss and Rorden Wilkinson, especially the following volumes: Julie Mertus, *The United Nations and Human Rights: A Guide for a New Era* (2005); Beth De Sombre, *Global Environmental Institutions* (2006); Bernard Hoekman and Petros Mavroidis, *The World Trade Organization: Law, Economics, and Politics* (2007); Steve Hughs, *The International Labour Organization: Coming in from the Cold* (forthcoming); Kelley Lee, *The World Health Organization* (2008); Gil Loescher, James Milner, and Alexander Betts, *UNHCR: The Politics and Practice of Refugee Protection into the Twenty-First Century* (2008); Chris May, *The World Intellectual Property Organization: Resurgence and the Development Agenda* (2006); Katherine Marshall, *The World Bank: From Reconstruction to Development to Equity* (2008); Timothy Shaw, *The Commonwealth(s) and Global Governance* (2008); Ian Taylor, *UN Conference on Trade and Development* (2007); and James Vreeland, *The International Monetary Fund: The Politics of Conditional Lending* (2007).

3. Thomas G. Weiss and Ramesh Thakur, *The UN and Global Governance: An Unfinished Journey* (Bloomington: Indiana University Press, 2010).

4. Thomas G. Weiss, Tatiana Carayannis, Louis Emmerij, and Richard Jolly, *UN Voices: The Struggle for Development and Social Justice* (Bloomington: Indiana University Press, 2005).

5. The United Nations Intellectual History Project, *The Complete Oral History Transcripts from UN Voices,* CD-ROM (New York: UNIHP, 2005).

6. Louis Emmerij, Richard Jolly, and Thomas G. Weiss, *Ahead of the Curve? UN Ideas and Global Challenges* (Bloomington: Indiana University Press, 2001), xi.

Introduction

1. See Article 1 of the Articles of Agreement of the International Bank for Reconstruction and Development, 22 July 1944, entered into force 27 December 1945, available at http://siteresources.worldbank.org/EXTABOUTUS/Resources/ibrd-articlesofagreement.pdf and in *United Nations Treaty Series* (New York: United Nations, 1947), 2: 134.

2. See Article 1(2)(c) of the Constitution of the Food and Agriculture Organization of the United Nations, 16 October 1945, available at http://www.fao.org/docrep/007/j2954e/

j2954e00.htm; and in W. E. Burhenne, ed., *International Environmental Law: Multilateral Treaties,* vol. 7 (Berlin: E. Schmidt, 1974-), 945:76.

3. *Oxford English Dictionary Online* (Oxford: Oxford University Press, 2007).

4. *Black's Law Dictionary,* 8th ed. (St. Paul, Minn.: West Group, 2004), 1056.

5. "Declaration on Permanent Sovereignty over Natural Resources," General Assembly resolution 1803 (XVII), 14 December 1962.

6. See Article 2 of the Convention on Biological Diversity, 5 June 1992, entered into force 29 December 1993, available at http://www.cbd.int/convention/convention.shtml; and in *International Legal Materials* 31 (1992): 822–841.

7. See *Glossary of Terms for Negotiators of Multilateral Environmental Agreements* (Nairobi: UNEP, 2007); or *Marine and Coastal Ecosystems and Human Well-Being: A Synthesis Report Based on the Findings of the Millennium Ecosystem Assessment* (Nairobi: UNEP, 2006).

8. See Report of the International Law Commission on the Work of Its Forty-Sixth Session, Chapter III on the law of the non-navigational uses of international watercourses, in *Yearbook of the International Law Commission, 1994,* vol. 2, Part Two (New York: United Nations, 1997), 118.

9. ICJ, *Legality of the Threat or Use of Nuclear Weapons,* Advisory Opinion, 8 July 1996, paragraph 29, available at http://www.icj-cij.org/docket/files/95/7495.pdf.

10. *Yearbook of the United Nations, 1948–1949* (New York: UN Department of Public Information, 1949), 482. Chapter 2 discusses the conference and its outcomes.

11. "Declaration of the United Nations Conference on the Human Environment," 16 June 1972, available at http://www.unep.org/Documents.Multilingual/Default.asp?DocumentID=97&ArticleID=1503 (italics added); and in *International Legal Materials* 11 (1972): 1416–1420.

12. "Declaration on Environment and Development," General Assembly document A/CONF.151/26, 12 August 1992.

13. *Report of the World Summit on Sustainable Development,* A/CONF.199/20, available at http://www.unctad.org/en/docs/aconf199d20&c1_en.pdf.

14. Kevin J. Gaston and John I. Spicer, *Biodiversity: An introduction,* 2nd ed. (Oxford: Blackwell Publishing, 2004), 4.

15. See Article 2 of the Convention on Biological Diversity.

16. See Article 1 of the United Nations Framework Convention on Climate Change, New York, 9 May 1992, entered into force 21 March 1994, available at http://unfccc.int/essential_background/convention/background/items/2853.php.

17. See the Separate Opinion of Vice-President Weeramantry in *Gabčíkovo-Nagymaros Project (Hungary/Slovakia),* Judgment, 25 September 1997, available at http://www.icj-cij.org/docket/files/92/7383.pdf.

18. Robert Costanza and Bernard C. Patten, "Defining and Predicting Sustainability," *Ecological Economics* 15, no. 3 (1995): 193–196. See also Klaus Bosselmann, *The Principle of Sustainability: Transforming Law and Governance* (Aldershot, UK: Ashgate, 2008); and Hans Opschoor, "Sustainability," in *Handbook on Economics and Ethics,* ed. Jan Peil and Irene van Staveren (Cheltenham, UK: Edward Elgar, 2009), 531–538.

19. See Robert U. Ayres, Jeroen C. J. M. van den Bergh, and John M. Gowdy, "Strong versus Weak Sustainability: Economics, Natural Sciences and Consilience," *Environmental Ethics* 23 (2001): 155–168.

20. See Mr. Chusei Yamada, Special Rapporteur, *Second Report on Shared Natural Resources: Transboundary Groundwaters,* General Assembly document A/CN.4/539, 9 March 2004; and Mr. Chusei Yamada, Special Rapporteur, *Fourth Report on Shared Natural Resources: Transboundary Groundwaters,* General Assembly document A/CN.4/580, 6 March 2007. Also see Article 2(b) of the 1997 United Nations Convention on the Law of the Non-Navigational Uses of International Watercourses, General Assembly document A/51/869, 11 April 1997, also reproduced in *International Legal Materials* 36 (1997): 700–702. The convention defines

an international watercourse as "a watercourse, parts of which are situated in different states." Article 122 of UNCLOS defines enclosed or semi-enclosed sea as a "gulf, basin or sea surrounded by two or more States and connected to another sea or the ocean by a narrow outlet or consisting entirely or primarily of the territorial seas and exclusive economic zones of two or more coastal States"; available at http://www.un.org/Depts/los/convention_agreements/texts/unclos/unclos_e.pdf and in *International Legal Materials* 21 (1982): 1261–1354.

21. See Principle 1 of UNEP, Environmental Law Guidelines and Principles on Shared Natural Resources (1978), available at http://www.unep.org/Law/PDF/UNEPEnvironmental-Law-Guidelines-and-Principles.pdf.

22. See Susan J. Buck, *The Global Commons: An Introduction* (Washington, D.C.: Island Press, 1998).

23. OECD Glossary of Statistical Terms, available at http://stats.oecd.org/glossary/index.htm.

24. Permanent Court of Arbitration, *Island of Palmas Case (Netherlands/United States of America),* Award, 4 April 1928, reproduced in *UN Reports of International Arbitral Awards,* vol. 2 (New York: United Nations, 1949), 829–871.

25. Dan Philpott, "Sovereignty," in *The Stanford Encyclopedia of Philosophy,* ed. Edward N. Zalta, available at http://plato.stanford.edu/archives/sum2003/entries/sovereignty/.

26. *Corfu Channel (United Kingdom of Great Britain and Northern Ireland v. Albania),* Judgment, 9 April 1949, available at http://www.icj-cij.org/docket/files/1/1645.pdf.

27. *Corfu Channel (United Kingdom of Great Britain and Northern Ireland v. Albania),* Separate Opinion by Judge Alvarez, available at http://www.icj-cij.org/docket/files/1/1649.pdf. See also J. P. Grant and J. C. Barker, eds., *Parry & Grant Encyclopaedic Dictionary of International Law* (New York: Oceana, 2004), 471.

28. See Nico J. Schrijver, *Sovereignty over Natural Resources: Balancing Rights and Duties* (Cambridge: Cambridge University Press, 1997), 3.

29. "Declaration on Permanent Sovereignty over Natural Resources," General Assembly resolution 1803 (XVII), 14 December 1962.

30. International Covenant on Economic, Social and Cultural Rights, Annex to General Assembly resolution 2200 (XXI), 16 December 1966; and International Covenant on Civil and Political Rights, Annex to General Assembly resolution 2200 (XXI), 16 December 1966.

31. See *Armed Activities on the Territory of the Congo (Democratic Republic of the Congo v. Uganda),* Judgment, 19 December 2005, paragraph 244, available at http://www.icj-cij.org/docket/files/116/10455.pdf. This case will be presented in detail in chapter 6.

32. "Declaration on Permanent Sovereignty over Natural Resources," General Assembly resolution 1803 (XVII), 14 December 1962.

33. "Charter of Economic Rights and Duties of States," General Assembly resolution 3281 (XXIX), 12 December 1974.

34. See, for example, Paragraph 4(b) of "Promotion of a Democratic and Equitable International Order," General Assembly resolution A/RES/61/160, 21 February 2007.

35. Schrijver, *Sovereignty over Natural Resources,* chapter 10.

36. See Antonio Cassese, *Self-Determination of Peoples: A Legal Reappraisal* (Cambridge: Cambridge University Press, 1995); and James Crawford, ed., *The Rights of Peoples* (Oxford: Clarendon Press, 1988).

37. "Declaration on the Granting of Independence to Colonial Countries and Peoples," General Assembly resolution 1514 (XV), 14 December 1960, paragraph 2.

38. "United Nations Declaration on the Rights of Indigenous Peoples," General Assembly resolution 61/295, 2 October 2007, Article 3.

39. Article 46(1) of the declaration has been expressly understood to limit the right to self-determination by excluding secession. Article 46(1) determines that "nothing in this Declaration may be . . . construed as authorizing or encouraging any action which would dismember or impair, totally or in part, the territorial integrity or political unity of sovereign

and independent States." See also statements of state representatives on the occasion of the adoption of the declaration at the 107th Plenary Meeting of the General Assembly, General Assembly document A/61/PV.107, 13 September 2007.

40. See "Question of Promoting the Peaceful Uses of the Sea-Bed and the Ocean Floor," *Yearbook of the United Nations, 1967* (New York: United Nations, 1969), 43; and "First Committee, 1515th Meeting, 1 November 1967," General Assembly document A/C.1/PV.1515, available at http://www.un.org/Depts/los/convention_agreements/texts/pardo_ga1967.pdf.

41. "Declaration of Principles Governing the Sea-Bed and the Ocean Floor, and the Subsoil Thereof, Beyond the Limits of National Jurisdiction," General Assembly resolution 2749 (XXV), 17 December 1970.

42. Edith D. Brown Weiss, *In Fairness to Future Generations: International Law, Common Patrimony, and Intergenerational Equity* (New York: Transnational Publishers, 1989).

43. World Commission on Environment and Development, *Our Common Future* (Oxford: Oxford University Press, 1987), 43. The chairperson was Gro Harlem Brundtland, the former prime minister of Norway.

44. See Nico Schrijver, "The Evolution of Sustainable Development in International Law: Inception, Meaning and Status," *Recueil des Cours de l'Académie de droit international de la Haye* 329 (2007): 366–374.

45. Donella H. Meadows, Dennis L. Meadows, Jørgen Randers, and William W. Behrens, III, *The Limits to Growth: A Report for the Club of Rome's Project on the Predicament of Mankind* (London: Earth Island Limited, 1972).

46. See also Nico Schrijver and Friedl Weiss, eds., *International Law and Sustainable Development: Principles and Practice* (Boston: Martinus Nijhoff Publishers, 2004).

1. Historical Background

1. See Ludwik A. Teclaff, *The River Basin in History and Law* (The Hague: Martinus Nijhoff, 1967), 20–21.

2. See Pierre Gerbet, "Rise and Development of International Organization: A Synthesis," in *The Concept of International Organization,* ed. G. Abi-Saab (Paris: UNESCO, 1981): 28–29.

3. Hans-Ulrich Scupin, "Peace, Historical Movements Towards," in *Encyclopedia of Public International Law,* ed. Rudolf Bernhardt, vol. 3 (Amsterdam: Elsevier, 1997), 914.

4. Hugo Grotius, *De jure belli ac pacis* (1625), English translation of quotation as provided in Hersch Lauterpacht, *The Function of Law in the International Community* (Oxford: Clarendon Press, 1933), 7n2.

5. Scupin, "Peace, Historical Movements Towards," 915–916.

6. See Inis L. Claude, *Swords into Plowshares: The Problems and Progress of International Organization,* 4th ed. (New York: Random House, 1971), 24–26.

7. See Shabtai Rosenne, *The Hague Peace Conferences of 1899 and 1907 and International Arbitration: Reports and Documents* (The Hague: TMC Asser Press, 2001); Joseph H. Choate, *The Two Hague Conferences* (Princeton, N.J.: Princeton University Press, 1913); Frederick W. Holls, *The Peace Conference at The Hague* (New York: Macmillan, 1900); James L. Tryon, "The Proposed High Court of Nations," *Yale Law Journal* 19 (1910): 145–155; A. Pearce Higgins, *The Hague Peace Conferences and Other International Conferences Concerning the Laws and Usages of War: Texts of Conventions with Commentaries* (Cambridge: Cambridge University Press, 1909); William I. Hull, *The Two Hague Conferences and Their Contributions to International Law* (Boston: Ginn & Co., 1908); James Brown Scott, ed., *The Proceedings of the Hague Peace Conferences: The Conference of 1907* (New York: Oxford University Press, 1921); and Yves Daudet, ed., *Topicality of the 1907 Hague Conference for the Second Peace Conference* (Leiden: Martinus Nijhoff, 2008).

8. However, no generally accepted definition of public international unions exists. See Philippe Sands and Pierre Klein, eds., *Bowett's Law of International Institutions,* 5th ed. (London: Sweet & Maxwell, 2001), 6.

9. Claude, *Swords into Plowshares,* 35.

10. For an interesting overview of systems established by ancient civilizations to manage water resources, see the separate opinion of Vice-President Weeramantry in *Gabčíkovo-Nagymaros Project (Hungary/Slovakia),* Judgment, 25 September 1997, available at http://www.icj-cij.org/docket/files/92/7383.pdf. These early forms of resource management, however, were not set up for managing resources shared between civilizations and could thus not be considered international, even in a remote sense.

11. Julio A. Barberis, "Water, International Regulation of the Use of," in *Encyclopedia of Public International Law,* ed. Rudolf Bernhardt (Amsterdam/Oxford: Elsevier, 1995), 4:1435.

12. Friedrich Meißner, "Rhine River," in ibid., 4:237.

13. For a detailed account, see Béla Vitányi, *The International Regime of River Navigation* (Alphen a/d Rijn: Sijthoff & Noordhoff, 1979).

14. Final Act of the Congress of Vienna, available in "General Treaty, Signed in Congress at Vienna, June 9, 1815, with the Acts Thereunto Annexed," reproduced in Thomas C. Hansard, *The Parliamentary Debates from the Year 1803 to the Present Time,* vol. 32 (1 February to 6 March 1816) (London, 1816), 71–215.

15. See Dietrich Rauschning, "Elbe River," in *Encyclopedia of Public International Law,* ed. Rudolf Bernhardt, vol. 2 (Amsterdam/Oxford: Elsevier, 1995), 50–52.

16. "General Act of the Berlin Conference Regarding Africa," reproduced in *The Map of Africa by Treaty,* 3rd ed., ed. Edward Hertslet (London: Cass, 1909), 62. See also generally Bonaya A. Godana, *Africa's Shared Water Resources: Legal and Institutional Aspects of the Nile, Niger and Senegal River Systems* (London: Frances Pinter, 1985), 124; and Béla Vitányi, *The International Regime of River Navigation* (Alphen a/d Rijn: Sijthoff & Noordhoff, 1979), 98–100.

17. This idea can be traced back to Hugo Grotius, who stated that a transboundary river "is the property of the people within whose boundaries it flows," but at the same time, Grotius wrote that "such a river, considered as running water, remains common property of all." Hugo Grotius, *De jure belli ac pacis* (1625), English translation provided in Béla Vitányi, *The International Regime of River Navigation* (Alphen a/d Rijn: Sijthoff & Noordhoff, 1979), 19. See further pages 31–33 on the idea of a community of riparians.

18. See Stephen C. McCaffrey, *The Law of International Watercourses: Non-Navigational Uses* (Oxford: Oxford University Press, 2001), 63.

19. See International Regulation Regarding the Use of International Watercourses for Purposes Other Than Navigation, 20 April 1911, available at http://www.cawater-info.net/bk/water_law/pdf/madrid_1911_e.pdf and in *Annuaire de l'Institut de Droit international* 24 (1911): 365.

20. See Articles IV and VIII of the Treaty between the United States and Great Britain Relating to Boundary Waters, and Questions Arising between the United States and Canada (1909), available at http://www.ijc.org/rel/agree/water.html (accessed 18 April 2009).

21. See Philippe Sands, *Principles of International Environmental Law,* 2nd ed. (Cambridge: Cambridge University Press, 2003), 28.

22. The first such commission was the International Commission for the Protection of the Rhine against Pollution, established in 1950. Other commissions soon followed, such as the International Commission for the Protection of the Mosel against Pollution (1961) and the River Niger Commission (1963). Most of these commissions still exist today. See Protocol Concerning the Constitution of an International Commission for the Protection of the Mosel Against Pollution, 20 December 1961, entered into force 1 July 1962, available at http://www.ecolex.org/server2.php/libcat/docs/multilateral/en/TRE000466.txt and in *United Nations Treaty Series* (New York: United Nations, 1974), 940: 211; Agreement Concerning the River

Niger Commission and the Navigation and Transport on the River Niger, 25 November 1964, entered into force 12 April 1966, available at http://www.docstoc.com/docs/2946001/AGREEMENT-CONCERNING-THE-RIVER-NIGER-COMMISSION-AND-THE-NAVIGATION- and in *United Nations Treaty Series* (New York: United Nations, 1967), 587: 8507.

23. Convention between the Grand Duchy of Luxembourg and Prussia Concerning the Regulation of Fisheries in Boundary Waters, 5 November 1892, reprinted in G. F. Martens, ed., *Nouveau recueil général de traités,* 2nd series, vol. 24 (Gottingen: Libraire Dietrich, 1899), 153.

24. Convention Concerning Fishing in the Bidassoa, Bayonne, 18 February 1886, reprinted in G. F. Martens, ed., *Nouveau recueil général de traités,* 2nd series, vol. 12 (Gottingen: Libraire Dietrich, 1887), 687.

25. Treaty Concerning the Regulation of Salmon Fishery in the Rhine River Basin, 30 June 1885, available (in French) at http://iea.uoregon.edu/pages/view_treaty.php?t=1885-RhineSalmon.FR.txt&par=view_treaty_html; and Final Protocol to the Treaty Concerning the Regulation of Salmon Fishery in the Rhine River Basin, reprinted in UN, *Legislative Texts and Treaty Provisions concerning the Utilization of International Rivers for Other Purposes Than Navigation* (New York: United Nations, 1963), treaty no. 112.

26. Convention between the Grand Duchy of Baden and Switzerland Concerning Fishing in the Rhine between Constance and Basel, 9 December 1869, reprinted in B. Rüster, B. Simma, and M. Bock, eds., *International Protection of the Environment: Treaties and Related Documents,* vol. 9 (Dobbs Ferry, NY: Oceana, 1975–1983), 4695.

27. Convention Concernant l'Exploitation et la Conservation des Pêcheries dans la Partie-Frontière du Danube, 15 January 1902, reprinted in F. Stoerk, ed., *Nouveau recueil de traités et autres actes relatifs aux rapports de droit international—Continuation du grand recueil de G. Fr. de Martens,* 2nd series, vol. 30 (Gottingen: Libraire Dietrich, 1904), 642.

28. Thomas W. Fulton, *The Sovereignty of the Sea* (Edinburgh, UK: William Blackwood and Sons, 1911), 695.

29. See Award of the Tribunal of Arbitration Constituted under the Treaty Concluded at Washington, the 29th of February 1892, between the United States of America and her Majesty the Queen of the United Kingdom of Great Britain and Ireland, 15 August 1893; reproduced in *International Environmental Law Reports* 1 (1999): 67; and *American Journal of International Law* 6 (1912): 233. Also available at http://www.archive.org/download/behringseaarbit00beriuoft/behringseaarbit00beriuoft.pdf.

30. Nonetheless, it is interesting to observe some of the arguments advanced by the United States. It maintained that "to destroy the sources from which any human blessing flows is a crime. . . . The earth being designed for the permanent abode of man, each generation is entitled only to its use, and the law of nature forbids that any waste should be committed to the disadvantage of the succeeding tenants." These submissions are reproduced in *International Environmental Law Reports* 1 (1999): 56.

31. See Stuart M. Kaye, *International Fisheries Management* (The Hague/Boston: Kluwer Law International, 2001), 45–46.

32. The ICES was initially established by a "gentleman's agreement" that was later formalized in the Convention for the International Council for the Exploration of the Sea, Copenhagen, 12 September 1964, entered into force 22 July 1968, available at http://www.ices.dk/aboutus/convention.asp and in *International Legal Materials* 7 (1968): 302.

33. Convention between the United States, Great Britain, Russia and Japan for the Preservation and Protection of Fur Seals, 7 July 1911, available at http://fletcher.tufts.edu/multi/sealtreaty.html. The convention was preceded by the Treaty for Protection and Preservation of Fur Seals between Great Britain and the United States, 7 February 1911; in *Papers Relating to the Foreign Relations of the United States with the Annual Message of the President Transmitted to Congress on December 7, 1911* (Washington, D.C.: Government Printing Office, 1918), 256–259.

34. Convention for the Preservation of the Halibut Fisheries of the Northern Pacific Ocean, 2 March 1923, entered into force 21 October 1924, available at http://www.iphc.washington.edu/halcom/history/treaty1923.htm and in *League of Nations Treaty Series,* vol. 32 (London: Harrison & Sons, 1925), 93.

35. See Convention for the Preservation of the Halibut Fishery of the Northern Pacific Ocean and Bering Sea, 9 May 1930, entered into force 9 May 1931, in *League of Nations Treaty Series,* vol. 121 (London: Harrison & Sons, 1931–1932), 45 and *American Journal of International Law: Supplement* 25 (1931): 188; and Convention Revising the Convention of May 9, 1930, for the Preservation of the Halibut Fishery of Northern Pacific Ocean and Bering Sea, 29 January 1937, entered into force 28 July 1937, in *American Journal of International Law: Supplement* 32 (1938): 71.

36. Convention for the Protection of Sockeye Salmon Fisheries, 26 May 1930, entered into force 28 July 1937, in *American Journal of International Law: Supplement* 32 (1938): 65.

37. Convention for Protection of Birds Useful to Agriculture, 19 March 1902, entered into force 6 December 1905, available at http://www.ecolex.org/ecolex/ledge/view/RecordDetails?id=TRE-000067&index=treaties and reprinted in F. Stoerk, ed., *Nouveau recueil de traités et autres actes relatifs aux rapports de droit international—Continuation du grand recueil de G. Fr. de Martens,* 2nd series, vol. 30 (Gottingen: Libraire Dietrich, 1904), 686.

38. Convention destinée à assurer la conservation des diverses espèces animales vivant à l'état sauvage en Afrique qui sont utiles à l'homme ou inoffensives (Convention for the Conservation of Wild Animal Species in Africa That Are Useful to Humankind or Harmless), 19 May 1900, in Bernd Rüster and Bruno Simma, *International Protection of the Environment: Treaties and Related Documents,* vol. 4 (Dobbs Ferry, N.Y.: Oceana, 1975–1983), 1607.

39. "Development of International Law," resolution adopted by the League of Nations Assembly, 22 September 1924, in *American Journal of International Law: Special Supplement* 20 (1926): 2.

40. For a collection of documents on the committee's work, see Shabtai Rosenne, ed., *League of Nations Committee of Experts for the Progressive Codification of International Law (1925–1928),* 2 vols. (New York: Oceana Publications, 1972).

41. José León Suárez, "Report on the Exploitation of the Products of the Sea," in Rosenne, *League of Nations Committee of Experts for the Progressive Codification of International Law,* 2:146–151. It is interesting to note that the rapporteur expressed doubts at the outset about whether the topic had been appropriately framed. While the committee entrusted Suarez "to enquire . . . whether it is possible to establish by way of international agreement rules regarding the exploitation of the products of the sea," Suarez thought that the inquiry should focus on whether "a special technical conference [should] be convened, to draw up immediately, without regard to the extension or maintenance of maritime jurisdiction extending to the three-mile limit, uniform regulations for the exploitation of the industries of the sea, whose wealth constitutes a food reserve for humanity, over the whole extent of the ocean bed forming part of the continental shelf" (146–147).

42. The Suárez quotes in this and the previous three paragraphs are from ibid., 147–149.

43. Hugo Grotius, *Mare Liberum* (1609), translation in Ralph van Deman Magoffin, *The Freedom of the Seas, or the Right Which Belongs to the Dutch to Take Part in the East Indian Trade* (New York: Oxford University Press, 1916).

44. Suarez, "Report on the Exploitation of the Products of the Sea," 149 and 147.

45. Ibid., 151.

46. "Report to the Council of the League of Nations on the Procedure to be Followed in Regard to the Question of the Exploitation of the Products of the Sea, 20 April 1927," in Hj. L. Hammarskjöld, ed., *American Journal of International Law: Special Supplement* 22 (1928): 44–45.

47. See discussions in the League of Nations Council and Assembly, reproduced in Rosenne, *League of Nations Committee of Experts for the Progressive Codification of International Law,* 1:lxxxi and xc.

48. Paragraph 3 of "Codification of International Law," resolution adopted by the Assembly, 27 September 1927, *League of Nations Official Journal* (*Special Supplement*), no. 53 (October 1927): 9–10; reprinted in *American Journal of International Law: Special Supplement* 22 (1928): 231.

49. See Daniel P. O'Connell and Ivan A. Shearer, *The International Law of the Sea,* vol. 1 (Oxford: Clarendon Press, 1982), 155–159.

50. Draft article 11 stipulated that "in virtue of its sovereign rights over the territorial sea, the riparian State shall exercise for itself and for its nationals the sole right of taking possession of the riches of the sea, the bottom and the subsoil"; reproduced in *American Journal of International Law: Special Supplement* 20 (1926): 119.

51. J. P. A. François, "Report of the Second Committee (Territorial Sea)," reproduced in *American Journal of International Law: Supplement* 24 (1930): 239.

52. "Decision of the 29th session, July 1929," *League of Nations Official Journal* 10 (1929): 1590. See also Appendix explaining the decision, at 1591–1596. See also the Preliminary Draft Convention for the Regulation of Whaling, prepared by a Committee of Experts and the Economic Committee, reproduced in *League of Nations Official Journal* 11 (1930): 1353.

53. Convention for the Regulation of Whaling, 24 September 1931, entered into force 16 January 1935, *League of Nations Treaty Series* 155: 349.

54. Ibid., Article 9.

55. Twenty-six states signed it (eight never ratified), and it was subsequently acceded to by ten others.

56. International Convention for the Regulation of Whaling, 8 June 1937, entered into force 7 May 1938, available in *American Journal of International Law: Supplement* 34 (1940): 106; Protocol Amending the International Whaling Agreement, 24 June 1938, published in *League of Nations Treaty Series* 196: 131.

57. International Convention Concerning the Regime of Navigable Waterways of International Concern, 20 April 1921, entered into force 31 October 1922, available at http://www.legislation.gov.hk/doc/multi_904v1.pdf and in *League of Nations Treaty Series* 7: 37.

58. Convention Relative to the Preservation of Fauna and Flora in their Natural State, 8 November 1933, entered into force on 14 January 1936, available at http://www.ecolex.org/ecolex/ledge/view/RecordDetails?id=TRE-000069&index=treaties and in *League of Nations Treaty Series* 172: 241.

59. A. Kiss and D. Shelton, *International Environmental Law* (Ardsley-on-Hudson, N.Y.: Transnational Publishers, 1999), 34.

60. On these developments, see Bhupinder S. Chimni, *International Commodity Agreements: A Legal Study* (London: Croom Helm, 1987), 16–21.

61. See particularly Patricia W. Birnie, *International Regulation of Whaling: From Conservation of Whaling to Conservation of Whales and Regulation of Whale-Watching* (New York: Oceana Publications, 1985), 105–141. Also see Ray Gambell, "Whale Conservation: Role of the International Whaling Commission," *Marine Policy* 1, no. 4 (1977): 301.

62. *World Economic Conference, Geneva, May 1927: Final Report* (Geneva: League of Nations, 1927), chapter 5 (Industry).

63. *Report of the Committee for the Study of the Problem of Raw Materials* (Geneva: League of Nations, 1937), 17–21; reproduced in *League of Nations Official Journal* 18 (1937): 1229.

64. *Report of the Committee for the Study of the Problem of Raw Materials* in *League of Nations Official Journal* 18 (1937): 1241.

65. Ibid., 1237.

66. Ibid., 1238.

67. Ibid., 1248.

68. See "Report on the Work of the Economic Committee at its Forty-Seventh Session, 28 January 1938," *League of Nations Official Journal* 19 (1938): 176.

69. Atlantic Charter of 14 August 1941, available at http://avalon.law.yale.edu/wwii/atlantic.asp and in "Official Documents: Great Britain–United States," *American Journal of International Law: Supplement* 35 (1941): 191.

70. *United Nations Conference on Food and Agriculture, Hot Springs, Va., 1943, Final Act and Section Reports* (Washington, D.C.: Government Printing Office, 1943). See report of Section III, Facilitation and Improvement of Distribution.

71. Statute of the Permanent Court of International Justice, 16 December 1920, available at http://www.worldcourts.com/pcij/eng/documents/1920.12.16_statute.htm and in *League of Nations Treaty Series* 6: 380. For a commentary on the statute and the work of the court, see Manley O. Hudson, *The Permanent Court of International Justice 1920–1942: A Treatise* (New York: MacMillan, 1943).

72. See Articles 34–36 of the Statute of the Permanent Court of International Justice.

73. The court had to rule on certain objections to the admissibility of the application by which the judicial proceedings were instituted and on its own jurisdiction. It found that only claims relating to the concessions of Jerusalem were admissible. See *Mavrommatis Palestine Concessions,* Objection to the Jurisdiction of the Court, Judgment, 30 August 1924, PCIJ, Ser. A, No. 2 (1924). The merits were decided in *Mavrommatis Palestine Concessions,* Judgment, 26 March 1925, PCIJ, Ser. A, No. 5 (1925), available at http://www.worldcourts.com/pcij/eng/decisions/1924.08.30_mavrommatis/.

74. *Case of the Readaptation of the Mavrommatis Jerusalem Concessions (Jurisdiction),* Judgment, 10 October 1927, PCIJ, Ser. A, No. 11 (1927), available at http://www.worldcourts.com/pcij/eng/decisions/1927.10.10_mavrommatis/.

75. *Phosphates in Morocco,* Judgment, 14 June 1938, PCIJ, Ser. A/B, No. 74 (1938), available at http://www.worldcourts.com/pcij/eng/decisions/1938.06.14_phosphates/.

76. *Case Relating to the Territorial Jurisdiction of the International Commission of the River Oder,* Judgment, 10 September 1929, at p. 27, PCIJ, Ser. A, No. 23 (1929), available at http://www.internationalwaterlaw.org/cases/river-oder.html.

77. *The Diversion of Water from the Meuse,* Judgment, 28 June 1937, PCIJ, Ser. A/B, No. 70 (1937), available at http://www.internationalwaterlaw.org/cases/meuse.html.

78. *Trail Smelter (United States v. Canada),* Arbitral Tribunal, 16 April 1938 and 11 March 1941, 3 UNRIAA (1947) 1905, at p. 1965; reproduced in *American Journal of International Law* 33 (1939): 182, and 35 (1941): 716.

79. The International Court of Justice later echoed this so-called no-harm principle as formulated in the Trail Smelter arbitration in more general terms in the *Corfu Channel Case (United Kingdom of Great Britain and Northern Ireland v. Albania),* Merits, Judgment, 9 April 1949, available at http://www.icj-cij.org/docket/files/1/1645.pdf. But the ICJ's most important pronouncement regarding protecting the environment appeared in *Legality of the Threat of Nuclear Weapons:* "The existence of the general obligation of States to ensure that activities within their jurisdiction and control respect the environment of other States or of areas beyond national control is now part of the corpus of international law relating to the environment" (paragraph 29). Advisory Opinion, 8 July 1996, available at http://www.icj-cij.org/docket/files/95/7495.pdf.

2. UN Involvement with Natural Resource Management at the National and Transboundary Levels

1. The chapter builds on "The Birth and Development of the Principle: The UN General Assembly as Midwife" in Nico J. Schrijver, *Sovereignty over Natural Resources: Balancing Rights and Duties* (Cambridge: Cambridge University Press, 1997).

2. This was in part pursuant to the recommendations of the League's Bruce report, *The Development of International Co-operation in Economic and Social Affairs: Report of the Special*

Committee (Geneva: League of Nations, 1939), Doc. A/23/1939. See also Ralph Townley, "The Economic Organs of the United Nations," in *The Evolution of International Organization,* ed. Evan Luard (London: Thames and Hudson, 1966), 248.

3. See Alain Pellet, "Article 55," in *La Charte des Nations Unies: Commentaire article par article,* ed. Jean-Pierre Cot and Alain Pellet, 2nd ed. (Paris: Economica, 1991), 843–853.

4. See Walter Sharp, *The United Nations Economic and Social Council* (New York: Columbia University Press, 1969).

5. UN Charter, Article 73.

6. Text in *Documents on American Foreign Relations (1941–42),* vol. 4 (Boston: World Peace Foundation, 1942), 10.

7. See Article I(iii) of the Articles of Agreement of the International Bank for Reconstruction and Development, 22 July 1944, entered into force 27 December 1945, available at http://siteresources.worldbank.org/EXTABOUTUS/Resources/ibrd-articlesofagreement.pdf and in *United Nations Treaty Series* 2: 134; and Article I(ii) of the Articles of Agreement of the International Monetary Fund, 22 July 1944, entered into force 27 December 1945, available at http://www.imf.org/external/pubs/ft/aa/index.htm and in *United Nations Treaty Series* 2: 39, and 726: 266.

8. "Control of World Oil Resources," in *Yearbook of the United Nations, 1947–1948* (Lake Success, N.Y.: UN Department of Public Information, 1948), 549.

9. ECOSOC document E/449 and Add.1, 31 July 1947.

10. "Control of World Oil Resources," in *Yearbook of the United Nations, 1947–1948,* 550.

11. The council merely took note of the proposal; see ECOSOC resolution 66 (V), 12 August 1947.

12. Paragraph 6 of "Recommendations Adopted [at the International Timber Conference]," reproduced in *Unasylva* 1, no. 2 (1947): 17. See also ECOSOC resolution 31 (IV), 29 March 1947. For a report on the conference, see "Timber Conference," in *Yearbook of the United Nations, 1947–1948,* 555.

13. "Conservation and Utilization of Resources," ECOSOC resolution 32 (IV), 28 March 1947. The conference was intended merely to provide an exchange of ideas and experiences about conserving and using resources without producing any resolutions and recommendations. See *Proceedings of the United Nations Scientific Conference on the Conservation and Utilization of Resources,* vol. 1, *Plenary Meetings* (Lake Success, N.Y.: UN Department of Economic Affairs, 1950).

14. *Report on the Conference by the Secretary-General,* ECOSOC document E/CONF.7/7 (1950), xvi, reproduced in *Proceedings of the United Nations Scientific Conference on the Conservation and Utilization of Resources,* vol. 1, *Plenary Meetings* (Lake Success, N.Y.: UN Department of Economic Affairs, 1950), xvi–xxiv.

15. *Yearbook of the United Nations, 1948–1949* (Lake Success, N.Y.: UN Department of Public Information, 1950), 481–482.

16. "Economic Development of Under-Developed Countries," *Yearbook of the United Nations, 1951* (New York: UN Department of Public Information, 1952), 417–419.

17. "Integrated Economic Development and Commercial Agreements," General Assembly resolution 523 (VI), 12 January 1952.

18. See *Anglo-Iranian Oil Co. (United Kingdom v. Iran),* Preliminary Objection, Judgment, 22 July 1952, available at http://www.icj-cij.org/docket/files/16/1997.pdf.

19. See M. A. Mughrabi, *Permanent Sovereignty over Oil Resources: A Study of Middle East Oil Concessions and Legal Change* (Beirut: Middle East Research and Publishing Center, 1966), 66–68; and G. Schwarzenberger, *Foreign Investments and International Law* (London: Stevens and Sons, 1969), 71.

20. "Economic Development of Under-Developed Areas," in *Yearbook of the United Nations, 1952* (New York: UN Department of Public Information, 1953), 387.

21. "Right to Exploit Freely Natural Wealth and Resources," General Assembly resolution 626 (VII), 21 December 1952.

22. ECOSOC document E/CN.4/L.24, 16 April 1952.

23. For progress in drafting the covenants, see "Draft International Covenants on Human Rights," in *Yearbook of the United Nations, 1955* (New York: UN Department of Public Information, 1956), 154–156; and "Report of the Working Party on Article 1," General Assembly document A/C.3/L.489 and Corr. 1 and 2. For an extensive report, see *Report of the Third Committee to the General Assembly,* 8 December 1955, General Assembly document A/3077, 20.

24. "International Covenants on Human Rights," in *Yearbook of the United Nations, 1966* (New York: United Nations, 1968), 406.

25. "Recommendations Concerning International Respect for the Rights of Peoples and Nations to Self-Determination," General Assembly resolution 1314 (XIII), 12 December 1958.

26. For a review and analysis of the work of the Commission on Permanent Sovereignty over Natural Resources, see Nico J. Schrijver, *Sovereignty over Natural Resources: Balancing Rights and Duties* (Cambridge: Cambridge University Press, 1997), 59–70.

27. *Report of the Commission on Permanent Sovereignty over Natural Resources* (New York: United Nations, 1962).

28. See "Sovereignty over Natural Resources," in *Yearbook of the United Nations, 1961* (New York: UN Office of Public Information, 1963), 530–533.

29. See "Permanent Sovereignty over Natural Resources," *Yearbook of the United Nations, 1962* (New York: UN Office of Public Information, 1964), 500–502.

30. UN Doc A/C.2/SR.858, 3 December 1962. See also *Yearbook of the United Nations, 1962,* 502.

31. Official Records of the General Assembly, 17th Session, 1193rd meeting, GA document A/PV.1193, 14 December 1962, p. 1124, para. 66.

32. Ibid. See also *Yearbook of the United Nations, 1962,* 502.

33. See "General and Specific Principles Recommended by UNCTAD I to Govern International Trade Relations and Trade Policies Conducive to Development," in *Proceedings of the United Nations Conference on Trade and Development: Geneva, 23 March–16 June 1964,* vol. 1 (New York: United Nations, 1964).

34. "Permanent Sovereignty over Natural Resources," *Yearbook of the United Nations, 1966* (New York: UN Office of Public Information, 1968), 329–333.

35. Rene-Jean Dupuy, *The Law of the Sea: Current Problems* (Leiden: Sijthoff, 1974), 9.

36. In "Proclamation by the President with Respect to the Natural Resources of the Subsoil and Sea Bed of the Continental Shelf, 28 September 1945," President Harry Truman declared: "Having concern for the urgency of conserving and prudently using its natural resources the United States regards the natural resources of the subsoil and sea-bed of the continental shelf beneath the high seas but contiguous to the coasts of the United States as appertaining to the United States, subject to its jurisdiction and control"; reproduced in *American Journal of International Law: Supplement* 40 (1946): 45.

37. "Proclamation by the President with Respect to Coastal Fisheries in Certain Areas of the High Seas, 28 September 1945," reproduced in *American Journal of International Law: Supplement* 40 (1946): 46.

38. For example, Mexico (1945), Argentina (1946), Nicaragua (1947), Chile (1947), Peru (1947), and Costa Rica (1948). For an analysis of these claims, see R. Young, "Recent Developments with Respect to the Continental Shelf," *American Journal of International Law* 42 (1948): 849–857. For an example of such a declaration, see "Argentina: Declaration Proclaiming Sovereignty over the Epicontinental Sea and the Continental Shelf," 9 October 1946, reproduced in *American Journal of International Law: Supplement* 41 (1947): 11.

39. Declaration on the Maritime Zone, 18 August 1952, in *United Nations Treaty Series* 1006: 326. The signatories—Chile, Ecuador, and Peru—declared that "they are responsible for the conservation and protection of their natural resources and for the regulation of the development of these resources in order to secure the best possible advantages for their respective countries" and that "it is also their duty to prevent any exploitation of these resources, beyond the scope of their jurisdiction, which endangers the existence, integrity and conservation of these resources to the detriment of the peoples who, because of their geographical situation, possess irreplaceable means of subsistence and vital economic resources in their seas." The declaration was complemented by the Joint Declaration Concerning Fishing Problems in the South Pacific, 18 August 1952, in *United Nations Treaty Series* 1006: 318.

40. Article 13(1)(a) of the UN Charter provides that the General Assembly "shall initiate studies and make recommendations for the purpose of . . . encouraging the progressive development of international law and its codification." To give effect to this article, the General Assembly established in 1947 the International Law Commission, which has "for its object the promotion of the progressive development of international law and its codification." See Article 1 of the Statute of the International Law Commission, adopted by General Assembly resolution 174 (II), 21 November 1947.

41. "International Technical Conference on the Conservation of the Living Resources of the Sea," General Assembly resolution 900 (IX), 14 December 1954.

42. *Report of the International Technical Conference on the Conservation of the Living Resources of the Sea, 18 April to 10 May 1955, Rome* (New York: United Nations, 1955), paragraphs 17–18.

43. General Assembly documents A/CONF.13/L52, A/CONF.13/L53, A/CONF.13/L54, and A/CONF.13/L55, 24 February–27 April 1958, reproduced in *United Nations Conference on the Law of the Sea Official Records,* vol. 2, *Plenary Meetings* (New York: United Nations, 1975–1984), 132–143.

44. Convention on the Continental Shelf, 29 April 1958, entered into force 10 June 1964, Articles 1 and 2, available at http://untreaty.un.org/ilc/texts/instruments/english/conventions/8_1_1958_continental_shelf.pdf and in *United Nations Treaty Series* (New York: United Nations, 1964), 499: 311.

45. Ibid., Article 2, paragraph 2.

46. Convention on Fishing and Conservation of Living Resources of the High Seas, 29 April 1958, entered into force 20 March 1966, available at http://untreaty.un.org/ilc/texts/instruments/english/conventions/8_1_1958_fishing.pdf and in *United Nations Treaty Series* (New York: United Nations, 1964), 559: 285.

47. Ibid., Article 2.

48. Ibid., Article 7.

49. The convention, however, stated that the joint breadth of the territorial sea and the contiguous zone shall not exceed twelve nautical miles.

50. The joint U.S.-Canadian proposal on a six-nautical-mile territorial sea plus a six-nautical-mile fishery zone adjacent to the territorial sea failed to receive the required majority by one vote (43 in favor, 33 against, with 12 abstentions); *Official Records of the Second United Nations Conference on the Law of the Sea,* vol. 1 (New York: United Nations, 1962), 152.

51. A number of Latin American states—Nicaragua in 1965, Ecuador in 1966, Argentina in 1966, Panama in 1967, Uruguay in 1969, and Brazil in 1970—either extended their territorial seas or established fishery zones to 200 nautical miles. See "Claims to Extended Territorial Waters or Fishing Zones since 1960 United Nations Law of the Sea Conference," reproduced in *International Legal Materials* 2 (1963): 1122; and "Limits and Status of the Territorial Sea, Exclusive Fishing Zones and the Continental Shelf," *FAO Fisheries Circular* 127 (1971), reprinted in *International Legal Materials* 10 (1971): 1255–1257.

52. "Exploitation and Conservation of Living Marine Resources," General Assembly resolution 2413 (XXIII), 17 December 1968. The resolution was adopted on the basis of a

proposal sponsored by Canada, Iceland, Libya, the Maldives, Malta, Mauritius, Norway, the Philippines, and the United Kingdom. See *Yearbook of the United Nations, 1968* (New York: United Nations, 1971), 434.

53. The Convention on Fishing and Conservation of the Living Resources of the High Seas, the last of the four Geneva Conventions, entered into force in 1966 and was signed by only thirty-eight parties (status as of 28 April 2009). See "Multilateral Treaties Deposited with the Secretary-General," Chapter XII, Law of the Sea, available at http://treaties.un.org/Pages/ParticipationStatus.aspx.

54. See Robert W. Smith, *Exclusive Economic Zone Claims: An Analysis and Primary Documents* (Boston: M. Nijhoff, 1986), 5; and Karin Hjertonsson, *The New Law of the Sea: Influence of the Latin American States on Recent Developments of the Law of the Sea* (Leiden: Sijthoff, 1973).

55. The United States and some other industrialized countries argued that seabed mining was one of the freedoms of the high seas to which article 2 of the Convention on the High Seas of 1958 indirectly referred with the phrase *inter alia*. However, there is little evidence for such an interpretation. In 1958, deep seabed mining was simply not yet an issue.

56. On the problems arising from rapid technological progress and the consequences of the latter on the outer limits of the continental shelf, see Juraj Andrassy, *International Law and the Resources of the Sea* (New York: Columbia University Press, 1970).

57. See "Question of Promoting the Peaceful Uses of the Sea-Bed and the Ocean Floor," *Yearbook of the United Nations, 1967* (New York: UN Office of Public Information, 1969), 41–48; and "First Committee, 1515th Meeting, 1 November 1967," General Assembly document A/C.1/PV.1515, available at http://www.un.org/Depts/los/convention_agreements/texts/pardo_ga1967.pdf.

58. See First Plenary Meeting, United Nations Conference on the Law of the Sea, General Assembly document A/CONF.13/SR.1, 1958, 3, reproduced in *United Nations Conference on the Law of the Sea, Official Records*, vol. 2, *Plenary Meetings*, 24 February–27 April 1958, 3.

59. "Examination of the Question of the Reservation Exclusively for Peaceful Purposes of the Sea-Bed and the Ocean Floor, and the Subsoil Thereof, Underlying the High Seas Beyond the Limits of Present National Jurisdiction, and the Use of Their Resources in the Interests of Mankind," General Assembly resolution 2340 (XXII), 18 December 1967.

60. "Question of the Reservation Exclusively for Peaceful Purposes of the Sea-Bed and the Ocean Floor, and the Subsoil Thereof, Underlying the High Seas Beyond the Limits of Present National Jurisdiction, and the Use of Their Resources in the Interests of Mankind," General Assembly resolution 2574 (XXIV), 15 December 1969.

61. "Declaration of Principles Governing the Sea-Bed and the Ocean Floor, and the Subsoil Thereof, Beyond the Limits of National Jurisdiction," General Assembly resolution 2749 (XXV), 17 December 1970.

62. "Reservation Exclusively for Peaceful Purposes of the Sea-Bed and the Ocean Floor, and the Subsoil Thereof, Underlying the High Seas Beyond the Limits of Present National Jurisdiction and the Use of Their Resources in the Interests of Mankind, and Convening of a Conference on the Law of the Sea," General Assembly resolution 2750 (XXV), 17 December 1970.

63. Some of these concerns were expressed as early as in 1957, when the World Meteorological Organization declared an International Geophysical Year, thereby focusing attention on the need for more research on the ozone layer in the light of pollution of the atmosphere and climate change. See "The World Meteorological Organization (WMO)," *Yearbook of the United Nations, 1957* (New York: UN Office of Public Information, 1958), 487.

64. One of the first books to call for international attention to the environment was Rachel Carlson's *Silent Spring* (Boston: Houghton Mifflin, 1962), which exposed the catastrophic effects of the use of DDT in agriculture, including the disappearance of many birds. The book is considered one of the more important events in the birth of the environmental movement.

65. "Economic Development and the Conservation of Nature," General Assembly resolution 1831 (XVII), 18 December 1962; and "Development and Conservation of Nature," in *Yearbook of the United Nations, 1962,* 268–269.

66. See "Problems of the Human Environment," General Assembly resolution 2398 (XXIII), 3 December 1968; and "Problems of Human Environment," in *Yearbook of the United Nations, 1968* (New York: UN Office of Public Information, 1971), 473–476.

67. See "United Nations Conference on the Human Environment," in *Yearbook of the United Nations, 1972* (New York: UN Office of Public Information, 1975), 318. In 1971, the General Assembly decided "to restore all its rights to the People's Republic of China and to recognise the representative of its government as the only legitimate representative of China"; see "Restoration of the Lawful Rights of the People's Republic of China in the United Nations," General Assembly resolution 2758 (XXVI), 25 October 1971.

68. *Report of the United Nations Conference on the Human Environment,* General Assembly document A/CONF.48/14/Rev.1, 16 June 1972; text reproduced in *International Legal Materials* 11 (1972): 1416–1420.

69. Enrique V. Iglesias, *Development and Environment: Report and Working Papers of a Panel of Experts Convened by the Secretary-General of the United Nations Conference on the Human Environment, Founex, Switzerland, June 4–12, 1971* (Paris: Mouton, 1972). See also Louis Emmerij, Richard Jolly, and Thomas G. Weiss, *Ahead of the Curve? UN Ideas and Global Challenges* (Bloomington: Indiana University Press, 2001), 90.

70. For a comprehensive analysis of the debates, see Louis B. Sohn, "The Stockholm Declaration on the Human Environment," *Harvard International Law Journal* 14 (1973): 423–515.

71. *Report of the United Nations Conference on the Human Environment.*

72. "Institutional and Financial Arrangements for International Environmental Cooperation," General Assembly resolution 2997 (XXIX), 15 December 1972.

73. See, for example, "Permanent Sovereignty over Natural Resources of Developing Countries," General Assembly resolution 3016 (XXVII), 18 December 1972; and "The Use and Development of Non-Agricultural Resources," in *Yearbook of the United Nations, 1972,* 347.

74. See "Permanent Sovereignty over National Resources," General Assembly resolution 3171 (XXVIII), 17 December 1973, especially paragraph 4: "*Deplores* acts of States which use force, armed aggression, economic coercion, or any other illegal or improper means in resolving disputes concerning the exercise of the sovereign rights." Meanwhile, the Security Council had met in an extraordinary session at Panama City, where on 21 March 1973 it adopted resolution 330, which noted "*with deep concern* the existence and use of coercive measures which affect the free exercise of permanent sovereignty over the natural resources of Latin American countries," recognized that such coercive measures may endanger peace and security in Latin America, and requested states to refrain from using or encouraging the use of any type of coercive measures against states of the region.

75. See "Permanent Sovereignty over National Resources," esp. paragraphs 3 and 7.

76. These documents were contained in UN document A/AC.166/L.47, 30 April 1974, and were reproduced in *Report of the Ad Hoc Committee of the Sixth Special Session,* General Assembly document A/9556, 30 April 1974.

77. See *Report of the Ad Hoc Committee of the Sixth Special Session.*

78. "Official Records UN General Assembly, Sixth Special Session, 2229th Meeting," 1 May 1974, General Assembly document A/PV.2229, 1 May 1974, para. 81.

79. "Declaration on the Establishment of a New International Economic Order," General Assembly resolution 3201 (S-VI), 1 May 1974; and "Programme of Action on the Establishment of a New International Economic Order," General Assembly resolution 3202 (S-VI), 1 May 1974.

80. See "Charter of the Economic Rights and Duties of States," UNCTAD resolution 45 (III), 18 May 1972.

81. "Charter of Economic Rights and Duties of States," General Assembly resolution 3281 (XXIX), 12 December 1974. See also Official Records of the General Assembly, 2315th Meeting, 12 December 1974, General Assembly document A/PV.2315, and an extensive report in "Charter of Economic Rights and Duties of States," *Yearbook of the United Nations, 1974* (New York: UN Office of Public Information, 1977), 381–407.

82. For an extensive review, see Robert F. Meagher, *An International Distribution of Wealth and Power: A Study of the Charter of Economic Rights and Duties of States* (New York: Pergamon Press, 1979); and Nico J. Schrijver, *Sovereignty over Natural Resources: Balancing Rights and Duties* (Cambridge: Cambridge University Press, 1997), 100–111.

83. This article was adopted by 100 votes to eight, with 28 abstentions, illustrating the controversy involved.

84. See Abdelaziz Megzari, "Negotiating the Common Fund for Commodities," in *Effective Negotiation: Case Studies in Conference Diplomacy,* ed. Johan Kaufmann (Dordrecht: Nijhoff, 1989), 205–230.

85. United Nations Convention on the Law of the Sea, 10 December 1982, entered into force 16 November 1994, General Assembly document A/CONF.62/122, available at http://www.un.org/Depts/los/convention_agreements/texts/unclos/unclos_e.pdf and in *International Legal Materials* 21 (1982): 1261.

86. Ibid., Preamble.

87. See "A Constitution for the Oceans," remarks by Tommy T. B. Koh, president of the Third United Nations Conference on the Law of the Sea, in *The Law of the Sea: Official Text of the United Nations Convention on the Law of the Sea with Annexes and Index: Introductory Material on the Convention and the Conference* (New York: United Nations, 1983), xxxiii.

88. Willem D. Verwey, "The New Law of the Sea and the Establishment of a New International Economic Order," *Indian Journal of International Law* 21 (1981): 387–423; Barbara Kwiatkowska, *The 200 Mile Exclusive Economic Zone in the New Law of the Sea* (Dordrecht: Nijhoff, 1989); Yuwen Li, *Transfer of Technology for Deep Sea-Bed Mining: The 1982 Law of the Sea Convention and Beyond* (Dordrecht: Nijhoff, 1994).

89. See, for example, the Montevideo Declaration on the Law of the Sea, 8 May 1970, reproduced in *International Legal Materials* 9 (1970): 1081–1083; or the Declaration of the Latin American States on the Law of the Sea, 4–8 August 1970 (also known as the Lima Declaration), reproduced in *International Legal Materials* 10 (1971): 207–214; and in S. H. Lay, R. Churchill, and M. Nordquist, eds., *New Directions in the Law of the Sea, Documents,* vol. 1 (Dobbs Ferry, N.Y.: Oceana, 1973), 237–239.

90. See the Declaration of Santo Domingo, 9 June 1972, reproduced in *American Journal of International Law* 66 (1972): 918. The declaration was a product of the Specialized Conference of Caribbean Countries Concerning the Problems of the Sea.

91. See "Conclusions in the General Report of the African States Regional Seminar on the Law of the Sea, Yaoundé, 20–30 June 1972," in *National Legislation and Treaties Relating to the Law of the Sea* (New York: United Nations, 1974), 602. See also Satya N. Nandan, "The Exclusive Economic Zone: A Historical Perspective," in *The Law and the Sea: Essays in Memory of Jean Carroz,* ed. Food and Agriculture Organization (Rome: FAO, 1987), 171–188.

92. See Satya N. Nandan, Shabtai Rosenne, and Neal R. Grandy, eds., *United Nations Convention on the Law of the Sea, 1982: A Commentary,* vol. 2 (Dordrecht: Nijhoff, 1993), 498; Karin Hjertonsson, *The New Law of the Sea: Influence of the Latin American States on Recent Developments of the Law of the Sea* (Leiden: Sijthoff, 1973); and Nasila S. Rembe, *Africa and the International Law of the Sea: A Study of the Contribution of the African States to the Third United Nations Conference on the Law of the Sea* (Alphen a/d Rijn: Sijthoff & Noordhoff, 1980).

93. UNCLOS, Article 56. At the same time, the coastal state has jurisdiction with regard to the establishment and use of artificial islands, installations, and structures; marine scientific research; and the protection and preservation of the marine environment.

94. Ibid., Article 76.

95. Ibid., Article 82. However, these payments are not due until after five years of production and do not apply to developing states, which are net importers of the minerals in question. It remains to be seen whether the International Seabed Authority will ever receive payments on this basis.

96. Ibid., Article 46.

97. This was enough to satisfy most Latin American and African states, which had previously claimed 200-mile territorial seas and had been the prime initiators in this rush to claim maritime resources. Following adoption of the convention, most coastal states enacted new legislation that accommodated these new arrangements.

98. The general obligation to protect and preserve the marine environment is articulated in UNCLOS, Article 192.

99. Ibid., Article 193.

100. See ibid., Articles 61 and 119.

101. Ibid., Article 194.

102. "Draft World Charter for Nature," General Assembly resolution A/RES/35/7, 30 October 1980.

103. "World Charter for Nature," General Assembly resolution A/RES/37/7, 28 October 1982. See also "Environmental Activities," in *Yearbook of the United Nations, 1982* (New York: UN Department of Public Information, 1986), 1024; and Wolfgang E. Burhenne and Will A. Irwin, *The World Charter for Nature: Legislative History and Commentary,* 2nd ed. (Berlin: Erich Schmidt Verlag, 1986).

104. These organizations also jointly published the World Conservation Strategy in 1980. IUCN, UNEP, World Wildlife Fund, FAO, and UNESCO, *World Conservation Strategy: Living Resource Conservation for Sustainable Development* (Gland, Switzerland: IUCN, 1980).

105. "Co-operation in the Field of the Environment Concerning Natural Resources Shared by Two or More States," General Assembly resolution 3129 (XXVIII), 13 December 1973; and "Decisions by UNEP Governing Council, Economic and Social Council and General Assembly," *Yearbook of the United Nations, 1973* (New York: UN Office of Public Information, 1976), 374–375.

106. See "Cooperation in the Field of the Environment Concerning Natural Resources Shared by Two or More States," General Assembly resolution 3129 (XXVIII), 13 December 1973; and "Co-operation in the Field of the Environment Concerning Natural Resources Shared by Two or More States," UNEP Governing Council decision 44 (III), 25 April 1975.

107. See "Charter of Economic Rights and Duties of States," *Yearbook of the United Nations, 1974* (New York: UN Office of Public Information, 1977), 381–407, in particular the explanation of votes on Article 3 on p. 397.

108. See "Co-operation in the Field of the Environment Concerning Natural Resources Shared by Two or More States," UNEP Governing Council decision 6/14, 19 May 1978, in Official Records of the General Assembly, Thirty-third Session, Supplement No. 25, General Assembly document A/33/25, annex I, 154–155.

109. UNEP, Environmental Law Guidelines and Principles on Shared Natural Resources (1978), available at http://www.unep.org/Law/PDF/UNEPEnvironmental-Law-Guidelines-and-Principles.pdf.

110. "Co-operation in the Field of Environment Concerning Natural Resources Shared by Two or More States," General Assembly resolution A/RES/34/186, 18 December 1979.

111. See Sharelle Hart, ed., *Shared Resources: Issues of Governance* (Gland, Switzerland: IUCN, 2008).

112. Convention on International Trade in Endangered Species of Wild Fauna and Flora (CITES), Washington, D.C., 3 March 1973, entered into force on 1 July 1975, available at http://www.cites.org/eng/disc/text.shtml#texttop and in *International Legal Materials* 12 (1973): 1085–1104.

113. Convention on the Conservation of Migratory Species of Wild Animals (CMS or Bonn Convention), Bonn, 23 June 1979, entered into force on 1 November 1983, available at http://www.cms.int/pdf/convtxt/cms_convtxt_english.pdf and in *International Legal Materials* 19 (1980): 15–32.

114. "Process of Preparation of the Environmental Perspective to the Year 2000 and Beyond," General Assembly resolution A/RES/38/161, 19 December 1983.

115. The commission was established in "Process of Preparation of the Environmental Perspective to the Year 2000 and Beyond." Its mandate included proposing long-term environmental strategies for achieving sustainable development and recommending ways of achieving greater cooperation among developing countries and between developing and developed countries.

116. "Report of the World Commission on Environment and Development," General Assembly resolution A/RES/42/187, 11 December 1987.

117. "UN Conference on Environment and Development," General Assembly resolution A/RES/44/228, 22 December 1989.

118. "Rio Declaration on Environment and Development," 14 June 1992, General Assembly document A/CONF.151/26, available at http://www.unep.org/Documents.multilingual/Default.asp?DocumentID=78&ArticleID=1163.

119. Ibid.; emphasis added.

120. See *Report of the United Nations Conference on Environment and Development,* General Assembly document A/CONF.151/26, 14 August 1992, available at http://www.un.org/documents/ga/conf151/aconf15126-1.htm. For more about the conference, see "UN Conference on Environment and Development," in *Yearbook of the United Nations, 1992* (New York: UN Department of Public Information, 1993), 670–681.

121. United Nations Framework Convention on Climate Change, 9 May 1992, entered into force on 21 March 1994, available at http://unfccc.int/resource/docs/convkp/conveng.pdf and in *International Legal Materials* 31 (1992): 851–853.

122. Convention on Biological Diversity, 5 June 1992, available at http://www.cbd.int/convention/convention.shtml and in *International Legal Materials* 31 (1992): 822–841.

123. Ibid., Article 2.

124. Ibid., Article 1.

125. See ibid., Articles 6, 8, 9, 10, and 15.

126. For insight into forest negotiations at the Rio Summit, see Deborah S. Davenport, "An Alternative Explanation for the Failure of the UNCED Forest Negotiations," *Global Environmental Politics* 5, no. 1 (2005): 105–130.

127. Article 2 of the Convention to Combat Desertification in Countries Experiencing Serious Drought and/or Desertification, Particularly in Africa, 14 October 1994, available at http://www.unccd.int/convention/text/convention.php and in *United Nations Treaty Series* (New York: United Nations, 1996), 1954: 3.

128. Convention on the Protection and Use of Transboundary Watercourses and International Lakes, 17 March 1992, available at http://www.unece.org/env/water/pdf/watercon.pdf and in *United Nations Treaty Series* (New York: United Nations, 1996), 1936: 269.

129. Agreement on the Co-operation for the Sustainable Development of the Mekong River Basin, 5 April 1995, available at http://www.mrcmekong.org/agreement_95/agreement_95.htm and in *International Legal Materials* 34 (1995): 864.

130. UN Convention on the Law of the Non-Navigational Uses of International Watercourses, 21 May 1997, available at http://untreaty.un.org/ilc/texts/instruments/english/conventions/8_3_1997.pdf and in *International Legal Materials* 36 (1997): 700–702.

131. Agreement for the Implementation of the Provisions of the United Nations Convention on the Law of the Sea of 10 December 1982 relating to the Conservation and Management of Straddling Fish Stocks and Highly Migratory Fish Stocks, 4 August 1995, available at http://daccessdds.un.org/doc/UNDOC/GEN/N95/274/67/PDF/N9527467.pdf?OpenElement and in *United Nations Treaty Series* (New York: United Nations, 2001), 2167: 3.

132. Agreement to Promote Compliance with International Conservation and Management Measures by Fishing Vessels on the High Seas, 24 November 1993, available at http://www.fao.org/docrep/meeting/003/x3130m/X3130E00.HTM and in *International Legal Materials* 33 (1994): 968.

133. Code of Conduct for Responsible Fisheries, adopted on 31 October 1995 by the FAO Conference, available at ftp://ftp.fao.org/docrep/fao/005/v9878e/v9878e00.pdf.

134. Kyoto Protocol to the United Nations Framework Convention on Climate Change, 11 December 1997, available at http://unfccc.int/resource/docs/convkp/kpeng.pdf and in *International Legal Materials* 37 (1998): 22–28.

135. See Barbara Ruis, "No Forest Convention but Ten Tree Treaties," *Unasylva* 52, no. 206 (2001): 3–13.

136. "Resolutions and Decisions Adopted by the General Assembly during Its 19th Special Session, 23 to 28 June 1997," General Assembly document A/S-19/33, 28 June 1997.

137. "Programme for the Further Implementation of Agenda 21," General Assembly resolution A/RES/S-19/2, 19 September 1997, paragraphs 4 and 5.

138. Ibid., esp. paragraphs 17 and 72.

139. "United Nations Millennium Declaration," General Assembly resolution A/RES/55/2, 18 September 2000. In the declaration, the world's leaders also stated that certain fundamental values are essential to international relations in the twenty-first century, of which respect for nature was one: "Prudence must be shown in the management of all living species and natural resources, in accordance with the precepts of sustainable development. Only in this way can the immeasurable riches provided to us by nature be preserved and passed on to our descendants. The current unsustainable patterns of production and consumption must be changed in the interest of our future welfare and that of our descendants" (paragraph 6).

140. For more information on the Millennium Development Goals, see http://www.un.org/millenniumgoals.

141. "10-Year Review of Progress Achieved in the Implementation of the Outcome of the UN Conference on Environment and Development," General Assembly resolution A/RES/55/199, 20 December 2000.

142. The Declaration and Plan of Implementation were adopted by consensus on 4 September 2002; they are reproduced in the *Report of the World Summit on Sustainable Development, Johannesburg, South Africa, 26 August–4 September 2002* (New York: United Nations, 2002), available at http://www.unctad.org/en/docs/aconf199d20&c1_en.pdf. For analysis of the outcomes of the Johannesburg World Summit, see Virginie Barral, "Johannesburg 2002: quoi de neuf pour le developpement durable?" *Revue Générale de Droit International Public* 107 (2003): 415–432; Mohammed K. S. Hussain, "World Summit on Sustainable Development, Johannesburg: An Appraisal," *Indian Journal of International Law* 42 (2002): 348–369; Kevin R. Gray, "World Summit on Sustainable Development: Accomplishments and New Directions?" *International and Comparative Law Quarterly* 52 (2003): 256–268; Paul Wapner, "World Summit on Sustainable Development: Toward a Post-Jo'burg Environmentalism," *Global Environmental Politics* 3, no. 1 (2003): 1–10.

143. See *Investing in the United Nations: For a Stronger Organization Worldwide: Report of the Secretary-General,* General Assembly document A/60/692, 7 March 2006, available at http://daccessdds.un.org/doc/UNDOC/GEN/N06/251/77/PDF/N0625177.pdf?OpenElement.

144. See Peter Hilpold, "Reforming the United Nations: New Proposals in a Long-Lasting Endeavour," *Netherlands International Law Review* 52 (2005): 389–431; see also Nico J. Schrijver, "UN Reform: A Once-in-a-Generation Opportunity?" *International Organizations Law Review* 2 (2005): 271–275.

145. See "World Summit Outcome Document," General Assembly resolution A/RES/60/1, 24 October 2005.

146. "2005 World Summit Outcome," General Assembly resolution A/RES/60/1, 24 October 2005, 11–12.

147. "United Nations Declaration on the Rights of Indigenous Peoples," General Assembly resolution A/RES/61/295, 13 September 2007, adopted by 143 to 4 votes, with 11 abstentions. For the particular role of African countries, see W. J. M. Genugten, "The African Move towards the Adoption of the 2007 Declaration on the Rights of Indigenous Peoples: The Substantive Arguments behind the Procedures," 1 March 2008, prepared for the Committee on the Rights of Indigenous Peoples of the International Law Association, available at http://ssrn.com/abstract=1103862.

148. See N. J. Schrijver, *Sovereignty over Natural Resources: Balancing Rights and Duties* (Cambridge: Cambridge University Press, 1997).

3. Management of the Global Commons

1. For more on the expedition, see A. L. Rice, "The *Challenger* Expedition: The End of an Era or a New Beginning?" in *Understanding the Oceans,* ed. Margaret Deacon, Tony Rice, and Colin P. Summerhayes (London: Routledge, 2001), 27–48.

2. For more information on these resources, see International Seabed Authority, "Marine Mineral Resources," available at http://www.isa.org.jm/files/documents/EN/Brochures/ENG6.pdf.

3. UNCLOS, Article 136 and Part XI, available at http://www.un.org/Depts/los/convention_agreements/texts/unclos/unclos_e.pdf.

4. On these controversies, see Yuwen Li, *Transfer of Technology for Deep Sea-Bed Mining: The 1982 Law of the Sea Convention and Beyond* (Dordrecht: Martinus Nijhoff Publishers, 1994), particularly chapter 8.

5. Agreement Relating to the Implementation of Part XI of the United Nations Convention on the Law of the Sea of 10 December 1982, 28 July 1994, adopted by General Assembly resolution 48/263, 17 August 1994, available at http://www.un.org/Depts/los/convention_agreements/texts/unclos/closindxAgree.htm.

6. See ibid., in particular Section 2 on the Enterprise, Section 5 on transfer of technology, Section 6 on production policy, and Section 7 on economic assistance. See also UNCLOS, Article 170(1), available at http://www.un.org/Depts/los/convention_agreements/texts/unclos/unclos_e.pdf; and Li, *Transfer of Technology for Deep Sea-Bed Mining.*

7. Ibid., Article 134.

8. UNCLOS defined "resources" as all solid, liquid, or gaseous mineral resources in situ in the area at or beneath the seabed, including polymetallic nodules; see Article 133(a).

9. UNCLOS, Article 137.

10. Ibid., Article 157.

11. The regulations were adopted on 13 July 2000 and are annexed to the Decision of the Assembly on the Regulations for Exploration and Exploitation for Polymetallic Nodules in the Area, ISA document ISBA/6/A/18, 4 October 2000. These regulations set out the legal rules that contractors and the ISA must follow in their work to locate and evaluate nodules and include provisions to protect the marine environment against possible harm from seabed activities.

12. UNCLOS, Articles 156–165; and Agreement Relating to the Implementation of Part XI of the United Nations Convention on the Law of the Sea of 10 December 1982.

13. UNCLOS, Article 170.

14. See International Seabed Authority, "Contractors for Seabed Exploration," available at http://www.isa.org.jm/files/documents/EN/Brochures/ENG3.pdf.

15. See Salvatore Arico and Charlotte Salpin, *Bioprospecting of Genetic Resources in the Deep Seabed: Scientific, Legal and Policy Aspects* (Yokohama, Japan: UN University, Institute

for Advanced Studies, 2005), available at http://www.cbd.int/doc/external/unu/unu-ias-mar-report-2005-en.pdf.

16. According to Article 86 of UNCLOS, the high seas comprise "all parts of the sea that are not included in the exclusive economic zone, in the territorial sea or in the internal waters of a State, or in the archipelagic waters of an archipelagic State."

17. UNCLOS, Article 87.

18. *Fisheries Jurisdiction (United Kingdom v. Iceland),* Merits, Judgment, 25 July 1974, paragraph 72, available at http://www.icj-cij.org/docket/files/56/6001.pdf; *Fisheries Jurisdiction (Federal Republic of Germany v. Iceland),* Merits, Judgment, 25 July 1974, paragraph 64, available at http://www.icj-cij.org/docket/files/55/5977.pdf.

19. UNCLOS, Articles 117 and 118.

20. Ibid., Article 116.

21. Ibid., Article 119(1). To ensure the availability of "best scientific evidence," UNCLOS also outlines the duty of states to exchange available scientific information, catch and fishing effort statistics, and other data relevant to the conservation of fish stocks; see Article 119(2).

22. Besides the possibility of recourse to the ICJ, the International Tribunal for the Law of the Sea, and arbitration tribunals, UNCLOS allows for the establishment of special arbitral tribunals (so-called Annex VIII Tribunals) to deal specifically with disputes concerning fisheries; see Part XV.

23. These steps led to the adoption of the Convention for the Prohibition of Fishing with Long Driftnets in the South Pacific, 24 November 1989, available at http://eelink.net/~asilwildlife/southpacific.html and in *International Legal Materials* 29 (1990): 1453–1461.

24. "Large-Scale Pelagic Driftnet Fishing and Its Impact on the Living Marine Resources of the World's Oceans and Seas," General Assembly resolution A/RES/44/225, 22 December 1989. See also "Large-Scale Pelagic Drift-Net Fishing and Its Impact on the Living Marine Resources of the World's Oceans and Seas," General Assembly resolution A/RES/46/215, 20 December 1991.

25. These include the *Estai* incident and the proceedings before the ICJ in *Fisheries Jurisdiction (Spain v. Canada),* 1998.

26. United Nations Agreement for the Implementation of the Provisions of the United Nations Convention on the Law of the Sea of 10 December 1982 Relating to the Conservation and Management of Straddling Fish Stocks and Highly Migratory Fish Stocks, 4 August 1995, entered into force 11 December 2001, available at http://daccessdds.un.org/doc/UNDOC/GEN/N95/274/67/PDF/N9527467.pdf?OpenElement and in *United Nations Treaty Series* (New York: United Nations, 2001), 2167: 3. The agreement was negotiated as a follow-up to the mandate of Chapter 17 of Agenda 21.

27. UNCLOS, Articles 2–3.

28. See particularly ibid., Articles 5–7.

29. Ibid., Articles 8–10.

30. For an overview of regional fisheries bodies, see "Fact Sheets on Regional Fisheries Bodies," available at http://www.fao.org/fishery/rfb/search/en.

31. On the role of RFMO/As, see "Regional Fishery Bodies (RFB)," available at http://www.fao.org/fishery/rfb/en.

32. Agreement to Promote Compliance with International Conservation and Management Measures by Fishing Vessels on the High Seas, 24 November 1993, entered into force 24 April 2003, available at http://www.fao.org/docrep/meeting/003/x3130m/X3130E00.HTM and in *International Legal Materials* 33 (1994): 968. The agreement mandates the adoption of measures to prevent reflagging of fishing vessels as a way of avoiding compliance and provides for strengthened international cooperation, particularly when exchanging information on high seas fishing. The agreement notes in its preamble that "under Agenda 21, States commit themselves to the conservation and sustainable use of marine living resources on the high seas."

33. Code of Conduct for Responsible Fisheries, adopted on 31 October 1995 by the FAO Conference, available at ftp://ftp.fao.org/docrep/fao/005/v9878e/v9878e00.pdf.

34. See "Sustainable Fisheries, Including through the 1995 Agreement for the Implementation of Provisions of the United Nations Convention of the Law of the Sea of 10 December 1982 Relating to the Conservation and Management of Straddling Fish Stocks and Highly Migratory Fish Stocks, and Related Instruments," General Assembly resolution A/RES/60/31, 10 March 2006.

35. *Oceans and the Law of the Sea: Report of the Secretary-General: Addendum,* General Assembly document A/62/66/Add.2, 10 September 2007, paragraphs 285–307, available at http://daccessdds.un.org/doc/UNDOC/GEN/N07/500/06/PDF/N0750006.pdf?OpenElement.

36. For an overview of current issues, see *Oceans and the Law of the Sea: Report of the Secretary-General,* General Assembly document A/63/63, 10 March 2008.

37. See UNCLOS, Articles 65 and 120. Some marine mammals are also listed as highly migratory species and are thus covered by Article 64, but Article 65 provides for a more general protection for all marine mammals.

38. Ibid., Article 65.

39. See Patricia Birnie, "International Legal Issues in the Management and Protection of the Whale: A Review of Four Decades of Experience," *Natural Resources Journal* 29 (1989): 903.

40. International Convention for the Regulation of Whaling, 2 December 1946, entered into force 10 November 1948, available at http://www.iwcoffice.org/commission/convention.htm and in *United Nations Treaty Series* (New York: United Nations, 1953), 161: 72.

41. The convention applies "to factory ships, land stations, and whale catchers under the jurisdiction of the Contracting Governments, and to all waters in which whaling is prosecuted by such factory ships, land stations, and whale catchers"; ibid., Article I, paragraph 2.

42. Ibid., Preamble.

43. In a sense, the convention predates the concept of sustainable use of natural resources, which later evolved into an essential element of the concept of sustainable development.

44. International Convention for the Regulation of Whaling, Preamble.

45. For an updated list of IWC members, see "IWC Members and Commissioners," available at http://www.iwcoffice.org/commission/members.htm.

46. See also Patricia W. Birnie and Alan E. Boyle, *International Law and the Environment,* 2nd ed. (Oxford: Oxford University Press, 2002), 667.

47. International Convention for the Regulation of Whaling, Article V.

48. These are twelve baleen whales—the bowhead (or Greenland right) whale, the North Atlantic right whale, the North Pacific right whale, the southern right whale, the gray whale, the blue whale, the fin whale, the sei whale, Bryde's whale, the common (or northern) minke whale, the Antarctic minke whale, and the humpback whale—and the largest toothed whale, the sperm whale.

49. Recommendation 33 of the Action Plan for the Human Environment (1972), available at http://fds.oup.com/www.oup.co.uk/pdf/bt/cassese/cases/part3/ch17/1204.pdf and in *International Legal Materials* 11 (1972): 1421.

50. For an account, see David D. Caron, "The International Whaling Commission and the North Atlantic Marine Mammal Commission: The Institutional Risks of Coercion in Consensual Structures," *American Journal of International Law* 89 (1995): 154–174.

51. See Paragraph 13 of the Schedule attached to the International Convention for the Regulation of Whaling (which forms an integral part of the latter), available at http://www.iwcoffice.org/_documents/commission/schedule.pdf. In 2007, the commission renewed for another five years the catch limits for the bowhead whales of the Bering-Chukchi-Beaufort Seas Stock, the Eastern North Pacific gray whales, the humpback whales taken by Saint Vincent and the Grenadines, the West Greenland fin whales, West and East Greenland common minke whales, and West Greenland bowhead whales. See *Oceans and the Law of the Sea: Re-*

port of the Secretary-General: Addendum, General Assembly document A/62/66/Add.1, 31 August 2007, paragraph 138, available at http://www.un.org/Depts/los/general_assembly/general_assembly_reports.htm.

52. Article VIII of the International Convention for the Regulation of Whaling states: "Notwithstanding anything contained in this Convention any Contracting Government may grant to any of its nationals a special permit authorizing that national to kill, take and treat whales for purposes of scientific research subject to such restrictions as to number and subject to such other conditions as the Contracting Government thinks fit." It also states that "the killing, taking, and treating of whales in accordance with the provisions of this Article shall be exempt from the operation of this Convention."

53. See "Special Permit Catches since 1985," available at http://www.iwcoffice.org/conservation/table_permit.htm. See also Philip J. Clapham et al., "The Whaling Issue: Conservation, Confusion and Casuistry," *Marine Policy* 31 (2007): 314–319.

54. See "Iceland and Commercial Whaling," available at http://www.iwcoffice.org/conservation/iceland.htm.

55. In fact, the convention's Preamble recognizes that "the whale stocks are susceptible of natural increases if whaling is properly regulated, and that increases in the size of whale stocks will permit increases in the number of whales which may be captured without endangering these natural resources."

56. For an account on the progress made with regard to the RMS, see "Information on the Background and Progress of the Revised Management Scheme (RMS)," available at http://www.iwcoffice.org/conservation/rms.htm.

57. See William Aron, William Burke, and Milton Freeman, "The Whaling Issue," *Marine Policy* 24 (2000): 179–192; and Sidney J. Holt, "Whaling: Will the Phoenix Rise Again?" *Marine Pollution Bulletin* 54 (2007): 1081–1086.

58. At its 2006 annual meeting, the IWC adopted a declaration that committed its members to work to normalize the functions of the commission based on the terms of the ICRW, to respect cultural diversity and the traditions of coastal peoples, and to respect the fundamental principles of sustainable use of resources. The declaration also affirmed the need for the science-based policy making and rule making that are accepted as the world standard for the management of marine resources. The declaration was adopted by a narrow majority of 33 votes to 32. For the text of the declaration, see http://www.iwcoffice.org/meetings/resolutions/resolution2006.htm.

59. See Mike Iliff, "Normalization of the International Whaling Commission," *Marine Policy* 32 (2008): 333–338; and Iliff, "Modernisation of the International Convention for the Regulation of Whaling," *Marine Policy* 32 (2008): 402–407. See also "Future of the IWC," available at http://www.iwcoffice.org/commission/future.htm.

60. Article 2 of Agreement on Cooperation in Research, Conservation and Management of Marine Mammals in the North Atlantic (NAMMCO), 9 April 1992, entered into force 7 July 1992, available at http://untreaty.un.org/unts/120001_144071/16/9/00013434.pdf and in *Law of the Sea Bulletin* 26 (1994): 66.

61. See ibid., Articles 4(2)(a) and 5(1).

62. Ibid., Article 9.

63. Participation in NAMMCO is in principle open to other states. However, acceptance of new members is subject to the consent of existing members (ibid., Article 10). Moreover, all decisions are to be taken unanimously (ibid., Articles 4 and 5).

64. See Caron, "The International Whaling Commission."

65. Article 2 of Agreement on the Conservation of Small Cetaceans of the Baltic and North Seas (ASCOBANS), 17 March 1992, entered into force 29 March 1994, available at http://www.ascobans.org/index0101.html and in *United Nations Treaty Series* (New York: United Nations, 1994), 1772: 217. The agreement covers all species, subspecies, or populations of toothed whales, including various species of porpoises and dolphins but excluding sperm whales.

66. The amendment, which was adopted on 22 August 2003, is available at http://www.ascobans.org/index0101.html. It entered into force on 3 February 2008.

67. Article II, paragraph 1 of Agreement on the Conservation of the Cetaceans of the Black Sea, Mediterranean Sea and Contiguous Atlantic Area (ACCOBAMS), 24 November 1996, entered into force 1 June 2001, available at http://www.cms.int/species/accobams/acc_bkrd.htm and in *International Legal Materials* 36 (1997): 777. The agreement applies to all cetaceans "that have a range which lies entirely or partly within the Agreement area or that accidentally or occasionally frequent the Agreement area," including large cetaceans such as fin or sperm whales.

68. Amendment of Annex 2 to the Agreement on the Conservation of Cetaceans of the Black Sea, Mediterranean Sea and Contiguous Atlantic Area, Related to the Use of Drift Nets, adopted at the Third Meeting of the Parties to ACCOBAMS, 22–25 October 2007, entered into force 22 March 2008, available at http://www.cms.int/species/accobams/acc_text.htm.

69. Article I(1)(a) of Convention on the Conservation of Migratory Species of Wild Animals, 23 June 1979, entered into force 1 November 1983, available at http://www.cms.int/documents/convtxt/cms_convtxt.htm and in *International Legal Materials* 19 (1980): 15.

70. Agreement on the Conservation of Seals in the Wadden Sea, 16 October 1990, available at http://www.cms.int/pdf/en/summary_sheets/cwss.pdf; and Memorandum of Understanding Concerning Conservation Measures for the Eastern Atlantic Populations of the Mediterranean Monk Seal, 18 October 2007, available at http://www.cms.int/species/monk_seal/monk_seal_bkrd.htm.

71. Memorandum of Understanding Concerning Conservation Measures for Marine Turtles of the Atlantic Coast of Africa, 29 May 1999, available at http://www.cms.int/pdf/AFRICAturtle_mou.pdf; and Memorandum of Understanding on the Conservation and Management of Marine Turtles and Their Habitats of the Indian Ocean and South-East Asia, 1 September 2001, available at http://www.cms.int/species/iosea/IOSEAturtle_bkgd.htm.

72. Memorandum of Understanding for the Conservation of Cetaceans and Their Habitats in the Pacific Islands Region, 9 September 2006, available at http://www.cms.int/species/pacific_cet/pacific_cet_bkrd.htm; Memorandum of Understanding on the Conservation and Management of Dugongs and Their Habitats Throughout their Range, 31 October 2007, available at http://www.cms.int/species/dugong/pdf/Annex_08_Dugong_MoU.pdf; and Memorandum of Understanding Concerning the Conservation of the Manatee and Small Cetaceans of Western Africa and Macronesia, 3 October 2008, available at http://www.cms.int/pdf/en/summary_sheets/wamm.pdf.

73. Convention on International Trade in Endangered Species of Wild Fauna and Flora, 3 March 1973, entered into force 1 July 1975, available at http://www.cites.org/eng/disc/text.shtml and in *International Legal Materials* 12 (1973): 1085.

74. Convention on the Conservation of European Wildlife and Natural Habitats, 19 September 1979, entered into force 1 June 1982, available at http://conventions.coe.int/Treaty/EN/Treaties/Html/104.htm and in *United Nations Treaty Series* (New York: United Nations, 1982), 1284: 209.

75. E.g., Agreement on the International Dolphin Conservation Program, 15 May 1998, entered into force 15 February 1999 (for more information, see http://www.nmfs.noaa.gov/ia/intlagree/aidcp.htm); Inter-American Convention for the Protection and Conservation of Sea Turtles, 1 December 1996, entered into force 2 May 2001, available at http://www.seaturtle.org/iac/intro.shtml; and Agreement Concerning the Creation of a Marine Mammal Sanctuary in the Mediterranean, 25 November 1999, entered into force 14 February 2002, available at http://untreaty.un.org/unts/144078_158780/4/7/12492.pdf.

76. On the important interplay between the ICRW and CITES, see *Oceans and the Law of the Sea: Report of the Secretary-General: Addendum,* General Assembly document A/62/66/Add. 1, 31 August 2007, paragraph 140.

77. FAO Guidelines to Reduce Sea Turtle Mortality in Fishing Operations, attached as Appendix E to the *Report of the FAO Technical Consultation on Sea Turtles Conservation and*

Fisheries (Bangkok, 29 November–2 December 2004), available at ftp://ftp.fao.org/docrep/fao/007/y5887e/y5887e00.pdf.

78. See "Peaceful Uses of Outer Space," in *Yearbook of the United Nations, 1958* (New York: UN Office of Public Information, 1959), 19.

79. "International Co-Operation in the Peaceful Uses of Outer Space," General Assembly resolution 1472 (XIV), 12 December 1959.

80. "Declaration of Legal Principles Governing the Activities of States in the Exploration and Uses of Outer Space," General Assembly resolution 1962 (XVIII), 13 December 1963. The declaration stated that the exploration and use of outer space shall be carried on for the benefit and in the interests of all mankind and that outer space and celestial bodies are free for exploration and use by all states on a basis of equality and are not subject to national appropriation by claim of sovereignty.

81. Articles I and II of the Treaty on Principles Governing the Activities of States in the Exploration and Use of Outer Space, Including the Moon and Other Celestial Bodies (Outer Space Treaty), 27 January 1967, entered into force 10 October 1967, available at http://untreaty.un.org/cod/avl/ha/tos/tos.html and in *United Nations Treaty Series* (New York: United Nations, 1967), 610: 205.

82. Agreement Governing the Activities of States on the Moon and Other Celestial Bodies (Moon Agreement), 5 December 1979, entered into force 11 July 1984, General Assembly document A/34/664, 12 November 1979, available at http://www.islandone.org/Treaties/BH766.html and in *International Legal Materials* 18 (1979): 1434–1441. The Moon Agreement has been ratified by Australia, Austria, Belgium, Chile, Kazakhstan, Lebanon, Mexico, Morocco, the Netherlands, Pakistan, Peru, the Philippines, and Uruguay.

83. Ibid., Article 11, paragraphs 1–3.

84. Ibid., Article 1.

85. Ibid., Article 4.

86. Ibid., Article 11, paragraph 4.

87. Ibid., Article 11, paragraphs 5 and 7.

88. Ibid., Article 11, paragraph 6.

89. Ibid., paragraph 8.

90. Article 6(2) of the Moon Agreement provides that in carrying out scientific investigations states shall have the right to collect and remove from the moon samples of its mineral and other substances that they may use for scientific purposes. The agreement notes the desirability of making these samples available to the international scientific community. It also states that states "may in the course of scientific investigations also use mineral and other substances of the moon in quantities appropriate for the support of their missions."

91. See Articles I and II of the Antarctic Treaty, 1 December 1959, entered into force 23 June 1961, available at http://www.nsf.gov/od/opp/antarct/anttrty.jsp and in *United Nations Treaty Series* (New York: United Nations, 1961), 402: 71.

92. Although the parties to the Antarctic Treaty did not renounce their previously asserted rights or claims to territorial sovereignty in Antarctica, they cannot rely on the acts or activities taking place on the basis of the treaty as a basis for asserting, supporting, or denying a claim to territorial sovereignty or any other rights of sovereignty over Antarctica (Article IV).

93. The consultative parties comprise the original parties to the treaty (i.e., the twelve nations active in the Antarctic during the International Geophysical Year of 1957–1958) and sixteen states that, in view of their substantial scientific activities, have demonstrated a special interest in Antarctica and have thus become parties to the treaty. The original parties to the treaty were the United Kingdom, South Africa, Belgium, Japan, the United States, Norway, France, New Zealand, the Soviet Union, Argentina, Australia, and Chile. Since then, Poland, Germany, Brazil, India, China, Uruguay, Italy, Spain, Sweden, Finland, Peru, South Korea, Ec-

uador, the Netherlands, Bulgaria, and Ukraine have obtained consultative status. In addition to these, eighteen other states are parties to the Antarctic Treaty but do not enjoy consultative status and thus cannot participate in the decision making at the consultative meetings.

94. Article IX(1)(f) of the Antarctic Treaty states that the parties to the treaty will meet at regular intervals "for the purpose of exchanging information, consulting together on matters of common interest pertaining to Antarctica, and formulating and considering, and recommending . . . measures in furtherance of the principles and objectives of the Treaty," including measures regarding "preservation and conservation of living resources in Antarctica."

95. The Agreed Measures for the Conservation of Antarctic Fauna and Flora, 2 June 1964, are available at http://sedac.ciesin.columbia.edu/entri/texts/acrc/aff64.txt.html and in *Treaties and Other International Acts Series,* no. 6058 (Washington, D.C.: U.S. Government Printing Office, 1964).

96. Convention for the Conservation of Antarctic Seals, 1 June 1972, entered into force 11 March 1978, available at http://sedac.ciesin.org/entri/texts/antarctic.seals.1972.html and in *International Legal Materials* 11 (1972): 251–261. The convention's preamble recognizes "the general concern about the vulnerability of Antarctic seals to commercial exploitation and the consequent need for effective conservation measures" and states "that the stocks of Antarctic seals are an important living resource in the marine environment which requires an international agreement for its effective conservation." Moreover, it recognizes "that this resource should not be depleted by over-exploitation, and hence that any harvesting should be regulated so as not to exceed the levels of the optimum sustainable yield."

97. Convention on the Conservation of Antarctic Marine Living Resources, 20 May 1980, entered into force 7 April 1982, available at http://sedac.ciesin.org/entri/texts/antarctic.marine.resources.1980.html and in *International Legal Materials* 19 (1980): 841–859.

98. Ibid., Article I(1). Article I(2) defines Antarctic marine living resources as the populations of fin fish, mollusks, crustaceans, and all other species of living organisms found south of the Antarctic Convergence, including birds.

99. Ibid., Article II.

100. Convention on the Regulation of Antarctic Mineral Resource Activities, 2 June 1988, available at http://sedac.ciesin.columbia.edu/entri/texts/acrc/cramra.txt.html and in *International Legal Materials* 27 (1988): 868–900.

101. Ibid., Article 2. Article 1(6) defines mineral resources as all nonliving natural nonrenewable resources, including fossil fuels and metallic and nonmetallic minerals.

102. Ibid., Articles 7, 8, 11–12, 55–59.

103. Article 7 of Protocol on Environmental Protection to the Antarctic Treaty, 4 October 1991, entered into force 14 January 1998, available at http://www.antarctica.ac.uk/about_antarctica/geopolitical/treaty/update_1991.php and in *International Legal Materials* 30 (1991): 1461. Article 24 prohibits reservations to the protocol. The protocol contains six annexes: Environmental Impact Assessment, Conservation of Antarctic Fauna and Flora, Waste Disposal and Waste Management, Prevention of Marine Pollution, Area Protection and Management, and Liability Arising from Environmental Emergencies.

104. See in particular Articles 2, 3, and 7. The protocol has been ratified by all twenty-eight consultative parties and by six nonconsultative parties to the Antarctic Treaty. The current status of ratifications is available at http://www.ats.aq/devAS/ats_parties.aspx?lang=e.

105. In 2004, the International Whaling Commission decided to continue the Southern Ocean Sanctuary for another ten years, after a proposal by Japan to change the status of the sanctuary failed to reach the required majority in the commission.

106. See *Oceans and the Law of the Sea: Report of the Secretary-General: Addendum,* General Assembly document A/62/66/Add.1, 31 August 2007, paragraph 137.

107. See "Communication Concerning Antarctica," in *Yearbook of the United Nations, 1958,* 109–110.

108. See "Other Political Questions: Antarctica," in *Yearbook of the United Nations, 1983* (New York: UN Department of Public Information, 1987), 387. Nonetheless, the General Assembly requested that a comprehensive, factual, and objective study be prepared by the Secretary-General on all aspects of Antarctica; see "Question of Antarctica," General Assembly resolution A/RES/38/77, 15 December 1983.

109. The initiative, which came in the OAU's resolution 988 (XLII) of July 1985, called on all OAU members to take appropriate steps at the 1985 General Assembly session to seek Antarctica's recognition as the common heritage of mankind. "Resolution on the Question of Antarctica," OAU document CM/Res/988 (XLII), available at http://www.africa-union.org/root/AU/Documents/Decisions/com/25CoM_1985b.pdf. See also "Other Political Questions: Antarctica," in *Yearbook of the United Nations, 1985* (New York: UN Department of Public Information, co-published by Dordrecht/Boston: Martinus Nijhoff Publishers, 1989), 389.

110. "Question of Antarctica," General Assembly resolution A/RES/40/156 (B), 16 December 1985, adopted by 92 to 0 votes, with 14 abstentions and 53 nonvoting.

111. "Question of Antarctica," General Assembly resolution A/RES/41/88 (A) and (B), 4 December 1986; and "Question of Antarctica," General Assembly resolution A/RES/42/46 (B), 30 November 1987. In 1987, Antigua and Barbuda also submitted (but subsequently withdrew) a draft resolution requesting that an authority be established for sharing Antarctica's resources. See "Other Political Questions: Antarctica," in *Yearbook of the United Nations, 1987* (New York: UN Department of Public Information, 1992), 359–360.

112. In its 1986 resolution, for example, the General Assembly requested that the consultative parties "keep the Secretary-General fully informed on all aspects of the question of Antarctica so that the United Nations could function as the central repository of all such information." "Question of Antarctica," General Assembly resolution A/RES/41/88 (A) and (B), 4 December 1986; "Other Political Questions: Antarctica," in *Yearbook of the United Nations, 1986* (New York: UN Department of Public Information, co-published by Dordrecht/Boston: Martinus Nijhoff Publishers, 1992), 372. See also "Question of Antarctica," General Assembly resolution A/RES/42/46 (B), 30 November 1987. In its resolutions of 1989 and 1990, the General Assembly again expressed regret that the Secretary-General or his representative had not yet been invited to the Antarctic Treaty Consultative Meetings. See "Question of Antarctica," A/RES/44/124 (B), 15 December 1989; and "Question of Antarctica," General Assembly resolution A/RES/45/78 (A), 12 December 1990.

113. "Question of Antarctica," General Assembly resolution A/RES/43/83A, 7 December 1988.

114. "Question of Antarctica," General Assembly resolution A/RES/44/124B, 15 December 1989; and "Question of Antarctica," General Assembly resolution A/RES/45/78 (A), 12 December 1990.

115. See General Assembly resolution A/44/124B, 15 December 1989.

116. "Question of Antarctica," General Assembly resolution A/RES/44/124B, 15 December 1989. In this resolution, the General Assembly also affirmed that "in view of the significant impact that Antarctica exerts on the global environment and ecosystems, any régime to be established for the protection and conservation of the Antarctic environment and its dependent and associated ecosystems, in order to be for the benefit of mankind as a whole and in order to gain the universal acceptability necessary to ensure full compliance and enforcement, must be negotiated with the full participation of all members of the international community." Similar views were expressed in "Question of Antarctica," General Assembly resolution A/RES/45/78A, 12 December 1990; and "Question of Antarctica," General Assembly resolution A/RES/46/41A, 6 December 1991.

117. The General Assembly expressed disappointment that the protocol was negotiated without the full participation of the international community and stated its concern about the fact that the Madrid Protocol on Environmental Protection lacked monitoring and implemen-

tation mechanisms to comply with its provisions and had not taken into consideration the call of the international community to permanently ban prospecting and mining in Antarctica. "Question of Antarctica," General Assembly resolution A/RES/46/41A, 6 December 1991. In subsequent resolutions, the General Assembly reiterated its call for the ban to be made permanent; see "Question of Antarctica," General Assembly resolution A/RES/47/57, 9 December 1992; and "Question of Antarctica," A/RES/48/80, 13 January 1994.

118. See "Question of Antarctica," General Assembly resolution A/RES/57/51, 22 November 2002; and "Question of Antarctica," General Assembly resolution A/RES/60/47, 6 January 2006.

119. Article III(2) of the Antarctic Treaty states that "every encouragement shall be given to the establishment of cooperative working relations with those Specialized Agencies of the United Nations and other technical organizations having a scientific or technical interest in Antarctica."

120. See reports of the Secretary-General: *Question of Antarctica: Report of the Secretary-General,* General Assembly document A/41/722, 17 November 1986; and *Question of Antarctica: Report of the Secretary-General,* General Assembly document A/60/222, 11 August 2005.

121. See, for example, *Question of Antarctica: Report of the Secretary-General,* General Assembly document A/60/222, 11 August 2005.

122. With regard to ice-covered areas, Article 234 of the Convention on the Law of the Sea states: "Coastal States have the right to adopt and enforce non-discriminatory laws and regulations for the prevention, reduction and control of marine pollution from vessels in ice-covered areas within the limits of the exclusive economic zone, where particularly severe climatic conditions and the presence of ice covering such areas for most of the year create obstructions or exceptional hazards to navigation, and pollution of the marine environment could cause major harm to or irreversible disturbance of the ecological balance. Such laws and regulations shall have due regard to navigation and the protection and preservation of the marine environment based on the best available scientific evidence." Available at http://www.un.org/Depts/los/convention_agreements/texts/unclos/unclos_e.pdf.

123. Agreement on the Conservation of Polar Bears, 15 November 1973, entered into force 26 May 1976, available at http://www.ecolex.org/server2.php/libcat/docs/multilateral/en/TRE000041.txt and in *International Legal Materials* 13 (1974): 13–18.

124. In any event, the skins of bears and other items of value resulting from taking of bears shall not be made available for commercial purposes; ibid., Article 3.

125. Agreement between the Government of the United States of America and the Government of Canada on the Conservation of the Porcupine Caribou Herd, adopted and entered into force on 17 July 1987, available at http://untreaty.un.org/unts/144078_158780/16/2/7177.pdf and in *United Nations Treaty Series* (New York: United Nations, 2002), 2174: 268.

126. Arctic Environmental Protection Strategy, 14 June 1991, available at http://arctic-council.org/filearchive/artic_environment.pdf and in *International Legal Materials* 30 (1991): 1624–1626.

127. See ibid., Article 2. The Arctic Environmental Protection Strategy outlined principles that were to guide the activities of states in the Arctic region. It stipulated that the activities related to management, planning, and development would provide for the conservation, sustainable utilization, and protection of the ecosystem and natural resources of the Arctic for the benefit and enjoyment of present and future generations, including indigenous peoples, and that the use and management of natural resources would be based on an approach that considers the value and interdependent nature of components of the ecosystem.

128. "Declaration on the Establishment of the Arctic Council," 19 September 1996 available at http://arcticcircle.uconn.edu/NatResources/Policy/decacouncil.html and in *International Legal Materials* 35 (1996): 1382–1384. The council's other objectives are to oversee and coordinate the programs established under the Arctic Environmental Protection Strategy, to

adopt terms of reference for and oversee and coordinate a sustainable development program, and to disseminate information, encourage education about, and promote interest in Arctic-related issues.

129. Arctic Offshore Oil and Gas Guidelines, 10 October 2002, available at http://old.pame.is/sidur/uploads/ArcticGuidelines.pdf.

130. Ilulissat Declaration, 28 May 2008, available at http://arctic-council.org/filearchive/Ilulissat-declaration.pdf.

131. Note that in the exclusive economic zone, states have sovereign rights for the purpose of exploring, exploiting, conserving, and managing (living or nonliving) natural resources of the waters superjacent to the seabed and of the seabed and its subsoil but not of the airspace above the exclusive economic zone; UNCLOS, Article 56.

132. On atmospheric resources as global commons, see John Vogler, "Future Directions: The Atmosphere as a Global Commons," *Atmospheric Environment* 35 (2001): 2427–2428.

133. See Principle 1 of UNEP, Environmental Law Guidelines and Principles on Shared Natural Resources (1978), available at http://www.unep.org/Law/PDF/UNEPEnvironmental-Law-Guidelines-and-Principles.pdf.

134. For early analyses of the effects of acid rain, see Roger W. Ferenbaugh, "Acid Rain: Biological Effects and Implications," *Environmental Affairs* 4 (1975): 745–758; and Fred Pearce, *Acid Rain* (Harmondsworth, UK: Penguin, 1987). For an early discussion of the problem from an international law perspective, see Irene H. van Lier, *Acid Rain and International Law* (Toronto: Bunsel Environmental Consultants, 1982). However, acid rain precipitation and the long-range transport of air pollution were familiar long before acid rain became the subject of international controversy. See Kenneth Hanf, "The Problem of Long-Range Transport of Air Pollution and the Acidification Regime," in *International Environmental Agreements and Domestic Politics: The Case of Acid Rain*, ed. Arild Underdal and Kenneth Hanf (Aldershot, UK: Ashgate, 2000), 23.

135. See Recommendations 72 and 73 of the Action Plan adopted by the United Nations Conference on the Human Environment, available at http://www.unep.org/Documents.Multilingual/Default.asp?DocumentID=97&ArticleID=1509&l=en.

136. Convention on Long-Range Transboundary Air Pollution, 13 November 1979, entered into force 16 March 1983, available at http://www.unece.org/env/lrtap/full%20text/1979.CLRTAP.e.pdf and in *International Legal Materials* 18 (1979): 1442–1455.

137. Ibid., Article 1(b).

138. Protocol to the 1979 Convention on Long-Range Transboundary Air Pollution on the Reduction of Sulphur Emissions or their Transboundary Fluxes by at Least 30 Per Cent, 8 July 1985, entered into force on 2 September 1987, available at http://www.unece.org/env/lrtap/full%20text/1985.Sulphur.e.pdf and in *International Legal Materials* 27 (1988): 707–711.

139. Ibid., Article 2.

140. Protocol to the 1979 Convention on Long-Range Transboundary Air Pollution Concerning the Control of Emissions of Nitrogen Oxides or Their Transboundary Fluxes, 31 October 1988, entered into force 14 February 1991, available at http://www.unece.org/env/lrtap/full%20text/1988.NOX.e.pdf and in *International Legal Materials* 28 (1989): 212–213.

141. Protocol to the 1979 Convention on Long-Range Transboundary Air Pollution on Further Reduction of Sulphur Emissions, 14 June 1994, entered into force 5 August 1998, available at http://www.unece.org/env/lrtap/full%20text/1994.Sulphur.e.pdf and in *International Legal Materials* 33 (1994): 1540–1541.

142. Article 1(7) of the Protocol to the 1979 Convention on Long-Range Transboundary Air Pollution Concerning the Control of Emissions of Nitrogen Oxides or Their Transboundary Fluxes defines critical load as "a quantitative estimate of an exposure to one or more pollutants below which significant harmful effects on specific sensitive elements of the environment do not occur according to present knowledge."

143. However, the critical loads were to be used as guidelines, while the actual achievement of critical loads was a long-term objective.

144. For a list of all protocols to the Convention on Long-Range Transboundary Air Pollution, see "Protocols to the Convention," available at http://www.unece.org/env/lrtap/status/lrtap_s.htm.

145. Protocol to the 1979 Convention on Long-Range Transboundary Air Pollution Concerning the Control of Emissions of Volatile Organic Compounds or Their Transboundary Fluxes, 18 November 1991, entered into force 29 September 1997, available at http://www.unece.org/env/lrtap/full%20text/1991.VOC.e.pdf and in *International Legal Materials* 31 (1992): 568–570.

146. Protocol to the 1979 Convention on Long-Range Transboundary Air Pollution on Persistent Organic Pollutants, 24 June 1998, entered into force 23 October 2003, available at http://www.unece.org/env/lrtap/full%20text/1998.POPs.e.pdf and in *International Legal Materials* 37 (1998): 505–510.

147. Protocol to the 1979 Convention on Long-Range Transboundary Air Pollution on Heavy Metals, 24 June 1998,entered into force 29 December 2003, available at http://www.unece.org/env/lrtap/full%20text/1998.Heavy.Metals.e.pdf.

148. Protocol to the 1979 Convention on Long-range Transboundary Air Pollution to Abate Acidification, Eutrophication and Ground-level Ozone, 30 November 1999, entered into force 17 May 2005, available at http://www.unece.org/env/lrtap/full%20text/1999%20Multi.E.Amended.2005.pdf. The protocol addresses multiple effects (acidification, tropospheric ozone formation, and eutrophication) and multiple pollutants (e.g., SO_2, NO_x, NH_3). For an appraisal, see J. Wettestad, *Clearing the Air: European Advances in Tackling Acid Rain and Atmospheric Pollution* (Aldershot, UK: Ashgate, 2002).

149. The "critical loads" under various protocols were computed with the help of the Regional Acidification Information and Simulation (RAINS) model, which was developed at the International Institute for Applied Systems Analysis in Austria. For a brief overview of RAINS and of the history of atmospheric pollution research at that institute, see http://gains.iiasa.ac.at/index.php/about-apd/history.

150. ASEAN Agreement on Transboundary Haze Pollution, 10 June 2002, entered into force 25 November 2003, available at http://www.aseansec.org/pdf/agr_haze.pdf and in *International Environmental Law: Multilateral Treaties* 2002: 44.

151. See Paul J. Crutzen, "The Influence of Nitrogen Oxides on the Atmospheric Ozone Content," *Quarterly Journal of the Royal Meteorological Society* 96 (1970): 320–325.

152. In 1995, Crutzen, Molina, and Rowland were awarded the Nobel Prize for Chemistry for their findings.

153. See transcript of the oral history of Mostafa K. Tolba, p. 47, in United Nations History Project, *The Complete Oral History Transcripts from UN Voices*, CD-ROM (New York: UNIHP, 2005).

154. Vienna Convention for the Protection of the Ozone Layer, 22 March 1985, entered into force 22 September 1988, available at http://www.unep.org/ozone/pdfs/viennaconvention2002.pdf and in *International Legal Materials* 26 (1985): 1529. Article 1(1) defines the ozone layer as "the layer of atmospheric ozone above the planetary boundary layer."

155. Ibid., Article 2(1).

156. See ibid., Preamble.

157. Transcript of the oral history of Tolba, p. 48, in UNIHP, *The Complete Oral History*.

158. Vienna Convention for the Protection of the Ozone Layer, Article 1(6).

159. For background on the negotiations and an early assessment of the protocol, see Jutta Brunnée, *Acid Rain and Ozone Layer Depletion: International Law and Regulation* (Dobbs Ferry, N.Y.: Transnational Publishers, 1988), 242–253.

160. The phase-out schedules for developed countries as contained in the Montreal Protocol on Substances that Deplete the Ozone Layer are as follows:

halons	phased out by 1994
CFCs	phased out by 1996
carbon tetrachloride	phased out by 1996
methyl chloroform	phased out by 1996
hydrobromoflourocarbons	phased out by 1996
bromochloromethane	phased out by 2002
methyl bromide	reduced by 25 percent by 1999, by 50 percent by 2001, by 70 percent by 2003, phased out by 2005
hydrochloroflourocarbons	reduced by 35 percent by 2004, by 75 percent by 2010, by 90 percent by 2015, and phased out by 2020, allowing 0.5 percent for servicing purposes during the period 2020–2030

161. The phase-out schedules for developing countries as currently outlined in the adjusted and amended protocol are as follows:

halon	freeze at average 1995–1997 levels by 1 July 1999, then reduce them by 50 percent by 2005, by 85 percent by 2007, and phase them out by 2010
CFCs	freeze at average 1995–1997 levels by 1 July 1999, then reduce them by 50 percent by 2005, by 85 percent by 2007, and phase them out by 2010
carbon tetrachloride	freeze at average 1995–1997 levels by 1 July 1999, then reduce them by 50 percent by 2005, by 85 percent by 2007, and phase them out by 2010
methyl chloroform	freeze at average 1998–2000 levels by 2003, then reduce them by 30 percent by 2005, by 70 percent by 2010, and phase them out by 2015
hydrobromoflourocarbons	phase out by 1996
bromochloromethane	phase out by 2002
methyl bromide	freeze at average 1995–1998 levels by 2002, then reduce them by 20 percent by 2005, and phase them out by 2015
hydrochloroflourocarbons	freeze at average 2009–2010 levels by 2013, then reduce them by 10 percent by 2015, by 35 percent by 2020, and by 67.5 percent by 2025 and phase them out by 2030, allowing for an annual average of 2.5 percent for servicing purposes during the period 2030–2040

162. See *Synthesis Report* of the 2006 assessments of the Scientific Assessment Panel, the Environmental Effects Assessment Panel, and the Technology and Economic Assessment Panel, UNEP document UNEP/OzL.Pro.WG.1/27/3, 22 February 2007, available at http://ozone.unep.org/Meeting_Documents/oewg/27oewg/OEWG-27-3E.pdf.

163. Ibid.

164. For the status of each amendment, see "Status of Ratification," available at http://ozone.unep.org/Ratification_status.

165. See UNEP, *2006 Assessment Report of the Technology and Economic Assessment Panel,* March 2007, available at http://ozone.unep.org/Assessment_Panels/TEAP/Reports/TEAP_Reports/teap_assessment_report06.pdf.

166. *A Success in the Making: The Montreal Protocol on Substances that Deplete the Ozone Layer* (Nairobi: UNEP, 2007), 11, available at http://ozone.unep.org/Publications/MP_A_Success_in_the_making-E.pdf.

167. The Montreal Protocol established an Implementation Committee, which receives, considers, and reports on submissions made by any party regarding another party's implementation of its obligations under the protocol and any information or observations forwarded by the secretariat in connection with the preparation of reports based on information submitted by the parties pursuant to their obligations under the protocol. The committee tries to reach amicable resolutions based on the provisions of the protocol and reports to the Meeting of the Parties, which may decide upon and call for steps to bring about full compliance with the protocol. The Meeting of the Parties might then take decisions about specific measures against a noncomplying party that include issuing cautions and suspending specific rights and privileges under the protocol. See Decision IV/5, Report of the Fourth Meeting of the Parties, UNEP/OzL.Pro4/15, 25 November 1992, reproduced in *International Legal Materials* 32 (1993): 874. See Decision IV/5 ("Non-Compliance Procedure"), Annex IV ("Non-Compliance Procedure"), and Annex V ("Indicative List of Measures that Might Be Taken by a Meeting of the Parties in Respect of Non-Compliance with the Protocol"), reproduced in *Report of the Fourth Meeting of the Parties to the Montreal Protocol on Substances that Deplete the Ozone Layer, Copenhagen, 23–25 November 1992,* United Nations document UNEP/OzL. Pro.4/15, 25 November 1992. For a general overview of noncompliance procedures under various multilateral environmental agreements, see P. Sands, *Principles of International Environmental Law,* 2nd ed. (Cambridge: Cambridge University Press, 2003), 205–210.

168. See IPCC, *Climate Change 2007: Synthesis Report* (Geneva: IPCC, 2007), available at http://www.ipcc.ch/pdf/assessment-report/ar4/syr/ar4_syr.pdf.

169. "Protection of Global Climate for Present and Future Generations of Mankind," General Assembly resolution 43/53, 6 December 1988.

170. The IPCC was not established to conduct research or monitor climate-related data. Rather, its role is "to assess on a comprehensive, objective, open and transparent basis the scientific, technical and socio-economic information relevant to understanding the scientific basis of risk of human-induced climate change, its potential impacts and options for adaptation and mitigation." See "Principles Governing IPCC Work," available at http://www.ipcc.ch/pdf/ipcc-principles/ipcc-principles.pdf.

171. See "Protection of Global Climate for Present and Future Generations of Mankind," General Assembly resolution A/RES/45/212, 21 December 1990.

172. United Nations Framework Convention on Climate Change, 9 May 1992, entered into force 21 March 1994, available at http://unfccc.int/resource/docs/convkp/conveng.pdf and in *International Legal Materials* 31 (1992): 851–873.

173. Ibid., Article 1(2) .

174. Ibid., Article 2. This objective captures the core of the multifaceted concept of sustainable development rather well.

175. Ibid., Article 3(1).

176. Ibid., Preamble.

177. Ibid., Article 4(1).

178. Ibid., Article 4(2)(a). The countries with economies in transition, however, are granted a certain degree of flexibility in fulfilling these obligations.

179. Ibid., Articles 4(3), 4(4), and 4(5).

180. Ibid., Article 3(4).

181. Ibid., Article 3(1), Preamble, and Article 3(3), respectively.

182. The text of the convention was adopted at United Nations Headquarters in New York on 9 May 1992. The convention entered into force on 21 March 1994 and has currently received 192 instruments of ratification.

183. Kyoto Protocol to the United Nations Framework Convention on Climate Change, 11 December 1997, entered into force 16 February 2005, available at http://unfccc.int/resource/docs/convkp/kpeng.pdf and in *International Legal Materials* 37 (1998): 32–43. For a

general commentary on the protocol, see Peter G. G. Davies, "Global Warming and the Kyoto Protocol," *International and Comparative Law Quarterly* 47 (1998): 446–461.

184. In Annex B to the Kyoto Protocol, the limitation or reduction targets are listed for each of the thirty-eight developed countries and for the European Community as a whole.

185. Kyoto Protocol, Article 3, paragraph 1. Some countries "undergoing the process of transition to a market economy" (i.e., former Eastern European countries) are allowed to select a base year other than 1990; see Article 3, paragraph 5. Moreover, any party included in Annex I may use 1995 as its base year for levels of hydrofluorocarbons, perfluorocarbons, and sulphur hexafluoride; see Article 3, paragraph 8.

186. Kyoto Protocol, Article 3, paragraph 4.

187. Ibid., Article 2, paragraph 1.

188. Ibid., Articles 3, paragraphs 3 and 4.

189. Ibid., Article 3, paragraph 1.

190. Ibid., Article 12.

191. Ibid., Article 6; see also Article 3, paragraph 10. However, Article 17 states that "any such trading shall be supplemental to domestic actions for the purpose of meeting quantified emission limitation and reduction commitments under that Article."

192. See "Principles, Nature and Scope of the Mechanisms Pursuant to Articles 6, 12 and 17 of the Kyoto Protocol," Decision 15/CP.7 (which forms part of the so-called Marrakesh Accords), reproduced in *Report of the Conference of the Parties on its Seventh Session, Held at Marrakesh from 29 October to 10 November 2001,* FCCC/CP/2001/13/Add.2, 21 January 2002, available at http://unfccc.int/resource/docs/cop7/13a02.pdf.

193. This is referred to as the Conference of the Parties serving as the meeting of the Parties to the Kyoto Protocol.

194. Kyoto Protocol, Article 25, paragraph 1.

195. IPCC, *Climate Change 2007: Synthesis Report,* available at http://www.ipcc.ch/pdf/assessment-report/ar4/syr/ar4_syr.pdf, 46–47.

196. See *Report of the Conference of the Parties on Its Thirteenth Session, Held in Bali, 3 to 15 December 2007: Addendum,* document FCCC/CP/2007/6/Add. 1, 14 March 2008, 3, available at http://www.unisdr.org/eng/risk-reduction/climate-change/docs/Bali-Action-plan.pdf.

197. Copenhagen Accord, 18 December 2009, UNFCCC Doc. Decision -/CP.15, available at http://unfccc.int/files/meetings/cop_15/application/pdf/cop15_cph_auv.pdf.

198. See various reports from the conference by Daniel Bodansky, including "Preliminary Thoughts on the Copenhagen Accord," available at http://opiniojuris.org/2009/12/21.

199. See "Copenhagen United Nations Climate Change Conference ends with political agreement to cap temperature rise, reduce emissions and raise finance," Press Release, available at http://unfccc.int/files/press/news_room/press_releases_and_advisories/application/pdf/pr_cop15_20091219.pdf.

200. See IPCC, *Climate Change 2007,* 64.

201. For an analysis of these principles, see Nico J. Schrijver, *The Evolution of Sustainable Development in International Law: Inception, Meaning and Status* (Leiden: Martinus Nijhoff Publishers, 2008).

4. The International Architecture for Environmental Governance and Global Resource Management

1. See Frank Biermann and Bernd Siebenhüner, *Managers of Global Change: The Influence of International Environmental Bureaucracies* (Cambridge, Mass.: MIT Press, 2009).

2. See Elizabeth R. De Sombre, *Global Environmental Institutions* (London: Routledge, 2006); Mostafa K. Tolba (with Iwona Rummel-Bulska), *Global Environmental Diplomacy: Negotiating Environmental Agreements for the World, 1973–1992* (Cambridge, Mass.: MIT Press, 1998); Regina S. Axelrod, David Leonard Downie, and Norman J. Vig, eds., *The Global Envi-*

ronment: Institutions, Law, and Policy (Washington, D.C.: CQ Press, 2005); Frank Biermann and Steffen Bauer, eds., *A World Environment Organization* (Aldershot, UK: Ashgate, 2005); and W. Bradnee Chambers and Jessica F. Green, eds., *Reforming International Environmental Governance: From Institutional Limits to Innovative Reforms* (Tokyo: United Nations University Press, 2005).

3. "Institutional and Financial Arrangements for International Environmental Co-operation," General Assembly resolution 2997 (XXVII), 15 December 1972.

4. See Daniel Bodansky, "Prologue to the Climate Change Convention," in *Negotiating Climate Change: The Inside Story of the Rio Convention*, ed. Irving M. Mintzer and J. A. Leonard (Cambridge: Cambridge University Press, 1994), 60.

5. See Naigzy Gebremedhim, "Lessons from the UNEP Regional Seas Programme," in *Comprehensive Security for the Baltic: An Environmental Approach,* ed. Arthur H. Westing (London: PRIO, UNEP, and Sage, 1989), 90–98. See also UNEP, "Regional Seas Program," available at www.unep.org/regionalseas/.

6. The central tool of UNEP's involvement in water resource management was the Environmentally Sound Management of Inland Water Programme (EMINWA), which was conceived in 1985. Within the umbrella of EMINWA, various subprograms were then established. One of the main subprograms was the African inland water program, which focused on water management and the reduction of the effect of droughts in Africa. As the first step in the implementation of this program, the Common Zambezi River System (ZACPLAN) was developed in 1985. See Mostafa K. Tolba, "Eminwa and Sustainable Water Development," *International Journal of Water Resources Development* 4 (1988): 76–79. Other subprograms were soon launched, such as the Environmentally Sound Management of Lake Environments Programme (1987).

7. See Agreement on the Action Plan for the Environmentally Sound Management of the Common Zambezi River System, adopted and entered into force 28 May 1987 available at http://www.fao.org/docrep/w7414b/w7414b0j.htm and in *International Legal Materials* 27 (1988): 1109.

8. The Global Plan of Action for the Conservation, Management and Utilisation of Marine Mammals (MMAP), which is currently under review, was developed between 1978 and 1983 jointly by UNEP and the FAO with the aim of promoting the effective implementation of a policy for conservation, management, and utilization of marine mammals. For more information, see "About UNEP and Marine Mammals," available at http://www.unep.org/regionalseas/Marinemammals/about/default.asp.

9. International Tropical Timber Agreement, 18 November 1983, entered into force 1 April 1985, UNCTAD document TD/TIMBER/l l/Rev.l (1984), available at http://www.itto.int/itta/#1994. The agreement was amended in 1994 and 2006.

10. See Alexander Timoshenko and Mark Berman, "The United Nations Environment Programme and the United Nations Development Programme," in *Greening International Institutions,* ed. Jacob Werksman (London: Earthscan, 1996), 38–54.

11. See also David L. Downy and Marc A. Levy, "UNEP at a Turning Point," in *The Global Environment in the Twenty-First Century: Prospects for International Co-operation,* ed. Pamela S. Chasek (Tokyo: United Nations University Press, 2000), 355–377.

12. At the Rio summit in 1992, the call was made to establish a commission "to ensure the effective follow-up of the Conference, as well as to enhance international cooperation and rationalize the intergovernmental decision-making capacity for the integration of environment and development issues and to examine the progress in the implementation of Agenda 21 at the national, regional and international levels." See Agenda 21, paragraph 38.11 in the section "International Institutional Arrangements," available at http://www.unep.org/Documents.Multilingual/Default.asp?documentID=52.

13. See "Institutional Arrangements to Follow Up the United Nations Conference on Environment and Development," General Assembly resolution A/RES/47/191, 22 December

1992; and "Establishment of the Commission on Sustainable Development," ECOSOC document E/1993/207, 12 February 1993.

14. See "Institutional Arrangements to Follow Up the United Nations Conference on Environment and Development."

15. Barbados Programme of Action for the Sustainable Development of Small Island Developing States, in *Report of the Global Conference on the Sustainable Development of Small Island Developing States,* General Assembly document A/CONF.167/9, 6 May 1994, available at http://www.un-documents.net/ac167-9.htm.

16. See *Report of the International Meeting to Review the Implementation of the Programme of Action for the Sustainable Development of Small Island Developing States* (New York: UN, 2005), available at http://www.sidsnet.org/docshare/other/20050622163242_English.pdf.

17. See Farhana Yamin, "The CSD Reporting Process: A Quiet Step Forward for Sustainable Development," in *Yearbook of International Co-operation on Environment and Development 1998–1999,* ed. Helge Ole Bergesen, Georg Parmann, and Øyestein B. Thommessen (London: Earthscan, 1998), 51–62; and Pamela S. Chasek, "The UN Commission on Sustainable Development: The First Five Years," in *The Global Environment in the Twenty-First Century: Prospects for International Co-operation,* ed. Pamela S. Chasek (Tokyo: United Nations University Press, 2000), 378–398.

18. For an early assessment, see Martin Khor, "The Commission on Sustainable Development: Paper Tiger or Agency to Save the Earth?" in *Green Globe Yearbook 1994,* ed. Helge Ole Bergesen and Georg Parmann (Oxford: Oxford University Press, 1994), 103–113.

19. See Preamble of the Constitution of the Food and Agriculture Organization of the United Nations, 16 October 1945, available at http://www.fao.org/docrep/007/j2954e/j2954e01.htm#P8_10 and in *International Environmental Law: Multilateral Treaties* 945: 76.

20. Article I.2(c) of the Constitution of the Food and Agriculture Organization of the United Nations.

21. The WFP was established to provide for food aid in support of economic and social development, to meet emergency and protracted relief food needs, and to promote world food security. See WFP General Regulations, available at http://one.wfp.org/aboutwfp/how_run/GeneralRegulations_E.pdf.

22. The Agreement for the Establishment of the Indian Ocean Tuna Commission (1993) was concluded under Article XIV of the FAO's constitution. Among the conventions for which the FAO acts as depositary are the International Convention for the Conservation of Atlantic Tunas (1966), the Convention on the Conservation of the Living Resources of the South-East Atlantic (1969), the Agreement for the Establishment of the Intergovernmental Organization for Marketing Information and Technical Advisory Services for Fishery Products in the Asia and Pacific Region (1985), the Regional Convention on Fisheries Cooperation among African States Bordering the Atlantic Ocean (1991), the Agreement for the Establishment of the Intergovernmental Organization for Marketing Information and Cooperation Services for Fishery Products in Africa (1991), the Constitution of the Centre for Marketing Information and Advisory Services for Fishery Products in Latin America and the Caribbean (1994), the Convention for the Establishment of the Lake Victoria Fisheries Organization (1994), the Agreement for the Establishment of the International Organization for the Development of Fisheries in Eastern and Central Europe (2000), the Convention on the Conservation and Management of Fishery Resources in the South East Atlantic Ocean (2001), and the Southern Indian Ocean Fisheries Agreement (2006). More information on conventions, agreements, and treaties deposited with the FAO is available at http://www.fao.org/Legal/treaties/treaty-e.htm.

23. See the Web site of the FAO's Committee on Fisheries at http://www.fao.org/fishery/about/cofi/en.

24. See *Report of the International Technical Conference on the Conservation of the Living Resources of the Sea, 18 April–10 May 1955, Rome,* General Assembly document A/CONF.10/6, July 1955, paragraphs 17–18. The relevant parts of this report are reproduced in M. M. White-

man, *Digest of International Law,* vol. 4 (Washington, D.C.: Department of State publications, 1965), 1099–1100.

25. See Jean Carroz, "Achievement of the FAO World Conference on Fisheries Management and Development," in *Proceedings of the Second Conference of the International Institute of Fisheries Economics and Trade,* vol. 1, ed. International Institute of Fisheries, Economics, and Trade (Corvallis: Oregon State University, 1984), 33.

26. Agreement to Promote Compliance with International Conservation and Management Measures by Fishing Vessels on the High Seas, 24 November 1993, entered into force 24 April 2003, available at http://www.fao.org/docrep/meeting/003/x3130m/X3130E00.HTM and in *International Legal Materials* 33 (1994): 968.

27. Code of Conduct for Responsible Fisheries, adopted on 31 October 1995 by the FAO conference, available at ftp://ftp.fao.org/docrep/fao/005/v9878e/v9878e00.pdf.

28. International Plant Protection Convention, 6 December 1951, entered into force 3 April 1952, available at https://www.ippc.int/IPP/En/default.jsp and in *United Nations Treaty Series* (New York: United Nations, 1952), 150: 67.

29. International Treaty on Plant Genetic Resources for Food and Agriculture, 3 November 2001, entered into force 29 June 2004, available at http://www.planttreaty.org/ and in *International Environmental Law: Multilateral Treaties (*2001): 28.

30. See the Web site of the Committee on Forestry at http://www.fao.org/forestry/cofo/en/.

31. The FAO's Web site also provides country maps that show types of forests and land mass devoted to forests; see http://www.fao.org/forestry/country/en/. The State of the World's Forests (SOFO) is FAO's flagship publication concerning the forest sector; it is available at http://www.fao.org/forestry/sofo/en/.

32. See "IFAD Strategic Framework 2007–2010," available at http://www.ifad.org/sf/strategic_e.pdf.

33. See IFAD, *Annual Report 2008* (2009), 87, available at http://www.ifad.org/pub/ar.htm.

34. Articles of Agreement of the International Monetary Fund, 22 July 1944, entered into force 27 December 1945, available at http://www.imf.org/external/pubs/ft/aa/ and in *United Nations Treaty Series* 2: 39 and 726: 266; and IBRD Articles of Agreement, 22 July 1944, entered into force 27 December 1945, available in *United Nations Treaty Series* (New York: United Nations, 1947), 2: 134.

35. IBRD Articles of Agreement, Article I(iii).

36. For further information, see the "About Us" section of the World Bank's Web site, available at http://www.worldbank.org.

37. "What Is the GEF?" available at http://www.gefweb.org/interior_right.aspx?id=50.

38. Ibid.

39. See GEF, *Financing the Stewardship of Global Biodiversity* (Washington, D.C.: GEF, 2008), 9, available at http://www.indiaenvironmentportal.org.in/sites/cse/files/13_0.pdf.

40. In response to the escalating local and international controversies over large dams, the World Bank and the IUCN established the World Commission on Dams in May 1998 to review the performance of large dams and assess alternatives for water resources and energy development and to develop guidelines for the future construction of new dams. In 2000, the World Commission on Dams issued its final report; see *Dams and Development: A New Framework for Decision-Making: The Report of the World Commission on Dams* (London: World Commission on Dams, 2000). See also Dana Clark, Jonathan Fox, and Kay Treakle, eds., *Demanding Accountability: Civil Society Claims and the World Bank Inspection Panel* (London: Rowman & Littlefield Publishers, 2003).

41. See Ibrahim Shihata, *The World Bank Inspection Panel: In Practice* (Oxford: Oxford University Press, 2000); and Dana Clark, Jonathan Fox, and Kay Treakle, eds., *Demanding Accountability: Civil Society Claims and the World Bank Inspection Panel* (London: Rowman &

Littlefield Publishers, 2003). See also Gudmundur Alfredsson and Rolf Ring, eds., *The Inspection Panel of the World Bank: A Different Complaints Procedure* (The Hague: Nijhoff, 2001).

42. For details, see "Inspection Panel," available at http://www.worldbank.org/inspectionpanel.

43. See the Compliance Advisor Ombudsman Web site at http://www.cao-ombudsman.org.

44. Constitution of the United Nations Educational, Scientific and Cultural Organization, Article I(1), available at http://www.icomos.org/unesco/unesco_constitution.html.

45. For a list, see UNESCO and MAB Secretariat, "Biosphere Reserves: World Network," available at http://www.unesco.org/mab/doc/brs/BRlist2008.pdf.

46. For more information, see UNESCO, "Biosphere Reserves," available at http://portal.unesco.org/science/en/ev.php-URL_ID=4801&URL_DO=DO_TOPIC&URL_SECTION=201.html.

47. "Oceans and the Law of the Sea," General Assembly resolution A/RES/60/30, 20 November 2005, paragraphs 89–96; see also "Assessment of Assessments," available at http://www.unga-regular-process.org.

48. For more information on the Global Ocean Observing System, see http://www.ioc-goos.org.

49. On the UN-Oceans mechanism, see http://ioc3.unesco.org/un-oceans/index.php?option=com_content&task=view&id=19&Itemid=42.

50. See "IOC Draft Medium-Term Strategy (2008–2013)," IOC resolution EC-XXXIX.1, 25 April 2008, available at http://www.ioc-unesco.org/components/com_oe/oe.php?task=download&id=3358 &version=1.0&lang=1&format=1.

51. See "International Hydrological Programme," available at http://typo38.unesco.org/index.php?id=240.

52. On UN-Water, see http://www.unwater.org.

53. On the UN World Water Development Report, see "The United Nations World Water Development Report (WWDR)," available at http://www.unesco.org/water/wwap/wwdr/.

54. See Article 2 of Convention of the World Meteorological Organization, 11 October 1947, as amended by subsequent resolutions in 1959, 1963, 1967, 1975, 1979, 1983, 2003, and 2007, available at ftp://ftp.wmo.int/Documents/MediaPublic/Publications/Policy_docs/wmo_convention.pdf.

55. See "The World Meteorological Organization (WMO)," in *Yearbook of the United Nations, 1957* (New York: UN Office of Public Information, 1958), 487.

56. See WMO, "World Climate Programme (WCP)," available at http://www.wmo.int/pages/prog/wcp/index_en.html.

57. For more information regarding the Global Climate Observing System, see http://www.wmo.int/pages/prog/gcos/index.php?name=AboutGCOS. For information on the Global Ocean Observing System, see http://www.ioc-goos.org/content/view/12/26/.

58. See Article 1 of the Convention on the Intergovernmental Maritime Consultative Organization, adopted in Geneva, 6 March 1948, available in *United Nations Treaty Series* (New York: United Nations, 1958), 289. After a long and uncertain ratification process, the convention entered into force on 17 March 1958.

59. For an account of the work of the International Maritime Organization, see Myron H. Nordquist and John Norton Moore, eds., *Current Maritime Issues and the International Maritime Organization* (The Hague: Nijhoff Publishers, 1999). See also the IMO's Web site at http://www.imo.org.

60. On these agreements, see Lucius C. Caflisch, "International Law and Ocean Pollution: The Present and the Future," *Revue belge de droit international* 8 (1972): 7–33.

61. For background on the MARPOL 73/78 and its annexes, see http://www.imo.org/Conventions/contents.asp?doc_id=678&topic_id=258.

62. For some earlier assessments of this problem, see for example Rebecca Becker, "MARPOL 73/78: An Overview in International Environmental Enforcement," *The George-*

town International Environmental Law Review 10 (1998): 625–642; and Gerard Peet, "The MARPOL Convention: Implementation and Effectiveness," *International Journal of Estuarine and Coastal Law* 7 (1992): 277–295.

63. For background information, see "The London Convention and Protocol: Their Role and Contribution to Protection of the Marine Environment," available at http://www.imo.org/includes/blastDataOnly.asp/data_id%3D21278/LC-LPbrochure.pdf.

64. For more information about these conventions, consult the IMO Web site at http://www.imo.org/Conventions/mainframe.asp?topic_id=260.

65. For the work of the Marine Environment Protection Committee, see "IMO and the Environment," available at http://www.imo.org/Environment/mainframe.asp?topic_id=197.

66. For a study of compliance, see Alan Khee-Jin Tan, *Vessel-Source Marine Pollution: The Law and Politics of International Regulation* (Cambridge: Cambridge University Press, 2006).

67. The Statute of the IAEA was approved on 23 October 1956 and came into force on 29 July 1957. It is available at http://www.iaea.org/About/statute_text.html. The text of the Agreement Governing the Relationship between the United Nations and the International Atomic Energy Agency is available at http://www.iaea.org/Publications/Documents/Infcircs/Others/infcirc11.pdf.

68. The IAEA is the only organization in the UN system with a mandate partly dedicated to energy issues. On the conspicuous absence of the topic of energy in the UN system, see Sylvia I. Karlsson-Vinkhuyzen, "The United Nations and Global Energy Governance: Past Challenges, Future Choices," *Global Change, Peace & Security* (2010) (forthcoming).

69. For historical background on the work of the IAEA and its achievements, see David Fischer, *History of the International Atomic Energy Agency: The First Forty Years* (Vienna: IAEA, 1997); and Russell B. Olwell, *The International Atomic Energy Agency* (New York: Chelsea House, 2008).

70. UNIDO was initially created as a special organ of the UN. See "United Nations Industrial Development Organization," General Assembly resolution 2152 (XXI), 17 November 1966. In 1979, it was transformed into a specialized agency with the adoption of the Constitution of the United Nations Industrial Development Organization, Vienna, 8 April 1979, available at http://www.unido.org/fileadmin/user_media/UNIDO_Header_Site/About/UNIDO_Constitution.pdf.

71. See Article 1 of its constitution; see also "UNIDO in Brief," available at http://www.unido.org/index.php?id=7840.

72. See "Introducing UNIDO," available at http://www.unido.org/fileadmin/user_media/UNIDO_Header_Site/About/IntrodUNIDO_July2009.pdf.

73. See Article 1 of the Constitution of the World Health Organization, adopted on 22 July 1946, entered into force 7 April 1948, available at http://www.who.int/governance/eb/who_constitution_en.pdf.

74. See "WHO Air Quality Guidelines," available at http://www.euro.who.int/air/activities/20050222_2.

75. For more information on this program, see WHO, "Climate Change and Health," available at http://www.wpro.who.int/sites/climate/home.htm.

76. See the activities of the Division of Healthy Environments and Sustainable Development, available at http://www.afro.who.int/des/index.html.

77. See UN Charter, Article 63, paragraph 2, and Article 64.

78. The membership of ECOSOC was increased in 1965 from 18 to 27; in 1973 it was increased to 54. See "Question of Equitable Representation on the Security Council and the Economic and Social Council," General Assembly resolution 1991B (XVIII), 17 December 1963; and "Enlargement of the Economic and Social Council," General Assembly resolution 2847 (XXVI), 20 December 1971.

79. See *Delivering as One: Report of the High-level Panel on United Nations System-wide Coherence in the Areas of Development, Humanitarian Assistance and the Environment,* General Assembly document A/61/583, 20 November 2006.

80. See "Management Review of Environmental Governance within the United Nations System," Joint Inspection Unit document JIU/REP/2008/3, 1 December 2008, available at http://www.unjiu.org/data/reports/2008/en2008_3.pdf.

81. "Establishment of the United Nations Conference on Trade and Development as an Organ of the General Assembly," General Assembly resolution 1995 (XIX), 30 December 1964.

82. On UNCTAD's activities and areas of work, see http://www.unctad.org.

83. See São Paulo Consensus, UNCTAD document TD/410, 25 June 2004, available at http://www.unctad.org/en/docs/td410_en.pdf, in particular paragraph 100. This mandate now complements the Bangkok Plan of Action, UNCTAD document TD/386, 18 February 2000, available at http://www.unctad.org/en/docs/ux_td386.en.pdf.

84. See "Consolidation of the Special Fund and the Expanded Programme of Technical Assistance in a United Nations Development Programme," ECOSOC Resolution 1020 (XXXVII), 11 August 1964; and "Consolidation of the Special Fund and the Expanded Programme of Technical Assistance in a United Nations Development Programme," General Assembly resolution 2029 (XX), 22 November 1965. The organizational structure and activities of the UNDP were subsequently redefined in "The Capacity of the United Nations Development System," General Assembly resolution 2688 (XXV), 11 December 1970.

85. See paragraphs 38.24 and 38.25 of Agenda 21.

86. See the UNDP's Web site on Environment and Energy for Sustainable Development, available at http://www.undp.org/energyandenvironment; and the various fact sheets available at http://www.undp.org/energyandenvironment/factsheets.htm.

87. Regarding the former, see the UNDP-UNEP Poverty-Environment Initiative Web site at http://www.unpei.org; regarding the latter, see UNDP/UNEP, *Partnership Initiative for the Integration of Sound Management of Chemicals into Development Planning Processes: Maximizing Return on Investment* (2009), available at http://www.energyandenvironment.undp.org/indexAction.cfm?module=Library&action=GetFile&DocumentAttachmentID=2310.

88. For an extensive examination of the UNDP and its work, see Craig N. Murphy, *The United Nations Development Programme: A Better Way?* (Cambridge: Cambridge University Press, 2006); and Olav Stokke, *The UN and Development: From Aid to Cooperation* (Bloomington: Indiana University Press, 2009), 186–250.

89. "Establishment of an International Law Commission," General Assembly resolution 174 (II), 21 November 1947.

90. Article 1, paragraph 1, of the Statute of the International Law Commission, 1947, available at http://untreaty.un.org/ilc/texts/instruments/english/statute/statute_e.pdf.

91. Ibid., Article 15.

92. See *Yearbook of the International Law Commission, 1953,* vol. 2 (New York: United Nations, 1959), 217–219.

93. UN Convention on the Law of the Non-Navigational Uses of International Watercourses, 21 May 1997, General Assembly document A/51/869, 11 April 1997, available at http://untreaty.un.org/ilc/texts/instruments/english/conventions/8_3_1997.pdf and in *International Legal Materials* 36 (1997): 700.

94. See ibid., Articles 5–9.

95. See ibid., Articles 11–19 and 20–28.

96. Draft articles on the Law of Transboundary Aquifers (2008), available at http://untreaty.un.org/ilc/texts/instruments/english/draft%20articles/8_5_2008.pdf. See in particular articles 4–8, 10, 12, and 14.

97. Draft articles on Prevention of Transboundary Harm from Hazardous Activities (2001), available at http://untreaty.un.org/ilc/texts/instruments/english/draft%20arti

cles/9_7_2001.pdf; and Draft principles on the Allocation of Loss in the Case of Transboundary Harm Arising Out of Hazardous Activities (2006), available at http://untreaty.un.org/ilc/texts/instruments/english/draft%20articles/9_10_2006.pdf.

98. ECOSOC resolution 1535 (XLIX), 27 July 1970.

99. On the work of the Committee on Natural Resources, see Nico J. Schrijver, *Sovereignty over Natural Resources: Balancing Rights and Duties* (Cambridge: Cambridge University Press, 1997), 115–118.

100. See "Restructuring and Revitalization of the United Nations in the Economic, Social and Related Fields," General Assembly resolution A/RES/46/235, 13 April 1992.

101. "Further Measures for the Restructuring and Revitalization of the United Nations in the Economic, Social and Related Fields," ECOSOC resolution 1998/46, 31 July 1998.

102. "Termination of the Work of the Committee on Energy and Natural Resources for Development," ECOSOC decision 2002/303, 25 October 2002.

103. See Barbara Ruis, "No Forest Convention but Ten Tree Treaties," *Unasylva* 52, no. 206 (2001): 3–13.

104. "Report of the Fourth Session on the Intergovernmental Forum on Forests," ECOSOC resolution 2000/35, 18 October 2000.

105. Ibid. The Collaborative Partnership on Forests is chaired by the FAO and is serviced by the UNFF Secretariat. More information can be found on the partnership's Web site at http://www.fao.org/forestry/cpf/en/.

106. These objectives seek to (1) reverse the loss of forest cover worldwide through sustainable forest management (including protection, restoration, afforestation, reforestation and an increase in efforts to prevent forest degradation); (2) enhance forest-based economic, social, and environmental benefits; (3) increase significantly the area of sustainably managed forests and the proportion of forest products derived from sustainably managed forests; and (4) reverse the decline in official development assistance for sustainable forest management and mobilize significantly increased new and additional financial resources. "Outcome of the Sixth Session of the United Nations Forum on Forests," ECOSOC resolution 2006/49, 28 July 2006.

107. "Non-Legally Binding Instrument on All Types of Forests," General Assembly resolution A/RES/62/98, 17 December 2007.

108. UNCLOS, Articles 156–157, available at http://www.un.org/Depts/los/convention_agreements/texts/unclos/unclos_e.pdf.

109. See ibid., Article 170; and Section 2, Annex, of the 1994 implementation agreement. The full text of the agreement is available at http://www.un.org/Depts/los/convention_agreements/texts/agreement_part_xi/agreement_part_xi.htm.

110. The other alternatives are the ICJ, Annex VII arbitration tribunals, and Annex VIII special arbitration tribunals. See UNCLOS, Article 287. The convention thus provides a menu of options for settling legal disputes.

111. The UN and ITLOS have entered into a cooperative agreement. See "Agreement on Cooperation and Relationship between the United Nations and the International Tribunal for the Law of the Sea," General Assembly resolution A/RES/52/251, 8 September 1998.

112. UNCLOS, Article 290. For more on provisional measures, see Shabtai Rosenne, *Provisional Measures in International Law: The International Court of Justice and the International Tribunal for the Law of the Sea* (Oxford: Oxford University Press, 2005).

113. *Southern Bluefin Tuna Cases (New Zealand v. Japan; Australia v. Japan)*, Provisional Measures, Order, 27 August 1999, available at http://www.itlos.org/case_documents/2001/document_en_116.pdf and in *International Law Reports* 117: 148.

114. *The MOX Plant Case (Ireland v. United Kingdom)*, Provisional Measures, Order, 3 December 2001, available at http://www.itlos.org/case_documents/2001/document_en_197.pdf and in *International Law Reports* 126: 259.

115. *Case Concerning Land Reclamation by Singapore in and Around the Straits of Johor (Malaysia v. Singapore)*, Provisional Measures, Order, 8 October 2003, available at http://www

.itlos.org/case_documents/2003/document_en_230.pdf and in *International Law Reports* 126: 487.

116. See UNCLOS, Article 76(8) and Annex II, particularly Article 3.

117. For an analysis of the impact of UN regional commissions on development thinking, see Yves Berthelot, ed., *Unity and Diversity in Development Ideas: Perspectives from the UN Regional Commissions* (Bloomington: Indiana University Press, 2004).

118. See "Terms of Reference and Rules of Procedure of the United Nations Economic Commission for Europe," 4th rev. ed., ECOSOC document E/ECE/778/Rev.4, available at http://www.unece.org/oes/mandate/Commission%20Rev4%20English.pdf. The ECE's terms of reference are based on "Workplan on Reform of the Economic Commission for Europe and Revised Terms of Reference for the Commission," ECOSOC resolution 2006/38, 27 July 2006.

119. See ECOSOC resolution 37 (IV), 28 March 1947.

120. ECOSOC resolution 1984/67, 27 July 1984.

121. For example, see the following ECLAC reports and studies: *The Water Resources of Latin America and the Caribbean and Their Utilization* (Santiago: UN Economic Commission for Latin America, 1985); *The Water Resources of Latin America and the Caribbean—Planning, Hazards and Pollution* (Santiago: UN Economic Commission for Latin America, 1990); *Development of the Mining Resources of Latin America* (Santiago: UN Economic Commission for Latin America, 1989).

122. See Web site of the division at http://www.eclac.org/drni/.

123. ECOSOC resolution 671 A (XXV), 29 April 1958.

124. See the division's Web site at http://www.uneca.org/eca_programmes/sdd/default.htm.

125. ECOSOC resolution 1818 (LV), 9 August 1973.

126. For an excellent review, see Rosemary Sandford, "International Environmental Treaty Secretariats: Stage-Hands or Actors?" in *Green Globe Yearbook 1994,* ed. Helge Ole Bergesen and Georg Parmann (Oxford: Oxford University Press, 1994), 17–29.

127. See Jacob Werksman, "The Conferences of Parties to Environmental Treaties," in *Greening International Institutions,* ed. Jacob Werksman (London: Earthscan, 1996), 55–68.

128. See "Management Review of Environmental Governance within the United Nations System," Joint Inspection Unit document JIU/REP/2008/3, 1 December 2008, available at http://www.unjiu.org/data/reports/2008/en2008_3.pdf.

129. International Tropical Timber Agreement, 18 November 1983, entered into force 1 April 1985, available at http://sedac.ciesin.org/entri/texts/tropical.timber.1983.html. This agreement was superseded by the International Tropical Timber Agreement, 26 January 1994, entered into force 1 January 1997, available at http://sedac.ciesin.org/entri/texts/ITTA.1994.txt.html. In 2006, the third International Tropical Timber Agreement was adopted (27 January 2006, available at http://untreaty.un.org/english/opening_signature/english_19_46.pdf). The 2006 agreement is expected to come into force in 2009.

130. See the ITTO's mission statement at http://www.itto.int/en/mission_statement.

131. Agreement Establishing the Common Fund for Commodities, 27 June 1980, entered into force 19 June 1989, available at http://www.legaltext.ee/text/en/PH0835.htm and in *International Legal Materials* 19 (1980): 896–937.

132. See Common Fund for Commodities, *Basic Facts 2008–2009* (Amsterdam: Common Fund for Commodities, 2008–2009), 10, available at http://www.common-fund.org/data/documenten/BF.08.09.pdf.

133. See "Official Records of the 43rd Session of the General Assembly," General Assembly document A/43/PV.6, 28 September 1988, 76.

134. See, for example, "Comprehensive System of International Peace and Security," General Assembly resolution A/RES/42/93, 7 December 1987, paragraph 10. The resolution was adopted by 76 to 12 votes, with 63 abstentions. See also "Comprehensive Approach to Strengthening International Peace and Security in Accordance with the Charter of the United

Nations," General Assembly resolution A/RES/43/89, 7 December 1988, adopted by 97 votes to 3 against (Israel, Japan, and the United States), with 45 abstentions.

135. See the description of comprehensive security in *A More Secure World: Our Shared Responsibility: Report of the High-level Panel on Threats, Challenges and Change,* General Assembly document A/59/565, 29 November 2004, page 2 of the summary, available at http://www.un.org/secureworld/.

136. See *Renewing the United Nations: A Programme for Reform: Report of the Secretary-General,* General Assembly document A/51/950, 14 July 1997.

137. See *United Nations Reform: Measures and Proposals: A New Concept of Trusteeship: Note by the Secretary-General,* General Assembly document A/52/849, 31 March 1998.

138. UNIDO was established by General Assembly resolution 2152 (XXI), 17 November 1966.

139. Because the United States was dissatisfied with certain trends in the policy, ideological emphasis, budget, and management of UNESCO, it withdrew from the organization in 1984. It was followed by the United Kingdom and Singapore a year later. The United Kingdom rejoined in 1997, the United States in 2003, and Singapore in 2007. For more on the controversy, especially from the U.S. perspective, see William Preston, Edward S. Herman, and Herbert I. Schiller, *Hope & Folly: The United States and UNESCO, 1945–1985* (Minneapolis: University of Minnesota Press, 1989). See also Maarten Mourik, "UNESCO: Structural Origins of Crisis and Needed Reforms," in *The UN under Attack,* ed. Jeffrey Harrod and Nico Schrijver (Aldershot, UK: Gower, 1988), 123–129.

140. For a good review of proposals for reform, see Toru Iwama, "Multilateral Environmental Institutions and Coordinating Mechanisms," in *Emerging Forces in Environmental Governance,* ed. Norichika Kanie and Peter M. Haas (Tokyo: United Nations University Press, 2004), 15–34. See also Lydia Swart and Estelle Perry, eds., *Global Environmental Governance: Prospects on the Current Debate* (New York: Center for UN Reform Education, 2007), particularly the contributions of Maria Ivanova and Jennifer Roy ("The Architecture of Global Environmental Governance"), Frank Biermann ("Reforming Global Environmental Governance"), and Nils Meyer-Ohlendorf and Markus Knigge ("A United Nations Environment Organisation"). See also Frank Biermann, "Strengthening Green Global Governance in a Disparate World Society: Would a World Environment Organisation Benefit the South?" *International Environmental Agreements* 2 (2002): 297–315. For a discussion of earlier proposals, see Nico J. Schrijver, "International Organisation for Environmental Security," *Bulletin of Peace Proposals* 20 (1989): 115–122.

141. See Niels M. Blokker and Henry G. Schermers, eds., *Proliferation of International Organisations: Legal Issues* (The Hague: Kluwer Law International, 2001).

142. Examples of how coordination could be achieved might be taken from the field of human rights. See Nigel S. Rodley, "United Nations Human Rights Treaty Bodies and Special Procedures of the Commission of Human Rights—Complementarity or Competition?" *Human Rights Quarterly* 25 (2003): 882–908; and Netherlands Advisory Council on International Affairs, *The UN Human Rights Treaty System. Strengthening the System Step by Step in a Politically Charged Context* (The Hague, 2007).

5. Natural Resources and Armed Conflict

1. For a detailed early review and analysis of this subject, see Arthur H. Westing, *Warfare in a Fragile World: Military Impact on the Human Environment* (London: Taylor & Francis, 1980). See also Arthur H. Westing, ed., *Global Resources and International Conflict: Environmental Factors in Strategic Policy and Action* (Oxford: UNEP/SIPRI/Oxford University Press, 1986).

2. Such views prevailed well into the 1980s. Particular examples include the Integrated Programme for Commodities, adopted by UNCTAD IV at Nairobi (1976), and the Agree-

ment Establishing the Common Fund for Commodities, 27 June 1980, entered into force 19 June 1989, available at http://www.legaltext.ee/text/en/PH0835.htm and in *International Legal Materials* 19 (1980): 896–937.

3. The term was coined in "The Dutch Disease," *The Economist*, 26 November 1977, 82–83. For a concise explanation of the phenomenon, see Christine Ebrahim-Zadeh, "Dutch Disease: Too Much Wealth Managed Unwisely," *Finance and Development* 40, no. 1 (2003): 1–38.

4. One of the most prominent examples of this literature is Jeffrey Sachs and Andrew Warner, *Natural Resource Abundance and Economic Growth* (Cambridge, Mass.: Harvard Center for International Development, 1997).

5. For a reexamination of these assumptions, see Jonathan DiJohn, "Mineral Resource Abundance and Violent Political Conflict: A Critical Assessment of the Rentier State Model," Working Paper no. 20, Crisis States Programme, Development Research Center, London, 2002.

6. The "resource curse" argument was introduced by Richard M. Auty in *Sustaining Development in Mineral Economies: The Resource Curse Thesis* (London: Routledge, 1993) and has recently been reexamined by economists Joseph Stiglitz and Jeffrey Sachs in *Escaping the Resource Curse* (New York: Columbia University Press, 2007). For criticism regarding the possible bias of such research, see Christa N. Brunnschweiler and Erwin H. Bulte, "Linking Natural Resources to Slow Growth and More Conflict," *Science* 320 (2008): 616–617.

7. This research produced a growing body of literature on the topic. See, for example, Paul Collier et al., *Breaking the Conflict Trap: Civil War and Development Policy* (New York: Oxford University Press, 2003); Roland Paris, *At War's End: Building Peace after Civil Wars* (Cambridge: Cambridge University Press, 2004); and Michael T. Klare, *Resource Wars: The New Landscape of Global Conflict* (New York: Metropolitan Books, 2001).

8. It is difficult to present a coherent picture without taking account of the different methodological and theoretical assumptions that underlie those studies. For an analysis of existing studies, see Michael L. Ross, "What Do We Know about Natural Resources and Civil War?" *Journal of Peace Research* 41, no. 3 (2004): 337–356.

9. For an early call to broaden the concept of security to encompass environmental aspects, see Jessica T. Mathews, "Redefining Security," *Foreign Affairs* 68, no. 2 (1989): 162–177. Robert D. Kaplan, "The Coming Anarchy—How Scarcity, Crime, Overpopulation, Tribalism and Disease Are Rapidly Destroying the Social Fabric of Our Planet," *The Atlantic Monthly*, February 1994, 44–76, was also influential in the "environmental security" debate.

10. Much of this research is inspired by Thomas F. Homer-Dixon, *Environment, Scarcity, and Violence* (Princeton, N.J.: Princeton University Press, 1999). See also Oli Brown, "The Environment and our Security: How Our Understanding of the Links Has Changed," May 2005, available at http://www.iisd.org/pdf/2005/security_env_peace_iran.pdf.

11. See also "Letter Dated 6 June 2007 from the Permanent Representative of Belgium to the United Nations to the Secretary-General," Security Council document S/2007/334, 6 June 2007.

12. The Chilean proposal was reproduced in General Assembly document A/AC.97/L.3/Rev.2, 18 May 1961. For more background on the difficulties with formulating the 1962 Declaration on Permanent Sovereignty over Natural Resources in an ideologically divided United Nations, see N. J. Schrijver, *Sovereignty over Natural Resources: Balancing Rights and Duties* (Cambridge: Cambridge University Press, 1997), 59–68.

13. "Permanent Sovereignty over Natural Resources," General Assembly resolution 1803 (XVII), 14 December 1962, paragraph 4.

14. See Thomas C. Hayes, "Confrontation in the Gulf: The Oilfield Lying below the Iraq-Kuwait Dispute," *New York Times*, 3 September 1990.

15. On this episode, see N. J. Schrijver, *Sovereignty over Natural Resources: Balancing Rights and Duties* (Cambridge: Cambridge University Press, 1997), 152–156.

16. See Nurit Kliot, *Water Resources and Conflict in the Middle East* (London: Routledge, 1994).

17. See particularly *Final Report of the Monitoring Mechanism on Angola Sanctions,* Security Council document S/2000/1225, 21 December 2000.

18. Philippe Le Billon, "The Political Ecology of Transition in Cambodia 1989–1999: War, Peace and Forrest Exploitation," *Development and Change* 31 (1999): 785–805.

19. Michael L. Ross, "Booty Futures: Africa's Civil Wars and the Futures Market for Natural Resources," 6 May 2005, 24, available at http://www.polisci.ucla.edu/faculty/ross/bootyfutures.pdf.

20. See *Report of the Panel of Experts on Sierra Leone Diamonds and Arms,* Security Council document S/2000/1195, 20 December 2000.

21. See, for example, "Letter Dated 15 October 2002 from the Secretary-General Addressed to the President of the Security Council," Security Council document S/2002/1146, 16 October 2002; "Letter Dated 26 January 2006 from the Chairman of the Security Council Committee Established Pursuant to Resolution 1533 (2004) Concerning the Democratic Republic of the Congo Addressed to the President of the Security Council," Security Council document S/2006/53, 27 January 2006; and "Letter Dated 18 July 2006 from the Chairman of the Security Council Committee Established Pursuant to Resolution 1533 (2004) Addressed to the President of the Security Council," Security Council document S/2006/525, 18 July 2006. See Mwayila Tshiyembe, "Kivu Conflict Shakes the Congo," and Delphine Abadie, Alain Deneault, and William Sacher, "This Is Not an Ethnic Conflict," both in *Le Monde Diplomatique,* 6 December 2008, 6.

22. "Letter Dated 7 November 2005 from the Chairman of the Security Council Committee Established Pursuant to Resolution 1572 (2004) Concerning Côte d'Ivoire Addressed to the President of the Security Council," Security Council document S/2005/699, 7 November 2005.

23. "Letter Dated 4 May 2006 from the Chairman of the Security Council Committee Established Pursuant to Resolution 751 (1992) Concerning Somalia Addressed to the President of the Security Council," Security Council document S/2006/229, 4 May 2006.

24. *Tenth Progress Report of the Secretary-General on the United Nations Mission in Liberia,* Security Council document S/2006/159, 14 March 2006.

25. See John Markakis, *Resource Conflict in the Horn of Africa* (London: Sage, 1998).

26. See, for example, "Climate Change and International Security: Paper from the High Representative and the European Commission to the European Council," EC document S113/08, 14 March 2008, available at http://www.consilium.europa.eu/ueDocs/cms_Data/docs/pressData/en/reports/99387.pdf.

27. For background on these disputes, see Mark Kurlansky, *Cod: A Biography of the Fish That Changed the World* (New York: Penguin, 1998); Peter G. G. Davies, "The EC/Canadian Fisheries Dispute in the Northwest Atlantic," *International and Comparative Law Quarterly* 44 (1995): 927–939; Dale D. Murphy, "The Tuna-Dolphin Wars," *Journal of World Trade: Law, Economics, Public Policy* 40 (2006): 597–617; and Marcos A. Orellana, "The Swordfish Dispute between the EU and Chile at the ITLOS and the WTO," *Nordic Journal of International Law* 71 (2002): 55–81.

28. "Question of the Reservation Exclusively for Peaceful Purposes of the Sea-Bed and the Ocean Floor, and the Subsoil Thereof, Underlying the High Seas beyond the Limits of Present National Jurisdiction, and the Use of Their Resources in the Interests Of Mankind," General Assembly resolution 2574 (XXIV), 15 December 1969.

29. See Press Release of U.S. president Richard Nixon entitled "Statement about United States Oceans Policy," 23 May 1970, available at http://www.state.gov/documents/organization/52602.pdf.

30. See Adrian Howkins, "Icy Relations: The Emergence of South American Antarctica during the Second World War," *Polar Record* 42, no. 221 (2006): 153–165.

31. See Francisco O. Vicuna, "Antarctic Conflict and International Cooperation," in *Antarctic Treaty System: An Assessment,* ed. Polar Research Board and National Research Council (Washington, D.C.: National Academy Press, 1986), 55–64.

32. It has been suggested that the United Kingdom instituted proceedings against the claims of Argentina and Chile in the full knowledge that the ICJ lacked jurisdiction to entertain the cases. The unilateral application of the United Kingdom met with no response from either Argentina or Chile. As a result, the court had no jurisdiction to decide the dispute. The unsuccessful application nevertheless served an important purpose, inasmuch as it recorded an official protest of the United Kingdom, which prevented any possible consolidation of Argentinean and Chilean claims to the disputed parts of Antarctica. Moreover, much of the historical and legal material that the UK compiled in its application remains of particular interest today and is conveniently available at http://www.icj-cij.org/docket/files/27/10783.pdf.

33. Article IV of the Atlantic Treaty. Nonetheless, seven states maintain historical claims to parts of the continent and (at least nominally) assert control over parts of Antarctica on the basis of sovereign jurisdiction.

34. The continental shelves of the sub-Antarctic Kerguelen Islands (France) and of Heard Island and Macdonald Islands (Australia) extend to the Antarctic area.

35. See UNCLOS, Article 3 of Annex II, available at http://www.un.org/Depts/los/convention_agreements/texts/unclos/unclos_e.pdf.

36. Not to mention the effects of the deliberate manipulation of natural phenomena for hostile purposes that has become possible with modern military technology. This is partly addressed by the Environmental Modification Convention.

37. "Declaration of the United Nations Conference on the Human Environment," available at http://www.unep.org/Documents.Multilingual/Default.asp?DocumentID=97&ArticleID=1503; "World Charter for Nature," General Assembly resolution A/RES/37/7, 28 October 1982; and "Rio Declaration on Environment and Development," 14 June 1992, General Assembly document A/CONF.151/26, available at http://www.unep.org/Documents.multilingual/Default.asp?DocumentID=78&ArticleID=1163.

38. Convention (IV) Respecting the Laws and Customs of War on Land and Its Annex: Regulations Concerning the Laws and Customs of War on Land, 18 October 1907, available at http://www.icrc.org/ihl.nsf/385ec082b509e76c41256739003e636d/1d1726425f6955aec125641e0038bfd6 and in *American Journal of International Law: Supplement* 2 (1908).

39. See *United Nations Treaty Series* (New York: United Nations, 1950): Convention (I) for the Amelioration of the Condition of the Wounded and Sick in Armed Forces in the Field, 12 August 1949, 75: 31; Convention (II) for the Amelioration of the Condition of Wounded, Sick and Shipwrecked Members of Armed Forces at Sea, 12 August 1949, 75: 85; Convention (III) relative to the Treatment of Prisoners of War, Geneva, 12 August 1949, 75: 135; Convention (IV) Relative to the Protection of Civilian Persons in Time of War, 12 August 1949, 75: 287. All four Geneva conventions are also available at http://www.icrc.org/ihl.nsf/CONVPRES?OpenView.

40. Article 22 of the Hague Convention of 1907. Or in the words of the Declaration of St. Petersburg of 1868, which codified this important precept for the first time, "the only legitimate object which States should endeavour to accomplish during war is to weaken the military forces of the enemy." Declaration Renouncing the Use, in Time of War, of Explosive Projectiles under 400 Grammes Weight, 29 November / 11 December 1868, available at http://www.icrc.org/ihl.nsf/FULL/130?OpenDocument and in *American Journal of International Law: Supplement* 1 (1907): 95–96.

41. See the ICRC study on customary humanitarian law, published as Jean-Marie Henckaerts and Louise Doswald-Beck, eds., *Customary International Humanitarian Law*, vol. 1, *Rules* (Cambridge: Cambridge University Press, 2005), in particular Rule 43, at p. 143. For an examination of the application of these principles to environmental protection, see Michael N. Schmitt, "Green War: An Assessment of the Environmental Law of International Armed Conflict," *Yale Journal of International Law* 22 (1997): 52–62; and Betsy Baker, "Legal Protections for the Environment in Times of Armed Conflict," *Virginia Journal of International Law* 33 (1992/1993): 359–367.

42. Article 23, paragraph (g) of Convention (IV) Respecting the Laws and Customs of War on Land and Its Annex: Regulations Concerning the Laws and Customs of War on Land.

43. Article 53 of ibid. A party to a conflict that, for example, destroys property protected by this provision and in so doing causes damage to the environment violates the convention if such destruction is not deemed "absolutely" necessary by military operations. If such destruction is "extensive," the act becomes a grave breach of the convention; see Article 147.

44. See Articles 28 and 47 of Convention (IV) Respecting the Laws and Customs of War on Land and Its Annex: Regulations Concerning the Laws and Customs of War on Land and Article 33 of Convention (IV) Relative to the Protection of Civilian Persons in Time of War. For a definition of pillage, see Pietro Verri, *Dictionary of the International Law of Armed Conflict* (Geneva: ICRC, 1992).

45. Article 55 of Convention (IV) Respecting the Laws and Customs of War on Land and Its Annex: Regulations Concerning the Laws and Customs of War on Land. The rules of usufruct, which are based in ancient Roman law, imply the legal right to use and derive profit or benefit from property that belongs to another person as long as the property is not damaged.

46. This principle is reaffirmed in Article 4 of Protocol Additional to the Geneva Conventions of 12 August 1949, and Relating to the Protection of Victims of International Armed Conflicts (Protocol 1), 8 June 1977, which states that "neither the occupation of a territory nor the application of the Conventions and this Protocol shall affect the legal status of the territory in question"; available at www2.ohchr.org. See also Yoram Dinstein, *War, Aggression and Self-Defence*, 4th ed. (Cambridge: Cambridge University Press, 2005), 168–169.

47. See Antonio Cassese, "Powers and Duties of an Occupant in Relation to Land and Natural Resources," in *International Law and the Administration of Occupied Territories: Two Decades of Israeli Occupation of the West Bank and Gaza Strip*, ed. Emma Playfair (Oxford: Clarendon Press, 1992), 420. See also the pleadings of Professor Philippe Sands in the Congo v. Uganda proceedings: *Armed Activities on the Territory of the Congo (Democratic Republic of the Congo v. Uganda)*, Public Sitting Held on Friday, 15 April 2005, CR 2005/5, p. 19, paragraph 12, available at http://www.icjcij.org/docket/files/116/4297.pdf.

48. Arthur H. Westing, *Ecological Consequences of the Second Indochina War* (Stockholm: Alinquiest & Wiksell, 1976); Willem D. Verwey, *Riot Control Agents and Herbicides in War: Their Humanitarian, Toxicological, Ecological, Military, Polemological, and Legal Aspects* (The Hague: Sijthoff, 1978).

49. "Convention on the Prohibition of Military or Any Other Hostile Use of Environmental Modification Techniques," General Assembly resolution A/RES/31/72, 10 December 1976, Articles I and II.

50. See Seymour M. Hersh, "Rainmaking Is Used as Weapon by U.S.; Cloud-Seeding in Indochina Is Said to Be Aimed at Hindering Troop Movements and Suppressing Antiaircraft Fire," *New York Times*, 3 July 1972, 1; and A. H. Westing, *Ecological Consequences of the Second Indochina War* (Stockholm: SIPRI/Almqvist & Wiksell International, 1976).

51. Protocol Additional to the Geneva Conventions of 12 August 1949, and Relating to the Protection of Victims of International Armed Conflicts (Protocol 1), Article 35(3).

52. Ibid., Article 55(1). Paragraph 2 of this article also prohibits attacks against the natural environment by way of reprisals. However, while these provisions protect the environment as such, they were inserted in relation to human beings, who are the principal concern of international humanitarian law.

53. See ibid., Articles 54(2) and 56(1). Although they do so indirectly, these two provisions prohibit causing damage to the environment even where the environment constitutes a military objective or where the damage to the environment may be considered as not excessive in relation to the military advantage anticipated. Apart from this, Articles 59 and 60 allow for the creation of specially protected zones that could encompass environmentally sensitive areas.

54. For example, Protocol for the Prohibition of the Use in War of Asphyxiating, Poisonous or Other Gases and of Bacteriological Methods of Warfare, 17 June 1925, available at

http://www.nti.org/e_research/official_docs/inventory/pdfs/genev.pdf and *League of Nations Treaty Series* (London: Harrison & Sons, 1929), 94: 65; Convention on the Prohibition of the Development, Production and Stockpiling of Bacteriological (Biological) and Toxin Weapons and on Their Destruction, 10 April 1972, available at http://www.opbw.org/convention/conv.html and in *United Nations Treaty Series* (New York: United Nations, 1976), 1015: 164; Convention on Prohibitions or Restrictions on the Use of Certain Conventional Weapons Which May be Deemed to be Excessively Injurious or to Have Indiscriminate Effects, 10 October 1980, available at http://www.icrc.org/IHL.nsf/FULL/500?OpenDocument and in *United Nations Treaty Series* (New York: United Nations, 1983), 1342: 137; Convention on the Prohibition of the Development, Production, Stockpiling and Use of Chemical Weapons and on Their Destruction, 13 January 1993, available at http://nti.org/e_research/official_docs/inventory/pdfs/cwc.pdf and in *International Legal Materials* 32 (1993): 800; Convention on the Prohibition of the Use, Stockpiling, Production and Transfer of Anti-Personnel Mines and on Their Destruction, 18 September 1997, entered into force 1 March 1999, available at http://www.nti.org/e_research/official_docs/inventory/pdfs/apl.pdf and *United Nations Treaty Series* (New York: United Nations, 1999), 2056: 211; and Convention on Cluster Munitions, 30 May 2008, available at http://www.clusterconvention.org/.

55. For example, Convention Concerning the Protection of the World Cultural and Natural Heritage, 23 November 1972, available at http://whc.unesco.org/en/conventiontext/ and in *International Legal Materials* 11 (1972): 1358–1366.

56. See Iain Scobbie, "Natural Resources and Belligerent Occupation: Mutation through Permanent Sovereignty," in *Human Rights, Self-Determination and Political Change in the Occupied Palestinian Territories,* ed. Stephen Bowen (The Hague: Nijhoff, 1997), 234.

57. See Protocol Additional to the Geneva Conventions of 12 August 1949, and Relating to the Protection of Victims of International Armed Conflicts (Protocol 1), Article 54, paragraph 5. Nonetheless, states remain bound by the prohibition on the use of "methods or means of warfare which are intended, or may be expected, to cause widespread, long-term and severe damage to the natural environment" pursuant to Article 35(3) of the same protocol.

58. Protocol Additional to the Geneva Conventions of 12 August 1949, and relating to the Protection of Victims of Non-International Armed Conflicts (Protocol II), 8 June 1977, available at www2.ohchr.org. The environment might indirectly be protected by Article 14 of the protocol, which prohibits attacks against "foodstuffs, agricultural areas for the production of foodstuffs, crops, livestock, drinking water installations and supplies and irrigation works," and Article 15, which prohibits attack against "installations containing dangerous forces . . . if such attack may cause the release of [such] forces." The diplomatic conference rejected a proposal to introduce provisions analogous to those in Protocol I. See Antoine Bouvier, "Protection of the Natural Environment in Time of Armed Conflict," *International Review of the Red Cross* 285 (1991): 576.

59. As the ICJ determined authoritatively in its Advisory Opinion on the *Legal Consequences of the Construction of a Wall,* the provisions of the Hague Convention of 1907 have now become part of customary international law. See *Legal Consequences of the Construction of a Wall in the Occupied Palestinian Territory,* Advisory Opinion of 9 July 2004, paragraph 89, available at http://www.icj-cij.org/docket/files/131/1671.pdf. A similar conclusion can be reached for the majority of the provisions of the 1949 Geneva Conventions, which have attracted a great number of parties.

60. Henckaerts and Doswald-Beck, *Customary International Humanitarian Law,* vol. 1, *Rules,* Rule 44, at p. 147.

61. Ibid., Rule 45, at p. 151. It is not clear whether a customary obligation exists with regard to this rule. Many important states that have been regularly engaged in armed conflicts—including India, Israel, Pakistan, and the United States—have not become parties to Protocol I, which lays down this obligation in Article 35(3). Moreover, many states have consistently objected to the provisions relating to the environment. For example, France, the United King-

dom, and the United States—three important members of the nuclear club—have held that these provisions are incompatible with the damage that would result from the use of nuclear weapons. See Yoram Dinstein, *The Conduct of Hostilities under the Law of International Armed Conflict* (Cambridge: Cambridge University Press, 2004), 185. See also "Joint Letter from John Bellinger III, Legal Adviser, U.S. Department of State, and William J. Haynes, General Counsel, U.S. Department of Defense, to Dr. Jakob Kellenberger, President, International Committee of the Red Cross, Regarding Customary International Law Study," 3 November 2006, reproduced in *International Legal Materials* 46 (2007): 514–531.

62. *Legality of the Threat or Use of Nuclear Weapons*, Advisory Opinion, 8 July 1996, paragraph 29, available at http://www.icj-cij.org/docket/files/95/7495.pdf.

63. See Arthur H. Westing, "Environmental Dimension of the Gulf War of 1991," in *Security and Environment in the Mediterranean: Conceptualising Security and Environmental Conflicts*, ed. Hans Günter Brauch, P. H. Liotta, Antonio Marquina, and Paul F. Rogers (Berlin: Springer, 2003), 523–534.

64. See *Report of the Secretary-General on the Protection of the Environment in Times of Armed Conflict*, General Assembly document A/48/269, 29 July 1993.

65. See Silja Vöneky, "A New Shield for the Environment: Peacetime Treaties as Legal Restraints of Wartime Damage," *Review of European Community & International Environmental Law* 9 (2000): 20–32. For an approach favoring an integration of international humanitarian law and international environmental law, see also Daniëlla Dam-de Jong, "International Law and Resource Plunder: The Protection of Natural Resources during Armed Conflict," *Yearbook of International Environmental Law* 19 (2008): 27–57.

66. *Legality of the Threat or Use of Nuclear Weapons*, Advisory Opinion, 8 July 1996, paragraph 30, available at http://www.icj-cij.org/docket/files/95/7495.pdf.

67. For the whole study, see UNEP, *Protecting the Environment during Armed Conflict: An Inventory and Analysis of International Law* (Nairobi: UNEP, 2009), available at http://postconflict.unep.ch/publications/int_law.pdf.

68. The PCA has recently prepared a set of rules aimed at resolving these kinds of disputes. See PCA, "Optional Rules for Arbitration of Disputes Relating to Natural Resources and/or the Environment," available at http://www.pca-cpa.org/upload/files/ENVIRONMENTAL%283%29.pdf.

69. UN Charter, Article 1(1).

70. Ibid., Article 25 and Article 24, paragraph 1.

71. Article 5, paragraph 1 of the Covenant of the League of Nations, stipulated that "decisions at any meeting of the Assembly or of the Council shall require the agreement of all the Members of the League at the meeting." Covenant of the League of Nations, 28 June 1919, available at http://avalon.law.yale.edu/20th_century/leagcov.asp and in *American Journal of International Law: Supplement* 13 (1919).

72. UN Charter, Article 27, paragraph 3 requires a majority of nine out of fifteen votes to adopt decisions on nonprocedural matters, including "the concurring votes of all permanent members." In order to avoid constant paralysis during the Cold War, a practice emerged that an abstention by one or more permanent members would not block the adoption of a legally valid decision by the council. (Before 1965, when the Charter amendments of 1963 entered into force, the required majority was seven out of eleven.) In 1971, the International Court of Justice confirmed this practice "as not constituting a bar to the adoption of resolutions." *Legal Consequences for States of the Continued Presence of South Africa in Namibia (South West Africa) Notwithstanding Security Council Resolution 276 (1970)*, Advisory Opinion, 21 June 1971, paragraph 22, available at http://www.icj-cij.org/docket/files/53/5595.pdf.

73. The council determined that the situation in Southern Rhodesia and the continued supply of arms to apartheid South Africa constituted threats to peace and ordered coercive measures in the form of comprehensive economic sanctions (Security Council resolution 232, 16 December 1966, and Security Council resolution 253, 29 May 1968) and an arms em-

bargo (Security Council resolution 418, 4 November 1977). On this change in the meaning of "peace," see Bert V. A. Röling, "International Law and the Maintenance of Peace," *Netherlands Yearbook of International Law* 4 (1973): 1–103.

74. See Security Council resolution 330 (1973), 21 March 1973.

75. This was the council's determination in the context of Iraq's repression of Kurds living within its borders; see Security Council resolution 688, 5 April 1991. See also Nico J. Schrijver, "Sovereignty versus Human Rights? A Tale of UN Security Council Resolution 688 (1991) on the Protection of the Kurdish People," in *The Role of the Nation-State in the 21st Century: Human Rights, International Organisations, and Foreign Policy,* ed. Monique Castermans-Holleman, Fried van Hoof, and Jacqueline Smith (The Hague: Kluwer Law International, 1998), 347–357.

76. For the former, see "Threats to International Peace and Security Caused by Terrorist Acts," Security Council resolution 1368, 12 September 2001; and "Threats to International Peace and Security Caused by Terrorist Acts," Security Council resolution 1373, 28 September 2001. For a subsequent anti-terrorism resolution, see "Proliferation of Small Arms and Light Weapons and Mercenary Activities: Threats to Peace and Security in West Africa," Security Council resolution 1467, 18 March 2003.

77. "The Situation in Somalia," Security Council resolution 1846, 2 December 2008; and "The Situation in Somalia," Security Council resolution 1851, 16 December 2008.

78. See "Note by the President of the Security Council," Security Council document S/23500, 31 January 1992.

79. For changes in the concept of threats to peace, see José E. Alvarez, *International Organizations as Law-Makers* (Oxford: Oxford University Press, 2005), 195–196; and Karel C. Wellens, "The UN Security Council and New Threats to the Peace: Back to the Future," *Journal of Conflict and Security Law* 8 (2003): 15–70.

80. Established by Security Council resolution 692, 20 May 1991. See also Section E of Security Council resolution 687, 8 April 1991.

81. The International Tribunal for the Prosecution of Persons Responsible for Serious Violations of International Humanitarian Law Committed in the Territory of Former Yugoslavia since 1991 was established by Security Council resolution 827, 25 May 1993.

82. The International Criminal Tribunal for Rwanda was established by Security Council resolution 955, 8 November 1994.

83. This has raised a number of fundamental legal questions, in particular regarding the need to balance human rights and due process concerns and the need for anti-terrorism measures. Moreover, it raises the issue of whether the Security Council has begun to take on a semi-judicial role. See "Strengthening Targeted Sanctions through Fair and Clear Procedures," annexed to General Assembly and Security Council document A/60/887-S/2006/331, 14 June 2006.

84. See Peter Wallensteen and Carina Staibano, *International Sanctions: Between Words and Wars in the Global System* (London: Frank Cass, 2005).

85. Security Council resolution 687, 3 April 1991, paragraph 16.

86. Ibid. For more on the UNCC and environmental claims, see Robin L. Juni, "The United Nations Compensation Commission as a Model for an International Environmental Court," *Environmental Law* 7 (2000/2001): 53–74.

87. *Report of Secretary-General Pursuant to Paragraph 19 of Security Council Resolution 687 (1991) of 2 May 1991,* Security Council document S/22559, 2 May 1991, paragraph 20. The UNCC's rules stated that commissioners were to apply Security Council resolution 687 (14 June 1991) and other relevant Security Council resolutions, the criteria established by the Governing Council for particular categories of claims, and any pertinent decisions of the Governing Council when considering claims. In addition, where necessary, commissioners were to apply other relevant rules of international law. See "Provisional Rules for Claims Procedure," UNCC Document S/AC.26/1992/10, 26 June 1992, Article 31.

88. The UNCC Governing Council identified six categories of claims: four of these were claims by individuals, one by corporations, and one by governments and international organizations. The latter, known as category F claims, related to losses incurred by governments and international organizations in evacuating citizens and providing relief to citizens as well as to damage to diplomatic premises and loss of and damage to other government property and damage to the environment. Category F claims were further divided into four subcategories. Of these, F4 claims related to claims for damage to the environment. See at "Category 'F' Claims," available at http://www.uncc.ch/claims/f_claims.htm.

89. See *Report and Recommendations Made by the Panel of Commissioners Concerning the Fifth Installment of "F4" Claims,* UNCC document S/AC.26/2005/10, 10 June 2005, paragraph 4; see also United Nations Claims Commission, "Category 'F' Claims," available at http://www.uncc.ch/claims/f_claims.htm.

90. *Report and Recommendations Made by the Panel of Commissioners Concerning the Fifth Installment of "F4" Claims.* For a brief commentary, see Cymie Payne, "UN Commission Awards Compensation for Environmental and Public Health Damage from 1990–91 Gulf War," *ASIL Insight,* 10 August 2005, available at http://www.asil.org/insights050810.cfm.

91. "The UNCC at a Glance," available at http://www.uncc.ch//ataglance.htm.

92. Comprehensive sanctions regimes were adopted with regard to Southern Rhodesia (Security Council resolution 232, 16 December 1966), Iraq (Security Council resolution 661, 6 August 1990), Federal Republic of Yugoslavia (Security Council resolution 757, 30 May 1992 and Security Council resolution 820, 17 April 1993), and Haiti (Security Council resolution 841, 16 June 1993).

93. The most well known is the sanctions regime against Al Qaeda and the Taliban pursuant to Security Council resolution 1267, 15 October 1999; Security Council resolution 1333, 19 December 2000; and subsequent resolutions.

94. Extensive non-economic sanctions were adopted with regard to the Federal Republic of Yugoslavia (Serbia and Montenegro) pursuant to Security Council resolution 757, 30 May 1992, which required states to reduce staff at diplomatic posts and consular missions in Serbia and Montenegro, take steps to prevent Serbia and Montenegro from participating in international sporting events, and suspend scientific and technical cooperation with and cultural exchanges and visits to Serbia and Montenegro.

95. For a recent overview of the Security Council's practice with regard to sanctions, see Jeremy M. Farrall, *United Nations Sanctions and the Rule of Law* (Cambridge: Cambridge University Press, 2007).

96. In the case of Libya, the Security Council imposed an embargo on technical equipment used to produce oil without directly banning exports or imports of petroleum as such. See Security Council resolution S/RES/883 (1993), 11 November 1993.

97. Such targeted sanctions were adopted at the end of 2008 with respect to the Democratic Republic of the Congo. See Security Council resolution 1857, 22 December 2008.

98. The Security Council has often established sanctions committees—composed of representatives of each member state of the council—to facilitate the administration, monitoring, and implementation of sanctions. There are currently eleven active sanctions committees, of which two are supervising sanctions related to natural resources. See "Security Council Sanctions Committees: An Overview," available at http://www.un.org/sc/committees/index.shtml. Although the mandates of these committees vary considerably, most of them report to the Security Council, make observations and recommendations on actions taken by member states to implement sanctions, and make decisions about exemptions. Sanctions committees have sometimes been assisted by groups of experts that are established for short periods to investigate the implementation of sanctions in practice, assess their effectiveness, and, if necessary, recommend measures for improving them. In some situations, peacekeeping operations have also been authorized to help monitor and enforce the relevant sanctions regimes. Part of the mandate of the United Nations Mission in Liberia, for example, was "to assist the transitional

government in restoring proper administration of natural resources"; Security Council resolution 1509, 19 September 2003, paragraph 3(r).

99. See *Final Report of the Monitoring Mechanism on Angola Sanctions,* Security Council document S/2000/1225, 21 December 2000.

100. "The Role of Diamonds in Fuelling Conflict: Breaking the Link between the Illicit Transaction of Rough Diamonds and Armed Conflict as a Contribution to Prevention and Settlement of Conflicts," General Assembly resolution A/RES/56/263, 9 April 2002. Likewise, the Security Council strongly supported the Kimberley Process Certification Scheme "as a valuable contribution against trafficking in conflict diamonds" and stressed the necessity of the widest possible participation in the scheme; Security Council resolution S/RES/1459, 28 January 2003.

101. The Kimberley Process Certification Scheme is an agreement between the representatives of forty-nine nations, the diamond trading community, the World Diamond Council, and some NGOs. Among its signatories are important diamond-producing countries such as Sierra Leone, Angola, Liberia, and the DRC as well as the United States and the EU, which have the most significant markets for diamonds. See http://www.kimberleyprocess.com/.

102. See *Report of the Group of Experts on the Democratic Republic of the Congo,* Security Council document S/2006/53, 27 January 2006, 27–28; and *Report of the Group of Experts on the Democratic Republic of the Congo,* Security Council document S/2006/525, 18 July 2006, 30–31.

103. For example, the Federal Institute for Geosciences and Natural Resources has conducted a pilot study financed by Germany to fingerprint coltan; see "Fingerprinting of Conflict Minerals: Columbite-Tantalite ('Coltan') Ores," *SGA News* 3 (June 2008), available at http://e-sga.org/fileadmin/sga/newsletter/news23/SGANews23.pdf. In the meanwhile, the Geology for an Economical Sustainable Development Centre, financed by Belgium, has also been working on developing practical methods for the traceability and certification of copper and cobalt ores; see "GECO (Geology for an ECOnomical Sustainable Development," available at http://www.gecoproject.org.

104. For the initiative of the DRC government, see Joe Bavier, "DRC Setting Up Scheme to Certify Colombo-Tantalite," available at http://www.mineweb.com:8080/mineweb/view/mineweb/en/page39?oid=49809&sn=Detail. For the initiative in the U.S. Senate, see "S.891: Congo Conflict Minerals Act of 2009," available at http://www.govtrack.us/congress/bill.xpd?bill=s111-891.

105. See Article 11 of the Protocol Against the Illegal Exploitation of Natural Resources, adopted on 30 November 2006, available at http://www.icglr.org/key-documents/democracy-good-gov/Protocol%20against%20the%20Illegal%20Exploitation%20of%20Natural%20Resources.pdf.

106. See Security Council resolution 1493, 28 July 2003, paragraph 28. In 2004, the Security Council reiterated its condemnation "of the continuing illegal exploitation of natural resources in the Democratic Republic of the Congo . . . which contributes to the perpetuation of the conflict" and reaffirmed "the importance of bringing an end to these illegal activities, including by applying the necessary pressure on the armed groups, traffickers and all other actors involved"; Security Council resolution 1533, 12 March 2004.

107. See "Letter Dated 26 January 2006 from the Chairman of the Security Council Committee Established Pursuant to Resolution 1533 (2004) Concerning the Democratic Republic of the Congo Addressed to the President of the Security Council," Security Council document S/2006/53, 27 January 2006; and "Letter Dated 18 July 2006 from the Chairman of the Security Council Committee Established Pursuant to Resolution 1533 (2004) Concerning the Democratic Republic of the Congo Addressed to the President of the Security Council," Security Council document S/2006/525, 18 July 2006.

108. The Security Council asked the group to prepare recommendations on feasible and effective measures, including a certificate of origin regime, that could be imposed to prevent

the illegal exploitation of natural resources to finance armed groups and militias in the eastern part of the Democratic Republic of the Congo; see Security Council resolution 1698, 31 July 2006, paragraph 6.

109. See *Interim Report of the Group of Experts on the Democratic Republic of the Congo, Pursuant to Security Council Resolution 1698 (2006)*, Security Council document S/2007/40, 25 January 2007.

110. *Report of the Secretary-General Pursuant to Paragraph 8 of Resolution 1698 (2006) Concerning the Democratic Republic of the Congo*, Security Council document S/2007/68, 8 February 2007.

111. Security Council resolution 1756 (2007), 15 May 2007, paragraph 7. The Security Council explicitly recognized the role that links between the illegal exploitation of natural resources, the illicit trade in such resources, and the proliferation and trafficking of arms played in fueling and exacerbating conflicts in the DRC and urged all states "to take appropriate steps to end the illicit trade in natural resources, including if necessary through judicial means" and called upon "the international financial institutions to assist the Government of the DRC in establishing effective and transparent control over the exploitation of natural resources" (paragraph 15).

112. The Secretary-General expressed these concerns in *Report of the Secretary-General Pursuant to Paragraph 8 of Resolution 1698 (2006) Concerning the Democratic Republic of the Congo*, paragraph 63.

113. See paragraph 4(g) of Security Council resolution 1857, 22 December 2008.

114. *Armed Activities on the Territory of the Congo (Democratic Republic of the Congo v. Uganda)*, Judgment of 19 December 2005, available at http://www.icj-cij.org/docket/files/116/10455.pdf. This case is discussed further in the next chapter.

115. "Declaration on Strengthening the Effectiveness of the Security Council's Role in Conflict Prevention," Security Council resolution 1625, 14 September 2005.

116. "Letter Dated 6 June 2007 from the Permanent Representative of Belgium to the United Nations to the Secretary-General," Security Council document S/2007/334, 6 June 2007.

117. "Statement by the President of the Security Council," Security Council document S/PRST/2007/22, 25 June 2007.

118. On the Charter's capacity for adaptation and informal modification in light of changed circumstances and new needs, see Nico J. Schrijver, "The Future of the Charter of the United Nations," *Max Planck Yearbook of United Nations Law* 10 (2006): 1–34.

119. See Lansana Gberie, Ralph Hazelton, and Ian Smillie, *The Heart of the Matter: Sierra Leone, Diamonds, and Human Security* (Ottawa: Partnership Africa Canada, 2000), available at http://www.reliefweb.int/library/documents/2001/pac-sie-jan00.pdf; and Greg Campbell, *Blood Diamonds: Tracing the Deadly Path of the World's Most Precious Stones* (Boulder, Colo.: Westview Press, 2004). For reports and other information, see Partnership Africa Canada, "Diamonds and Human Security," available at http://www.pacweb.org/pub-diamonds-nr-e.php.

6. The Role of the International Court of Justice in the Settlement of Natural Resource Disputes

1. *Fisheries (United Kingdom v. Norway)*, Judgment, 18 December 1951, p. 133, available at http://www.icj-cij.org/docket/files/5/1809.pdf.

2. *Fisheries Jurisdiction (United Kingdom of Great Britain and Northern Ireland v. Iceland)*, Merits, Judgment, 25 July 1974, paragraph 69, available at http://www.icj-cij.org/docket/files/55/5977.pdf; and *Fisheries Jurisdiction (Federal Republic of Germany v. Iceland)*, Merits, Judgment, 25 July 1974, paragraph 61, available at http://www.icj-cij.org/docket/files/56/6001.pdf. In view of certain differences between the positions of the United Kingdom and Ger-

many and their respective submissions, the court decided not to join the proceedings in the two cases, even though the basic legal issues in each case appeared to be identical. As a result, the court delivered two separate judgments, which however contained identical wording on a number of points.

3. *Fisheries Jurisdiction (United Kingdom of Great Britain and Northern Ireland v. Iceland)*, paragraph 71; and *Fisheries Jurisdiction (Federal Republic of Germany v. Iceland)*, paragraph 63.

4. *Fisheries Jurisdiction (United Kingdom of Great Britain and Northern Ireland v. Iceland)*, paragraph 72; and *Fisheries Jurisdiction (Federal Republic of Germany v. Iceland)*, paragraph 64; emphasis added.

5. See "Current Legal Developments," *International and Comparative Law Quarterly* 25 (1976): 687.

6. *North Sea Continental Shelf (Federal Republic of Germany/Denmark Federal Republic of Germany/Netherlands)*, Judgment, 20 February 1969, paragraph 17, available at http://www.icj-cij.org/docket/files/52/5561.pdf. The two cases were joined and the court delivered one judgment.

7. Ibid., paragraph 97.

8. Ibid., paragraph 101(D)(2).

9. *Continental Shelf (Tunisia/Libyan Arab Jamahiriya)*, Judgment, 24 February 1982, paragraph 106, available at http://www.icj-cij.org/docket/files/63/6267.pdf.

10. Ibid., paragraph 107.

11. *Continental Shelf (Libyan Arab Jamahiriya/Malta)*, Judgment, 3 June 1985, paragraph 50, available at http://www.icj-cij.org/docket/files/68/6415.pdf.

12. Ibid.

13. *Delimitation of the Maritime Boundary in the Gulf of Maine Area (Canada/United States of America)*, Judgment, 12 October 1984, paragraph 194, available at http://www.icj-cij.org/docket/files/67/6369.pdf.

14. Ibid., paragraph 40.

15. Ibid., paragraph 232.

16. Ibid., paragraph 237.

17. Ibid., paragraph 238–239.

18. *Maritime Delimitation in the Area between Greenland and Jan Mayen (Denmark v. Norway)*, Judgment, 14 June 1993, paragraph 72, available at http://www.icj-cij.org/docket/files/78/6743.pdf.

19. Ibid., paragraph 75.

20. Ibid., paragraph 76.

21. *Maritime Delimitation and Territorial Questions between Qatar and Bahrain (Qatar v. Bahrain)*, Merits, Judgment, 16 March 2001, paragraphs 235–236, available at http://www.icj-cij.org/docket/files/87/7027.pdf.

22. *Continental Shelf (Tunisia/Libyan Arab Jamahiriya)*, Judgment, 24 February 1982, paragraphs 117–119.

23. Ibid., paragraph 133(B)(4).

24. *Land and Maritime Boundary between Cameroon and Nigeria (Cameroon v. Nigeria; Equatorial Guinea intervening)*, Judgment, 10 October 2002, paragraphs 302–303, available at http://www.icj-cij.org/docket/files/94/7453.pdf.

25. Ibid., paragraph 304.

26. Ibid.

27. *Territorial and Maritime Dispute between Nicaragua and Honduras in the Caribbean Sea (Nicaragua v. Honduras)*, Judgment, 8 October 2007, paragraphs 238–254, available at http://www.icj-cij.org/docket/files/120/14075.pdf.

28. *Maritime Delimitation in the Black Sea (Romania v. Ukraine)*, Judgment, 3 February 2009, paragraphs 189–196, available at http://www.icj-cij.org/docket/files/132/14987.pdf.

29. Ibid., paragraph 198. The court referred to the decision of the Arbitral Tribunal in the case between Barbados and Trinidad and Tobago (2006), which observed that "resource-related criteria have been treated more cautiously by the decisions of international courts and tribunals, which have not generally applied this factor as a relevant circumstance." See paragraph 241 of *Arbitration between Barbados and the Republic of Trinidad and Tobago,* Award of 11 April 2006, available at http://www.pca-cpa.org/upload/files/Final%20Award.pdf.

30. Ibid.

31. *Frontier Dispute (Burkina Faso/Republic of Mali),* Judgment, 22 December 1986, paragraph 150, available at http://www.icj-cij.org/docket/files/69/6447.pdf.

32. Ibid., paragraph 162.

33. *Kasikili/Sedudu Island (Botswana/Namibia),* Judgment, 13 December 1999, paragraphs 103–104, available at http://www.icj-cij.org/docket/files/98/7577.pdf.

34. *Land, Island and Maritime Frontier Dispute (El Salvador/Honduras; Nicaragua intervening),* Judgment, 11 September 1992, paragraph 58, available at http://www.icj-cij.org/docket/files/75/6671.pdf.

35. *Sovereignty over Pulau Ligitan and Pulau Sipadan (Indonesia/Malaysia),* Judgment, 17 December 2002, paragraph 145, available at http://www.icj-cij.org/docket/files/102/7714.pdf.

36. *Frontier Dispute (Benin/Niger),* Judgment, 12 July 2005, paragraphs 81 and 137, available at http://www.icj-cij.org/docket/files/125/8228.pdf.

37. *Territorial and Maritime Dispute between Nicaragua and Honduras in the Caribbean Sea (Nicaragua v. Honduras),* Judgment, 8 October 2007, paragraphs 195–196, available in http://www.icj-cij.org/docket/files/120/14075.pdf.

38. Ibid., paragraphs 204 and 207.

39. *Western Sahara,* Advisory Opinion, 16 October 1975, paragraphs 87–88, available at paragraphs 195–196.

40. *Gabčíkovo-Nagymaros Project (Hungary/Slovakia),* Judgment, 25 September 1997, paragraph 78, available at http://www.icj-cij.org/docket/files/92/7375.pdf.

41. Ibid., paragraph 78.

42. Ibid., paragraph 85.

43. Ibid., paragraph 152.

44. Ibid., paragraph 140.

45. *Dispute regarding Navigational and Related Rights (Costa Rica v. Nicaragua),* Judgment, 13 July 2009, paragraph 88, available at http://www.icj-cij.org/docket/files/133/15321.pdf.

46. Ibid., paragraph 89.

47. Ibid.

48. Ibid., paragraph 144.

49. Ibid., paragraph 141.

50. Ibid.

51. Ibid., paragraph 143.

52. *Pulp Mills on the River Uruguay (Argentina v. Uruguay),* Request for the Indication of Provisional Measures, Order, 13 July 2006, paragraph 80, available at http://www.icj-cij.org/docket/files/135/11235.pdf.

53. *Armed Activities on the Territory of the Congo (Democratic Republic of the Congo v. Uganda),* Judgment, 19 December 2005, paragraph 242, available at http://www.icj-cij.org/docket/files/116/10455.pdf.

54. Ibid., paragraphs 243–245.

55. Ibid., paragraph 246.

56. The court was referring to "Permanent Sovereignty over Natural Resources," General Assembly resolution 1803 (XVII), 14 December 1962; "Declaration on the Establishment of a New International Economic Order," General Assembly resolution 3201 (S.VI), 1 May 1974; and "Charter of Economic Rights and Duties of States," General Assembly resolution 3281 (XXIX), 12 December 1974.

57. *Armed Activities on the Territory of the Congo (Democratic Republic of the Congo v. Uganda),* Judgment, 19 December 2005, paragraph 244.

58. Ibid., paragraph 242.

59. *Armed Activities on the Territory of the Congo (Democratic Republic of the Congo v. Uganda),* Declaration of Judge Koroma, 19 December 2005, paragraph 11, emphasis in the original, available at http://www.icj-cij.org/docket/files/116/10459.pdf.

60. *Armed Activities on the Territory of the Congo (Democratic Republic of the Congo v. Uganda),* Dissenting Opinion of Judge ad hoc Kateka, 19 December 2005, paragraph 56, available at http://www.icj-cij.org/docket/files/116/10473.pdf.

61. *Legality of the Threat or Use of Nuclear Weapons,* Advisory Opinion, 8 July 1996, paragraph 29, available at http://www.icj-cij.org/docket/files/95/7495.pdf.

62. Ibid., paragraphs 30–32.

63. *Legal Consequences of the Construction of a Wall in the Occupied Palestinian Territory,* Advisory Opinion, 9 July 2004, paragraph 133, available at http://www.icj-cij.org/docket/files/131/1671.pdf.

64. Ibid., paragraphs 134–135.

65. Ibid., paragraphs 149–153.

66. The United Kingdom requested that the court declare that the Iranian government was under an obligation to submit the dispute to arbitration or to declare that the decision of the Iranian government to nationalize was contrary to international law.

67. See *Anglo-Iranian Oil Co. (United Kingdom v. Iran),* Request for the Indication of Interim Measures of Protection, Order, 5 July 1951, available at http://www.icj-cij.org/docket/files/16/2013.pdf.

68. *Anglo-Iranian Oil Co. (United Kingdom v. Iran),* Preliminary Objection, Judgment, 22 July 1952, available at http://www.icj-cij.org/docket/files/16/1997.pdf.

69. *Aegean Sea Continental Shelf (Greece v. Turkey),* Jurisdiction, Judgment, 19 December 1978, paragraph 12, available at http://www.icj-cij.org/docket/files/62/6245.pdf.

70. *Certain Phosphate Lands in Nauru (Nauru v. Australia),* Preliminary Objections, Judgment, 26 June 1992, available at http://www.icj-cij.org/docket/files/80/6795.pdf.

71. *East Timor (Portugal v. Australia),* Judgment, 30 June 1995, available at http://www.icj-cij.org/docket/files/84/6949.pdf.

72. *Fisheries Jurisdiction (Spain v. Canada),* Jurisdiction of the Court, Judgment, 4 December 1998, available at http://www.icj-cij.org/docket/files/96/7533.pdf.

7. The UN's Conceptual Contribution

1. Examples include not only environmental treaties such as the United Nations Framework Convention on Climate Change and the Convention on Biological Diversity but also economic treaties such as the Agreement Establishing the World Trade Organization of 1994, available at http://www.wto.org/english/docs_e/legal_e/04-wto.pdf.

2. In *Gabčíkovo-Nagymaros Project,* the court observed: "This need to reconcile economic development with protection of the environment is aptly expressed in the concept of sustainable development." Judgment, 25 September 1997, paragraph 140, available at http://www.icj-cij.org/docket/files/92/7375.pdf.

3. "Human Rights Council," General Assembly resolution A/RES/60/251, 3 April 2006, adopted by 170 votes to 4, with 3 abstentions.

4. UN Security Council resolution 687, 3 April 1991.

5. The Group of Experts, which was appointed by the Secretary-General to monitor the implementation of the sanctions regime in the DRC, was established by Security Council resolution 1533 (2004) and subsequently renewed by Security Council resolutions 1552 (2004), 1596 (2005), 1616 (2005), 1654 (2006), 1698 (2006), 1771 (2007), 1807 (2008), and

1857 (2008). The Group of Experts supports the Sanctions Committee and reports directly to the Security Council.

6. See Security Council resolution 1625 (2005), 14 September 2005; and Security Council resolution 1653 (2006), 27 January 2006.

7. Examples of land boundary disputes that have come before the court include *Kasikili/Sedudu Island (Botswana/Namibia)* (1999) and *Land and Maritime Boundary between Cameroon and Nigeria (Cameroon v. Nigeria: Equatorial Guinea intervening)* (2002), examined in chapter 6 of this volume.

8. For example, the *North Sea Continental Shelf (Federal Republic of Germany/Netherlands)* (1969), *North Sea Continental Shelf (Federal Republic of Germany/Denmark)* (1969), *Fisheries Jurisdiction (Federal Republic of Germany/Iceland)* (1974), *Fisheries Jurisdiction (United Kingdom of Great Britain and Northern Ireland/Iceland)* (1974), *Delimitation of the Maritime Boundary in the Gulf of Maine Area (Canada/United States of America)* (1984), *Continental Shelf (Libyan Arab Jamahiriya/Malta)* (1985), *Maritime Delimitation in the Area between Greenland and Jan Mayen (Denmark v. Norway)* (1993), and *Maritime Delimitation and Territorial Questions between Qatar and Bahrain (Qatar v. Bahrain)* (2001). See chapter 6 for further analysis of these cases.

9. *Legality of the Threat of Nuclear Weapons,* Advisory Opinion, 8 July 1996, paragraph 29, available at http://www.icj-cij.org/docket/files/95/7495.pdf.

10. *Gabčíkovo-Nagymaros Project,* Judgment, 25 September 1997, paragraph 140.

11. *Armed Activities on the Territory of the Congo (Democratic Republic of the Congo v. Uganda)* (2005), Judgment, 19 December 2005, available at http://www.icj-cij.org/docket/files/116/10455.pdf.

12. See General Assembly document A/CONF.13/SR.1 (1958), 3.

13. See Nico J. Schrijver, *Sovereignty over Natural Resources: Balancing Rights and Duties* (Cambridge: Cambridge University Press, 1997); and Nico J. Schrijver, "Natural Resources, Sovereignty over" in *Encyclopedia of Public International Law* (Oxford: Oxford University Press, forthcoming), available online at http://www.mpepil.com.

14. See Edith D. Brown Weiss, *In Fairness to Future Generations: International Law, Common Patrimony, and Intergenerational Equity* (New York: Transnational Publishers, 1989); and Catherine Redgwell, *Intergenerational Trusts and Environmental Protection* (Manchester: Manchester University Press, 1999).

15. See chapters 2 and 4 for more details on the UN's involvement with these activities.

16. Oscar Schachter, *Sharing the World's Resources* (New York: Columbia University Press, 1977); and Weiss, *In Fairness to Future Generations* are pioneering books in this field.

17. Compare Pieter VerLoren van Themaat, *The Changing Structure of International Economic Law* (Dordrecht: Martinus Nijhoff), 31–33, and Peter M. Haas, Norichika Kanie, and Craig N. Murphy, "Conclusion: Institutional Design and Institutional Reform for Sustainable Development," in *Emerging Forces in Environmental Governance,* ed. Norichika Kanie and Peter M. Haas (Tokyo: United Nations University Press, 2004), 263–281.

Index

Italicized page numbers indicate figures.

About the Author

Nico Schrijver holds the Chair of International Law and is Academic Director of the Grotius Centre for International Legal Studies at Leiden University. He is a member of the Royal Netherlands Academy of Arts and Sciences and the Permanent Court of Arbitration. He serves as a member of the UN Committee on Economic, Social and Cultural Rights and of the UN's High-Level Task Force on the Implementation of the Right to Development and has regularly appeared as counsel and expert before various international courts and tribunals. In 2009–2010, he was a member of the Independent Committee of Inquiry on the War in Iraq, established by the Dutch Government. His research interests focus on international law, collective security, environmental conservation, international development cooperation, and human rights. He is author of numerous publications, including *Sovereignty over Natural Resources: Balancing Rights and Duties* and *The Evolution of Sustainable Development in International Law: Inception, Meaning, and Status.*

About the United Nations Intellectual History Project

Ideas and concepts are a main driving force in human progress, and they are arguably the most important contribution of the United Nations. Yet there has been little historical study of the origins and evolution of the history of economic and social ideas cultivated within the world organization and of their impact on wider thinking and international action. The United Nations Intellectual History Project is filling this knowledge gap about the UN by tracing the origin and analyzing the evolution of key ideas and concepts about international economic and social development born or nurtured under UN auspices. UNIHP began operations in mid-1999 when the secretariat, the hub of a worldwide network of specialists on the UN, was established at the Ralph Bunche Institute for International Studies of The CUNY Graduate Center.

UNIHP has two main components, oral history interviews and a series of books on specific topics. The seventy-nine in-depth oral history interviews with leading contributors to crucial ideas and concepts within the UN system provided the raw material for this volume and other volumes. In addition, complete and indexed transcripts are available to researchers and the general public in an electronic book format on CD-ROM available through the secretariat.

The project commissioned fifteen studies about the major economic and social ideas or concepts that are central to UN activity, which have been published by Indiana University Press.

- *Ahead of the Curve? UN Ideas and Global Challenges,* by Louis Emmerij, Richard Jolly, and Thomas G. Weiss (2001)
- *Unity and Diversity in Development Ideas: Perspectives from the UN Regional Commissions,* edited by Yves Berthelot with contributions from Adebayo Adedeji, Yves Berthelot, Leelananda de Silva, Paul Rayment, Gert Rosenthal, and Blandine Destremeau (2003)
- *Quantifying the World: UN Ideas and Statistics,* by Michael Ward (2004)
- *UN Contributions to Development Thinking and Practice,* by Richard Jolly, Louis Emmerij, Dharam Ghai, and Frédéric Lapeyre (2004)

- *The UN and Global Political Economy: Trade, Finance, and Development,* by John Toye and Richard Toye (2004)
- *UN Voices: The Struggle for Development and Social Justice,* by Thomas G. Weiss, Tatiana Carayannis, Louis Emmerij, and Richard Jolly (2005)
- *Women, Development, and the UN: A Sixty-Year Quest for Equality and Justice,* by Devaki Jain (2005)
- *Human Security and the UN: A Critical History,* by S. Neil MacFarlane and Yuen Foong Khong (2006)
- *Human Rights at the UN: The Political History of Universal Justice,* Roger Normand and Sarah Zaidi (2008)
- *Preventive Diplomacy at the UN,* by Bertrand G. Ramcharan (2008)
- *The UN and Transnational Corporations: From Code of Conduct to Global Compact,* by Tagi Sagafi-nejad in collaboration with John H. Dunning (2009)
- *The UN and Development: From Aid to Cooperation,* by Olav Stokke (2009)
- *UN Ideas That Changed the World,* by Richard Jolly, Louis Emmerij, and Thomas G. Weiss (2009)
- *Global Governance and the UN: An Unfinished Journey,* by Thomas G. Weiss and Ramesh Thakur (2010)
- *Development without Destruction: The UN and Global Resource Management,* by Nico Schrijver (2010)

The project also collaborated on *The Oxford Handbook on the United Nations,* edited by Thomas G. Weiss and Sam Daws, published by Oxford University Press in 2007.

For further information, the interested reader should contact:
UN Intellectual History Project
The CUNY Graduate Center
365 Fifth Avenue, Suite 5203
New York, New York 10016-4309
212-817-1920 Tel
212-817-1565 Fax
UNHistory@gc.cuny.edu
www.unhistory.org

Printed and bound by CPI Group (UK) Ltd, Croydon, CR0 4YY

16/04/2025

14658362-0001